most of the work would
5 and 9 o[clock]. All the morning would
be at your own disposal. The morphologist
here does not speak English! And this place
is never without a hundred doctors. At
present there are over 300 in the various
branches. I have become attached to the
University; this will necessitate my
remaining here 3 months longer than
I expected. Do give the place a week's trial
or even 5 days!

The reasons for suggesting to forward MS
[are] that I don't know enough German
to steer it thro the press; the English is
quainter than [our] Holy Office; the
MS. is not confined altogether to verse [quin]
later I shall make arrangements for
whatever tour time will permit me [to make]

Sincerely Yours,

[signature]

Oliver St.John Gogarty

the man of many talents

Oliver St John Gogarty from a portrait by Sir William Orpen, *c*, 1911. Courtesy of Oliver D. Gogarty.

Oliver St.John Gogarty

the man of many talents

A Biography

J.B. Lyons

Blackwater Dublin

The Blackwater Press
Folens Publishers
Airton Road
Tallaght
Co. Dublin

Printed in the Republic of Ireland by Folens Printing Co. Ltd.

To Muriel

'To do the useful thing, to say the courageous thing, to contemplate the beautiful thing: that is enough for one man's life.'
T.S. Eliot — *The Use of Poetry and the Use of Criticism.*

'It may be that, perhaps, you will not be praised as you should be until about fifty years after you are dead. . .'
James Stephens — *Letter to Oliver St. John Gogarty.*

Acknowledgements

As the book grew my debt to individuals and institutions increased steadily. The former, whom it is a pleasure to thank, include Seamus Cahalane, Alan Denson, P.J. Gavin, Nora Hoult, Norma Jessop, Denis Johnston, Alf McLoughlin, James Mays, Countess Moltke, Ulick O'Connor, Niall Sheridan and Mervyn Wall. My general research was facilitated by the helpful staffs of the National Library of Ireland and the libraries of the Royal Dublin Society and the Irish Colleges of Physicians and Surgeons. Access to manuscript material was generously permitted by the National University of Ireland; the British Library; the New York Public Library; the libraries of Bucknell University, Cornell University, Delaware University, Harvard University and Yale University. The extracts detailed in the notes are reproduced with their permission.

Quotations from W.B. Yeats's correspondence with Gogarty are permitted by Senator Michael Yeats. Senator Yeats and the Oxford University Press have allowed me to use extracts from *Letters from W.B. Yeats to Dorothy Wellesley*. Some lines from *Chamber Music* are used by consent of Jonathan Cape and Mr. Liam Cosgrave, T.D., has permitted quotation from W.T. Cosgrave's letters.

Much of the material used for illustrations was processed by David Smyth of Sir Patrick Dun's Hospital, and the Green Studio. The typescript prepared by my secretary, Brid Kennedy, has had the expert attention of Tom Turley and Brigid Pike in Blackwater's editorial department. The letters to James Joyce and Shane Leslie which form the end papers are reproduced by permission of Cornell University and Bucknell University respectively.

Professor James F. Carens opened for me an Aladdin's cave of Gogartiana in Lewisburgh, Pennsylvania. Professor Zack Bowen's home proved a hospitable oasis during American peregrinations.

My greatest debt is to Oliver D. Gogarty, S.C. and his sister, Mrs. Brenda Williams, for making many documents, letters and photographs available to me and for allowing me to quote freely from copyright material. The final word of thanks goes to my wife for her gentle tolerance of many abstracted and untidy hours of authorship.

John Benignus Lyons
M.D., F.R.C.P.I.
Autumn, 1979.

Department of the History of Medicine,
Royal College of Surgeons in Ireland,
St. Stephen's Green,
Dublin.

Contents

List of Illustrations

Frontispiece: Oliver St John Gogarty from a portrait by Sir William Orpen, *c,* 1911. Courtesy of Oliver D. Gogarty.

19 15 Ely Place, Dublin, from a water colour by Flora N. Mitchell. Courtesy of Oliver D. Gogarty.

20 Renvyle House, Connemara.

21 East 61st Street, New York.

22 National Maternity Hospital, Holles Street.

23 The Richmond Hospital.

24 Allgemeines Krankenhaus, Vienna.

25 Meath Hospital.

26 Dust jacket of *Selected Poems* by Bip Pares.

27 Dust jacket of *As I was Going Down Sackville Street* (American edition).

28 Letter to James Joyce signed 'Caddie Rouselle'. Courtesy of Cornell University.

29 Holograph of *To T. Gillman Moorhead* by Oliver St John Gogarty. Courtesy of the Royal College of Physicians of Ireland.

30 Autograph poem by Oliver Gogarty.

31 Certificate of attendance at National Maternity Hospital, 1903.

32 From bronze medallion by Spicer Simpson. Courtesy of National Gallery of Ireland.

33 Detail from cartoon by Gordon Brewster, 1935. Courtesy Medical Board, Meath Hospital.

34 86 St. Stephen's Green, Dublin — formerly University College.

35 The Campanile, Trinity College, Dublin.

36 Testimonial of Royal Humane Society.

37 Left to right: Sir Hamilton Harty, Oliver St John Gogarty, W.B. Yeats and Count John MacCormack in New York, 1932.

38 Beth Israel Hospital, New York.

39 Ballinakill Lake, Connemara.

40 Connemara — "The lanes that end on hill or strand . . ."

41 Gogarty's tombstone, Ballinakill Cemetery, Connemara.

42 Plaque on 5 Parnell (Rutland) Square.

Preface

Ironically, for he had observed that one should not 'after Caesar skulk in Rome', Oliver St. John Gogarty outlived most of his contemporaries and all his older friends. It was his good fortune, or the reverse, to spend almost a score of years in New York City away from the irritations of Irish political life but separated from Ireland's springs of inspiration and from the younger writers who might have found in his companionship reasons to voice his commemoration. Nor did he escape the disadvantages of longevity, hostility to new ideas and new moods in art, and an incontinence of speech which betrays the inescapable rigidity of age.

Always a controversial figure, but latterly a neglected one, Gogarty to-day is a man remembered for one book, *As I Was Going Down Sackville Street,* and that not his best. His verses are overlooked by readers who pay fealty only to post-Eliot measures, or if read are narrowly evaluated. His characterization as 'Buck Mulligan' in James Joyce's *Ulysses* served him ill, that brilliant but malicious portrait masking a kinder and more sensitive personality.

Ulick O'Connor's biography achieved some redress for the surgeon-poet and obtained a reprieve from a sentence of oblivion that appeared to threaten his literary reputation. Nevertheless in the fifteen years since its publication there has been little evidence of the resurgence of interest that might have been expected as we approached the centenary of his birth.

The present neglect is the outcome of complex factors among which fashion and envy rank high: the arid modes of contemporary poetry are at variance with his music-making rhythms; his ebullience in life was so strong (not to speak of his mordant humour), his material and social success so apparent, that faint-hearted critics have been content not to stir the shadows or disturb the silence that surround him. The exceptions include James F. Carens,[1] A. Norman Jeffares and Vivian Mercier.

Gogarty's departure to America coincided with my own arrival in Dublin to study medicine in 1939: I never knew him personally.

I read a borrowed copy of *Tumbling in the Hay* soon after its publication and laughed uproariously. I recall, too, the striking dustjacket of *I Follow Saint Patrick* in the bookshops but could not afford to purchase it; *Sackville Street,* following the legal action, was unobtainable.

His name cropped up from time to time in medical circles, his admirers equalled by his detractors, but it was not until some years after his death that, in the course of a study eventually published as *James Joyce and Medicine,* I became convinced that a major contributor to Anglo-Irish literature was being short-changed. An invitation from Professor James F. Carens to write a monograph on Gogarty for Bucknell University's Irish Writers series necessitated further acquaintance with Gogartiana published and unpublished, which augmented my conviction that a fascinating (repelling, some undoubtedly would say) character was being under-valued.

Although cast in biographical form the emphasis of the present study is bibliographical, my intention to place a detailed survey of Gogarty's publications before the general reader and the student of Anglo-Irish literature in the hope that the former will be prompted to seek out the original works and that the latter, in due course, will find some of them worth critical attention.

Commonly a poet's juvenilia do not merit more than cursory attention while marginalia of a bawdy nature tend to be seen as unfortunate aberrations to be glossed over and forgotten. Gogarty's juvenilia have not survived but since sexuality is an integral part of the human condition, a well spring of passion, tenderness and ceaseless laughter, it would seem a pity to exclude some very funny lines which formerly might have invited censorship. His own disagreements with the notorious Irish censors were lukewarm but by 'censoring' a nursery-rhyme he succeeded in showing that the censor's blue pencil can create prurience where it does not exist:

> *Goosey, Goosey, Gander*
> *Where do you ****
> *Upstairs and ****
> *In a lady's ****

Civilization imposes masks on us that become habitual; caution leaves us tongue-tied. Gogarty's lively mind, however, refused to be convention's slave; he spoke when others would have remained silent. And his humorous fantasy was such that it magnified the lewd and barbed thoughts that occur secretly to all of us, giving them immediate vent in speech or on paper — for he was an incessant letter-writer — to the delight of his confidants. Their repetition after the lapse of years, removed from the chuckles of his contemporaries, all of whom were capable of equal malice, and out of the context of his times, may lead to misinterpretation. This risk must be taken in the study of an exuberant, accomplished, and complex personality.

PART ONE

1

Once Upon a Time

One of his medical colleagues said that Oliver St. John Gogarty was a first-class writer, a second-class patriot and a third-class surgeon. It is a judgement that could be argued endlessly: is it likely that a third-class surgeon could have attained teaching hospital appointments, or that Arthur Griffith would have taken to a 'patriot' of low calibre? And what of the laurel crown so facilely bestowed? The sparing comments of present-day *literati*, the niggardliness of contemporary Irish anthologists, suggest that his right to it might be disputed.

When this versatile man took a medical degree at Trinity College, Dublin, in June 1907 he was observing a family tradition. Almost three-quarters of a century previously, Robert Graves[1] lecturing on scarlet fever in the Meath Hospital during the session 1834—35 remarked, 'Dr. Gogerty (of Nobber, County Meath) has had many fatal cases, and the disease has been very prevalent'. The Gogertys or Gogartys are a branch of a County Tipperary ruling sept, MacFogarty, which on moving to County Meath changed its name to O'Gogarty or Gogarty. The 'Dr. Gogerty' to whom Graves alluded was either Dr. Henry Gogarty or his son James, physician to the family of Viscount Gormanstown.

Dr. James Gogarty, a man of great charm, married Elizabeth Kelly, a daughter of Richard Kelly and his wife Maria Theresa Duffy. Miss Duffy's father, Bernard, was a Dundalk merchant and her husband, who was given Drummond, a considerable estate at Kelly's Vale near Kingscourt, County Cavan, by his kinsman and godfather Colonel Coote, was in affluent circumstances.[2] Miss Duffy herself had a talent for music, languages and poetry.

Dr. and Mrs. James Gogarty had seven children. Their eldest son, Henry Joseph Kelly Gogarty, was born in 1844 and studied medicine in Dublin at the Ledwich School and became a Licentiate of the Royal College of Surgeons in Ireland in 1864. He took the coveted Fellowship of this College two years later and in 1877 added to his qualifications the Licence of the Royal College of Physicians of Edinburgh.[3] He practised in Dublin at 66 Blessington Street, moving to 5 Rutland Square, East in 1869 — a testimony of success. In this opulent neighbourhood where the householders included twelve doctors and more than twice as many lawyers, Dr. Gogarty's immediate neighbours were Colonel Crofton Vandeleur, M.P., and the Hon. Sterne Ball Miller, judge in the Court of Bankruptcy. The most distinguished of the local notabilities were the Earl of Charlemont and the Rt. Hon. Thomas O'Hagan, Lord High Chancellor of Ireland.

Henry Gogarty married Margaret Oliver in 1876. His bride was the daughter of John Oliver of Eyre Square, Galway, a prosperous miller. Their eldest child who was born on 17 August 1878 was called Oliver St. John Joseph, taking two of his given names from his grandfather and father respectively, the unusual addition possibly a sign of rank owing to a descendant of the Galway Olivers and the Kellys of Drummond, (there was once a Lord Deputy of Ireland, Oliver St. John).

At what stage young Oliver became conscious of caste and aware of his relatively privileged position in a city where the professional classes regarded themselves as separated only narrowly, if at all, from the aristocracy which remained in Ireland after the Union one cannot even surmise, but later in life he certainly took pride in his lineage. He boasted to Shane Leslie that if W.B. Yeats could make much of a forebear who had jumped overboard 'after a ragged hat in Biscay Bay', he too could claim the blood of wild buccaneers.

> Fitzdominick Oliver uncle of my Grandfather it was who seized Lord Edward Fitzgerald and dumped him into Salem. He took him from Aldingham House Galway and accused him or Wolfe Tone or one Foley of betraying him for standing in with the privateers of Britanny; and reminded him that for all his patriotism he did not hestitate to turn his guns on the women and children of Boston; for Lord Edward served in the fleet. He took Jute, an American who was spying for the British from his forecastle and strung him to the yardarm and emptied his 'gun' into him. These Fitzdominicks were of the De Burgo, now Burke, who married Granuale (Grace O'Malley) and made it possible for her to hold the Western Ocean.[4]

His Aunt Imelda, a sister in the Dominican Convent, Taylor's Hill, Galway, disapproved of his research into genealogy and refused to tell him 'how to reach from my Grandfather to Oliver Oge' and there the matter rests whether it be a romantic legend or a fact.

Such musings were of his maturity. The pattern of little Oliver's life and that of his sister, Mayflo, and two brothers, Henry and Richard,[5] was that of the children in a well-to-do Dublin family which had some entry into 'Society' and lived in a tall, red-brick Georgian house, well provided with servants to cook and clean and wait on table and carry the coal and hot water, with nurses to take their charges for walks keeping them from under their parents' feet, and grooms to look after the horses.

The family album[6] gives hints that if Oliver enjoyed the amenities and the comforts of an upper-middle-class household he was also at risk to the whims of a mother who enjoyed parading her children at fancy-dress balls in costumes which pleased her but may have merited their undeclared resentment. Thus, we find Mayflo and Oliver decked out in solemn absurdity as Maritana and Don Caesar de Bazan, and again in droll costume at the Countess of Aberdeen's garden-party. But neither these, nor the earliest lessons in the kindergarten, nor the Mass-going on Sundays and Holidays of Obligation that was part of the routine of a Catholic household, were what remained in his mind. He remembered instead an Easter Sunday when he waited for the sun to dance and saw it dancing on the bedroom ceiling; he remembered playing with his sister beneath the blossoms of the currant bushes in the garden behind 5 Rutland Square; he remembered sitting on a horse outside the stables. Earliest of all, when he could have been no more than a baby, he remembered a green wave over his head when his mother dipped him in the sea in Salthill near her home in Galway.[7]

A feature of such an upbringing is the conspiracy existing between the children and the servants who grow to love them. They share secrets, and it was Michael, the man-servant, who told Oliver that Dr. Gogarty had purchased Fairfield, a country-house in Glasnevin, standing in seven acres and bounded by a stream.

Fairfield House was two stories high with a gable in the middle and a hall door in a rounded tower at one end. Another tower half as high led into the garden. The hall was level with the ground. Behind the house was the most wonderful garden I ever saw. A huge yew hedge many hundreds of years old separated it from the kitchen garden. Fully grown yew trees sheltered it from the north. The yew hedge was mysterious: there were tunnels in it where you found hollow eggs. Blackbirds nested in it, and in the big yews at the end of the garden low down in the branches little birds slept 'all the night with open eyes'.[8]

This paradise stirred the boy's poetic sensibility, though not as yet into recorded words. He would lie under great elms looking up into a spread of green branches and watching the finches and linnets. He was happy to be alone beneath the trees or drifting on the Tolka in a tin bath that served as a boat.

The broad acres belonging to his father's friend in County Meath also helped to make town-bred Oliver something of a countryman, but Farrell O'Reilly's Kilbeg was almost too big for a child, its river reedy and dark.

> *My Father no sooner would talk of Kilbeg*
> *And carefully measure the charge for each cartridge,*
> *Than I saw myself strutting behind with the bag*
> *And heard the men talk as they walked up the partridge.*
> *The coveys were scarce, and the cause of the trouble*
> *Was 'Farell O'Reilly's too proud to have stubble'.*
>
> *O thick-sodded fields that have fattened the herds*
> *From the days of the kings in the dawn of our time,*
> *O fields of Moynalty, The Plains of the Birds,*
> *None ever drew plough through your land on the lime!*
> *King Leary of Tara just over the way*
> *Knew more about Meath than the men of to-day.*
>
> *My young eyes were good and rejoiced at the sight*
> *Of a drake with the sun all a blaze on his green*
> *That flew on a sudden from left to the right:*
> *What banging! But only a feather was seen.*
> *When each man exclaimed to the other, 'Bad luck!'*
> *I could not help thinking 'twas good for the duck.*[9]

The day's shooting was likely to finish with little Oliver's volunteering to carry a game-bag but being carried in the end himself, tired and happy.

> *Wood, river and well — the wild things of the fields;*
> *The lis with its lonely and wind-twisted thorn,*
> *Enchanted me early; . . .*

Less enchanting, presumably, were the obligations of the schoolroom that approached as he grew older.

Whether or not Dr. Gogarty was a man with social aspirations he had a fund of practical commonsense which led him to invest

money in bricks and mortar in Botanic Road and to select practical
teachers for his sons. Unlike John Stanislaus Joyce, the feckless
father of a promising son, who despised the Christian Brothers
and their demotic schools ('Is it with Paddy Stink and Mickey
Mud?'), Henry Gogarty sent his boy in 1890 to the O'Connell
School, North Richmond Street, convenient to Fairfield. Here the
long-remembered advice of the president, Dr. Swan, to his pupils
was 'Chisel your words', and Oliver found Euclid a help towards
unambiguous expression. He learned Irish but, reading a translation
of *The Youthful Exploits of Finn,* was mystified by the opening
sentence: 'Cumhal left pregnant his wife'. What could that possibly
mean? His friends at this school included Tom Kettle whom he
came increasingly to admire.

Dr. James Gogarty had died suddenly after vaulting a fence on
his way to visit a patient. Dr. Henry Gogarty's death from appendi-
citis in 1891 was less sudden but equally unexpected. His widow was
left with four children to rear but evidently in comfortable financial
circumstances. There was no change in her way of life, Fairfield and
5 Rutland Square both being retained. Oliver, however, experienced
a drastic change. His happy days at the Richmond Street School
and the countless hours spent fishing for gudgeon with a bent pin
with local lads on an island near Tolka Bridge came to an end.
   No stories of indiscipline at this stage have survived, however
many there were to be later, but it may have been decided by the
family council, now comprised of Mrs. Gogarty and the children's
aunt ('who had not only the Almanac de Gotha by heart but Burke's
Landed Gentry as well') that Oliver needed male supervision in a
boarding-school. In 1892 he exchanged the relative freedom of
Fairfield and North Richmond Street for Mungret, an Irish provincial school near Limerick run by the Jesuit Fathers, where Oliver
disliked the food and chafed against the rigidly imposed law-and-
order. When the boy lost weight his mother relented only in so far
as to transfer him to Stonyhurst College, a leading English Catholic
school standing picturesquely on the slope of Longridge Fell in
Lancashire's Ribble Valley.
   The testimony of his contemporaries in adult life is that Oliver St.
John Gogarty glowed with high spirits and was effervescent with
puckish good humour. It is difficult, then, to envisage the fourteen-
year-old so thoroughly miserable as he would have a correspondent
believe, referring to his years at Stonyhurst, in later life: 'That school
was the scene of such unhappiness that I accepted unhappiness as

the norm! I have never mentioned it to anyone. It is amazing how you heard of it: Stonyhurst the Accurst.'[10] He found outlets on the playing fields, in the swimming-pool and in the gymnasium. Translating Plato in the classroom he sardonically underlined, 'Knowledge which is acquired under compulsion obtains no hold on the mind', but he held on to enough to acquit himself successfully at the matriculation examination of the Royal University of Ireland in the summer of 1896.[11]

Although now eligible to taste the freedoms of undergraduate life the fact that during 1896-7 we find him boarding at Clongowes Wood College requires a note of explanation. The Royal University was an examining body which accepted candidates from many institutions and it was not uncommon in those days to take the First Arts examination from boarding-school. The extra year of disciplined supervision appealed, understandably, to many parents in that time of rigid morals and obligatory restraints. Oliver was happy at Clongowes. The First Arts students (there were two others, Hugo V. Flinn and James N. Meenan) would have been privileged and by now Gogarty was a first-class athlete, an accomplished cricketer and footballer, attributes which make life more than tolerable in Irish schools. Furthermore, scanning the new faces during his early days in Clongowes he recognised the familiar features of Tom Kettle and a friendship was renewed.

The term commenced in rainy weather on 1 September. Cricket played in unsuitable temperatures gave way to football a few weeks later. Meanwhile the annual retreat given by the Rev. Bernard Vaughan, S.J., commenced on 16 September and concluded on 20 September with general communion.[12] The year was to be a successful one for Tom Kettle who ended it as gold-medallist, all-Ireland Exhibitioner, and winner of the Higher Line essay prize with an essay on Owen Roe O'Neill. Oliver Gogarty was more impressed, however, by his friend's prowess as a cyclist — 'There comes under my eyelid a moving picture of his grey-clad figure scorching round and round the gravel cycling track of his school, his long legs pushing power into the pedals, his brown face bright with exercise, a glow in his dark eyes that could light a room'[13] — and he was soon imitating him, stripping down a roadster to serve as a racing bicycle.

School re-opened after the Christmas holidays on 14 January and the major distraction during the worst cold of the winter was skating and ice-hockey on the frozen pond. A major sporting disappointment was the soccer match against Bohemians, Dublin's leading amateur team. The game was played on a windy day with a blinding sun.

Winning the toss, Clongowes had the wind and the sun behind them; their passing was rapid and accurate and for most of the first half they kept the ball near their opponents' goal-mouth. It seemed that they must score but half-time came without one goal. The greater stamina and strength of the older men told in the second half when the Clongowes boys faced the wind. At the final whistle 'Bohs' had three goals to their opponents' one, which Gogarty had scored. Nevertheless it was generally conceded that Clongowes had the better forwards and the Bohemians' selectors asked O'Shaughnessy and Gogarty to play for them in a coming match against Belfast's Cliftonville. Oliver also played for Bohemians in their cup final and won a gold medal that Tom Kettle would have envied.

In those spartan times Easter holidays had not been introduced. The days preceding the Feast were days for recollection. Father Fegan preached the Good Friday sermon; he spoke on the history of the Sacred Passion and held the boys' attention for more than an hour. On Holy Saturday the choir gained plaudits for a rendering of Regina Coeli. It is unlikely that the sun danced on the ceiling of Gogarty's dormitory in Clongowes, on Easter Sunday morning, as it had long ago in Rutland Square, but it was a day for celebration, with roulette, raffles, target-shooting and sports until rain spoiled the fun. Oliver Gogarty won the Higher Line 120 yards hurdles race but what must have delighted him even more was to beat Tom Kettle (the scratch man) into second place in the three-mile cycle race.

Towards the end of April, after some weeks of coaching, cricket began in earnest on one of the finest pitches in the country. Gogarty, a strong bowler, was in the first eleven. In the match against the Curragh Brigade he was caught for a duck by Sgt. Major White but made amends by his bowling. His greatest feat was on 20 May against the Dublin Garrison. Their star bat, Captain Bonham Carter, had scored forty-six against previous bowlers but his wicket went down to Gogarty's first ball. He dismissed two other batsmen for eight and three and Lieutenant Comyn had scored five when he was caught by Treacy off Gogarty's bowling.[14]

The serious business of the year, however, lay ahead — the public examinations. The subjects for the First University Examination were Latin, Greek or another language, mathematics, natural philosophy (physics) and English. The essays set by Professor Thomas Arnold were ironically apposite — 'Pope as a friend or as an enemy', 'The Parliamentary career of Edmund Burke', 'The evils of excessive novel-reading' — for satire, politics and literary distractions were to compete with medicine in Gogarty's own career.

The three Clongowes candidates for the First University Examination were successful[15] and Oliver St. John Gogarty's hybrid existence as an over-mature schoolboy was completed. The world was his oyster now and he proceeded to open it with verve.

2

And a Very Good Time

Through the National Library's Lawrence Collection the city in which Gogarty grew to manhood as the nineteenth century drew to a close can be recovered. Dublin's bone structure remains unaltered, though it has run to flesh and its integuments have changed, the cobbles have vanished, the water-troughs have been removed, the great draught horses, the horse-buses and their later electrically-driven counterparts which swayed through the streets like galleons, replaced by dense motor traffic, the stables transformed into garages.

A wanton conception of raiding Vikings, Dublin sprawled in infancy at the Liffey's mouth until adopted in childhood by the Normans. Growing, it voiced its own legislative needs. Its heyday, perhaps, was under the Georges in the eighteenth century when it attained maturity and a claret-coloured complexion, before the emasculating Act of Union ushered in a decline not yet fully repaired. A chattel of the British, there were extremes of wealth and poverty in its residential squares and squalid slums; a flourishing red-light district catered for the garrison and others; in taverns and presbyteries, common-rooms and salons, wherever ideas were debated, the most-prized weapon was wit; it was indulgent towards eccentricity and characters were encouraged.

From Rutland Square the thoroughfare sloped down to Sackville Street, Dublin's widest boulevard, dominated then by the Nelson Pillar at the base of which sat shawl-clad flower-sellers crying their wares. Crossing O'Connell Bridge, which to the east might afford the sight of windjammers tied up at the quays, it divided into D'Olier Street and Westmoreland Street both of which led to Trinity College, Elizabeth the First's foundation. The university's splendid facade looked on to College Green and Dame Street at the other end of which Dublin Castle was a symbol of British power, fawned on and execrated.

Half way up Dame Street a complex of narrow lanes led to Cecilia Street where a building which formerly served as the Apothecaries' Hall housed the Catholic University Medical School, its ill-favoured site and cramped conditions mute witness of a struggle with the ascendancy. A mile or so away, containing the other faculties of Newman's Catholic University, by then a re-named constituent of the Royal University, University College was situated more favourably on the south side of St. Stephen's Green, a pleasant neighbourhood favoured by the clubs of the well-to-do.

Eventually Oliver St. John Gogarty was to live in Ely Place in the vicinity of St. Stephen's Green but by then all connection with University College and the Royal had been long since severed. According to himself the contretemps causing his defection stemmed from Professor Ambrose Birmingham's curtness when Mrs. Gogarty called to Cecilia Street to register Oliver for the medical course. A brilliant anatomist who combined the duties of registrar, 'Ambie' was an over-worked man who suffered fools and ladies badly. He was brusque with Mrs. Gogarty who beckoned her still dutiful son and flounced out of his office. She was more graciously received by Dr. Anthony Traill, a future Provost of Trinity College, who had the good manners to mention that he had known her late husband. Little things may decide large issues and Oliver entered Trinity.[1]

That at any rate is the received explanation but though his name appears in Trinity's *Entrance Book* on 5 July 1897 he remained an arts student at the Royal for another year and failed the second arts examination in 1898.[2] During that year he became acquainted with a group of young men who were more unruly than those in College Park.

Despite Cecilia Street's tradition of unruliness it also had many earnest students including a quartet of inseparables, Dolan, James Hegarty, McCluskey, and Roger Dwane who were called 'the Halogens' because like chlorine, fluorine, bromine and iodine they were never found free in Nature, always combined. They were serious and hard-working which did not endear them to Gogarty and the more raffish element. James Hegarty was singled out for particular disapprobation with a mocking 'Hah! Hegarty!' whenever there was a hush in class.

In Professor Sigerson's class in University College the students devised an ingenious scheme of dividing the extensive zoology textbook into boroughs or constituencies; each student was elected representative for a borough and was expected to answer questions about the creatures in his borough, even when the question was not addressed to him. Because of a growing reputation as a racing cyclist, Gogarty was elected to represent snails.

George Sigerson who had a long flaxen beard was a versatile man; a medical practitioner and translator of Charcot's *Diseases of the Nervous System,* he was himself a poet and the author of *The Poets and Poetry of Munster* and *Bards of the Gael & Gall.* The last-named was published in 1897 when Sigerson was sixty-one but he was to live to a great age and sit with Gogarty in the Irish Free State Senate. His venerable appearance did not make him immune to pranks but students tempted to treat him with disrespect came off second best. It was his habit when lecturing to place his silk hat upside down on the desk before him. When his back was turned a student dropped a card into it inscribed 'donkey'. At the end of the class Sigerson picked out the card, read it and said, 'I see that one of you gentlemen has left his card'. On another occasion a student with a mirror amused himself in an attempt to shine a beam of light on the professor's beard evoking Sigerson's comment, 'I see a student's feeble intellect flickering on the wall'. Gogarty recalled his saying, 'I have noticed that those who are most noisy in class are most silent in examinations'.

An oasis of peace walled off from the turmoil of the city's centre and the stridency of its commercial life, the green lawns, the cobbled quadrangles and the grey masonry of Trinity College provided Oliver St. John Gogarty with an ideal background for his studies had he had a mind to settle down to them. But there were distractions causing unconscionable delays, the unprojected byproducts of which included *Tumbling in the Hay*.

The five-year medical course entailed passing 'the Previous Medical or Half M.B. Examination' (the subjects for which were physics, chemistry, biology, anatomy and physiology), and the Final Examination. It was customary to take physics, chemistry and biology in the junior freshman year, completing 'the Half' as a senior freshman. Three nine-month sessions of clinical work followed. Candidates for the M.B. degree also had to take the B.A. but the arts course could be taken concurrently.

In 1897-8 the Provost of Trinity was George Salmon, D.D.; the Senior Fellows included John Kells Ingram, Ll.D., Litt.D., still remembered for his poem 'The Memory of the Dead'. The Junior Dean was Edward Gwynn, a member of the family which gave so many distinguished sons to the University that a wit said it should be called 'Gwynnity'. The chairs of chemistry and physics were held by James Emerson Reynolds and George Francis FitzGerald respectively. Professors E.P. Wright and H.W. Mackintosh taught botany and physiology. Speaking of George Francis FitzGerald who made important contributions to the development of electro-magnetic theory, John Butler Yeats said, 'he was a true scientist, that is, a poet as well'. His praise for the Provost was less enthusiastic:

> ....The late Dr. Salmon was a great man and a great mathematician but it was well known that tho' he was an infallible judge of every kind of investment he paid no attention to what is called the artistic values being exclusively a man of science and therefore a philistine. Mathematicians are as a rule philistines and are apt to think that there is nothing in life valuable except the utilities, and that what is called efficiency is the chief of human faculties. A friend of mine, a fine classical scholar, told me that in his experience, mathematicians could only talk of the price of things — tell them, he said, what you pay for your boots. I once met Dr. Salmon at dinner and was much flattered by his taking me aside and asking me what I paid for my lodgings.....[3]

Unlike the painter, Oliver Gogarty saw no poetry in the physics laboratory or if he did its idiom had little appeal for him; instead, his lively mind eventually found inspiration in the B.A. course where he was still bound to English literature and the classics, while on the cycling-track he experienced that thrust of power and rush of speed which is the body's equivalent of the sublimity of verse. It may be mentioned here that he was also a strong swimmer. He received the Royal Humane Society's bronze medal in 1898 'for having saved life from drowning'; in the following year he went to the assistance of a Mr. John Meeke who had got into difficulty in the sea off Balbriggan, County Dublin, but due to the clumsy handling of a boat which was sent out to help them Meeke was lost. On 22 June 1901 he dived into the Liffey and saved the life of a Mr. Max Harris.

His approach to his medical studies was, to say the least of it, leisurely. He sat an examination in botany and zoology in the autumn of 1898 passing comfortably with 62 per cent, the second highest mark awarded, but it was three and half years before he contemplated the next.[4] Rather than attribute this either to indolence or hedonism, though it is likely that elements of both were present, we should bear in mind that the more accommodating regulations of the time probably explained his apparent detachment. Even though he took no exams he was allowed to take out lectures in clinical subjects and so could hope to recover the lost time.

As a senior freshman in 1898-9 he attended lectures in systematic and practical anatomy (dissecting three 'parts'), practical chemistry and practical histology. In the following year the junior sophister attended lectures in physiology and anatomy and gained further credits for dissection. He commenced clinical work at the Richmond Hospital in October 1899.

During 1900-01, in addition to physiology and applied anatomy, he attended 'Boss' Bennett's surgery lectures and those of the professor of medicine, James Magee Finny. Credits for pathology and midwifery lectures were gained in the following year, and in 1902 he fulfilled the requirements for operative surgery and practical pathology.

Oliver Gogarty was now in the unusual position that he had more or less completed the requirements of the entire medical course but had not yet taken 'the half'. What is particularly difficult to understand is why he had not yet sat physics and chemistry, subjects he should have been rid of in the junior freshman year. He entered for anatomy and physiology in the Hilary term of 1902 but did not sit the examination; he failed dismally (23%) in the summer exam. In the autumn he passed in physics and chemistry.

He received instruction in midwifery and gynaecology at the National Maternity Hospital, Holles Street, between July 1903 and January 1904. The regulations required attendance at thirty-two maternity cases and personal responsibility for twelve the first of which, the delivery of Mrs. Cullen's male infant (vertex presentation) at 35 Wentworth Place, he conducted on 3 July 1903 assisted by Nurse Lutterell.[5]

Meanwhile a gift for parody and a facility in turning out bawdy verses had established Gogarty as a character in undergraduate circles. These talents were effectively combined in a salacious send-up of Arthur O'Shaughnessy's well-known 'Ode':

> *We are the masturbators*
> *We are the dreamers of dreams*
> *Spending in secretive places,*
> *Our totally purposeless streams;*
> *And one with a mind at leisure*
> *Can roger an ancient Queen*
> *And make from a moment's pleasure*
> *A map on the damascene.*[6]

Another *tour de force* was a long scatological verse-narrative, 'Sinbad the Sailor', of which only fragments have survived. His propensity for this genre was so great that he ran the risk of being credited with every naughty rhyme and limerick that circulated wherever men gathered in Dublin.[7]

Rumours of this antic figure eventually penetrated the portals of the senior common-room. Whatever his failings in certain scholastic areas, an athlete with a ribald sense of humour, an effortless memory for verse and a feeling for the classics could be forgiven much by the middle-aged dons. They sought him out and invited him into their company. At first a cautious and irreverent disciple, with maturity he attained the friendship of Mahaffy, Tyrrell and Macran.

The Rev. John Pentland Mahaffy, the most formidable of this trio, was sixty at the turn of the century. He was a Hellenist and historian who himself judged that his greatest talent was for music; his publications included *The Principles of the Art of Conversation* and his celebrity as a wit spread far beyond the College confines. Speaking of what might be expected of a Viceroy in Ireland he said, 'We have no use for a man who does not waste both his time and his money'. Pointing to the blank page of the *Book of Kells* where Queen Victoria had been invited to sign her name he said 'Behold the quintessence of snobbery!' Rebuking a student for swearing he said, 'My dear fellow, you should not swear. By doing so you may lose your immortal soul, and, what is worse, be fined two and six pence'.[8]   When Mahaffy asked Gogarty at a College meeting. 'Are you rising on a point of order?' Gogarty said, 'No, on the spur of the moment', a reply which the master-wit must have appreciated.

Mahaffy lisped and his social faults included a vein of snobbery which Gogarty satirized in 'The Death of Diogenes, the Doctor's Dog' (a parody of Swinburne's 'Atalanta in Calydon') published anonymously in the College Magazine on 14 February 1903 —

> *When I wambled awound*
> *In the gwound that was Gweece*
> *I was given the hound*
> *By the King's little niece;*
> *And rather were fined ere I found him to gaze on his saddest surcease.*
> *Chorus (Scholars of the House)*
> *He was given the hound*
> *By the seed of a king*
> *For the wisdom profound*

Of his wide wandering.
But was it the donor, or owner, or dog that was led by a string?

And so it ran on for many stanzas.

Mahaffy's reaction to the St. Valentine's Day lampoon is conjectural but on another occasion, years later, the joke was on Gogarty who had entertained the don in Ely Place. Mahaffy, a connoisseur of claret, praised the wine and asked where Gogarty had obtained it. Gogarty said he had bought it at an auction. 'I never heard of such a thing,' Mahaffy said. 'Laying down a cellar by haphazard. My friend, you are not worthy of your wine. I will send my man to remove it.' Which he did.[9]

Gogarty thought Henry Stewart Macran, the professor of moral philosophy, almost as omniscient as Mahaffy but more gentle. Yet there was that about him which another friend neatly summed up:

You could be all things
But a good and wifely man,
And that you would not if you could
We know, Macran.[10]

His gentleness was inconstant, especially when in his cups. 'You filthy asses!' he admonished the barmen in Jammet's at closing time when they cried *Time, please.* 'You are speaking of that the nature of which you do not know. Time is the moving shadow of eternity.'

It was, however, the Regius Professor of Greek, Robert Yelverton Tyrrell, who interested Gogarty most of all. He has described their first meeting after an English examination at which Tyrrell awarded the undergraduate an unprecedented ten marks out of ten.

He sat in a room off the Hall, a full-browed figure with a prominent forehead, 'rich-crowned with memory': light blue eyes in a clear pink countenance. This was the renowned Professor Tyrrell, the greatest Greek and diseur of his day, a 'worthy' if ever there was one, kalos k'agathos, which as everyone knows, means comely and worthy, and is the Greek for a gentleman. His knowledge of the structure of the metres of classical poetry was equalled only by his knowledge and love of English poetry.[11]

Tyrrell was the editor of the Bacchae and Troades of Euripides and of Plautus's *Miles Gloriosus* but, even more than his classical learning, Tyrrell's urbanity and love of sport attracted Gogarty.

Another quality which endeared Tyrrell to the younger man and which perhaps rubbed off on him was a flair for invective. He described Sir William Wilde as 'a small pithecoid fellow who skulked behind his wife's petticoats', and said of his own contemporary, Traill, that he was either a buffalo turned man or a man degenerating into a buffalo but he could never be certain which. Poor Traill who was appointed Provost in 1904 was anathema to Mahaffy who said when told that the Provost was ill, 'nothing trivial, I hope'. Frequently he referred to Traill as a bigot and a beast. He said audibly to Augustine Birrell in Traill's presence, 'Our Provost is a Beast', adding on observing Birrell's embarrassment, 'but he's a deaf beast'.

Mahaffy's biographers[12] cast reasonable doubt on the authenticity of a much-quoted comment — 'James Joyce is a living argument that it was a mistake to establish a separate university for the aborigines of this island, for the corner-boys who spit into the Liffey' — but it serves to remind us of the undeniable gulf then existing in Dublin between Trinity and University College, between the School of Physic and Cecilia Street. Gogarty's favoured position among the dons left an imprint on his character but, despite his English schooling and relative affluence, his grass-roots were those of the Catholic youths of St. Stephen's Green, not those of the mannered students of College Park. It was to his advantage to run with both groups, and to do so separately. The stamp on the obverse is just as clearly delineated and as valid.

The National Library in Kildare Street and the pubs were general clearing-houses for gossip and ideas. In these places he used to meet his friends from 'the Royal' who included Francis Sheehy Skeffington, Tom Kettle and also the group which is featured in *Tumbling in the Hay,* Simon Broderick, John Elwood, Vincent Cosgrave and James Joyce.

Gogarty's admiration for Tom Kettle never faltered:

Of all the wits and worthies I have met, and they were quite a few, one of the outstanding ones was Tom Kettle. He was young, buoyant, laughing, carefree, and gifted with an astounding power of breaking through an enemy's front with a wit like lightning.[13]

When, arguing about religion, an opponent expressed surprise that such an intelligent man should remain a Roman Catholic instead of picking and choosing, Kettle said, 'It's a matter of table d'hôte or à la carte'. He defined the United Arts Club as 'infinite bitches in a little room'. When he was carpeted for being inebriated in uniform he said, 'You do not know the roll of honour when you see it'.

John Elwood, a native of Carrowbehy, County Roscommon, took the first University Examination from Summerhill College, Sligo, coming to University College in 1901. He was successful in the first professional examination in 1902 but then 'Citizen' Elwood (his customary greeting was 'Citizen!') rested on his laurels and for years was a chronic medical student. On his departure to Buenos Aires Gogarty wrote: *Oh, send to bring the Springtime back/Your basic old subliming knack*[14] — but to everyone's relief his exile was brief. ' "Senor, be gob," shouted the Citizen, exalted by his dream of himself.' Heavily moustachioed, wearing sheepskin gaucho trousers, and brandishing silver-mounted pistols he made a mock-raid on the Cecilia Street dissecting-room on his first day back to be confronted by Professor Birmingham who was not amused and summoned the police. Elwood eventually took the Licentiate of the Apothecaries' Hall in 1915 and settled in his native place where he practised medicine and earned a reputation for his knowledge of land reclamation.

When Oliver Gogarty was introduced to James Joyce in the National Library in 1901 he found the latter's shyness 'as great as the diffidence of a lay brother in a monastery', but their homes lay in the same direction and from time to time he ran into Joyce in the street or on the tram. They had a bond in poetry and, strolling together on the North Side pavements and chatting in the shade of the trees at Fairfield, companionship warmed into a friendship that would last some years.

The younger by four years, Joyce's mocking gravity amused Gogarty who called him according to his mood 'Dante' or 'Kinch' or 'the virginal kip-ranger'. He celebrated his friend's waywardness in a limerick:

> *There is a young fellow named Joyce*
> *Who possesseth a sweet tenor voice.*
> *He goes to the Kips*
> *With a psalm on his lips*
> *And biddeth the harlots rejoice.*

The wayward and unrestrained characters of 'Monto', the redlight district which existed between Gloucester Street and Montgomery Street (east of the present Gardiner Street), had an infinite appeal for undergraduates who were themselves in undeclared revolt against years of rigidly enforced rectitude and constraints, and they have been memorialized imperishably by Gogarty in pages and verses which succeed in portraying the abandon behind the Edwardian facade, not neglecting to hint at the squalor of 'the long rancid hell, the frowsy pores of whose awful denizens tainted even its polluted air'.

> *O there goes Mrs. Mack;*
> *She keeps a house of imprudence,*
> *She keeps an old back parlour*
> *For us poxy medical students,*
> *To show, to show*
> *That we are medical students.*
> *To show, to show,*
> *That we medical students don't give a damn.*

One takes it that the devil-may-care attitude is a pose, for even if concupiscence now and then conquered, the medicals had seen enough horrid examples to make them dread the lethal pathology exuding from the diseased brothels of Night-town.

> *Tyrone Street of the crowded doors*
> *And Faithful Place so infidel...*
> *There's nothing left but ruin now*
> *Where once the crazy cabfuls roared;*
> *Where new-come sailors turned the prow*
> *And Love-logged cattle-dealers snored;*
> *The room where old Luke Irwin whored*
> *The stairs on which John Elwood fell...*[15]

The Madams, their 'drunken girls delectable' and the assorted clients are presented in Gogarty's now well-known poem 'The Hay Hotel'. When a bookie objected that Becky Cooper had been left out he added an unpublished stanza:

> *Shall Becky Cooper be forgot*
> *Have I forgotten Liverpool Kate*
> *And all the foam she used to frot*
> *Were she for one night celebrate?*
> *I often tried to dam that spate*
> *When 'Fuck me like a horse!' she'd yell*
> *And who was I to remonstrate*
> *Before I sought the Hay Hotel.*

Razed like the rest, the Hay Hotel (so named after its 'window stuffed with hay' for the cab-horses) belongs to a roistering past. Even its exact site is now unknown but it probably stood in Great Britain Street on the boundary of Night-town, not far from Rutland Square. Perhaps it was from this dubious hostelry that Gogarty returned homeward unsteadily on a night that he stumbled upstairs and muttered, 'Oliver falls the first time...'; there is said to have been a second fall and a third. The noise brought Mrs. Gogarty from her room to hear her prostrate son say indistinctly, 'Oliver meets his afflicted mother'.

3

And that Sweet City with her Dreaming Spires

Oliver Gogarty's pedestrian record in the medical school was compensated for in considerable measure by his victories on the cycling track and his unparalleled success as a contender for the Vice-Chancellor's Prizes.

At the turn of the century cycling was a popular sport with prizes attracting semi-professional attitudes. Gogarty's record as a cyclist has been detailed by Ulick O'Connor[1] and is referred to in *Tumbling in the Hay*. Essentially a sprinter, training added the stamina that made him a champion in the longer distances. His sense of style made him use red custom-made cycling shoes and an individually-designed jersey but the dandy was a match for the toughest opponents.

> I was watching Larry Oswald's calves very carefully as we circled in a bicycle race round the College Park. Larry, who was one of the best all-round athletes in Ireland, was leading. I lay next behind him, waiting for the least increase in the tension of the muscles in his long shapely calves. Then I'd be off. It was the third round, and we were coming to the bell which rings to announce the last lap. I had been floating along half mesmerised by muscular fitness which made it possible to move on the grass at twenty miles an hour as in a dream. The grass — what is this the Professor of Weeds called the grass in his last lecture? Yes, *Poa pratensis,* meadow grass, that was it. I was doing twenty on *Poa pratensis.*

Despite his vigilance the leaders were beaten in the last leg by Alfred Emerson Reynolds, son of the professor of chemistry. The defeat made Gogarty determined to win the ten mile race up north in Ballyneighfeigh where the prizes were better than the lobster knives he had given to his aunt. In the event he was hemmed in and nearly killed as he tried to take the lead. He spread his elbows in self defence touching the handlebars of a man who was crowding him against the curb; '... he changed his mind as suddenly as his direction'.

When Oliver was suspended by the Amateur Athletic Association for 'bad language' he gave his time to literature and won the Vice-Chancellor's Prize for English Verse in 1902 with a ten-stanza poem on Robert Louis Stevenson which is a very pale reflection of Shelley's 'Adonais':

No tears for him, for he has persevered
'Gainst adverse storms; no tears, for he has won,
Though weak and wearied, and become endeared
With Goldsmith with Scotland's darling son
To mankind's common heart. Safely he steered
To 'Treasure Island', in whose blue lagoon
Shining far brighter than she e'er appeared
To us, floats holily the pure faced moon.

The king beneath his ponderous pyramid
Has not as grand a sepulchre as thine;
A coral island rising sheer amid
A realm no earthly monarch may confine:
Nor were the works of this great king who bid
His myriads raise a puny mountain high,
As great as thine in living bosoms hid,
And which as long as hearts beat shall not die.

Gogarty took the B.A. in 1903 but having done badly in anatomy in 'the Half' he did not bother to sit physiology. However, he won the Vice-Chancellor's Prize again in 1903 — the subject was 'The Death of Shelley' — and in the same year, urged by James Joyce who pointed out his eligibility, he entered successfully for the Royal University's Gold Medal for English Verse which he promptly pawned. The subject was 'The Death of Byron'. Neither of these prize-winning poems has survived.

Encountering R.W. Lee, a Fellow of Worcester College, in Macran's rooms the idea of entering for Oxford University's Newdigate Prize germinated in Gogarty's mind and he spent two terms at Oxford in 1904. On the evening of his arrival, stepping on to the railway platform, he noticed that 'a falling star streamed down the blue vault'. An omen perhaps? 'If so, an omen of what?' Evidently it was not an omen of victory but the interlude broadened his horizon and introduced him to some new friends including Christopher Stone, Compton Mackenzie and Samuel Chenevix Trench.

It seems to have been a holiday — undeserved some would say — for Gogarty told Joyce in a letter, 'I'm reading for a Litt. D. which I don't intend to take out but it enables me to read with the lady students'.[2] He played soccer and toured the neighbourhood on a motor-bicycle hired from the creator of Morris cars, the future Lord Nuffield.

He found that behaviour was more important than intellect at Oxford, where conduct was ruled by 'good form' rather than reason, a higher level example of what Winston Churchill had in mind when he said that 'England is a Laocoon strangled by the Old School Tie'. Not surprisingly, Gogarty found himself in breach of some footling rule — it was, for instance, bad form to pun or make classical allusions in the dining-hall — and he was given the alternative of drinking the 'sconce' (a five-and-a-half-pint tankard) in one draught or being fined. The challenge was irresistible to a Dubliner who, as he himself said, 'had been weaned on pints':

I planted my elbows firmly on the table and raised the silver tankard to my mouth. I took a deep breath. I began to drink. The first two pints went down pleasantly enough. It would have been enjoyable if there had not been so much depending on the draught. You would never guess what affected me most. Not a feeling of repleteness. No. You could never guess. It was the awful cold that hurt me on both sides of the throat and went up into my ears... I held on, conscious still. If this goes on I will pass out; but on it had to go. I suppose it took two or three full minutes, and two minutes are enough to die in. Look at the second hand of your watch to realise how long two minutes can be. To me, whatever time it was seemed ten times longer. At last I reached the bottom and I put my head back to drain the thing so that it would not drip when I held it upside down.[3]

The feat added to Gogarty's popularity in Oxford but he missed Dublin's matter-of-fact ways — 'I can't be an aristocrat for more than ten days at a time'.

Various stratagems to enable James Joyce to join him in his carousals in Oxford failed but on one or other of his visits to London he met Dermot Freyer who introduced him to Francis Willoughby Tancred. The latter, who knew every word written by Herrick, worked in the Stock Exchange and wore a bowler instead of the helmet which would have suited him better. 'Tancred looked jointed,

as if he were accustomed to move only in armour.' His poetic endeavours included a New Year's resolution praiseworthy in more than
one sense: *My assets shall not gild the reticule/of any rose-lipped
daughter of misrule.*[4]

Dermot Freyer was the son of a distinguished surgeon, Sir Peter
Freyer, a native of Connemara who served in the Indian Medical
Service before returning to Harley Street to specialize in genito-
urinary surgery and who was the first to make removal of the prostate gland a practical procedure. Dermot shared Gogarty's consuming
interest in poetry and more than a little of his waywardness. His own
literary output would in time include *Rhymes and Vanities, Sunlit
Leaves, In Lavender Covers* and *Not All Joy.* Freyer who was some
years younger than Gogarty was captivated by the latter's personality
and they continued to meet and correspond for many years.

Gogarty's capacity for friendship is evident in the numerous
letters he dashed off effortlessly, their style bearing a not-so-subtle
relationship to the personality of the recipients. From Oxford he
sent James Joyce a bawdy parody of W.B. Yeats's 'The Pity of
Love', further obscene fragments concerning Medical Dick and
Medical Davy, and intimations (or perhaps wishful thinking) of
carnal consolations:

> Stone walls do not a prison make
> Nor iron bars a cage
> If in a tilt for sweet Love's sake
> The slavey will engage.
>
> If I have freedom in my love
> Who in my love am free
> The Connoisseur who rules above
> Knows no such liberty.

Regretfully he conveyed to Joyce the outcome of the poetic contest
which blighted his expectation of prize-money:

> This Danaan Druid, O Wandering Aengus, obtained but 2nd
> place in the Newdigate! further cause for impecuniosity. My
> Alexandrines I think are not traditional — hence these tears —
> Damn tradition, and the impenetrability of Professors' souls
> but perhaps to damn tradition is to wreck Rome and England,
> and we must have the one as we must have lingerie — on ladies
> — and we require the other as the ladies themselves. However,
> good luck.... O Aengus of the Birds. Sing sweetly so that the
> stones may move and build a causeway to Oxford.[5]

He did not lose hope that Joyce would find some way to join him and continued to exhort him: 'Bluff some respectable person and come over here before the blossoms have all gone down on the water. The place is lovely now. I am to meet the fellow who won the Newdigate. I will see if he can be made a poet. Of course if he descended to Pope's metre or teetotalism this cannot be done.' George Kennedy Allen Bell, the Christ Church student whose 'Delphi' had been preferred to the Irishman's, turned out to be a congenial companion and their friendship survived their departure from Oxford. Bell, a son of the Manse, was destined to become an ecumenical churchman, and Bishop of Chichester.

Gogarty had interrupted his Oxford idyll to sit 'the half' at the end of the Hilary term, only to fail, though with a better mark, 44 per cent. And now with mounting debts to settle he wrote again to 'the wandering Aengus' as the summer term ended:

> *I thought beloved, to have brought to you*
> *A gift of quietness, and ten and six;*
> *Cooling your brow and your landlady too,*
> *With ready spondulicks.*
> *Homeward I go not yet, because of those*
> *Who will not let me leave lest they repine:*
> *Far from the Bank the 'stream of quiet' flows*
> *Through hands that are not mine.*
> *But, O my Knight! I send to you the stars*
> *That light my very creditable gains.*
> *And out of Oxford — though 'on my arse' —*
> *My scorn of all its praise.*[6]

He explained his difficult position, equally concerned by his own problems and his inability to help James Joyce. 'Since I came back I have not had an ½d from home.... In town here I owe about 30 £. I can't pay Starkey whom I love with thee his 10/6 until I get back. O'Leary Curtis is *intangible?* If not "touch him". By the Christ crust I'm sorry that I cannot "make haste to help you." ' He had no hope of a prodigal son's welcome on his return. 'I am cut off from my domicile by the Mater. So keep room in that dust-bin of yours.' He excused himself from sitting 'the half' on the plea of illness and when he did sit it a few weeks later it was to fail again.

Fortunately his long-suffering mother relented and by the end of June Oliver was reinstalled in the comfort of 5 Rutland Square, his equanimity restored, his days free for swimming and literary pursuits which were combined in excursions to Sandycove and Howth.

On Howth summit, looking down on Lambay Island and the distant northern hills, mundane affairs seemed remote as he gained poetic inspiration from a girl's auburn hair.

> *When the sun shines on Mary's hair*
> *Her splendour seems to own*
> *That solid rays of sunlight there*
> *Are blended with the brown;*
> *And in the golden coil of it*
> *A thousand little rainbows sit.*
> *Then neither wonder that my sight*
> *On her is wholly shed,*
> *When she can take the heaven's light*
> *To bind abut her head;*
> *Or that to her I captive fall*
> *Who holds the rainbows in her thrall.*[7]

During the summer he wrote an essay on 'Mythology — theories as to its origin and development' which won the Vice-Chancellor's Prize for English prose in 1904 and he was already drafting a poem on 'Cervantes — Tercentenary of Don Quixote' for the 1905 competition. 'To Stella' the first poem to appear under his own name in a periodical issued for general circulation was published in *Dana* in August 1904.

> *Stars by the light they shed*
> *Only are known,*
> *Songs by the verse they wed*
> *Time have outgrown;*
> *And that my verse may be*
> *Tuned to eternity,*
> *Shining with love of thee*
> *Light me alone.*
>
> *Life to the lute of Love*
> *Only will sing,*
> *Few are the songs that move*
> *After the Spring;*
> *And if the Spring be frore —*
> *Spring that so soon is o'er —*
> *What shall the Winter store*
> *From harvesting?*

Some weeks previously he had sent G.K.A. Bell a letter of introduction to W.B. Yeats whom Bell was anxious to meet. He regretted
that he could not send the manuscript of a lyric that Yeats had
written out for him on the top of the piano one evening in Rutland
Square. Yeats, who first met Gogarty at a play-reading in the Nassau
Hotel ('No one formally introduced us,' Gogarty was to write later.
'We just met.'), occasionally put up at the Cavendish Hotel, a few
doors from the Gogarty residence, and over a number of years their
slight acquaintanceship deepened into friendship. But in 1904
Gogarty, a disciple of Swinburne, told Bell, 'Don't mind Yeats, the
Swins the thing!'[8]

Another of his older literary acquaintances was George Moore,
the novelist, who, disgusted by the Boer War, had returned to Ireland
in 1901 and lived in Ely Place. Gogarty dined with Moore early in
August. 'By Jove, Gogarty,' exclaimed Moore, 'that Newdigate you
showed me was splendid!' Gogarty was preparing to be bashful when
his host's next words made him realize that Bell's poem was being
praised. 'You couldn't possibly have won it!'

And so the summer wore on.... The only cloud on the horizon was
'the half' which had to be faced again in November. But meanwhile a
major diversion was approaching.

4

A Voice within the Tower

Setting out from Dublin on a tour that would be incorporated in *Rambles in Eirinn,* William Bulfin was told by his companion as they cycled towards Dalkey 'of two men living in a tower down somewhere to the left who were creating a sensation in the neighbourhood. They had ... assumed a hostile attitude towards the conventions of denationalisation, and were, thereby, outraging the feelings of the *seoinini.*' It was a lovely Sunday morning in September 1904; the cyclists were in no hurry and Bulfin's friend suggested they should call on these unconventional settlers.

There was no necessity to repeat the suggestion, so we turned off to the left at the next crossroads, and were soon climbing a steep ladder which led to the door of the tower. We entered, and found some men of Ireland in possession, with whom we tarried until far on in the morning. One of them had lately returned from a canoeing tour of hundreds of miles through the lakes, rivers, and canals of Ireland, another was reading for a Trinity College degree, and assiduously wooing the muses, and another was a singer of songs which spring from the deepest currents of life. The returned marine of the canoe was an Oxford student, whose button-hole was adorned by the badge of the Gaelic League — a most strenuous Nationalist he was, with a patriotism, stronger than circumstances, which moved him to pour forth fluent Irish upon every Gael he encountered, in accents blent from the characteristic speech of his alma mater and the rolling blas of Connacht. The poet was a wayward kind of genius, who talked in a captivating manner, with a keen, grim humour, which cut and pierced through a topic in bright, strong flashes worthy of the rapier of Swift. The other poet listened in silence, and when we went on the roof he disposed himself restfully to drink in the glory of the morning.

This little-known vignette captures the atmosphere created in the Martello Tower, Sandycove, by the extravagant patriotism of Samuel

Chenevix Trench, the ceaseless repartee of Oliver Gogarty, and the taciturnity of James Joyce the observer who, in the opening pages of *Ulysses,* described such a morning as seen by Haines, Buck Mulligan, and Stephen Dedalus. The Tower, one of many coastal towers built as a defensive measure during the Napoleonic wars, has come to be called 'the Joyce Tower', for his book has attracted countless literary pilgrims, but the enterprise of leasing it was almost entirely Gogarty's.

Early in July he had mentioned to Bell that he was in correspondence with the War Office and proposed to rent the Martello Tower and live there with Joyce. 'He must have a year in which to finish his novel. I'll send photos when we house the bard securely. The Tower stands on a high rock over the sea.'[1] Later in the month he told Bell that Joyce and he expected to take up residence in a week or so but there may have been an unexpected delay; it is unlikely that Gogarty took possession of it before his birthday, 17 August, on which date he executed the deed of covenant.[2] By this time his friendship with Joyce had cooled; the latter was not in the group which took up occupancy in August and consisted of Gogarty, Trench, and James Starkey now better known under his pseudonym Seumas O'Sullivan.

Situated near the 'Forty Foot Hole', a bathing-place reserved for men, the Tower commands a splendid view of Dublin Bay, facing Howth Head where not so many weeks before Gogarty was mixing 'light purple rhododendron leaves in a girl's red brown hair'. The colour of the promontory changed from pink to purple or cerulean when clouds veiled the sunlight, and at other times it gleamed as if covered with yellow corn fields.

He described his new abode for Bell:

> I should have enclosed some photos of this Tower but that they were not ready; soon I hope to send them. It is a white granite Martello Tower built on a rocky promontory on the south arm of Dublin Bay. Sandycove seems to have been a cynical euphemism because there are sheer rocks all here — composed of beautiful granite. The sea here is 'crystaline' on account of Sandycove being sandless; and the bathing is excellent. I swim 3 or 4 times a day for from ½ to ¾ hours at a stretch. I find it a splendid pastime — [3]

Trench, a Balliol student whom Gogarty had met in Oxford where they were both members of the St. Patrick's Club, was a grandson of Richard Chenevix Trench, Archbishop of Dublin, 1814-1884. His father, Major-General Trench, who had a distinguished military career, committed suicide in 1894. Generally called Samuel his given names were Richard Samuel Chenevix to which in March 1903 he was to add by deed poll an additional christian name, Dermot. A fervent member of the Gaelic League his *What is the Use of Reviving Irish?* was published in 1907. Two·years later he died by his own hand.

Starkey/O'Sullivan, a less complicated person, would have been an easier room-mate. The son of William Starkey, M.D., physician and apothecary, his own profession of pharmacy was to come a poor second to literary interests which found a major outlet in the *Dublin Magazine* which he founded in 1923. Gogarty communicated with him from time to time in verse and 'To Leave Rathmines' may have beguiled him to the Tower.

> *To leave Rathmines and come down to the sea*
> *I would persuade thee, Starkey, with these lines*
> *So that men won't forget me who got thee*
> *To leave Rathmines.*
>
> *Here green trees drink the sea-blue air, and we*
> *May look on rain or mountain when it shines*
> *And it will shine for me if thou'll agree*
> *To leave Rathmines.*[4]

This trio, or perhaps just Gogarty and Trench, was joined by James Joyce on or about 7 September. His stay was short. On 15 September he wrote to Starkey from Cabra: 'My trunk will be called for at the Tower to-morrow (Saturday) between 9 and 12. Kindly put into it a pair of black boots, a pair of brown boots, a blue peaked cap, a black cloth cap, a black felt hat, a raincoat and the Ms of my verses which are a roll on the shelf to the right as you enter. Also see that your host has not abstracted the twelfth chapter of my novel from my trunk. May I ask you to see that any letters coming to the Tower for me are re-directed to my address at once?'[5]

Joyce's cold letter has an air of finality about it. Gogarty's attempts to patch up their quarrel will be referred to in a later chapter and for the moment it suffices to describe the startling events which caused his abrupt departure. Disturbed by a vivid nightmare Trench woke and took a pot-shot at an hallucinatory black panther. Gogarty took the gun from him but compounded the folly by shooting at tin cans which clattered down on Joyce who, terrified of dogs and thunder, and now of gun shots, quickly dressed and left. Trench was punished by his characterization as the unlikeable Englishman, Haines, in *Ulysses* and Gogarty was made to pay an even greater price for his impulsive and dangerous prank but that lay in the future. Joyce's departure was likely to have restored a cordial atmosphere. He was never an easy companion.

There were other visitors. Arthur Griffith swam with Gogarty at the Forty-Foot; AE (George Russell) did an oil painting of the splendid seascape from the roof of the Tower; Dermot Freyer, then a Cambridge undergraduate, photographed them and had amusing stories to tell of W.B. Yeats at Cambridge.

Gogarty and Trench got on well together. 'Trench is delightful' the former told Bell, 'erratic and neurotic but this latter is getting better with the sea air'. The Oxford man stayed on until mid-October by which time Gogarty who planned to stay there with Starkey during the winter had returned temporarily to the city 'to read for the satisfaction of some Doctors.'⁶

Bad luck and a prejudiced examiner are favourite excuses for academic failure. Gogarty's most celebrated jape was his arrival at the Examination Hall in a shutter-drawn cab from which he emerged blindfolded to be led into the Hall, a stratagem devised, he explained, to avoid seeing a certain red-haired person who was his hoodoo. In *Tumbling in the Hay* he charges Andrew Francis Dixon (lightly disguised as McNought) with prejudice against an athlete:

> As we circled, my eye caught sight of a tall, red-headed man in knickerbockers with grey stockings. He stood under a tree smoking a pipe. Slow-burning tobacco! It was McNought, the Professor of Anatomy. He was watching the race with the greatest disapproval. Larry didn't care who was watching, for he was a Fellow Commoner and had independent means, which means that his money made him independent of a profession and professors. He also had a private cycling track in his grounds somewhere out in Bray. But my case was far different. I was dependent on professors; and the Professor of Anatomy was anything but a sport. He did not like the spectacle of muscle in action. He preferred still life. I knew the moment he saw me that I had lost my next 'Half', my anatomy exam, before it was held. I was wasting my time in the College Park when I should have been behind it in his one-storeyed building, picking

with a forceps and displaying with a knife the nerves or the arteries, filled with red lead, of some unclaimed pauper's well-flayed, dark-red corpse.

Such delusions are an inevitable part of the paranoia of examination candidates and Oliver Gogarty's accusation cannot be sustained. Dixon may have raised the standard considerably when he took the Chair in 1903 (thirteen of the nineteen candidates were rejected at Michaelmas), but Gogarty was equally weak in physiology, and before 1904 his marks are so bad that he cannot have been trying. After that an element of mischance might have entered or he may have been branded a 'chronic', but most examiners are lenient with this ilk, glad to pass them if only to get them off their hands. Be that as it may, Gogarty was ploughed again but, fortunately, he could continue his clinical studies.

The so-called Richmond Hospital which Gogarty attended comprises three hospitals named after the Viceroys holding office at the time of their establishment, the Earl of Hardwicke, the Duke of Richmond and the Earl of Whitworth. The Hardwicke (1803), Richmond (1811) and Whitworth (1817) Hospitals developed in association with Dublin's House of Industry for treatment of fevers, surgical and medical disorders respectively. In the years of their foundation they offered what refuge then existed from the disasters of illness. The early years of the twentieth century afforded the boons of anaesthesia and aseptic surgery but the spectacles of misery visible to students walking the wards were indescribable — 'ghosts of cripples like those that Hogarth drew haunt its wards'. Festering wounds, unalignable fractures, and the stink of osteomyelitis were surgical commonplaces while in the medical wards the rapid cachexia of diabetes, the wasting fever of pulmonary tuberculosis, the choking terror of diphtheria, the enervation and *cafe-au-lait* pallor of bacterial endocarditis, the progressive languor of pernicious anaemia presented heart-rending sights. Syphilis, the most versatile of diseases, was to be encountered daily in one or other of its three stages, the early genital sore, the widespread rash with 'snail-track' mucosal ulcers which developed some weeks later, or the depredations of the tertiary phase in bones, blood-vessels, and brain.

A protective shell of professional detachment was obligatory and in *Ulysses* we find Buck Mulligan speaking airily of death:

— And what is death, he asked, your mother's or yours or my own? You saw only your mother die. I see them pop off every day in the Mater and Richmond and cut up into tripes in the dissecting-room. It's a beastly thing and nothing else. It simply doesn't matter.

Gogarty's teachers at the Richmond included Sir Thornley Stoker, Professor Joseph O'Carroll and Sir Thomas Myles. A brother of Bram Stoker the author of *Dracula,* Sir Thornley was a patron of the arts. He selected a motto to be carved over a door in the entrance hall which originally read *Necessitati haud gratiae haec portae patent;* when Gogarty translated this irreverently as 'It is unnecessary to grease these patent doors' Sir Thornley ticked him off for his flippancy but the surgeon was devastated when the student pointed out tactlessly that the Latin was incorrect and *haec* should be *hae.*[7]

Professor O'Carroll, generally referred to as 'Joc' by his students, was a small lean man with a pointed grey beard and an ascetic appearance. There was an element of pedantry about him. He liked to dwell on the etymology of medical terms deriving them from their Greek and Latin roots. 'Get your Greek right and you have learned half of medicine.' He also thought it incumbent upon himself to make it clear to his students what a medical vocation entailed:

The sunny days will not be yours any longer but days in the crowded dispensaries, the camp of the miner or of the soldier where, unarmed, you must render service in the very foremost positions. It is in the darkened pathological department of some institution that you, some of you, will spend your lives in tireless investigation of that microcosmic world which holds more numerous and more dangerous enemies of man than the deep. Your faces will alter. You will lose your youthful smirks; for, in the end, your ceaseless traffic with suffering will reflect itself in grave lines upon your countenance. Your outlook on life will have none of the deception that is the unconscious support of the layman: to you all life will appear in transit, and you will see with clear and un-deceived vision the different stages of its devolution and its un-divertible path to the grave.

You can never remain in solitude or find leisure for contempla-tion. You can never retreat from the world, which is for you a battlefield on which you must engage in a relentless and unceas-ing war from which you know that you can never emerge victorious. You must confront the sightless myriads of the air in the invisible battle from which no medical man turns back. For this you must be prepared to sacrifice more than your lives. You must sacrifice your delight in Beauty; for, as you gaze on it, your knowledge tempts you to see beneath its bloom the intimations of decay.[8]

By contrast, Sir Thomas Myles was a huge man. He had gone to sea in his youth and sailed before the mast, a robust cure for threatened tuberculosis; he had also been a redoubtable boxer. Though Surgeon to the King in Ireland, he saw no contradiction in patriotic feelings and used his yacht, the *Chotah,* to run guns for the Irish nationalists in 1914.

Sir Thomas's surgery has been described as 'bloody, bold and resolute' and he used his own considerable knowledge of Shakespeare to enliven his teaching.

> The diagnosis here is not in doubt, nor the aetiology, as it might have been in Falstaff's case, when he invoked 'A gout on this pox, or a pox on this gout.' We may exclude the gout. Now the question is, what to do for this poor fellow who has got what is known in Dublin as 'the bad disorder'. He makes no bones about telling us that he got it. He cannot remember where. 'A little unremembered act of kindness and of love'. He is more straighforward than the clerical gentleman who asked me, 'Could you get this in a water-closet?' 'You could, my friend, but it's a damn dirty place to take a lady'.[9]

Cutting away a sloughing ulcer he might say, 'Rank corruption undermining all beneath doth infect unseen'; and at the end of an operation turning to his blood-stained assistants he was likely to remark, 'Bloody ruffians, marvellously ill-favoured'.

Teachers of general medicine and surgery demand a major part of their students' time, the more specialized clinicians attracting less attention, so that when Gogarty developed the habit of dropping in to the Ear, Nose and Throat Clinic where Mr. (later Sir Robert) Woods worked he had the great man to himself and acquired not only a splendid teacher but also a friend who determined the direction of his career.[10]

By now Oliver Gogarty had an open invitation to the 'literary evenings' which were Dublin's nearest equivalents to the Paris salons. At Yeats's, seeing Maurice Joy[11] correcting an Oxford scholar, he had moments of insight recalling his own behaviour. 'Joy is an awful warning to me — my early flippancies incarnated and I realising am shocked. Joy now was certainly what I was three to two years ago or last year.'[12]

At George Moore's where the company talked unaffectedly, he was struck by the way Yeats managed to impart a heroic value to commonplace words and was captivated when the poet read a passage from 'Deirdre', the play he was then writing. 'He forgot himself and his face seemed tremulous as if an image of impalpable fire — and not red, black and white coloured Yeats. His lips are dark cherry red and his cheeks too, take colour and his eyes actually glow black and then the voice gets all vibrating as he sways like a Druid with his whole soul chanting.... I know no more beautiful face than Yeats' when lit with song.'[13]

At 'An Stad', a tobacconist's shop in North Frederick Street close to Rutland Square, he kept in touch with another group whose verses were in Gaelic. The conversation of those who gathered in 'An Stad' concerned the Gaelic revival and the cause of Irish freedom, objectives which were pursued on the playing field by broad-shouldered, strong-limbed Michael Cusack ('the citizen' of Joyce's *Ulysses*), the founder of the G.A.A., who invariably carried with him an iron-bound hurley stick, and in the political arena by Arthur Griffith whose *The Resurrection of Hungary* was published in 1904. Jokingly Gogarty attributed his own participation with the National Freedom movement to his admiration for Michael Cusack's calves and Arthur Griffith's character.

A sonnet 'O'Connell Bridge' which appeared in the November issue of *Dana* reflects his association with this group:

> *I gazed along the waters at the west,*
> *Watching the low sky colour into flame,*
> *Until each narrowing steeple I could name,*
> *Grew dark as the far vapours; and my breast*
> *With silence like a sorrow was possessed,*
> *And men as moving shadows went and came;*
> *The smoke that stained the sunset seemed like [shame]*
> *Smouldering, or some great evil unexpressed.*

> *Then with a longing for the taintless air,*
> *I called that desolation back again,*
> *Which reigned when Liffey's widening banks were bare;*
> *Before Ben Edair gazed upon the Dane,*
> *Before the Hurdle Ford, and long before*
> *Fionn drowned the young men by its meadowy shore.*

As the year ended he was working on 'Cervantes: Tercentenary of Don Quixote' his entry for the Vice-Chancellor's English Verse Prize:

Three hundred years since first your rare Knight started
Are passed, since first on his adventurous quest
He rose in hope with Sancho simple-hearted
To wound wrong-doers and to heal distressed:

To raise his Lady's name beyond all others
To fight for her and guard her from disgrace
To set men free imprisoned, men his brothers,
That each one might behold her heavenly face.

To complete it in time he had to write 112 lines in eight days but there was a mix-up and his nom-de-plume was missing when the result appeared. Fortunately he could prove that his poem had been sent in by 1 January. A re-contest was declared and he was named the third-time winner. Professor Tyrrell, 'the Benign Doctor', gave a celebratory dinner for him and amused his guests with limericks in Greek.

Unfortunately this auspicious start to 1905 was not sustained. Though his marks in physiology were adequate at the Hilary term examination, he came a cropper in anatomy. To aggravate his feeling of intense disappointment he was obliged to submit to his mother's will when she insisted towards the end of February that he should make a week's retreat in a Cistercian monastery.

The unworldly atmosphere of dedication and prayer at the Abbey of St. Marcellin which Canon Sheehan described movingly in *The Queen's Fillet* did not in a twentieth-century Irish setting have the slightest appeal for Oliver Gogarty. He found the grey monastery cold and forbidding; the dramatic sight of sixty white-robed monks filing silently through a pointed Gothic side-door into the choir to sing vespers brought him no insight into the realities of the contemplative life. Gogarty had nothing of the mystic in his make-up a knowledge that makes men best who face it: a knowledge that our oddly pessimistic. 'Surely not the least part of the cross each man must take up and bear is the knowledge that life is at best a burden: a knowledge that makes men best who face it: a knowledge that our greatest from Sophocles to Matthew Arnold have not shirked.'[14]

Having placated his mother he left the 'dreadful monastery' with relief, and to breathe freely set off on a three-day walking tour in the glens of Wicklow. In March he received a copy of George Moore's new novel, *The Lake*, the main character of which is a Father Oliver Gogarty. Being afraid to leave it around in case Mrs. Gogarty should see it and sue Moore for libel he sent it to Bell.[15]

When Seumas O'Sullivan's *The Twilight People* was published in the spring Gogarty puffed it in an article on the Irish literary revival in the *Evening Mail*. He also contributed poems to *Dana* and *The Venture*.

Seeking W.B. Yeats's consent, on Bell's behalf, for inclusion of some poems in an anthology, he called on the poet in his hotel early in April. Yeats and Miss Horniman were in the parlour amid papers, books, sweets for Yeats's throat, and smelling salts. Yeats showed him an accumulation of letters. 'Miss Horniman writes all my letters now,' he explained. 'I leave them for a week and then we answer them all in an afternoon.'

'Do you know, Mr. Gogarty,' Miss Horniman said archly, 'that sometimes we have to go out to ask how to spell a word.'

Yeats then embarked on a long and useful lecture on modern literary languages and the avoidance of archaisms and inversions.[16]

With examination-time approaching Gogarty was in the dissecting-room every morning at eight but later in the month he got away to London for a few days. With Dermot Freyer he visited the 'Rose and Crown' in Wimbledon but to their regret Swinburne had just left. They sat in the corner which he customarily favoured and their hilarity annoyed the landlord who refused to give them the headed notepaper they requested.

Soon after his return he wrote to Freyer:

> Poor dear old Trench: it would be a dreadful and for me irreparable calamity if anything happened to him. He overworks himself and troubles too much. How few of us value the best of all evangels. *'Consider* the lilies of the field?'. I went out to consider them to-day. As there were none in the place I considered a wild cherry-tree instead. It was like a frozen fountain: all white bloom branched and sprayed like some tree on a white star might be. I could see the blue and the clouds up thro it as I lay supinely 'considering' it.[17]

Evidently Gogarty was enough of a clinician to understand the potential seriousness of Trench's emotional disturbance and he had already expressed his concern about him to Bell: 'If I had an opportunity I could talk to and perhaps cheer a friend of ours — Trench — who is suffering and downcast latterly. His nerves are ailing and I am afraid he may shoot himself in a fit of despondency at the futility of his labours — pamphlets etc'.

As an anatomist, however, he remained lacking and went down again at the summer examination. By this time the format of 'the half' had been reviewed; in future the 'Intermediate Medical Examination' as it was henceforth to be called would be taken in two parts. This may have suited Gogarty better; he took Part I successfully in the autumn of 1905 and passed Part II early in 1906. Then, as if transformed by success, he sat the primary examination for the Fellowship of the Royal College of Surgeons in Ireland, a most difficult and ambitious undertaking, and satisfied his examiners.[18]

Under the pseudonyms 'Omega' and 'Alpha' Gogarty contributed political pieces to the *United Irishman* in 1905 and he participated in the first Annual Convention of the National Council of Sinn Féin which was held in the Rotunda on Tuesday 28 November 1905.[19]

After the President, Edward Martyn, had spoken, Arthur Griffith proposed, as the National Council's policy, national self-development through the recognition of the duties and rights of citizenship on the part of the individual, and by the aid and support of all movements originating within Ireland, instinct with national tradition and not looking outside Ireland for the accomplishment of their aims. Gogarty spoke in support of this proposal: 'There was yet in Ireland, in spite of extraordinary, persistent and pernicious attempts to crush it, an idea that we were in our own right entitled to be free and separate people.... '

He singled out the educational system as contributing most to denationalization. Money was taken from the Irish people by forced taxation to supply the needs of Irish education. How was the Irish money used to educate Ireland? The language of Ireland was suppressed, the history of Ireland ignored or misstated, the attention of Ireland was turned to a foreign country, the character of the Irish tradition, the focus of national life was set in London. 'England dare not educate us as Irishmen,' he declared. 'She would be raising up judges to denounce her and condemn.' He threw a bouquet to the Christian Brothers as being Ireland's best educators with an understanding of our needs. Their scope if extended could embrace the needs of primary and secondary education. His dual experience of Trinity and the Royal placed him in an admirable position to comment on Ireland's university system and his speech reflects acutely an awareness of his ambiguous position in College Park:

As regards a remedy for the University system, the first thing to be understood was that the difficulty of nationality was the most important: one had to identify himself mentally several times a day, and recall to mind to whom he belonged, if he

would avoid being changed into one of those nationless nonen-
tities such as the Universities in Ireland were tending to produce.

He maintained that an exclusively Catholic university would be a
wrong against the national Protestant population just as an essentially Protestant university was a wrong against the Catholics. 'The
University should be for all classes without distinction, national from
the very centre outwards.'

The St. James's Brass Band and the York Street Brass Band played
a selection of national airs to entertain the crowd which gathered at
the Rotunda in the evening for the public meeting. When Edward
Martyn took the chair at eight twenty p.m. he said that they had
assembled 'to endorse the Sinn Féin policy which may be defined
as the awakening of a sense of justice in our rulers by the force
of passive resistance'. Ireland had reasoned with England in parliament and elsewhere unavailingly and now it was time to see what
passive resistance would do. This would include an anti-enlisting
policy. Latterly they had heard a good deal about flogging in the
navy; 'as regards ourselves, it does not matter very much whether
the English flogged each other or not, but the Irishman who enters
the army or navy of England deserves to be flogged'.

When the cheers subsided, Mr. John Sweetman, Chairman of
Meath County Council, proposed 'that the Irish are a free people and
that no law made without their authority and consent is or can ever
be binding on their conscience...'. This resolution was seconded by a
Wexford Catholic curate, Father Harpur, whose message to England
was, 'Curse your concessions, we want our country'. The next to
express his support for the resolution was Oliver St. John Gogarty
whose stirring speech was cheered repeatedly.

Gogarty said that the resolution was a conception so rarely expressed in public as to be almost new to the public, although by no
means a new idea. 'The law of the oak is not the law for the ash and
the law of England is not the law for Ireland. If an ash be uprooted
from its mountain glade and transplanted in harsh or marshy soil
its growth will be stunted and its development checked in proportion as the conditions favourable to it and the laws of its growth are
lacking.'

He asserted that in Ireland the British government was a tyranny
because it forced upon the unwilling Irish people a legislation they
repudiated. 'Now England is a pedlar, selling statues of right and
wrong in Ireland. We buy them because we have forgotten our own

statues and when we find the seller a cheat we forget that the chalk things are rotten, too, and hesitate to break and bundle them out.'

He insisted that no matter how beneficial foreign laws might be, the Irish were not intended by God to be beggars dependent upon foreign charity. 'England's Good is Ireland's Bad and England's Right is Ireland's Wrong and no matter on what principle England tries to do good for Ireland her benefits are as dangerous as the Siren's song.' Predictably his sentiments were cheered.[20]

5

My Heart's Delight

With 'the half' behind him Gogarty's affairs took a leap forward. True, he stumbled again when he attempted Part 1 of the Final Examination but a Benedict must be forgiven much. The salient events of 1906-07 were compressed into a sentence for Freyer's benefit: 'As to me I have been to America since I wrote to you; I got qualified, married; and I have an only begotten son in whom I am well pleased'.[1]

The purpose of his American trip is unrecorded. Earlier in 1906 he had visited friends in London who had lost heavily in the San Francisco earthquake. Could his journey have been in that connection or was it a bachelor's final splurge, or his reward for 'the primary Fellowship'? Despite a general outspokenness Gogarty seems to have been reticent about his own personal affairs.

He sailed in the *Caronia* 'a palace pushed into the sea' and delighted in the colours created by its stem cleaving the waves.

> To see the black-green water furrowed into April green and white — snow in Spring; and an everlasting rainbow shine above the changing waters was a sight that will nourish the soul that may never be able to describe it. And then above the dim red sunset the tranquil yellow evening star. When the great long slow moving waters moaned away on either side of the prow one could see beads like strings of pearl stretched from their crests — before they broke — to their bases. This in the evening with Hesperus calm must have been beheld by Lovell Beddoes when he wrote that lovely lyric 'How many times do I love you?' At night the phosphorescent stars were really scintillating planets of the ocean or glow-worms of the night of the main. I am looking forward to going back! Is this native?[2]

Being yet relatively untravelled he was amazed by America and found that the opulence of the Waldorf Astoria, where he stayed, put anything he knew in London in the shade. Like many visitors

60

from Europe he thought that most of what he saw was tasteless and pretentious. His comment about the American female (surely the outcome of a restricted glance at a very particular group) is oddly reminiscent of Evelyn Waugh's later descriptions of the aberrant moments of high society.

> The American women too, are superficial and untamed in spite of all their elegance. I sometimes think when I see the strange movements of their mincing gait that if I but turned my head they would relapse into a wild and ungovernable cake-walk. They are threatened by the primitive things. Beautifully manicured hands and Parisian costumes cannot make me quite assured that they are really civilized — but who was the cynic that said woman was the only animal we had not tamed? On his head be my ungallant imaginings![3]

His letter to Joyce on 14 June declares an intention of travelling to the West but this may have been merely blow for two days later he is telling Bell that he may catch the *Campania* on the twentyseventh. He adds that he hopes to be able to visit Wells, Somerset, (where G.K.A. Bell was at Divinity School) in August — 'things are very indefinite at present: but if they permit of my inclination having its way you know nothing could give me more pleasure than a visit to you.'

Sooner or later the most indefinite honeymoon plans must take shape and Oliver Gogarty was now engaged to marry Martha Duane of Ross Dhu, Moyard, County Galway. It is further evidence of his avoidance of the personal that there is no direct allusion in these letters to 'That not impossible She' who might also have been expected to be readily identifiable in his romantic verses. For the present, however, these had not been more than poetic exercises, compliments in rhyme and metre that any young man might wish to pay to the exquisiteness of feminine beauty, giving no hint that the heart rather than the eye has been touched.

The following lines belong to an empty tradition which glorifies the unrequited lover:

> *Not the lightness of the air*
> *Which the smallest pinion stirs,*
> *Nothing know I light and fair*
> *With a motion like to hers.*
> *Not the leaf that frames the bud*

Kindling on the swinging linde
Mete her matchless maidenhood
And can satisfy my mind.

Slender as the spring-time moon,
Pure and slender bright and fleet
Furthest from the plenilune
With one star beneath her feet
Goes she always in the sun
Pure and slender bright and free
Thoughtless as she hastens on
That she leaves the night to me.

She must ever hasten on
We may never meet and rest
As the azure-sandalled moon
Flies the night adown the West
Since we are the thralls of Time
Let me love her for her flight
Though the love that turns to rhyme
Leaves me wrapped around with Night.[4]

Their vacuity is such that they remained unpublished. A shorter love poem of very superior quality may have been withheld from publication for a different reason; the involvement, though mutual, must be kept secret.

Powder your neck lest there be seen
The marks where kissing lips have been.
But have a care the powder be
Matched to your round neck's ivorie
Lest by the difference of hue
Suspicion fall on me and you.[5]

Unlike George Moore of whom it was said that 'he told but did not kiss' Gogarty was the soul of discretion. With the exception of Alice Steele, an Islip barmaid whose prettiness is praised in 'Winifred', published in *Dana* in 1904, the lassies to whom he paid his tributes in rhyme remain unnamed.

Present-day newly-weds are unlikely to send their friends more than a picture postcard from Marbella or the Greek islands. The Gogartys did not venture so far but Oliver kept up his correspondence. He expressed satisfaction to Bell with his 'recent good luck' and his friends. He chided Starkey for missing the nuptials. 'You should have at least set out for the Wedding Feast if only to be interrupted by an Ancient Mariner.'[6]

The honeymoon began in Oxford. The couple put up at the Mitre but in summer the university city seemed enervating. They moved soon to Teignmouth and paid a visit to Dean Prior where Herrick had been vicar. Next they went to Paris where, as Oliver confided to Starkey, he hoped to ask a printer to print 'as much of Sinbad as he has sailed.' He sent for Starkey's amusement a quatrain entitled 'Helen's lamp', which Herrick would not have disowned:

> *A little lamp: but the great sun*
> *Sees not half I gaze upon.*
> *On me these kisses Paris traced*
> *For Helen by night light looks best —*

then recollecting his circumstances he added, 'O Hymen, Hymen! what am I saying?'[7]

Finally, before returning to their new home in Earlsfort Terrace, the Gogartys went to Moyard, Connemara, where for the first time Oliver met his in-laws. He also met the parish priest who wanted fifty pounds compensation because Gogarty's bride had married outside the parish. But Gogarty dug his toes in, as he explained to Starkey: 'He has not sweated a farthing out of me, to the immeasurable delight of my father-in-law, an American civil war pensioner...'. Away from this human conflict Gogarty had his first experience of the beauty of Connemara to which he would come back again and again. The lakes and ocean mirrored green hills and blue mountains in a way that challenged verbal description but it seemed to him that any attempt to recapture it in words was an impertinence.

The rapture of the body stilled, the visual ravishment of Paris and Connemara ended, events led back inevitably to the commonplace exercise of the Final Medical Examination, Part 1. The subjects were materia medica, medical jurisprudence and pathology and he did badly in all. His total mark was 40 per cent and he was rejected. Fortunately this was to be his last academic set-back and certainly it was high time he settled down, with a wife as well as a mother to placate and please. Early in 1907 he saved face by taking second place (with 61½%) when he re-sat Part 1.[8]

Meanwhile, at 17 Earlsfort Terrace, he assumed the new dignity of householder and had some unexpected callers including Mrs.

Dowden and Lady MacCabe who rather overawed the young couple. G.K.A. Bell accepted his invitation and came to Dublin in October. Oliver, perhaps with the approaching examination on his mind, set about roping in Starkey to ease the situation.

> Don't fail me on Sunday 1.30. I want you to take charge of Bell for a few hours (no! he is not like Trench). It is very hard times on me that I am unable to entertain him and that I have to appeal to a friend who is so reluctant to be entertained. But you said you would come, and, as my wife is neither dusty nor man-eating you must come now....[9]

He was disappointed by Yeats's *Deirdre* which the Abbey staged towards the end of November — 'he has whorified a fine old lover with little lascivities'. In his letter to Bell he hints at his personal trials:

> My dear Bell: There is whiskey mixed with the ink not without soda, so I don't know how this letter will wear until it reaches you. My inkpot was dry from disuse and reviving it, I revived also with the barley my failing life....[10]

Having disposed of Finals, Part 1, he straightaway sat the midwifery examination which proved to be a cake-walk. Dr. Richard Dancer Purefoy, whom the students called 'Pig-eye' Purefoy, was an indulgent examiner. Recalling Dr. Henry Gogarty's beautiful setters he put Oliver at ease by talking about the prize-winning Rufus and Garryowen before asking questions which were answered (sometimes with the help of mime) to his complete satisfaction. With 67 per cent Gogarty took third place in midwifery and gynaecology.

He completed Finals in June 1907, passing the examinations in medicine and surgery comfortably, and tying for first place in mental diseases. Whereupon, being of M.A. standing, and having spent the requisite time in the medical school, he used the lost years to his advantage. Under the obtaining regulations he was entitled to claim, in addition to the M.B., the M.D. degree by reading a thesis. On 29 June he became Oliver St. John Gogarty, M.D. The following month brought the additional dignity of fatherhood when the Gogartys' first child, a son, was born at Fairfield on 23 July.

To succeed in surgery in Ireland at the turn of the century it was necessary, after a period of study abroad, to take the Fellowship of the Royal College of Surgeons. London, Paris, and Berlin attracted many prospective specialists but they were outshone by Vienna, then the world's most prestigious medical centre — the city of Semmelweis, conqueror of child-bed fever; of Billroth, creator of modern gastric surgery; of Freud who opened new doors to self-knowledge. The Allgemeines Krankenhaus, a great repository of human suffering, provided unrivalled opportunities to gain experience and had a respected scientific tradition. Here it was that Ferdinand von Hebra had laid the foundations of dermatology and Josef Skoda had perfected methods of physical diagnosis. The latter, a complex crusty bachelor, wore ill-fitting clothes all his life rather than offend his tailor who was also a friend, but he sued a clergyman for a fee. Carl Rokitansky who devoted himself to the study of pathology was a more genial person; he had four sons, two physicians and two singers of whom he said, *'Die Einen heilen, die Anderen heulen'*.

Despite these nineteenth-century advances the great hospital boasted few cures: it was a time of therapeutic nihilism when to those within the citadel the ideal and sufficient objective seemed to be an exact diagnosis confirmed by post-mortem examination. Even when Oliver Gogarty was there in 1907-08 things had not changed greatly. The flag which was to be flown over the hospital if a day passed without a death was never unfurled.

The direction of Gogarty's professional career had been determined, as we have seen, by his fortuitous meeting and subsequent association with Mr. Robert Woods in the Richmond Hospital's ill-equipped Ear, Nose and Throat Dispensary. 'I am going strong at the Throat, Nose and Ear branch of the profession', he explained to Dermot Freyer. 'I intend doing ½ or ¾ of a year in Vienna, and then looking in at some of the London Hospitals. If you know any nose-man, or if you have a rhinologist at your own hospital take me round to that rhinoceros.'[11]

The Gogartys took their infant to be admired by his grandparents in Connemara in September, preparatory to their departure for Austria, and Oliver with his usual wish to have his friends about him urged Starkey to join them even for a few days.

It would only cost you your train fare — £1.12.6. return. If you didn't care to come here (as I know you by this) what the bloody hell is there to prevent you coming to the Letterfrack hotel for 3 or 4 days? I will see you through. (After all I owe you a few quid in little unremembered touches extending over several years.) The sea-bathing is splendid here — Atlantic, and the colours and the air Hymethan. We could spend a few digestive days together .... Remember, I'll be gone for ½ a year or longer — and Hades is an indifferent trysting place. So come down to Letterfrack for 3 or 4 days....[12]

Early in October he acknowledged the gift of Dermot Freyer's *Rhymes and Vanities — Verses in Lighter Vein* with an amusing villanelle:

> *I got a book of verse*
> *In lighter vein from Freyer,*
> *(It wasn't very de-ar,*
> *I didn't disemburse);*
> *A friend can oft amerce*
> *The price of papi-er:*
> *I got a book of verse*
> *In lighter vein from Freyer.*
>
> *I got a book of verse*
> *He wrote with half an eye,*
> *The other — Misey Die!*
> *He couldn't get it worse!*
> *I don't want to asperse*
> *His spotless Characteer*
> *(Iritis is a curse;*
> *Rheumatic? — very queer).*
> *I got a book of verse*
> *Writ well by Dermot Freyer.*
> *Well, Thamyris was blind*
> *Likewise Maeonides.*
> *One very rarely sees*
> *A poet's eye defined*
> *With all those 'fine frenzies',*
> *(And other little sprees*
> *That one could call to mind:)*
> *Well, Thamyris was blind*
> *Likewise Maeonides!*
>
> *I got a book of verse*
> *And I was much elate:*
> *But not at that hard fate;*
> *Boys will be — dissipate!*

> *I'd like to ask the nurse.*
> *My fancy dares to scarce,*
> *Though free, emancipate,*
> *To whisper — lips won't purse —!*
> *'How deli — delicate!'*[13]

A nurse was provided for little Oliver who remained in Earlsfort Terrace under the additional supervision of a doctor friend when his parents set out for Vienna. They arrived in London on 11 October and stayed in the Langham Hotel where they were joined by Freyer and Tancred. A visit to Cooks and other essential errands interfered with Oliver's wish to call to Swinburne's local, the Rose and Crown in Wimbledon, and 'pounce on the poet'.

They stopped again at Nurnberg the lovely town of Dürer, Fischer, and Hans Sachs the greatest of the Meistersingers. On the terrace of the inn, Oliver quickly adapted to local custom: *'Goodbye to Murray mild, my cheer/Is changed to Nurnberger beer!'*

Before resuming the journey he sent Freyer a further *jeux d'esprit* from the Hotel Maximilian:

> *Dear, Freyer, scythed Time has, hang him,*
> *Borne me afar, since at the Langham*
> *Both you, and he whose new-found verse*
> *Is rich, Catullus-like and terse,*
> *And sings in strains each gay lady*
> *Of Les Belles Dames du temps jadis*
> *As did their poet erst in France,*
> *But with more tired elegance. Ah me, a tear*
> *Unborn of Nurnburger beer,*
> *Mantles of eyne as, mantling yours,*
> *That darkened glass your gaze obscures*
> *And makes one waver in his faith*
> *To think no lady caused the scaith*
> *To eyes that, one night could not choose*
> *But wander from a lady's shoes*
> *To — where no married man should go:*
> *But Lord Christ save us all from woe!*
> *Write me anon a line of grace*
> *From that your proud prostatic place,*
> *A word about yourself and Tancred*
> *Who sang for sons of fathers chancred.*

Write to Vienna, be not lax:
This leaves the city of Hans Sachs.

The Gogartys rented chambers in Vienna which had been Krafft-Ebing's, a favourable omen perhaps. Between classes and work in the dispensary his time was fully occupied and he worked an eight-and-a-half hour day at least, finding much that was new to him in the surgical line. His teachers in otology included Barany and Alexander; Hajek and Ottaker von Chiari instructed him in disorders of the nose and throat. His progress was such that he planned to set up in practice in Dublin in the spring.

Unfamiliarity with the language was a major draw-back. He was one of many in this plight and in a letter to Joyce in Trieste he suggested that it would be worth his while to come to Vienna to teach the English-speaking students German. 'I would willingly give 38 kr a week to have German while here: but what would be of more importance to you — I could give you an introduction to the Medical Society which would put you in the way of getting as many tuitions as you could take, if you cared.'[15]

Lack of fluency in German also hindered his participation in the social life he encountered in the Cafe Klinik and elsewhere. But though Vienna is a byword for music and song he found the Viennese more hard-working than the Dubliners and their hours too long. The cafes might remain open until early morning but by then they were empty and cheerless. What a contrast to Dublin! 'Really, we know not how to be thankful for the well-attended chucking-out at 11 or 10, darkling! The murmuring groups at their eternal task of trying to end those immortal conversations!'

Such moments of nostalgia did not stop him from planning a visit to Venice ('Joyce lives in bawdry in Trieste. Perchance I might see him.') or a week in Greece before returning home and he tried unsuccessfully to enlist Starkey's interest.

The Gogartys were in Dresden in the New Year and stayed at the Continental Hotel where with his effortless ease in light-hearted verse Oliver dashed off a lengthy poem to Starkey which he finished in time to catch the post.

O you who in the times we love;
Make Sirmio of Sandycove!
Take safely to that dear resort
This freight of verse; and bring to port
My pinnace stuffed, as I opine,

Far down beneath the waterline
With ballast tremblingly consigned
To break against your Western Wind
That brings your poesies precise
But pungent with the ancient spice
Which mocks an ear you think rebels
'Gainst your hendecasyllables;
And moor it 'neath St. Carson's Mount,
Its cargo will discharge account,
You'll find your fillet on the bows —
When you're in Murray's Custom House.

First, from beneath its leaky planks,
Accept, unwaterlogged, my thanks
For song, that could it burst its traces,
Had impregnated all the Graces
And made them fain to grace your seaside
And rival Carson — on the leeside...

Tell me the latest from the Lan'
Who's gone, and Who's the coming Man
Where a Reviewer Colum calls
The Irish Burns (without the balls);
Where Kettle 'thinks' inside the Church
Lest its priests leave him in the lurch:
But tells outside it many a story
Because he's self-contradictory (!)
Is t'Pledge-bound Party speechless, dumb?
Or plays it still the Kettledrum?
And have they left the hazel down
Who erst exploited Hazelton?

Send me a word from that isle spent
In still delightful merriment
As one who nods between the jinks
Half sad to think that still he thinks
Vowing to higher things to climb
Before the sudden: 'Gentlemen, Time!'
Tell me if Maurice Joy's now well
Who brought the cold to Newcastle;[16]
And does he in his bardic feats
Still emulate the end of Keats
(Who, Marvellous!, the Muses sung

Although he hadn't got a lung)
Or seeks he now the loves of Herrick
Adown the docks, behind a derrick;
Or — what the Devil does he do?
From him I heard not — scarce from you.

I know that Starkey lately, squiffy,
Rolled down the lea, over the Liffey...
Sent a great Idyll here to me
Reverberate with Kelly's Quay,
And sang a Sailor loud in prose
Who not to sea but Mooney's goes...

Thank you my friend, for the delight
Caused by accounts of Christmas night
When you all let Soracte go —
To Hell! — in altitudes of snow;
And warmed for many a crackling hour,
The quaint recesses of the Tower
Where not Childe Roland ever came,
But chivalrous McCurdy lame
Who wore the buskin, not the sock
Of old when he demanded hock;
And lifted from his dismal state
That Oxford man disconsolate.

Write me again, ere time is called,
Some letter to the Wiener Wald
And hear me still apologise
In that I did materialize
And write the raucous rhyme at last
That should have been in days now past
Ported and stamped and sent to sea,
Save for my irregularity!
In many ways I could excuse
These aberrations of the Muse
But now the Porter, beer-bereft,
Mumbles I've but ten minutes left.
You'll see me in a Neptune's day
(If Kepler spells it in that way!)
By which I only 'try to mean'
That in a month I will be seen
And show you: 'Hell-A Miracle Play'
By Oliver St. John Gogarty.[17]

The Gogartys returned to Vienna towards the end of January. By then Oliver had a university research appointment which he expected would keep him occupied until March. After that he was free to return to Dublin and by May that inveterate theatre-goer and observer, Joseph Holloway had noted in his diary, 'Oliver Gogarty has passed his medical exam and is showing great promise as a throat specialist. He has taken Deane's house in Ely Place and sports a motor.'[18]

Ely Place, a cul-de-sac extending between Merrion Row and Smith's Buildings, housed an assortment of occupiers, a coal-and-coke merchant, a number of solicitors and land-agents, the Irish Land Commission, Miss Hempel's Boys Preparatory School, and the Y.W.C.A. Employment Agency. Add to this Sir Thornley Stoker, the surgeon who lived in a splendid mansion, Ely House, Henry Lionel Barnardo, J.P., the furrier, and the novelist George Moore who rented 4 Ely Place Upper, and it is understandable that another man with a potential for distinction would be a welcome resident. Sir Thornley Stoker had drawn Gogarty's attention to the advantages of 15 Ely Place where Sir Thomas Deane a distinguished architect had lived. What could be better than an architect's house built by an architect? Oliver Gogarty bought this house in the silent cul-de-sac and practised from it for the better part of thirty years.

The motor, a butter-coloured Rolls Royce, was not altogether an advertisement (a doctor's only legitimate advertisement) for it also reflected Gogarty's enthusiasm for motor-cars. He had already owned a twenty horse-power Argyll.

6

Situate at Nullnull, Medical Square

To be born with a caul implies good luck which for Oliver St. John Gogarty took the forms of abounding energy, an antic disposition — Yeats said that Gogarty came drunk from his mother's womb — and it was to his additional good fortune when Robert Woods confined his commitments to Sir Patrick Dun's Hospital as an honorary consultant, leaving a vacancy at the Richmond to which Gogarty was appointed.

Woods proved to be an ideal exemplar. The careers of master and pupil had a good deal in common and if the younger man never attained his teacher's pre-eminence in science and surgery he excelled him in the arts, while both were to do a stint in politics. Robert Henry Woods who was born in Tullamore, County Offaly, in 1865 had taken a degree in physics before qualifying in medicine in 1889.[1] He became President of the Royal College of Surgeons in Ireland in 1910 and was knighted in 1913. Elected member of parliament for Dublin University in 1918, Sir Robert incurred unpopularity in the House of Commons in 1920 by pointing out that the King's writ no longer ran in Southern Ireland. He objected to General Macready's demand for information from hospital doctors about the wounded men under their care and the order was never enforced.

His participation in the arts — he contributed articles to the *Dublin University Magazine* under the pseudonym 'Euphemist' and showed a talent for sculpture — never trespassed on the field of his major endeavour, nor rivalled his contributions to surgical literature which included 'Restoration of Nose by Modified Indian Operation', 'Excision of half the Larynx' and 'Ear Disease with Intracranial Complications'.

Sir Robert Woods was the first Dublin surgeon to devote himself exclusively to ear, nose and throat surgery, a speciality which has developed in close association with eye surgery. Sir William Wilde, Oscar's father, by excelling in both had set a pattern still followed in Dublin when Oliver Gogarty set up in practice. F. Odevanie, A.H. Benson (who prescribed James Joyce's first spectacles) and

1 John Oliver, grandfather.

2   Dr. Henry J.K. Gogarty, father.

3 Margaret Gogarty, mother.

4   Mayflo and Oliver.

5   Mayflo and Oliver in fancy dress.

6   Clongowes Cricket XI, 1897. Oliver is on extreme right of middle row.

7   Champion cyclist.

8   Oliver St John Gogarty as a young man.

9   Neenie Gogarty, Brenda, Noll (sitting) and Dermot.

10 Neenie Gogarty from a portrait by Augustus John, 1915, Courtesy of Oliver D. Gogarty.

John B. Story practised ophthalmic and ear, nose and throat surgery at St. Vincent's Hospital, Baggot Street Hospital and Dr. Steevens' Hospital respectively. Horace Law and Patrick Dempsey at the Adelaide and Mater Hospitals, like Woods, confined themselves to ear, nose and throat surgery and Gogarty did well to follow the modern trend. He was admitted to the coveted Fellowship of the Royal College of Surgeons in Ireland on 19 March 1910.

The Dublin Corporation's wish to have a Catholic doctor appointed ear, nose and throat surgeon to the Meath Hospital was to be Gogarty's next piece of good fortune. The Corporation's nominee was unacceptable to the Meath's largely Protestant staff but Gogarty, Papist though he might be, was a Trinity graduate which in their eyes made a difference. By inviting him to apply they spiked the Corporation's guns; Oliver St. John Gogarty, M.D., F.R.C.S.I., the better-qualified man (and a Catholic) was appointed.[2] His work at the hospital was unpaid but the servants of the best people attended the Meath and, in health matters, upstairs often followed down-stairs, but to private consulting-rooms.

Efficiency and knowledge make for success which is greatly expedited by infectious cheerfulness. Fed by Sir Thornley Stoker, his influential neighbour, Gogarty's practice grew quickly and to bread and butter soon was added jam. Hospital services elsewhere in the country were rudimentary. Dublin specialists enjoyed a mono-poly and Gogarty's increasing reputation put him in a position to benefit from it. Eventually he had a very large and remunerative practice with many well-satisfied patients.

A teaching hospital consultant is expected to treat patients, to instruct students, and to engage in research relevant to his speciality. By handling large numbers of patients he increases his expertise; by teaching he remains knowledgeable and makes relationships with the general practitioners of the future, potential purveyors of private patients; research is part of a tradition to which he has become ac-customed and appeals to inventive men capable of original thought.

The Meath Hospital has a distinguished record in research and at least two of its nineteenth-century physicians, Robert Graves and William Stokes, attracted post-graduate students from abroad. The former gave his name to a disorder of the thyroid gland, 'Graves disease', and Stokes described a particular type of cardiac compli-cation, 'Stokes-Adams syndrome', and the disordered breathing which often heralds death, 'Cheyne-Stokes respiration'. William Stokes also earned the gratitude of generations of Irishmen by his kindness to the stricken James Clarence Mangan whom he placed in a special room in the Meath Hospital and ensured that he received every care in his last illness.

Gogarty, who also had the example of Sir Robert Woods to follow, was soon occupied with a problem of diagnosis. Suppurative sinusitis, a menacing infection, is easily overlooked in its chronic form unless special procedures are carried out to isolate it. Gogarty collected 200 cases with no symptoms other than simple catarrh in which, had he not punctured and washed out the antrum, the disease would have remained unsuspected. He made these the subject of an address to the British Medical Association's Annual General Meeting in Aberdeen in July 1914 which was later published in the *British Medical Journal*, 'Latent Empyemeta of the Nasal Accessory Sinuses'.

One wonders what the British ear, nose and throat surgeons thought of the ebullient Irishman who recalled the meeting in later years: 'I remember a cross-section of the skull which I drew on a blackboard to demonstrate something. Someone asked me what the *Crista galli* [a prominence in the ethmoid bone resembling a miniature cock's comb] was. I told him it represented "the Cock of the North"; nobody laughed but the Scotsmen'.

He made a vigorous protest against operative injury of the inferior turbinate body which leads to loss of what he called the 'air-taste' in the nose. But in the subsequent discussion his recommendation of the use of strong solutions of cocaine suggests that, like many doctors at the time, he was unaware of the dangers of addiction.

His paper in the *British Medical Journal* was a contribution to the practical management of sinusitis rather than a major advance in knowledge and far less important than his repeated pleas relating to social conditions and aspects of preventive medicine. Unlike many doctors who become so obsessed by the eternal pursuit of disease and so fascinated by its therapy that they forget what health should look like, Gogarty could look beyond the under-nourished visages of the adenoidal children from the slums who crowded his clinics and see the glowing faces of normality.

Unlike the majority of doctors of his time who saw themselves as individual purveyors of health he saw clearly the immense potential of social reforms and his powerlessness without them. He took 'The Need of Medical Inspection of School Children' as the subject of an address introductory to the Winter Session at the Meath Hospital in 1911. 'Ireland is the only civilized country', he told his audience, 'which, while providing money to the Treasury for schools, receives in return no guarantee that the schools will not be a menace to the health of the children. If there be money enough to supply and support schools, and to make attendance at them compulsory, we should be better off without the schools, if, through being neglected, they become a danger to those who are bound by law to live in them during the most important and susceptible period of their lives.'

It was more important, he stressed, that children should be healthy than that they should be able to read and write. 'I fight not with learning, but with the inability to learn which results from preventable and unrecognised disease.' He described some ill-effects of chronic adenoidal disease — mouth-breathing, facial disfiguration and pigeon-chest — all of which were avoidable but, if permitted to develop, led to an impaired physique susceptible to later ailments.

In this city of street stables (there are 228 open stables or hazards in Dublin) and small cobble stones, which create an irritating, stony dust when chipped by traffic, there is less escape from chronic pulmonary disease than in other and better ordered towns. It is here in the schools that the soil is prepared for the tuberculosis of adult life. And it is the school children that should be protected by those who would save the nation from what has come to be regarded as our national disease.

Gogarty's compassion was easily touched and it was evident to him that the majority of the patients in the dispensaries of the Meath and the Richmond Hospitals were suffering children, and the great part of their suffering and ailments could be traced to the contained strain of long and hungry hours on their growing systems. 'Torturing with teaching a little starving child affects both the mind and body.' Not only should there be school medical inspections but school meals must be provided. 'These children are the Nation of to-morrow. Save it!'

A preface which Gogarty contributed to D. Houston's *The Milk Supply of Dublin* in 1918 relates to another aspect of his concern for public health and describes how about ten years earlier he had gone along to the City Laboratory with an obviously contaminated specimen of milk. 'A stout porter in livery stopped me in the hall and asked my business. I said that I wished to see Sir Charles Cameron. Why did I wish to see Sir Charles? Didn't I know that Sir Charles was not there to be seen by everybody? Though the fellow became abusive and ruffianly, I persisted and reached a room upstairs set apart for the purpose of analysis. To a small boy who was alone on duty I explained that as the milk stained every cloth it touched, I wished to have it analysed, so that the presence of any chemical preservative might be detected.'

Gogarty reported the functionary's insolence to the Town Clerk but between the jigs and the reels his specimen was mislaid and he was obliged to leave the porter 'to the congenial task of making the world safe for delinquency'.

He drew attention in the preface to the absence of precautions to ensure a clean milk supply. No investigation was ever held until typhoid fever broke out in a barracks or other institution 'and then the dairymen are changed and not the milk'.

To form three or four distributing stations where milk would be subject to daily testing, and where it could be distributed daily to motor vans, would improve the quality and lessen the cost by getting rid of the expensive horse and cart for every ten gallons or so, as well as the absurd system of pouring it in public streets made of mud and manure — perfectly harmless, if dry weather did not change them into dust and dessicated dung which pervade houses and utensils, are wafted at nightfall into the upper stories by means of revolving brush provided by the Cleaning Department. What would happen to Dublin were it not for its rainfall!

His strictures on the Department of Public Health 'to whose ineptitude thousands of little children are yearly sacrificed and slowly, painfully, unobtrusively put to death', seem by no means unwarranted even when seen through the softening glass of hindsight. But such vigorous condemnation usually results in raised hackles rather than official reforms. The better way of drawing public attention to the need to ameliorate social conditions, especially in the slums, was through laughter and this was Gogarty's principal object when his first play, *Blight — the Tragedy of Dublin,* was staged in the Abbey Theatre on 11 December 1917.

Meanwhile he had developed a reputation for surgical prowess. On Friday 17 December 1910 at a meeting of the section of surgery of the Royal Academy of Medicine in Ireland he reported the successful treatment of a case of chronic facial neuralgia. This thirty-one year-old man hd been tormented by pain in the left side of the face for thirteen years. Various procedures had been resorted to unavailingly before Dr. T.G. Moorhead asked Gogarty to exclude involvement of the sinuses. Local examination and transillumination revealed nothing. 'On the antrum being washed out,' Gogarty reported, 'both antrum and frontal sinuses were sound. It was decided to open the ethmoidal cells. Pus came away freely when this was done....' The patient became completely free of pain.

His colleagues received the report with great interest and it was discussed by his former teacher, Sir Thomas Myles, by Mr. E. H. Taylor and the president of the section and Mr. (later Sir John) Lentaigne. They agreed that Gogarty's paper deserved wide circulation.

'He's the King of antrum operations', an admiring anaesthetist eventually declared. 'Well, hardly!' a rival demurred, 'maybe the old Pretender!' There are fashions in surgery and Gogarty's fashion concerned sinuses; he insisted that all antra must be washed out. He made it almost a fetish and spoke and lectured about it, establishing a sort of cult especially among up-and-coming vocalists that unless the antra were washed out the timbre of the voice would suffer.

John Mc Cormack refused to have his tonsils removed by Gogarty but he submitted to antra punctures. Gogarty charged high fees for this operation but a Richmond pupil recalled that 'he was most generous and would take me or some other penniless student to assist him at private nursing homes and afterwards would slip a fiver into one's hand'.[3] Such was the haphazard way in which Dublin consultants made their livings but many of them, including Gogarty, earned large incomes.

Unlike many doctors who dislike treating relatives and friends, feeling that ties of affection may impair their clinical judgement, Gogarty did not hesitate to give medical advice to his acquaintances. Observing the enlarged glands at the *back* of Synge's neck he thought a diagnosis of tuberculosis unlikely and suspected Hodgkin's disease. Their informal consultation (for he was not Gogarty's patient) cheered Synge — 'I met Dr. Gogarty the other day,' he reported to Marie O'Neill, 'and he says I ought to get the glands out as soon as ever I can and that I will be all right then' — but his optimistic prognosis owed more to kindness than to science.[4]

Many of his patients became his friends. When Gerald Brockhurst, the Birmingham-born artist, was living in Ireland Gogarty's treatment improved his hearing which had been impaired since childhood. The doctor commissioned drawings of his children and canvassed sitters for Brockhurst.

He removed W.B. Yeats's tonsils in 1920 and according to the patient did so 'with exuberant gaiety' chatting with him about literature until the anaesthetic took effect and resuming the discussion as soon as the poet regained consciousness. Gogarty called on Yeats six times in the afternoon with various proposals for a dying speech.

He could handle patients with panache. When he was consulted by a musician who had lost his voice and could make no sound nor utter a syllable Gogarty suspected hysteria. He examined the man's throat carefully shining his light into the dark recess. Then he said with great deliberation: 'Your parents had syphilis'. 'They did not!' exclaimed the musician. 'You're cured,' said Gogarty.

Shane Leslie recalled sending him a patient. 'In those days I cast him to a beautiful singer losing her voice. The result was an instantaneous success. She could only describe her experience as "a scream!" No doubt he made her choke with bawdy stories but she sat up singing more shrilly than ever.'[5]

When Frank O'Connor, to his distress, was ordered into hospital for a throat operation a mutual friend suggested that he should go to Gogarty for a second opinion.[6]

'Jesus Christ!' Gogarty muttered at the conclusion of a thorough examination of the writer's throat. 'There are doctors in this town that don't know the difference between cancer and a sore toe.'

Then according to O'Connor, he 'sprang into rumbunctious life'.

'There's nothing wrong with you only Indian tea,' he said. 'I'll write it out for you — you can get it at Roberts' — Lap sang-soo-Choong.'

O'Connor was pleased with the reprieve from surgery but the diagnosis could have been corrected by Gogarty without such incontinent dismissal of his colleagues. The remark was not in the best tradition of professional etiquette and is a good example of the regrettable trait that caused someone to say that Oliver Gogarty had 'the kindest heart in Dublin and the dirtiest tongue'.

A constant object of derision was Mr. Keogh, a rival ear, nose and throat surgeon. 'Oh - Keogh!' he would say, to the amusement of the students, shining a light on a damaged palate or tonsil bed. 'Look at the snot doctor!' he remarked unfeelingly when the unfortunate Keogh emerged from his hall-door as Gogarty drove past. There may have been an element of justice, however, in his comment about another doctor with a disproportionately large practice. 'He dislikes walking in Stephen's Green because on his approach the ducks always cry "quack!" ' And his remark about a senior colleague at the Meath should be seen as an inspired example of the tongue-in-cheek gallow's-humour that circulates in all hospitals. Several of Sir Lambert Ormsby's beds were occupied by Gogarty's patients and a junior house-surgeon ventured to protest to the ear, nose and throat surgeon, saying that it was Sir Lambert's duty week and he needed the beds. 'Beds!' Gogarty exploded. 'He needs slabs.'[7]

In 1921 his privately published pamphlet, *A Suggested Operation For Turbinal Catarrh,* advocated a modification of the Caldwell-Luc operation as a cure for otherwise intractable nasal obstruction and catarrh. 'I have operated thus on more than a thousand cases — double and single — I have never seen septic pneumonia follow. The only untoward sequelae were neuralgia, or the necessity of washing out the antra for three weeks or more on account of the original infection persisting beyond the usual time or the ethmoiditis being either chronic or slow to recede.'[8] To support his emphatic advocacy of adequate drainage of the antrum he mentioned that he had himself submitted to an antrum operation to cure recurring colds. 'The result is so satisfactory and the relief so sudden that I can now realise how insidious can be the progress of the disease that can increase imperceptibly for years until life becomes miserable and strength and energy are depressed.'

Despite the annoying colds which the antrum operation cured, Oliver Gogarty's own health was good, his vitality inexhaustible, and his need for sleep minimal. Even when he stayed out carousing with some of his more dissolute companions he would rise early and go for a swim in Tara Street Baths or horse-riding on Merrion Strand. Then after a pint of buttermilk he was as ready to face the day as the most sober of his colleagues.[9]

From time to time he spoke on health legislation in the Senate and he gave the inaugural address at the Meath Hospital in 1937. On that occasion he protested that health was too much in the limelight and had become wistful and coy like a spoiled young girl. He maintained that despite a falling population the hospital records showed that more cases than ever were being treated. He complained of the unimaginable growth of the stock-pot of the manufacturing chemist and the advertisements in the daily papers which caused people to lose their individuality and become infected with whatever diseases the patent pills purported to cure. With considerable foresight he declared that one might be led to the conclusion that treatment was a cause of disease.

But writing to Dermot Freyer in December 1908 he made light of a recent misfortune. 'That I did not at once reply blame not me but my Appendix which narrowly escaped Chirurgery! I lay abed 8 days what time fair maids thrust ivory bobbins in behind and "threw up" turpentine! O Alfred Douglas!! I am better now.' It was a temporary reprieve for a few months later he wrote again from the Elpis Private Hospital:

My dear Freyer: they have carried me kicking from my own house, muzzled me with alien airs and cut the appendix out of me! These things were done last Wednesday week — a day after your letter came — I have been so interested in myself since that I have been unable to write until now, and now with difficulty. But you who have sucked in surgery from your first youth up to extreme old age will understand what shaketh the poetic hand in this novel way.....
I am rather weak but will be up in about 8 days and then will write long and lovingly to you.... Forgive my unpunctuality but when one's caecum perforates it is no time for mirth.[10]

He was seriously ill again in the spring of 1915, possibly with typhoid fever, and was a patient in the Meath Hospital from where he wrote to Seumas O'Sullivan in his customary high spirits: 'I am entering my third week — the Lethean week — of it now. Naturally, I will meet death with dignity (not to mention diarrhoea)!!'

> *I sickened with the clear intent*
> *To aid my printer, Seumas*
> *And gain the rare advertisement*
> *Of writing works posthumous*
>
> *So pale as that most watery bard*
> *Who wrote about Rathangan;*
> *I took up lodgings in the ward*
> *That saw the last of Mangan*
>
> *But you wrote on of dying vexed*
> *Before you print or etch it —*
> *When if you live to print the text*
> *You'll certainly die wretched.*[11]

Fortunately he did not suffer Mangan's fate, nor that of another Irish writer, Brendan Behan, who in a later day died prematurely in the Meath Hospital. He convalesced in Seaview (now Capri), Sorrento Road, Dalkey, a compact cottage where the Gogartys lived between 1915 and 1917. During that period the surgeon let 15 Ely Place and moved his consulting rooms to 32 St. Stephen's Green. The nearby Shelbourne Hotel facilitated conviviality, while in Dalkey it was a short distance along the Vico Road to the men's bathing place. To his additional joy, Henry Stewart Macran, 'The Master of Those Who Know', lived in Sorrento Terrace.

7

With Flowers and Wine, and Cakes Divine

Gibbon selected as the Golden Age the period between the death of Domitian and the accession of Commodus, but coming closer to our own times the years leading up to the first World War seem to have offered a degree of ease and privilege and an abundance of solid comfort to upper-middle-class society that could not today be readily commanded by a millionaire. A pound, or better still a golden sovereign, bought a week's groceries; coal was cheap and only the best families aspired to motor cars. Tradesmen were civil, and reliable; servants were undemanding, and knew their place.

The household at 15 Ely Place had been enlarged by the births of Dermot and Brenda and the employment of the staff necessary to enable the wife of a fashionable specialist to fulfil the duties expected of her which included a good deal of entertaining at home and some voluntary work on the Ladies Linen Guild and similar time-occupying committees in her husband's hospitals.

The Gogartys' close neighbours included, as we have seen, Sir Thornley Stoker and George Moore. Oliver extracted a good deal of fun from 'Moore-baiting'. He contrived that a series of greatly-desired dinner invitations be sent to him during a period when Moore was confined to his house for health reasons. He liked to repeat Tyrrell's gibe that the unlettered author of the projected *Ave atque Vale* thought that *atque* was a Roman centurion, but balanced it with the story of Moore's encounter with Thomas Cook in the Holy Land. The travel agent's offer of a guide to take him to the site of the Holy Sepulchre was refused by the novelist who expressed a preference to see the place where the woman was taken in adultery.

A state of armed neutrality, which Gogarty observed with amusement, existed between Sir Thornley and George Moore who annoyed the surgeon by drawing his cane noisily against the railings when he walked past Ely House and irritated him by unpunctuality when invited to dine there. But Moore went rather too far on an evening when Augustine Birrell, Gogarty and others were Sir Thornley's guests. Birrell was teasing his host about the success of Bram Stoker's *Dracula* when the dining-room burst open and an elderly nude woman ran in crying 'I like a little intelligent conversation!' Two female attendants followed and bundled Lady Stoker out of the room. This sudden appearance of his demented wife upset Sir Thornley but recovering he addressed his guests.

'Gentlemen, I hope you'll keep this mortifying incident completely to yourselves. And I must specially ask you, Moore —'

'But it was charming, Sir Thornley! I demand an encore.'

Furious, Stoker rose and taking Moore by the shoulder he showed him the door.[1]

Another immediate circle of acquaintances was formed by colleagues whom Gogarty met almost daily in the Meath and Richmond Hospitals. These included, in the latter, his old teachers, Dr. Joseph O'Carroll and Sir Thomas Myles, and younger men such as Dr. Frank Purser, international rugby-footballer and neurologist, and Mr. Adams McConnell, Ireland's first brain-surgeon. At the Meath the senior physician and surgeon were respectively, Sir John William Moore, editor of the *Irish Journal of Medical Science* and author of a *Textbook of Meteorology,* and Sir Lambert Hepenstal Ormsby, inventor of a pocket ether inhaler and a new form of pile clamp.

These were intelligent men, and good company, but unlike many doctors Gogarty took his closest friends from outside the profession and from many levels of society. The dons in Trinity still claimed his affection; there was, too, the company he met in Fanning's pub in Lincoln Place and in the Bailey Restaurant — poets, businessmen of literary tastes, politicians; and gradually the circle of his friends was to extend to include county families like the Leslies of Glaslough, County Monaghan, and aristocrats such as Lord Dunsany of Dunsany Castle, County Meath. Gogarty would not have denied the vein of snobbery[2] in his make-up but it is a testimony to his character that he so easily established himself as a desired guest at the tables of the elite where in the absence of wealth the attributes of a talented and pleasing personality may prove an acceptable substitute.

From time to time he lunched with Robert Yelverton Tyrrell at the Dolphin Hotel and elsewhere, and we find Tyrrell writing almost crossly to protest at Gogarty's generosity: 'There is no way of getting even with you. It was my turn and overdue. Yet when I went to pay Johnston, I found that the bill was already paid by "the Doctor". Knowing you I should have squared Johnston before I left the room. But it did not occur to me that you would spring this surprise on me. Will you give me a chance (difficult to achieve in your case) of playing my (with you) unaccustomed part of host on Wed. 5 at the Dolphin at one?"[3]

Another of Tyrrell's letters evidences his pleasure in his young friend's increasing social success:

> I wanted to tell you that you are now recognised as the diner-out, the *diseur,* the man without whom no dinner party is complete. I have had many proofs of this — one from Charlie Ball, who said he had met you twice, and you were the star of the dinner table.[4]

When Gogarty took him to lunch at Boss Croker's the host, a self-made man, was boastful. 'Do you see them ivories?' he said. 'Them is from the biggest elephant cemetery in Portuguese East, in Africa, I mean. One of their tusks weighs 160 pounds.... Let me show you something else. Them gold medals is produced in the statue of the bull pup that won them in Madison Square Garden. I had her statue made to life. It's gold, silver, and bronze.'

Afterwards Tyrrell said, 'Neither gold nor ivory amazed me so much as his use of "them" as an adjectival pronoun. He insisted on calling me "Perfessor". Probably he thought it was more emphatic than "Pro." '[5]

Tyrrell was ill in bed when the news reached him that Edward Dowden, Trinity's professor of English, had died. 'All my life', he said to his wife, 'Dowden has been held up to me as a model because he abstained from alcoholic drinks. And he's dead. Bring me another bottle!'

The professor of moral philosophy, Henry Macran, who had been Gogarty's tutor at Trinity and whose omniscience had earned him the title 'The Master of those Who Know' continued to value the company of the ex-pupil who had outgrown his patronage but whom he still addressed as Fasolt (himself posing as Fafner, another of the giants from Wagner's *Das Rheingold*), or, in a different mood, 'You filthy brute!'[6] Macran's knowledge, urbanity and waywardness never ceased to fascinate Gogarty. 'Sauternes', he would say, before pulling the cork, 'is more suited to the morning than Guinness's stout'. More suited, too, to the unhurried life of a Trinity don than to the crowded hours of an ear, nose and throat specialist.

Tea, rather than wine, was to be expected in the decorous atmosphere of the literary salons held by George Russell (AE) and Yeats, and, later, James Starkey (Seumas O'Sullivan). The Gogartys selected Fridays for their own literary evenings and this weekly event at 15

Ely Place was well attended by the established poets and their friends, a mixed company of well-mannered people.

Mrs. Starkie's musical 'At Homes' at Melfort, Blackrock, were another popular feature of Dublin's social life. Enid Starkie who was then a child has described her brother Walter playing the violin to the accompaniment of Edith Boxwell. She especially recalled Oliver Gogarty wandering among the guests, 'a twentieth-century Horace Walpole'. She enjoyed listening to his witty stories and admired his capacity 'to show us our great heroes *en pantoufles*'.[7]

A very different, and exclusively masculine, atmosphere, free of restraint, prevailed in Gogarty's favourite public-house, Fanning's of Lincoln Place, which was within walking distance of his home, easy to call to after consulting hours to meet cronies such as George Redding, James Montgomery, George Bonass, Kevin Smyth and Dr. Joe Boyd Barrett.

Fanning, the proprietor, defined nothing as 'a bunghole without a barrel' and expressed himself so freely that his tavern was known to its habitués as 'Indignation House'.[8] Kevin Smyth worked for Cantrell & Cochrane, a firm of mineral water manufacturers, but he preferred plain water with his whiskey. George Redding, a silent Ulsterman, worked in Guinness's Brewery and became general manager of its Port Royal Branch. He was a poet whose unpublished verses, according to Gogarty, were 'so few, but roses all!' Jimmy Montgomery was one of Dublin's wits, his best-known remark being the dry comment that the trees along the canal, a favourite trysting-place for lovers, were 'more sinned against than sinning'. When appointed film censor he said that he was 'between the devil and the Holy See'. Gogarty, incidentally, was on the Censorship Board.

Conversation in Fanning's was amusing, discursive and uninhibited. When the publican called 'drinks on the house' on an occasion of celebration Gogarty said, 'They also stand who only serve and wait'. And when told of the accidental death of an electrican who drank in the pub but had fallen from a roof-top in nearby Nassau Street while mending the Oxo sign, one of Dublin's first illuminated advertisements, Gogarty thought for a moment and composed an epitaph:

Here's my tribute to 'lectrician Joe,
Who fell to his death through the O in Oxo
He's gone to a land which is far far better
And he went, as he came, through a hole in a letter.[9]

The ambience of the Bailey Restaurant, a popular chop-house in Duke Street, was different again, more exclusive than an ordinary tavern. Here Gogarty's group was often joined by Arthur Griffith, an increasingly important political figure. A room where casual customers could not disturb them was set aside for their use, and when James Stephens was added to the company he heard for the first time, as he recalled later, 'poetry spoken of with the assured carelessness with which a carpenter talks of his planks and of the chairs and tables and oddments he will make of them'.

At the sale of Sir Thornley Stoker's collection of antiques in 1912 Gogarty met Lord Dunsany's agent who had come to the auction to buy back a valuable vase, one of a pair which was among the treasures of Dunsany Castle until Stoker claimed one of them as a fee. Soon after this the Gogartys were invited to a ball at the Castle. Tiring of the dancing, for Oliver was antipathetic to large-scale group enjoyments, he went in search of a quiet place to sit and encountered a tall, fair-haired young man doing likewise. The stranger proved to be his host and soon Gogarty and Lord Dunsany were reciting for each other their favourite verses of Herrick and Kipling.

Lord Dunsany who was Gogarty's exact contemporary having been born in London 24 July 1878 was a nephew of Sir Horace Plunkett, the founder of the Irish Co-operative Movement and employer of AE an association which led Dunsany to write *My uncle has a poet and he keeps him on a string,/And what do you think he keeps him for?/He keeps him for to sing.*

Dunsany's first play, *The Glittering Gate,* had been staged in the Abbey Theatre in 1909; two years later *King Arginenes and the Unknown Warrior* was accepted by the same management but then the association ceased for rightly or wrongly Dunsany felt that Yeats and Lady Gregory did not bring the same enthusiasm to the production of his work that they devoted to their own plays. This, according to Gogarty, was the basis of Dunsany's dislike for Yeats which was reciprocated and, despite his friendship with the older poet, Gogarty gradually came to realize the validity of Dunsany's opinion.

Gogarty and Dunsany were both men of action for whom poetry was an important daily interest but not an exclusive concern. The doctor did not aspire to the landowner's prowess at blood sports nor did he, of course, have the means and leisure that permitted Dunsany to hunt and travel. Nevertheless, they had many tastes in common and became good friends. He had an open invitation to Dunsany Castle, County Meath, and addressed a sonnet to its owner —

> *The twin dunes rise before it, and beneath*
> *Their tree-dark summits the Skene river flows,*
> *And old divine earth exaltation glows*
> *About it, though no longer battles breathe.*
> *For Time puts all men's swords in his red sheath,*
> *And softlier now the air from Tara blows;*
> *Thus in the royalest ground that Ireland knows*
> *Stands your sheer house in immemorial Meath.*
>
> *It stands for action done and days endured;*
> *Old causes God, in guiding Time, espoused,*
> *Who never brooks the undeserving long.*
> *I found there pleasant chambers filled with song,*
> *(And never were the Muses better housed)*
> *Repose and dignity and Fame assured.*[10]

Another who had treasured memories from those delectable days before Armageddon was the much-admired Beatrice Elvery (later Lady Glenavy) who in *To-day We Will Only Gossip* refers to Gogarty as a boon companion of William Orpen the painter and recalls picnics in the Dublin mountains, lunches and dinners in Jammet's, bathing parties in Howth and golden Portmarnock, and drives here and there about the country in Gogarty's big, butter-coloured Rolls Royce.

A quarrel terminated Orpen and Gogarty's companionship.[11] The latter's talent for friendship seems to have been paralleled by a flair for instinctive dislikes. The victims of his scorn included the Sinclair twins, Jewish dealers in works of art, plate and jewellery at 47 Nassau Street. With George Redding's encouragement he made a particular pastime of poking fun at William ('Boss') Sinclair who married Cissie Beckett:

> *Your dream of Beatrice Elvery*
> *Your business in old ivory,*
> *Your bachyderm; your spouse*
> *Who trumpets your sagacity —*
> *Thus Nassau Street has come to see*
> *A second Elephant House!*[12]

The first World War hardly affected Gogarty's life materially. Many of his Dublin colleagues assisted the Armed Services either locally or in France. At the Richmond Hospital Dr. Frank Purser was a Royal Army Medical Corps neurologist and Sir Thomas Myles saw no contradiction between his gun-running and support of the Crown Forces; Dr. Adrian Stokes took a motor-bicycle and sidecar with him to France and provided the Royal Army Medical Corps' first mobile laboratory; Dr. T.G. Moorhead was posted to Cairo.

Among the thousands of Irishmen who volunteered to fight for England none was more strongly moved by Christian idealism than Gogarty's friend, Tom Kettle, who was killed at Ginchy on 9 September 1916, meeting the death he had anticipated, ... *not for flag nor king nor emperor,/But for a dream born in a herdsman's shed,/ And for the secret scripture of the poor.*

When Gogarty thought of Kettle, his school friend, his opponent on the cycling track, his fellow-undergraduate at University College, he remembered 'his spirits which constantly were high, his wit that was as good-natured as himself, and his attitude to life that is a revelation to those who cannot but think of it as being as humdrum as themselves. There is a different land from this and a life to be lived therein, and it took Tom Kettle to reveal it to us with all his blithe strength'.[13]

On hearing that Gogarty had originated a project to erect a memorial to Kettle, Stephen Gwynn[14] wrote to him from the National Liberal Club to say he had been talking about Kettle to a number of friends 'who admired his work and still more his death' and that Lady Scott, widow of the Polar explorer had offered to help so that the subscription need only cover the cost of material and erection.[15] Eventually a bronze bust on a limestone pediment was erected in St. Stephen's Green where in fine weather Kettle used to lecture to his students.

The Gogartys spent Easter 1916 in the West. Oliver's return journey on Easter Monday was repeatedly interrupted and rumours of an insurrection spread through the train. A delay at Athlone to expedite the despatch of artillery from the barracks confirmed that something serious was happening. At Mullingar the passengers were told that the line had been cut and the train could go no further.

At an exorbitant price Gogarty managed to hire a car which he shared with Larry Ginnell, the local member of parliament, who was summoned to attend an emergency meeting at the House of Commons. His thoughts as he reached the suburbs, uncertain of what was happening, were of Lord Edward Fitzgerald, Wolfe Tone, Emmet and the succession of Irishmen who had risen and given their lives in Ireland's cause but it sobered Oliver when bullets whined above the car as they entered the city and one of them shattered the windscreen. The

rifles had been aimed at them by Irishmen mistaking their car for an
army vehicle.

Later he walked in the city and listened to the rumours of victory
for the insurgents and the counter-claims of the many who favoured
the military. Lord Dunsany, a serving soldier, making his way to join
an army group was shot and wounded. Another friend, the pacifist
Francis Sheehy-Skeffington, was to be brutally executed at the order
of a deranged British officer.

Gogarty read the hastily-printed Proclamation of Independence:
'... *We declare the right of the people of Ireland to the ownership
of Ireland and to the unfettered control of Irish destinies to be
sovereign and indefeasible....*' The names of the signatories, with the
exception of James Connolly's, meant little to him.[16] Next day he
talked about them to Hicks, a craftsman and cabinet-maker in Lower
Pembroke Street. Tom Clarke, an old Fenian, was alright they decided, but there were no Tones among them, no Emmets.

Medical practice was disrupted, and besides he decided that if
there was to be a general uprising he should look to the protection
of his wife and family. The Dublin-Galway train took him back as far
as Oranmore and he gradually made his way to Connemara.

Then Britain's miscalculated and bloody revenge extracted an Irish
victory out of defeat and surrender by creating martyrs. The ground-
swell of public opinion, previously hostile or indifferent towards
the insurgents, was vocalized by W.B. Yeats who declared motley
out-moded and saw the nascent glow of 'a terrible beauty' lighting
the Georgian facades. Some lesser poets contributed to *Aftermath
of Easter Week* and Gogarty paid his tribute in 'The Rebels', reminiscent of Hilaire Belloc's lapidary sonnets:

> *Not that they knew well, when they drew the blade
> That breaks for victory if gain were planned,
> You never gave without a trembling hand;
> But when they heard of sacred truth waylaid,
> And meanness with grandiloquence gainsaid,
> And Freedom, in the name of Freedom, banned;
> And Friendship in this foulness, this, England —
> This was the cause of that good fight they made.*
>
> *They heard your mobsters mouthing at the hordes,
> Who care not so the fight increase their store,
> Hawking your honour on the sandwich boards;
> But their's is safe, and to these things unlinked*

They stood apart; and Death withholds them more,
Separate for ever and aloof — distinct.

Oliver Gogarty's concern as a doctor for the public weal, and his sympathy for the oppressed, is acknowledged by a letter of appeal sent to him in October 1917 by Dr. Thomas J. Lenehan, a retired Royal Army Medical Corps officer, who was Medical Officer to Kilmainham Jail.[17]

Dear Gogarty: I am again in trouble. I found a poor devil of a Dublin voluntarily enlisted soldier lying in his cell about a week ago semi-collapsed and on the hunger-strike. He has been wounded and his right arm is withered, hand purple and trophic ulcers at tips break out from time to time. I sent him to Hospital and he was forcibly ejected from there this afternoon and sent back to Kilmainham Jail (condemned for the lowest criminals) — It is called Kilmainham Det. Bks. and I am the unfortunate Medical Officer   — to-morrow I expect this poor devil to be semi-collapsed and on the hunger-strike. You must protect me if I call on you to do so. My nerves won't stand forcible feeding and I have never passed a stomach tube in my life...

Lenehan proceeded to describe the deplorable conditions in 'this stinking Jail' which had totally inadequate facilities for the many prisoners meriting hospital attention but was nevertheless expected to take 'the venereal prisoners of Portobello' who were put into small cells where at the beginning of the war there had been an epidemic of cerebrospinal meningitis. He added, 'They would hang me for telling you all this'.

To cleanse that Augean Stable was far beyond Gogarty's powers.

8

Learn your Trade

Among the multifarious activities and undertakings, social, literary
and clinical, which Gogarty crowded into his restless days two events
have particular significance, the publication of *Hyperthuleana*[1] in
1916 and the purchase of a house in Connemara in the following
year. They finalize the early literary period and open the threshold
for new achievements. Before describing Renvyle House and its
interesting history it is proposed to take a retrospective glance at
Gogarty's early literary phase.

His verses from the first decade of the century are in three genres:
indifferent academic exercises and those composed to sell to the
editors of commercial journals for 'pin money' (or pint money) as
Professor Carens[2] has it; the bawdy which circulated in the oral
tradition of the Dublin pubs (many are preserved in his unpublished
papers); the more ambitious light lyrics and humorous poems which
found reputable initial publication and which often re-appear in later
collections.

We might expect to find some of his work in *T.C.D.: A College
Miscellany* and in view of his talent for parody it is tempting to
attribute to Gogarty the unsigned 'To Lucasta on going to the War',
concerning love ending in financial settlement (1902): *I could not
pay thee, dear, so much, loved I not freedom more,* and a sonnet
commencing *Long have I basked in Idleness, and my drowsy soul in
dormant lethargy.* Such attributions must be resisted. The first
example of Gogarty's work in *T.C.D.* which can be positively identified (and this may be Gogarty's first appearance in print), apart from
the privately-published prize-winning poem on Robert Louis Stevenson, is 'The Death of Diogenes, the Doctor's Dog'. 'Virgil', published
in the *Miscellany* on 21 November 1903, is a more ambitious lyric
and of particular interest because it shows that he was then sufficiently competent to write a sonnet worthy of subsequent inclusion
in *Collected Poems:*

From Mantua's meadows to Imperial Rome
Came Virgil, with the wood-light in his eyes,
Browned by the suns that round the hillside home
Burned on the chestnuts and the illices.
And these he left, and left the fallows where
The slow streams freshened many a bank of thyme,
To found a city in the Roman air,
And build the epic turrets in a rhyme.
But were the woodland deities forgot,
Pan, Sylvan, and the sister nymphs for whom
He poured his melody the fields along?
They gave him for his faith a happy lot:
The waving of the meadows in his song
And the spontaneous laurel at his tomb.

He was something of a pot-hunter but, despite W.B. Yeats's admonitions to the contrary (unheeded by Jack B. Yeats who sold drawings to *Comic Cuts* for a few shillings), is it not understandable that a needy student should be attracted by cash prizes? The Vice-Chancellor's prizes provided an annual bonus.

Poetic response to a set subject is unlikely to be inspired. The prize-winning poems on Stevenson and on the Don Quixote Tercentenary abound in facile rhymes and images: there are too many 'adowns' and some execrable lines — *Over waves that ebb not as they flow* — but also occasional lines *(the long perennial gospel of your glee)* and stanzas promising that better will follow:

You saw when rose leaves blow the Rose is broken
The Star that touches Earth is quenched and dead
The thought transferred is fettered by the Token,
You saw the rapt Knight bruised and buffeted.

Details of the chronology of Gogarty's poetic endeavours are readily extracted from *Many Lines to Thee,* his letters to G.K.A. Bell edited by J.F. Carens, and from unpublished letters to Freyer. In his letters to Bell, whose tastes differed from James Joyce's, Gogarty eschews the Rabelaisian, sending instead sensitive lyrics. His output was copious; evoking Swinburne he told Bell 'I shall send you dozens if you will but send me one type of "clear chryselephantine verse", if you will "send but a song oversea to us!" ' and again he pleaded for a 'lyric of thine, or a marble verse....'

> *Thy heart is as light as a leaf of a tree*
> *But mine giveth forth amongst seagulls hollow*
> *To the place of the slaying of Itylus*
> *Thou art classic, romantic is Gogarty.*

'To Stella', quoted in an earlier chapter, was sent to Bell in July 1904 together with the far more original 'To Maids Not to Walk in the Wind' and 'To Lilian to Cozen Time'. Other tributes to maidenhood, 'Winifred' and 'Molly', were published in *Dana* in November 1904 and February 1905 respectively. The 'Two Songs' commencing *My love is dark, but she is fair* and *Gaze on me though you gaze in scorn*, published in John Baillie's *The Venture* contain far finer lyrics. His initial arrangement with Baillie was that 'Delphi', his Newdigate offering, should be published but when the editor found it too long and asked for shorter poems, 'The Bardic pride melted and complied,' as Gogarty admitted to Bell.

On 22 July 1904 he mentioned an essay on Shakespeare's style that he was writing for the Shakespeare Society and a tragedy 'Beside the Ford' which he expected to be printed and bound by the following Spring. In August he sent a copy of *Ireland* 'to which I was driven to contribute' and an unfinished poem with a title partly derived from Herrick, 'To Maidens not to be kind about his tower'. He was invited to send an article on Dublin to *London Opinion* but never wrote it.

The unsigned commercial effusions in *Ireland* positively identifiable as Gogarty's are 'Song' and 'On the Death of a Favourite Race Horse' (September 1904):

> *The limbs that strove, the heart that pressed*
> *With such intense desire,*
> *Have reached a place of lasting rest,*
> *Where they no more shall tire...*

'Foreword' (April 1904), and the Kiplingesque 'Ireland's Welcome to the Fleet' (September 1904), may also be his, but they are poor stuff and would have been better consigned to the waste-paper basket.

The fragments which he sent to Bell in Autumn 1904, *O ye who dig for treasure trove/Amid the rocks of Sandycove..., Like those vestals of the sky/ Fallen before the days go by...*, are reproduced in *Many Lines to Thee; 'To a Sailor'* was re-titled 'The Isles of Greece' when he sent it with 'Dolly' in 1908 to Freyer who published both in *The Gambolier*. 'Folia Caduca', re-published in *An Offering of*

Swans, was delivered to Bell, with the letter that also contained 'Ringsend', a sonnet written on 12 December 1904 (and issued privately 'prettily misprinted for 10/6' in 1905):

> *At midnight when the coal dust on the Quay*
> *Blackens their sea-spun raiment, and the air*
> *Thick with the blustering torchlights' echoing flare*
> *Is withering up their brightness, noisily*
> *The fish are cast ashore and left to be*
> *Hurled into many a cart with careless care*
> *That shall in crushed glory landward bear*
> *The tribesman of the chainless realm of sea.*
>
> *And yet the fires that here lie heaped and hurled,*
> *Winnowed the waters in Corinthian bays,*
> *Tasting the forest freshets in the blue —*
> *They fret the wavering sunshine, and they knew*
> *The ever-during quiet of the ways*
> *Made green with all the verdure of the world!*

Next day Gogarty forwarded a stanza from 'At Burford', an extravaganza which remained an airy nothing. Meanwhile he was still working on the tragedy that never materialized: 'The Play is really well schemed or made mythical. The myth is good. One whose energies have been chiefly intellectual feels the longing to record action in deeds...'. Early in 1905 he dashed off 'Adieu to George Moore', thought of attempting a rhymed translation of the Chorus from 'The Clouds' by Aristophanes, and was encouraged when a London musician sought permission to put two of his poems to music.

As winter passed into spring his letters to Bell continued to reflect his preoccupation with literature. 'For reading — Matthew Arnold yet holds me — Horace, the construction of his Odes — not the metrical construction — is taking some of my attention; the rest, too much alas, is given to the medicine.' In due course he sent Bell news of a visit to the dentist and other tidings: 'Now it is over I am like Swinburne's Marlowe — "gold on his mouth and morning in his eyes." My exam too is over....My next residence may be for 3 months in a private asylum where I shall reside without being "an inmate": Everything is possible in a lunatic asylum. My friends are unanimous regarding the appropriateness of my dwelling.'

In October 1905 he was preparing an essay for the Vice-Chancellor's prose prize but this undertaking was delayed when he turned to 'Sir Dinedan's song for Sir Tristram',eventually included in *Hyper-thuleana* and the *Collected Poems*. He still had on hand the tragedy 'Beside the Ford', a political pantomime 'The Cows', and 'Iseult in Ireland'. He took in good part (he could hardly have done other-wise) Bell's warning that he was diffusing his talents:

> It is good of you to touch me on the ear and admonish me con-cerning my penny sonnets. I am really making an effort to get something done. But so many themes rise before me with such equal allurings that I can rarely do more than play an interlude.

Two of Gogarty's more spectral creations should be mentioned: the bawdy 'Sinbad the Sailor', a fragment of which Joyce received from Vincent Cosgrave in October 1905, and the 'Song of the Cheerful (but slightly sarcastic) Jesus' which Cosgrave also forward-ed. Writing from New York city on 14 June 1906 Gogarty informed Joyce, 'the American edition of "Sinbad" is out. It runs to 230 stanzas'.[3] Are we to conclude that Gogarty asked an American printer to execute a commission he would not have dared to place in Dublin? If so, there is no record of an existing copy. And besides, he mentioned, as we have seen, to Starkey that he would look for a printer in Paris.

By altering Gogarty's title and quoting it incompletely, Joyce's version of the 'Ballad of Joking Jesus' in *Ulysses,* as Carens has pointed out, conceals the serious purpose of this amusing if un-orthodox poem which is an anticlerical satire on commercial Christ-mas.[4]

> *The more men are wretched the more you will rule*
> *But thunder out 'Sinner' to each bloody fool;*
> *For the Kingdom of God (that's within you) begins*
> *When you once make a fellow acknowledge he sins.*

His letters to Freyer contain many light-hearted fragments which remain unpublished, such as *The prostate is expensive/Here both Love and Lust are mated;/But O it never costs so much/As when enucleated*[5] but 'When Clearance was intended to the Kips' (sent for Freyer's opinion in April 1908) and 'At the Abbaye la Trappe' (November 1910) are included in *Hyperthuleana* where 'City' has edged out the franker 'Kips'.

The commitments of his growing surgical practice left little time for poetry but, like Dr. William Carlos Williams, he sometimes wrote verses on his prescription pad between consultations. The poet's mantle does not fit snugly over a doctor's white coat, however, and he used pseudonyms when 'A Line from Rabelais' (1911) and 'To his Friend the Apothecary Poet' (1912) were published in *The Irish Review*. The seven-stanza echo of Rabelais (dedicated to George Moore in *Hyperthuleana*) is an amusing homily which shows Gogarty's flair for light humorous verse:

> *God is displeased with Koska's wife —*
> *She's yielded to that man again:*
> *A worthier villain on my life*
> *Ne'er merited the Extreme Pain!*
> *But my good Joan the Chatelaine*
> *She calls my penance mere restraint*
> *And swears, ere April buds be spent*
> *To find a way to vex a saint*
> *Faire and Softly passeth Lent*

Through his appointment as Surgeon to the Meath Hospital Gogarty had an official connection with the School of Physic but, in any case, it would have been difficult to find a more suitable person to write the 'Ode on the Bicentenary of the Medical School' which was read by Professor Tyrrell as a Prologue to a performance of *She Stoops to Conquer* in the Queen's Theatre on 4 July 1912. It aimed to celebrate the city, the School, and those who had served it.

> *Like Nicholson who could divine*
> *What smallest wort or seaward pine*
> *Of heathful balm supplies;*
> *Helsham whose book beyond it peers*
> *Taught science for a hundred years;*
> *And Molyneux who earned*
> *Two fames that leave him unforgot,*
> *A scholar and a patriot*
> *Whose book the hangman burned...*

One of his longer poems (208 lines), but a form with which he was never really comfortable, the ode lacks the ease and lightness which are Gogarty's characteristics. The descriptive passages are its best feature:

> *The rose-red Georgian houses seem*
> *To catch a glory and to gleam*
> *As when their lights of old*
> *Shone out, with many a taper's blaze*
> *On Dublin of the bounteous days.*
> *Built by the liberal and the bold*
> *In spacious street and square.*
> *What memories are theirs to hold*
> *Of gallant and of fair:*
> *Each room a house, each house a town*
> *Each hall a thoroughfare!*

Matter, metre and music are a 'Blessed Trinity' which Gogarty thought all poets should respect, a fealty evident in *Hyperthuleana* where despite classical leanings he addresses a Muse that is Irish and, one suspects, a slattern:

> *Dublin and Dublin's lanes'*
> *Typical daughter*
> *Fair, for the blood of Danes*
> *Moistened the mortar;*
> *As that rose-scattering*
> *Queen, the Italian's,*
> *Tall, though your shawl may bring*
> *Rhubarb and Scallions.*

This collection, privately published in a minuscule edition in 1916, allows us to see Gogarty for the first time in the round, greeting friends and castigating enemies:

> *With your regrets don't move my mirth*
> *That Beauty walks no more on earth,*
> *For you would be revealed at once*
> *In your true colours as her ponce.*

— already a master of the mock-heroic but not yet realizing his full lyric gifts. His advice 'To his Friend the Apothecary Poet' — *When you compound a verse or song/Make it translucent, not too strong;/ Pour the full measure gauged right;/ That it have body, yet be light* — is a prescription which he himself utilized.

The matter of his verse includes virulent satire, the celebration of the ordinary (for what, at first sight, could seem less poetic than the

object successfully hymned in 'To a Mushroom'?), the magnification
of the universal absurdity embodied in that relentless lover, the barn-
yard cock, a gaudy focus, perhaps, for an incongruity inherent in all
amorous affairs, suburban or legendary:

> *Strange that a small brown hen*
> *Should charm you thus! For men*
> *Great beauty shines, as when*
> *The Argive valleys*
> *Bore her limbs for whom Greece*
> *For ten years knew no peace,*
> *Or our own Western seas*
> *Bore Grace O'Malley's,*

He pokes fun at a land 'where sex is sin and virtue epicene,' hails a
friend, Kasimir Dunin Markievicz, with a sonnet:

> *Kasimir, a name that clashes like a sword*
> *Through skulls of dullards and brings back old joy!*
> *Kasimir, the great eternal-hearted boy!*
> *A centaur laughing on his mountain sward*
> *Could just as little with our life accord*
> *As you can with the little peoples here...*

He sends a generous host a graceful tribute:

> *Your table like a moon silvern*
> *Shows what a kitchen sun you burn*
> *An alternating sun that heats*
> *The growing herbs and lowing meats.*

He presents us with a matchless parody of Keats, 'On first looking into
Kraft Ebbing's (sic) Psychopathia Sexualis', scolds a bearded art-
dealer in lines that are prototypes of libels to come, and ends with
a self-mocking epilogue:

> *Inheritors of this our Song!*
> *Inhabitants of larger day!*
> *If you sometimes look back and long*
> *That you had met us, hear me say:*
> *You're happy though you may not know it,*
> *To have the Verse and not the Poet.*

Another anonymous collection, *Secret Springs of Dublin's Song* (1918), contains several of Gogarty's early and inferior poems, written for the most part before Yeats impressed on him the need to avoid the timeworn conventions of verse, the inversions and 'didst' and 'hast'. This volume may be what Gogarty had in mind when he informed Bell in 1904 that he and Seumas O'Sullivan intended to bring out a book of poems before Christmas. 'None of the verses are to be signed as this country will not stand criticism...' Ballantyne would print a thousand copies for £15. 'There's a market now for Irish eggs, butter and poetry'.[6] Towards the end of the year he again referred hopefully to a privately published volume of his own verses — Sullivan's 'Twilight People' (1905) was probably then with the printer — but he turned down an offer from a publisher in 1906. 'At present I do not wish to masquerade as a Poet. There are so many already in Dublin that they have "swamped the sacred poets with themselves." Next September, perhaps, I may appear in print.' From Vienna on 26 October 1907 he sought Joyce's aid: 'What about finding a printer and steering some lighter verses through the press for me?', a plea reiterated in November: 'If you would undertake to see some M.S. through the Press I would arrange with you on behalf of myself and some others who think of bringing out *Ditties of No Tone* very quaint'. When Joyce, in Trieste, signified a willingness to help, Gogarty explained: 'The reasons for suggesting to forward M.S. are that I don't know enough German to steer it through the press: the English is quainter than your Holy Office; the M.S. is not altogether confined to verses of mine'.[7] Freyer in Edinburgh was the next hope; he attempted to recruit his interest and Tancred's in 1909, promising 'a fiver' towards expenses and sending a suitable Foreword:

> *Reader, lest you read amiss*
> *Prithee to remember this,*
> *Culture in the height of Greece*
> *Gave us Aristophanes,*
> *Martial in the Roman day,*
> *And Religion Rabelais.*
>
> *Then if pleased you will not be*
> *Blame your day for our degree,*
> *Your small religion and less culture*
> *And these lesser Times' sepulture.*[8]

Secret Springs does not feature anything to compare with the cathartic 'Holy Office'; Gogarty's contributions include parodies, Moore-baiting, and an irreverent elegy:

> *O ye, who disinterested plant*
> *This mortal remnant of my Aunt,*
> *And planting her, grow dry,*
> *Suspend your vacant pensiveness,*
> *And turn those thoughts to my distress*
> *Which pints preoccupy.*

The pick of the bunch is 'To the Maids not to Walk in the Wind' which reappears in the *Collected Poems*.

Poetry was Gogarty's absorbing interest but even in the early phase, as we have seen, he sometimes turned to prose, a more difficult medium for the inexperienced writer, and especially for one temperamentally given to overstatement. An article published in the Dublin *Evening Mail* on 4 March 1905, 'The Irish Literary Revival', commences soberly enough with the sensible complaints of lack of critical standards concerning literary merit, confusion about what makes literature national and disagreement about the conception of drama. 'We are content to compare and not to criticise, with the result that when confronted with any form of art to which we cannot immediately apply a precedent we are puzzled.'

He cites as an example the Abbey audience's failure to appreciate *The Shadowy Waters* because it had neither action nor crisis and because it was not dramatic. 'I who was aware that no claim had been made for the dramatic excellence of the piece, appreciated and enjoyed it as a new and charming form of art — a lyric staged; a dream and not a drama.' He found fault with *On Baile's Strand* as an example of experiments 'which tend to lilliputianise our legends'; he thought Cuchullain was transformed into 'a trivial, peckish, and wavering old man'.

Passing to lyric poetry he found the prospect brighter: Yeats was the most powerful influence from Ireland on London; AE because of his 'strong personality, genius, and large humanity', the greatest influence at home. The remainder of the article was devoted to *The Twilight People*.

The technique of the verses alone would almost warrant my saying that as Mr. Yeats is devoting his attention persistently to literature of another kind, his magic mantle seems to have fallen on no unworthy shoulders. The mental climate of the particular country whence any poetry springs was never represented by any poet more faithfully than Seumas O'Sullivan represents the mood of the Irish mind. It is an expression such as this is of a nationality that constitutes national literature.

So far, so good! But he threw moderation to the winds and launched himself into the deep purple. It wouldn't be his fault if his friend's book didn't sell.

> The sentiment of the evergreen hills in the vespertine quiet of our old land has never found more faithful or tender wording. Metrical music rather than words is his vehicle; a music as of twilight moods audible; a twilight which makes more beautiful the cold divine stars.

Most of his contributions to *Sinn Féin* in 1906 were the stuff of hard-hitting polemical journalism, magnifying the imagined fault, indulging in unfounded generalities to the approval of an already converted readership, but convincing nobody else. The first article in the series 'Ugly England' was written during his honeymoon ('Mrs. Gogarty mustn't have been very entertaining,' was Joyce's ill-mannered comment to his brother Stanislaus). Having described the red earth of Devon and the villages hidden in the folds of the hills he makes it clear that this is a picture of the past, for the arrival of a wagonette of trippers from a manufacturing town destroys it.

> When I saw that wagonette with its full load of swollen men, I was as much moved as if I had actually seen a hearse pass by with the dead body of England and Empire. They were not dead, but those are signs of death, nevertheless. And I will tell you why. These are the English middle-class, the common men than whom the world cannot show more ugly or more animal human beings. The class that are devouring England even as they eat its roast beef. The class whose only cult is that of Beecham, Carter, or the fruit-salt seller, Eno: the over-fed, aperient people.

It is for the common Englishman, whom Gogarty prefers to call 'Sludge' than John Bull, that we 'have turned our country into grazing lots; it is for him that we connive at permitting our youth to enlist or associate with soldiers; it is for him that the best of our peasantry have become renegades, and, by selling their strength and manhood as a woman might her beauty, enter the ranks of the R.I.C.'

Using the pseudonym 'Mettus Curtius', his target is the British soldier who 'when he is not a disease is a shopwalker':

Was it in England I saw it, the anthropoid thing? It was in a khaki suit, and its nature accorded with its coat. Its legs were swathed in bandages of like colour, but the ankles were as thick as the knees, and no calf muscle held the 'putties' firm. So it walked along, and I noticed its greenish face, and reflected that the red blood must have been spilt in imaginary wars. There were many of these — soldiers a person called them.

The profession of arms is an honourable one when the soldier fights for motives which are chivalrous and sublime. 'But England makes incursions and enslaves peoples only because they are weaker, only because they can be despoiled, only because she must get buyers for the goods by trading which she lives. But England says it is for Liberty and Progress. She has even stolen the labels off the virtues and perverted the values of things.'

Whether simulated or not, for Gogarty had many British friends and was aware of England's virtues, his indignation has a Swiftian quality and not all his charges were unfounded. Nobody is more self-righteous than Sludge. 'And also as he remains with his eyes devoutly lifted he cannot perceive that at his very feet in India are slave-compounds, where women are incarcerated with more than the horrors of a harem to be debauched at the good pleasure of the Army, a body of men who, as their own statistics show, are already more than half leprous from venereal excess.'

Gogarty may have contributed several unsigned pieces to Arthur Griffith's paper but a short story 'The Gardeners', published in *Sinn Féin* on 26 May, appeared, regrettably, under his name. This unsuccessful tale describes two old men in an autumnal garden laughing over their ageing master's discomfiture on finding a goat owned by his young wife in the garden. There is a plethora of adjectives, a striving after misplaced lyricism; the best that can be said of it is that it presents age making a contented submission to inexorable nature. 'Sweet is the sight of children playing or of the salient water that blows forever and can return again; but for us who do not return the goodliest sight of all is an old man contented. Rest them deeply Earth for they tended you well.' Gogarty's exhortation seems uncharacteristic of this Rabelaisian galliard but it is an early token of an awareness of mutability and death, a note which echoes more plaintively in his verses.

By 1906 he was approaching graduation and aware that the traditions of his chosen profession discouraged its members from cultivating publicity. This may explain why the articles in *The Shanachie* attributed to Gogarty by Cathal O'Shannon[9] were published under the pseudonym 'Oliver Gay'. O'Shannon also said that the poet contributed verses to *The Voice of Labour*. This seems an unlikely repository for Gogartiana — 'They have the rhythm of labour without its work', was his comment on labour leaders — and a search in that journal's files has been unrewarding.

PART TWO

9

Smiling Public Man

A modern road system enables present-day motorists to sweep from one end of Connemara to the other in two or three hours. The cratered, winding roads which Oliver Gogarty knew were very different, although immeasurably better than those laid down by Alexander Nimmo in the early nineteenth century. But when Henry Blake the original owner of Renvyle House came to inspect his ancestral property in 1811 no road whatsoever existed.[1]

Young Blake travelled on horseback through the Joyce country, traversed the pass of Maam Cloughaloon and followed the bed of a mountain stream to the pass of Maam Turc. He explained his decision to build a house to replace the then existing one, a low, thatched dwelling-place, in *Letters from the Irish Highlands* with an amusing reference to phrenology. 'The heir of fortune is seldom content until he has pulled down what was built by his immediate predecessors. Gall and Spurzheim would attribute this unlucky propensity to the absence of the organ of habitativeness, and the prevalence of that of constructiveness.' His real reason for doing so was the realization that unless he lived on the property it would be despoiled.

Henry Blake settled into his new house in 1819 and whatever his relations with his tenants were they could not have been worse than the unhappy situation which prevailed after the emergence of the Land League when Mrs. Blake, a strong-minded woman who was then the owner, was boycotted and had cattle, sheep and horses driven on to her land. She sat it out and gained some measure of victory, but to make ends meet she was obliged to open Renvyle House as a hotel.

One week in the 1890s her guests included the inspired cousins, Violet Martin and Edith Somerville, who drove over from Ross House in a governess cart and were greatly impressed to find 'a long grey, two-storey house, with low Elizabethan windows, and pale weather-slated walls, wholly unexpected, and altogether unique, as far at all events, as this part of Ireland is concerned'.

A little distance from the iron-studded door was a 'lake "shtiff" with brown trout' and beyond it the Atlantic.[2] Entering the house the heavy door led into a hall fitted with oaken props for guns and rods; an open fire heated the low-ceilinged, mahogany-panelled sitting room.

By purchasing Renvyle House in 1917 Oliver Gogarty put the seal on his professional success and acquired a unique holiday house which he was proud to show off to his friends. While never attempting to rival Lady Gregory's Coole Park it provided a second major literary focus in the West, and Connemara left its impress on his writing, charming him to the point of enchantment as in the past it had done to Maria Edgeworth, Thackeray the wordmaster who was obliged to accept its beauty as indescribable, and Sir William Wilde, and would in the future capture the imagination of Richard Murphy the poet of High Island and the Cleggan disaster.

His property included many acres of land situated on the northern side of the Renvyle peninsula near its tip, and was reached by turning off the main Clifden-Westport road at Letterfrack and following a narrow road, then hardly more than a boreen, that wound westward for some miles, flanked by rocks and moorland with here and there clusters of green fields where animals could graze or hard-won crops be cultivated, passing through the spartan villages of Tully Cross and Tully and climbing a hill by the deserted Coastguard Station from which the first glimpse of the roofs and chimneys of Renvyle House was gained. Half-a-mile further on a bleak and rutted avenue curved between ragged fuschia hedges towards a commodious and stoutly-built dwelling set between lake-water and the ocean.

Nothing can be more desolate, or more magnificent, than this area which had an instinctive and instant appeal for something that under-lay Gogarty's urbanized exterior. Sodden green fields merge with the purples and browns of the rising moorland; the whins flaunt their gaudy yellow among the vast abounding granite slabs and boulders. The crumbling castle of the O'Flahertys stands, a useless sentinel, at Renvyle Point; to the south Tully Mountain shuts out Ballynakill Bay and northwards across a sweep of the Atlantic the eye passes from Inish Turk and Clare Island to the distant coastal ranges of County Mayo, Slieve More in far-away Achill, the Corraun peninsula, the coned peak of Croagh Patrick, Ireland's holy mountain, and the massive bulk of Muilrea, the tallest mountain in Connacht.

Nothing can be so memorable, and yet so fugitive, as the beauty of Connemara, a region vulnerable to drenching rains which in a matter of moments blot out all its loveliness, replacing it with a grey, impenetrable pall lasting for days before sunshine rends the veil liberating vast white cloud-galleons to sail the skies, casting their wind-swept shadows across the dancing grass, the moving heather and the steady peaks of the Beanna Beola.

Gogarty brought the ageing Mahaffy to Renvyle House to marvel at the 'plum-coloured hills'; W.B. Yeats and his bride were offered it for their honeymoon; Augustus John absorbed the landscapes and regurgitated them on canvas; the Bodkins and many others came and went; the Gogartys' hospitality was endless and evidently undiminished by political cross-currents that were to lead to the Anglo-Irish War.

Gogarty came down with a severe attack of influenza in the pandemic of 1919. 'It is a mixture of spotted fever without the aesthetic advantages of the pattern the spots make, and consumption without the bobsleighs of Davos Platz. Headache and lung trouble mixed! Horrible.' He went to Renvyle to convalesce early in March and was pleased to hear that Lady Leslie had accepted an invitation to visit Connemara. She was one of the three celebrated American-born Jerome sisters who through their marriages to Lord Randolph Churchill, Sir John Leslie and Moreton Frewen became the mothers of Winston Churchill, Shane Leslie and the sculptress Clare Sheridan, respectively.

Dear Lady Leslie: the best news I have had for a long time is that you are coming here at Easter. It is really delightful; and to you who have descended to the cellar dining-room of Ely Place it will be endurable. After all it is no worse than living in College at Oxford.[3]

Arthur Griffith, who dressed badly and was a dull, uninspired orator, may seem an unlikely figure to have commanded Gogarty's undeviating respect and admiration but it is surely no more than the caprice of history that permits 'the greatest architect of modern Ireland', as a modern historian calls him, to remain undervalued.[4] He may not have cut a dash but his qualities were apparent to Gogarty who never treated him with the levity reserved for other eminent friends, and who was a loyal supporter of Sinn Féin. In 1906 , when Gogarty was still an impecunious student, he urged Dermot Freyer to support the *United Irishman*. 'I have raised the furtive fiver! I am taking a debenture share in the new U.I. Go thou and do likewise: it will be a pleasant thing to consider that you have a finger in the dissolution of tyranny in Ireland.'

Whatever his deficiencies as a speaker, and these may have been exaggerated, for it has been said that he had a remarkable facility for incisive statements which could clear the air 'like a flash and a thunderclap', Arthur Griffith, the son of a Dublin printer, was a consummate political journalist. His verbal style which did not eschew violence and the manipulation of facts was in contrast to his political policy of non-violent resistance and abstention from Westminster.

Griffith, who was elected President of Sinn Féin in 1911, joined the Irish Volunteers in 1913. Since he saw its role as a defensive one his association with the Volunteers as a rank-and-file member was quite consistent with his advocacy of non-violent measures. He participated in the Howth gun-running and hid a rifle in his home. His opposition to the Great War and to the possibility of conscription in Ireland led to the suppression of *Sinn Féin,* but the irrepressible editor followed it with *Eire-Ireland, Scissors and Paste* and *Nationality*.

Understandably, in 1916 this outspoken man of peace, although working close to Seán MacDermott and in receipt of funds from Clan na Gael and the IRB, was not told of the secret plans for an Easter Rising. He had heard nothing until Saturday 22 April and then his immediate instinct was to support Eoin MacNeill's countermanding order. Nevertheless, on Easter Monday, prepared to give what support he could to his comrades, he made his way to the General Post Office but was convinced by Seán MacDermott and others that he could best serve the cause by returning home in the hope that he would remain free to carry on his work and propaganda in the not unlikely event of the Rising's failure.

Griffith was arrested in due course and incarcerated in Reading Gaol where he remained until the Christmas release of 1916. When *Nationality* reappeared in February 1917 his basic convictions were unchanged and he hoped to settle Ireland's problems through an appeal to the post-war peace conference.

Three groups, the declining parliamentarians, non-violent Sinn Féin, and the liberated insurgents now contended for leadership of the Freedom movement. Count Plunkett's success in the North Roscommon by-election was followed by three other victories on the abstentionist ticket in 1917. These were almost mortal blows for the parliamentarians and signal triumphs for Griffith who had working with him Michael Collins, an increasingly prominent organizer whose attitudes and arguments were to minimize Griffith's moderating influence. Despite a personal constancy to his original policies, increasing cohesion made it difficult to see light between the doves and the hawks; the Sinn Féin label began to cover the wider group in consideration of which Griffith unselfishly stood down from the presidency at the annual convention on 27 October 1917 and was replaced by Eamonn de Valera the senior surviving commandant of the Easter Rising.

The subsequent sweep of events included the threat of conscription which united all parties; Griffith's election as abstentionist M.P. for East Cavan while serving a prison sentence with others in Gloucester Gaol; the increasing power of men like Collins and Harry Boland in the absence of the moderates; Armistice Day and the general election when Sinn Féin took seventy-three of the Irish seats; the first meeting of Dáil Éireann in the Mansion House, which might have been seen as the vindication of Griffith's policy but for the shooting of two members of the R.I.C. at Soloheadbeg which from his prison cell he condemned, prophetically, as the kind of outlaw action which would end by Irishmen shooting one another.

Released in March 1919, Griffith returned to Dublin where he held the post of Home Minister and, ironically, in view of his willingness to place the mantle of leadership on de Valera's shoulders, from June he was acting-President during de Valera's protracted absence in America. The Anglo-Irish war escalated following the arrival of the 'Black and Tans' in mid-1920 and the first of Ireland's 'Bloody Sundays' occurred in November. Despite his reputation as a 'moderate', Griffith was arrested in December and incarcerated in Mountjoy Gaol until 30 June 1921. Meanwhile, until de Valera's return to Ireland in March, Michael Collins had full control of the political and military wings of Sinn Féin.

Following the Truce in July 1921 a new ministry of six, which included William T. Cosgrave, was set up; despite de Valera's position as President it fell to Griffith to lead the Irish delegation which between 11 October and 6 December 1921 negotiated a treaty in London. The subsequent long, recriminatory and bitter debate in the Dáil ended on 7 January 1922 and it was voted to accept the Treaty by 64 votes to 57; Griffith was chosen as President in preference to de Valera by an even narrower margin, 60 to 58.

The participants in this drama who influenced Oliver St. John Gogarty were Arthur Griffith, W.T. Cosgrave and, in an ugly and possibly negative sense, Eamonn de Valera. He admired Michael Collins greatly and when on the run Collins could depend on shelter and security in Ely Place.[5] Another dimension of 'the troubles' in both pre- and post- Treaty phases was made evident to him through his friendship with Lord Dunsany and Talbot Clifton of Kylemore House, Connemara.

The deepest and most permanent influence on Gogarty was Griffith's and while one does not wish to draw a parallel between their virtues, other than that they both abhorred physical violence, it is possibly relevant to say that many of Griffith's faults were magnified in Gogarty. Both were assertive, capable of narrowmindedness and prone to strong dislikes; neither was prepared to concede much to an opponent's arguments, or change his own even when facts seemed to have gone awry. Gogarty's apprenticeship, such as it was, in polemical journalism, may not have been the best foundation for a literary career.

This condensation of political data is intended to provide a background against which certain events in Oliver St. John Gogarty's life can be set, a sombre background which his mercurial temperament helped him to endure. He would not have aspired to share Griffith's sensitivity. 'He had not the armour with which I, for one, was invested be it irony or motley. His sincerity was a bow and his belief an arrow which, if deflected, slew his faith.'[6]

Returning now to Renvyle House where he sat for Augustus John in 1917, we find Gogarty pondering on his portrait and wondering by what creative miracle his external features traversed the artist's cerebral cortex to re-emerge, passively, with unmistakable identity.

> *Image of me according to John*
> *Back from the world behind his brow,*
> *Back from the boulevards of his brain,*
> *My painted wraith, what ails you now?*
> *Whom have you met with or discerned;*
> *Where have you bivouacked or lain,*
> *Who look like Caesar late returned*
> *Exhausted from a long campaign?*
> *Where were the tropic fields you fought?*
> *What hostels heard your jibes and jests?*
> *Alas! my wraith, you answer not;*
> *But on your face a pallor rests.*[7]

Gogarty had known Augustus John since the summer of 1912 when, at the suggestion of Orpen the artist, he had gone to look for him in the Bailey when he was visiting Dublin, and was impressed by John's genius which had about it elements of manic-depression.[8]

He examined John professionally and decided that his ears were the seat of his melancholy. John agreed that this might be so but that the oppression of Gogarty's incessant monologue was contributory. On their arrival in Galway in 1917 he flung a bowl of nuts in the doctor's face to compel silence.[9]

The corniche road leading from Tully Cross towards Lettergesh was the route of John's absent-minded drive, distracted by the superb landscape:

> *And your driving not your drawing*
> *Was what there might be flaw in —*
> *Like a God a little cloud*
> *Held you, as with speed endowed*
> *You drove on through the divine*
> *Light of day above the shine*
> *Of the green and grapy sea,*
> *Whose translucent greenery*
> *Broke on crescent sands remote,*
> *Goldener than Helen's throat.*

Later in this year the doctor appears in the role of aspirant playwright. One could not, today, expect a theatre to accept a play and stage it within weeks but writing to Lady Gregory on 9 November 1917 Oliver Gogarty foresaw no obstacles:

A friend of mine has a Dublin play nearly ready. I have had a hand in it. It is of the slums and public boards and likely to cause a stir. If it is to take on it should be on the stage by Xmas. If the Abbey refuse it the Irishwomen's reform league may take the Gaiety for it. I want the Abbey to have it if you think it good enough. May I send you two Acts to read?[10]

Evidently Lady Gregory expressed interest. Gogarty sent her his 'morality play' explaining that 'the third [act] is laid in the Board Room of one of the Dublin Hospitals and shows how the Board which is allotting a sum of money to improvements is interrupted by the returned soldier whose children have been neglected during his absence abroad. Misapplied philanthropy is one of the motives; the other — to put a true picture of Dublin conditions on the stage.' She found the play 'very stirring' and having received the improved third act felt it would be successful. 'Some may fall on us, but we shall suffer in a good cause — '

Blight — The Tragedy of Dublin by Alpha and Omega was staged at the Abbey Theatre on 11 December 1917; it ran for a week and was put on again for the first three days of January 1918. Joseph O'Connor, a Dublin barrister, participated in its authorship to a minor degree.[11] The producer, Fred O'Donovan, played Stanislaus Tully, the chief character, Micheál MacLiammóir had the part of Jimmy, his crippled son, and other celebrities from those early Abbey days included Maureen Delaney (Mrs. Larissey), Barry Fitzgerald (a labourer) and Arthur Shields (Medical Dick).

Tully, a rogue who lives by his wits, is presented not unsympathetically, for all his villainy. Gogarty recognized that the Tullys of this world are to some degree the products of their blighted environments. Similarly, he softens the defects of long-suffering Mrs. Foley and her daughter, Lily — a street-walker who provides clinical interest for Medical Dick and Medical Davy when she develops a syphilitic chancre on her lip. He reserves his malice for Miss Maxwell-Knox, a district visitor, and for the dogooders on the Hospital Board, an exception being Tumulty whom Gogarty uses to express his own opinions.

Stanislaus Tully may have contributed something to the creation of Joxer Daly and Fluther Good, for Sean O'Casey was in the first-night audience, and if he lacks the uniqueness of those two immortals he portrays well a certain type of Dubliner — physical laziness backed by an active mind, quick to see his own advantage and ready to defend the indefensible, which in Tully's case is drink. He upbraids the district visitor who would take away 'me night's rest and me morning's breakfast', and with the eloquence of his type points out what drink has done for Dublin:

What built Findlater's Church? Was it preaching or drink? Drink. And the new hostel in Hatch Street? Drink. What put a roof on Christ Church Cathedral? Drink. What renovated Stephen's Green — Drink — and the ducks swimming in it! Drink doesn't keep us poor, but poverty makes us drink...

A clever malingerer, Tully sees his advantage in a trivial back injury and is awarded generous compensation with which he purchases the tenement he lives in, planning to sell it to the governors of the local hospital where an extension is being planned. But first he must become a member of the Dublin Corporation which affords him an opportunity to moralize — 'D'ye want me to believe that there's neither science nor charity nor the love of God in Dublin?' — and to expatiate on the machinations of politics:

They must have something to blame like the gods in the Queen's Theatre. The great secret of politics is to provide them with heroes and villains, and to take care that the villains are far enough away and the heroes within reach.

Eventually we are introduced to the Townsend Thanatorion which has received a legacy of £30,000 which might provide a new operating theatre, a wing for skin cases, or an observation ward where, as a char-woman remarks, 'they put you to wait for a disease'. The governors, however, want to spend it on a mortuary chapel. Tumulty is the exception; he thinks it would be better spent in demolishing the slums, a breeding-place for diseases:

As long as you leave the corpse-converting slums, all the money spent in charity might as well be spent in decorating dead-houses, which are a symbol of the inefficiency and petuousness of the whole system.

Tumulty trenchantly expressed Gogarty's own thoughts on the inadequacy of the voluntary hospitals system ('Are the lives of the poor to depend on the sufferance of your goodwill? Is charity to be ever an escape from responsibility?) and the evil of the slums — 'Tenement property in Dublin is like cheese that grows in value as it rots.'

Today the social message in *Blight* does not seem overstated. How curious, at this distance, the rumour that it might be suppressed after its first performance! Even that somewhat blinkered playgoer, Joseph Holloway, conceded that despite 'a certain amount of crude realism' its message hit home. The box-office takings for the week's run were £190; the authors gave the £10 they received to the Boot Fund.

Towards the end of December 1917 Gogarty mentioned a new idea to Lady Gregory:

I wrote a short play yesterday. It has gone to be typed. I am now engaged in putting Trinity College on the stage. The idea is this: — the Board send to Oxford for a professor to fill the Chair in history. He comes, but after discovering such evidences of a national culture as are in the College Library he begins a 'Kultur Kampf'. In other words he becomes a Sinn Feiner and his influence is seen in the ladies' dresses (like Dun Emer productions) at a Garden Party in College to which the Lord

Lieutenant comes! Consternation of the Board which is increased by the fact that to send him back with his message to
Oxford is unthinkable, besides he has become engaged to the
daughter of the only nonentity in Dublin who is indispensible
to the Government as a recipient of honours that cause no
controversy.

Neither the satire nor Lady Gregory's opinion of it has survived.
Gogarty may have tired of it and instead presented the Abbey with
A Serious Thing, a one-act play attributed to Gideon Ousley,[12]
which was staged on 19 August 1919. Set in Judea during the Pro-
curatorship of Pontius Pilate, the curtain rises on a Roman soldier
who is guarding the tomb of Lazarus and who is joined by a centurion and a second Roman soldier, a Jewish conscript. For Roman
read British and Gogarty's purpose is apparent. It amused him to
see two rows of British officers in the house and to hear them
joining in the general laughter unaware that their legs were being
pulled.

The centurion/British subaltern is endowed with some of the
utterances of Gogarty's friend, Talbot Clifton, 'Hah! Lookey here
now!' The Roman/British Tommy is an indoctrinated professional
whose dialogue with the conscript allows Gogarty to score off
empire builders:

Second Roman: 'Vell, why are we here?'
First Roman: To preserve peace and stamp out sedition.
Second Roman: But it is because we are here that people are
seditious .... I'm thinking it's an extraordinary thing that
every country we occupy seems to be inhabited exclusively
by rebels.
The Voice of God, off-stage raises Lazarus from the dead.
The first Roman soldier cries, 'Halt!' his less resolute companion cries 'Help!'
First Roman: Halt! And present your permit. Halt! or I fire.
Second Roman: Oh, don't fire, that might make it worse! Don't
fire on the dead.
First Roman: All right, Lazarus! I can identify you. You'll be
courtmartialled for being within a military area without a
permit....

The risen Lazarus, a symbol of the dead of Easter 1916 and of the
Irish nation, poses a new threat: 'If this movement amongst the

dead is not stamped out, what is to become of Rome?' And the Roman soldier's sentiment, 'If there is to be no more death, there can be no more valour,' re-echoes in one of Gogarty's poems:

> But for your Terror,
> Where would be Valour?
> What is Love for
> But to stand in your way?
> Taken and Given,
> For all your endeavour
> You leave us with more
> Than you touch with decay![13]

It was preceded by Padraic Colum's *The Fiddler's House*. A critic wrote: 'The only irresistibly funny episode of the night was "A Serious Thing" — a farcical play by a gentleman who conceals his identity under the title of Gideon Ousley. It is very brief, and simply kept the house in shrieks of laughter in which they indulged with all the greater gusto perhaps because of the melancholy experiences of the early part of the night.'

Lady Gregory who had sent a copy of *Blight* to George Bernard Shaw[14] in 1918 wrote to Gogarty from Coole Park on 15 October 1919, in connection with another one-act play, *The Enchanted Trousers*:

I must apologise for not having acknowledged the play at once. It came on Saturday (just a day too late for G.B.S. I am sorry to say for I should have liked his opinion and criticism). I did not write then, as I intended to read it at once, and did read it in the evening with great enjoyment. It amused me very much. At the same time I think you could do a great deal to improve it. I have been thinking it over, and meant to consult Yeats, but now I had better send it straight to you. These are my suggestions....The first is a trivial thing. I think spitting is mentioned too often. An audience gets tired of repetition. And your mind is so full of originality, I think you should get a good deal more richness into the dialogue, just as you would if you were talking on the subject....Another trivial think, I don't think Minister of Spraying is good. Perhaps it should be a fancy title such as super organizer. But you will think of something better.[15]

Lady Gregory expressed the hope that it would all 'be as good as your talk. There ought not to be a bald sentence in it, there isn't in your conversation.' But when the *Enchanted Trousers* was staged on 25 November 1919 neither the spits nor the Minister for Spraying had been expunged; its theme was jobbery in Clare-Galway, the likelihood that an Englishman would fill the sinecure inspiring Humphrey Heavy, an unemployed actor, to masquerade as an Englishman. His brother assures him that: 'You'll have the most appreciative audience for an Englishman in the world. An Irish audience, who, instead of criticising you will be finding points to admire and be looking to you for a lead.' The legitimate presence of a stage-Irishman and a stage-Englishman affords an opportunity for comparing national attitudes:

> Every Englishman is in a worse predicament than you'll be. Not once or twice in his rough island story but he has been so for centuries. He never knows what moment his armies may peacefully penetrate and annex some highly civilised country.
> He never knows the moment when he may be called on to be superior to the most cultured race in existence. How does he protect himself? What does he do? What do you know about Chemistry? What did he know about Hindustani? What do you know about copper-sulphate? What did he know about Arabic? And yet he owns India and Egypt. Do you think he learnt the language before taking over those countries to save them from themselves? Not at all.

Attired in a borrowed garment which the local police sergeant wore prior to his promotion, the bogus Englishman gets the job. But the enchanted trousers effect a character change and influenced by a newly-acquired integrity he turns his back on his conspirators.

This is the slightest of Gogarty's plays and the last to be staged.[16] A fourth play, *Wave Lengths,* is mentioned by James F. Carens 'probably written at the very close of the "thirties"; the manuscript was unaccountably lost, and it was re-written in a shorter and inferior version after Gogarty settled in America.' A one-act farce, *The Incurables,* based on the discovery of a restorative elixir, is included in a *Week-end in the Middle of the Week* (1958).[17]

In a letter to Lady Gregory in 1918 Father Pádraig de Brún remarked:

Our friend Dr. Gogarty is achieving a public reputation as a poet in spite of himself. His five privately printed poems have already been reviewed by AE in the *Homestead,* and by Hone in the *Nation,* as both reviewers thought the book was to be republished. And the remarks of the *Homestead* have been copied in the *Tuam Herald.* So he might as well have made money on the Muse instead of paying for the printing.[18]

The reference was, of course, to *The Ship and Other Poems* (illustrated by Jack B. Yeats) published by the Talbot Press.[19]

A.E. wished that the booklet were three times as large and singled out 'The Old Goose' for particular praise, impressed by the poet's ability to mirror nature in verse:

> *Now gleams the frozen reek*
> *With blue beyond the peak*
> *Oh, take on breast and beak*
> *The night's dark onset.*
> *Washed in the mauve twilight*
> *O'er some far western bight*
> *Where islands rest in light*
> *Long after sunset!*

He chided Gogarty for being miserly to the public with his lyrical talent and said that 'if he had written a score of lyrics like *'The Old Goose'* and *'The Ship'* he would take his place with the best singers in Ireland to-day.' Within the next decade the poet was to oblige and the score of poems AE demanded can easily be found in *An Offering of Swans* (1923) and *Wild Apples* (1928) by which time he had become a notable public figure in the new polity.

10

Sortes Virgilianae

'It is not in falling between two stools that the tragedy consists, but in falling off each stool in turn.' Gogarty's remark applied to Lord Dunsany who having been wounded by the insurgents during the Easter Rising was now arrested by the Black and Tans for the unauthorized possession of arms, the sporting guns with which he indulged his passion for snipe shooting. His mistake was to boast that he was having an exceptional season and to send gifts of game to his envious friends in the Kildare Street Club who, angry to find he was still using his guns (the possession of which could merit the death penalty), reported him.

The Black and Tans drove up to Dunsany Castle to find that his Lordship was not at home. Actually he was in the bog with an offending weapon shooting snipe. 'Whom shall I say called?' Mander the butler asked as the armoured lorries rolled away.[1] But when Dunsany was eventually taken to Dunshaughlin where Gogarty visited him the peer extracted little comfort from the doctor's reminder that he could demand to be hanged with a silken rope. Nor at first did he wish Gogarty, who was identified with the Sinn Féiners, to prejudice the situation by going bail for him. A local grocer and butcher bailed him out.

When Gogarty reported to him that a Major Lane had said to him, 'Oh yes, Dunsany! It's rather a joke isn't it?' Lord Dunsany would not accept the remark at face value.[2] He reasoned that Major Lane, a professional soldier, could not take a Field General court martial lightly and that he must have been attempting to draw Gogarty out. He declared that 'Styx rolling stormily' would have been more appropriate than his friend's comforting telegram, 'Mincius sliding smoothly.'

Dunsany regarded the threatened court martial as 'fiddling while Rome is burning' and even though the officer had thought it rather funny, the authorities might adopt a 'he-must-be-made-to-see' policy and impose a sentence of at least a year. Besides, on 26 January 1921, fourteen men had come to Dunsany Castle looking for a roomful of German automatic pistols. The cache of arms was just as insubstantial as the 'German plot' which was the pretext for Griffith's arrest, but who could say how it would be used?

Despite representations on his behalf to persons in high places a hearing was finally arranged at Kilmainham court and he was led to understand that he was going to be found guilty and given bail on two sureties of £250 each. He asked Gogarty to be one of his bailsmen.

When Lord Dunsany had eventually extricated himself from the absurd charges he sent Gogarty a present of a Grecian vase and wrote to him from the Hotel des Anglais, Cannes, where he had joined his wife and mother-in-law. He harboured no bitterness but was filled with a reflective wonder which compared to their disadvantage the upper-class acquaintances who had caused him such trouble with the local peasants who had given him much sympathy. 'Whenever I saw that my hat, or my ways, or the cut of my hair, displeased the Kildare Street Club I never thought otherwise than that their ways must be wiser than mine. I accepted the judgement of cold glances as infallible. But henceforth whenever I go there, I, who would never have betrayed one of my own class and occupation and party to the danger that threatened me, shall have — for what it is worth — that slight feeling of moral superiority to those around me, which some men prize.'[5]

Arthur Griffith enlisted Gogarty's aid in July 1921 when General Smuts was due to arrive in Dublin. Griffith proposed to intercept him before he reached Dublin Castle; Gogarty was to provide transport. Gogarty met the welcoming-party, which included Robert Barton and the Lord Mayor, Larry O'Neill, outside the church in Lower Merrion Street at four-thirty a.m. and they drove in his Rolls Royce to Kingstown Pier. The mail boat was being tied up as they arrived. The discreet approach which Griffith had intended was spoiled by the Lord Mayor who dashed up the gangway.

'Tell General Smuts the Lord Mayor of Dublin wishes to greet him.'

'General Smuts is not on board', a steward said stonily.

Having examined the passenger-list unavailingly for clues they decided to breakfast in the saloon and remain on board until eight o'clock when everybody must disembark. They caught no sight of Smuts.

'Where to now?' asked Gogarty.

Griffith made no reply, so certain was he that Smuts had made the crossing.

'Where do you want to go now, Mr. Griffith?' asked the Lord

Mayor.

'Number Five Merrion Square.'

Gogarty recognized the address of Dr. Robert Farnan, a leading gynaecologist who was professor of midwifery in University College. Having deposited his passengers at Farnan's he promised to join them when he had garaged his car. The big Rolls might give the show away to intelligence agents.[4]

As things transpired it was a wise but hardly necessary precaution. On his arrival Gogarty found de Valera breakfasting with Farnan. Some moments later the phone rang, 'Could Dublin Castle speak to Mr. de Valera?' So much for secrecy!

'Is your car at the door?' de Valera asked.

'I'm not quite such a fool!' Gogarty repudiated the insinuation.

The purpose of the phone-call was to arrange a meeting at the Mansion House between the Irish leaders and General Smuts who had concealed himself on the boat-deck to avoid the advance party.

The need for secrecy was temporarily lessened by the Truce and on the eve of the Dáil's Treaty debate a group of people which included Professor E.H. Alton, Father Dwyer and others had assembled in the Gogartys' drawing-room to discuss the problematical future. Speaking of omens it was decided to resort to the *Sortes Virgilianae,* an ancient and scholarly form of crystal gazing in which the *Aeneid* is opened at random with a pointer and the answers to posed questions are read off from the line where the tip of the pointer rests.

Gogarty produced a folio from his study and supplied a key as a pointer which must be inserted by a child, a chaste person, or a priest. He gave the book to Father Dwyer.[5]

And the question? 'What will happen to Arthur Griffith?' There was nothing they wished to know more.

The priest inserted the pointer and passed the *Aeneid* to Alton — '*Spretae quo munere.*' (Spurned by which gifts.)

Suddenly the room was tense. Did this mean Griffith's repudiation? They could not stop now. They framed the next question. 'What will de Valera do?'

Father Dwyer inserted the key and Alton translated the chance selection —

'Rouse thee now and with joyful heart bid thy young men arm themselves and move to the fray....'

As the glasses were replenished and the faltering conversation was slowly resumed the general feeling was that *Sortes Virgilianae* was irrational and hardly respectable and nobody suggested posing a third question.

Early in February 1922 Oliver Gogarty sent a bundle of papers to his American cousins, 'the anti-treaty papers as well as those for it. We are for it only so far as it is better than no bread and that England will let go only by degrees.'

On February 14th England has to ratify the treaty by Bill. This date will show if there be any dodge up his sleeve. At present the Cabinet is anxious for a brisk settlement, but as it is an opportunistic body it will form its policy on the amount of the majority here for the Treaty. No one is fully satisfied with a treaty that divides the country, puts four Gibraltars on its shores, forbids a single wireless communication with the outer world....We only take it as a stepping-stone remembering the feudalism and savagery of the English character. This is often overlooked by the critics of the Treaty: the character of the opposing party. But if what the Treaty offers be honestly ratified by England a degree of freedom can be reached here and maintained that will be impossible to obliterate.[6]

The narrow affirmative margin for the Treaty left a considerable body of dissidents in a country with no experience of democratic methods which now hovered on the brink of civil war. On 13 April 1922 a party of 'Irregulars' led by Rory O'Connor seized the Four Courts and held it defiantly as a fortified post, unchallenged by the new government for a time in the hope of averting a debacle.

The assassination of Field Marshal Sir Henry Wilson in London on 22 June was generally thought to have been ordered by Rory O'Connor.[7] There was a strong feeling of public outrage and an increasing awareness that the I.R.A. presence in the centre of the city could be no longer permitted.

In a note to Clare Sheridan, then a roving reporter for an American paper, on 27 June Gogarty pointed out that O'Connor could be contacted by calling Sir John Ross's phone number, or merely by asking the telephone exchange to put a call through to the Four Courts. 'You should ring him up in the name of your paper and ask him to justify himself to America or to the Arabian Knights and ask that you be not kept waiting at the side gate. This is an interminable and intolerable thing.'[8]

Next morning shelling of the Four Courts began and Mrs. Sheridan reported how she enlisted Gogarty's aid:

At nine o'clock I was at Dr. Oliver Gogarty's.... He was not up. Dublin was blasé about gun-firing — but I made him get

up and take me in his car down the quays. There was a good
crowd and the rifle bullets came whistling close and chipping off
bits of the wall next to us. A bullet whizzing too near made
the crowd retreat like one man, but only to surge back again.
We might have been dodging sea spray on a pier. It is extraordinary with what fatalism one can place oneself in danger;
the other fellow may be hurt, but oneself, impossible.[9]

Returning to the car they drove towards the Richmond Hospital,
their route taking them behind the Four Courts. Gogarty stopped at
a street corner to allow his passenger to speak to a crowd of working-
class women who stood there, Dublin fashion, babies cradled in their
arms.
'Do you know y're in the line of fire?' a woman asked Clare Sheridan. 'A man was shot dead just where you're standing.'
'And what about yourselves?' she asked.
'Ah, it's no matter, it's the will of God...'
Meanwhile Gogarty spoke to some men who pointed out the danger of snipers mistaking his car for a Free State general's. Discretion
prevailed and they proceeded to the hospital where casualties were
beginning to arrive, a ten-year-old boy shot through the heart, a
labourer bleeding torrentially from a wounded leg.
Later, as they were leaving a strange procession approached, its
centre a group of men staggering under the weight of a limp body.

Women swathed in shawls followed wailing. I seemed to have
seen something of the kind on a Greek bas-relief, or maybe it
was some well-known painting of the descent from the Cross.
The women's wailing had the cadence of music.
'Ah, the poor man, the poor man! There was no better man.
The poor old man!' Their words faded into a weird 'Keening',
and they moaned over a blood-drenched sheet and cursed the
name of Rory O'Connor.[10]

When the Four Courts surrendered two days later Rory O'Connor
and other anti-treaty I.R.A. executives were taken prisoner. Fighting
continued elsewhere in the city and soon the civil war had become
general.
Long accustomed to the crude thrills of guerilla warfare many
extremists, on both sides, were sustained by a familiar excitement
even though now their enemies were, sometimes literally, their
brothers. For Arthur Griffith,[11] the apostle of non-violent methods,

not even the conviction that a legal government has a duty to defend itself could assuage a sense of horror. Though a non-combatant he was unable to cling to the semblance of normal living but existed in the discomfort of semi-siege conditions in government buildings in Merrion Street.

When Oliver Gogarty was called to see the President professionally early in August he looked into the muzzle of a sentry's pistol and was then ushered into a room sheeted with bullet-proof steel. When his credentials were authenticated he was taken to Griffith whom with a glance he saw to be seriously ill. This was no place, he decided, for a sick man. 'You are going to be decorated for the first time in your life with carpet slippers,' he told him and with the permission of general headquarters arranged for his admission to the Sisters of Charity's private nursing-home, 96 Lower Leeson Street, under the care of Dr. Jim Magennis, a leading physician.

Griffith fretted under restraint and insisted on receiving Cabinet reports. On 12 August he was found collapsed, comatose and dying on the landing outside his bedroom. Surgeon Meade, summoned urgently from the general hospital, made an incision in the forearm to open an artery, an emergency measure then favoured for the treatment of brain haemorrhage or confirmation of death.

Gogarty was also sent for; on his arrival Griffith's dead body had not been moved and lay surrounded by nuns and nurses who could not credit this sudden calamity.

'Take up that corpse at once,' Gogarty ordered harshly, softening his instruction immediately as his grief struggled to overmaster anger. 'Take the President's body into the bedroom.'

Walking to the window Gogarty laid his head in his hands and wept. 'My poor Arthur!' he exclaimed, 'my poor Arthur!' But within moments he had regained a stoical composure partly engendered by his medical training, partly the reflection that life's hurts must be endured, or sublimated in verse. He expressed his deeper feelings in elegaic lines:

> *He fought as many fights as Conn the Fighter;*
> *And all alone he fought*
> *Without a friend to make his sword arm lighter,*
> *Unblindable, unbought.*
> *He held his shield until the waves resounded,*
> *The men of Ireland woke.*
> *He made the loud tyrannical foe dumb-founded*
> *And to relax his yoke.*

Inglorious in the gap: by many a hater;
The scoffing word was said.
He heard from those who had betrayed him "Traitor!"
The cross-grained and cross-bred.

He shook from off him with a grand impatience
The flesh uncomforted;
And passed among the captains in whom nations
Live when these men are dead.

He's down, he's down! The silent heart is broken,
Death's pang his forehead warps.
O let the foe snatch neither spoil nor token;
But rally round his corpse![12]

In a fine eulogy he recalled Griffith as he had known him. 'He was gentle and simple and lovable. He was terrible, unpersuadable and right. And when one thinks of his gentleness and simplicity and of all he renounced, and when one remembers the long, solitary fight he made of it the heart almost breaks to think of the cruel suffering Fate imposed on this shy, modest, uncomplaining little man.'

Despite the offer of a remunerative editorship in New York Griffith had endured poverty to serve the Irish people —

When I looked on the dead face with the straight lines in the forehead that Lavater knew to be signs of genius and leader-ship, the marble features that were the clear hieroglyphics of forcefulness and nobility of soul; the great strength of character in the jaw and the fine outline of it all, I felt with my memory full of their ingratitude and fickleness inclined to ask if he had not won for the Irish people a position in Europe beyond their deserts....

Now that his never comforted body, broken by the weight of raising and re-building the Nation has been borne to its last resting-place through the thronged city that he loved; now that the poor he lifted and set on a road that leads from their poverty have gazed at the tricoloured coffin surrounded by soldiers of his making, and followed by the representatives of the Nation he renewed, have paid it the last tribute of reverence and awe; and now that his splendid soul glows with the splendour of God, it remains for Ireland to become worthy of Arthur Griffith.[13]

The unworthiness of at least some of its citizenry was made manifest not many days after the appearance of Gogarty's words in *An Saorstat* by the death of Michael Collins, killed by anti-Treaty foes at Beal-na-mBlath between Macroom and Bandon: *Now Death holds in a net/What England could not get/For forty thousand pounds upon his head.*

Communications with Cork other than by sea were cut off and with others Gogarty waited in the dark for the arrival of the S.S. *Classic*, the boat,

> *That bore his body as its dearest freight!*
> *And, with long time to wait,*
> *I cast in mind our country's horoscope,*
> *Striving to find the future from the past,*
> *From courage to the people known by rote:*
> *The laughing heart, the unimpeded mind,*
> *The heart that slew itself through being kind;*
> *Until she loomed at last*
> *With light on either mast*
> *And turned our Liffey to a Styx of hope.*[14]

A gun-carriage received the coffin and carried it through the dark streets to the City Hall. Early the following morning Gogarty accompanied by Desmond Fitzgerald, the Minister for Defence, undertook the task of embalming the dead patriot and carried out a post-mortem examination which confirmed that Collins had been slain by a ricocheting bullet which struck him on the back of the head.

After the funeral, as he confided to Lady Leslie, 'We had Lady Lavery in widow's weeds full of confidences of Collins. Lady Fingall made her go home and leave the arena to Kitty Kiernan.'[15]

The powers formerly vested in Arthur Griffith and Michael Collins were now assumed by William T. Cosgrave and Kevin O'Higgins. The former nominated Oliver Gogarty as a member of the Irish Free State Senate which first met on 11 December 1922. His friendship with W.T. Cosgrave permitted Gogarty to exert influence on behalf of AE and W.B. Yeats. When offered a seat, Russell said, 'I must consult the Gods' and eventually rejected it; Yeats was prepared to accept the honour. Calling to confirm his friend's nomination Gogarty found nobody at home and inscribed 'Senator W.B. Yeats' with his finger on the moist hall-door surface.

Had other prospective senators displayed the prudence of AE
and consulted omens they might have had second thoughts about
accepting an honour which made their lives and homes important
targets for the anti-Treaty forces who in November had declared
that public representatives who had voted for the emergency powers
would be shot on sight. A week later, on 7 December, two T.D.s
were shot at as they set out for the Dáil from their hotel and one
of them, Sean Hales, was killed. The cabinet's immediate and drastic
measure of reprisal, the execution without trial of Rory O'Connor,
Liam Mellowes, Richard Barrett and Joseph McKelvey may have prevented a score of slayings. Writing to Shane Leslie towards the end of
December Gogarty referred to the government's Draconian action
with qualified approval:

> I am sure that Justice-protesting and confessing England must
> have been shocked at the execution of the four prisoners. In
> terms of Justice it cannot be defended but in as much as Justice
> comes after order has been established and the humanities, this
> prescription for Chaos was inevitable; and, when you think of
> the policy of assassination that confronted every member, it is
> impossible to suggest any other remedy. As Mrs. Wyse-Power
> says: 'I don't agree with it but Glory be to God, wasn't it
> wonderful!' It stopped the murders anyway.[16]

The execution of Erskine Childers, whom Griffith spoke of in a
moment of uncharacteristic exasperation as 'that damned Englishman', caused Gogarty no misgivings. 'I cannot see or excuse him
from any standpoint but from that from which Savonarola was
condemned. There was nothing mystical at all in Childers. He was
one of those self-contained, unsmiling men whose doom seems to
be written on their faces.' He extended his strictures to include
Mrs. Childers. 'To her political sadism he owes his death. There is a
tribe of thrill-seeking women who are intensely mischievous; vapid
and selfish. They have lost touch with sincerity to such an extent
that they can only be interested by terrible happenings. Mrs. Childers
is doubtless thinking of the effect *she* will have in Boston when she
is lionized there.'
Senator Oliver St. John Gogarty had sufficient of a sense of the
ridiculous to realize that it might surprise some of his friends to see
him in a role traditionally characterized by *gravitas*. He made light
of his selection in his correspondence with Leslie:

You are wondering why such an indiscreet person was ever placed in the Senate. So am I. As far as I have had the immodesty to inquire, I think it was for disliking the Provost who caused such a scandal by preferring the 30 pieces of silver to the 39 Articles. Either this, or for disliking golf. Fastidious people are indispensable at this juncture in our history....[17]

He expressed the belief that Ireland would survive even her senators and a determination to cultivate silence. 'Already I can trace a curve between the whiteness of the hair and the length of the speeches, between prostatitis and polylallia in fact. Yeats too is not exempt.' In the event, however, and predictably, Gogarty's tongue ran away with him and Yeats proved to be more silent.

Shane Leslie's mother, Lady Leslie, being indisposed was advised by Gogarty either to come to Dublin to a nursing-home or to have Dr. T.G. Moorhead down to Glasslough, which would cost sixty guineas.

If you come to Dublin for treatment it would mean going into Ivanhoe or 26, Upper Pembroke Street near the stained glass of which we are never done hearing:

> Life like a dome of many coloured glass
> Stains the white radiance of eternity!

The 'divine Sarah' would be your visitor there. What a pity you don't get an ailment in my department. It would benefit both of us. You would save sixty guineas and I would have a salve for my conscience for leaving my work and going up to Glasslough.[18]

Gogarty's conviction that the government's reprisal measures had stopped the murders may have given him a false sense of security although he had received warnings from different sources that his name was on an assassination list. He was given a colt revolver but felt that an armed doctor was a ridiculous spectacle. The fact that his home was a doctor's house increased his vulnerability for legitimate callers might be expected at anytime.

He was taking a bath on a cold January evening in an empty house, for his family were in the country, when a trench-coated gunman ordered him out at pistol point. He dressed and was handed a fur-lined leather driving coat which his assailants had taken from the hallstand. He was forced to walk to a waiting car and driven to a house on the river bank at Islandbridge. 'Death by shooting is a very good death', one of the men said pressing his gun into Gogarty's side. 'Isn't it a fine thing to die in a flash', said another. A third asked, 'Have we any chance of a Republic, Senator?'

'Shall I tip the driver?' Gogarty's assumed insouciance annoyed his captors as they motioned him out of the car and towards a dark cellar which he judged to be about twenty yards from the water. He felt his feet sticking to the ground with fright but managed to face the gunmen, now seven in number, unflinchingly.

A fire was lighted from broken timber and torn-up music books. Gogarty protested that the smoke would choke him. Then on the pretext of an urgent call of nature he asked to be taken outside. Two guards were detailed to accompany him.

In the darkness Gogarty slipped his arms out of the coat-sleeves. He squatted as if to relieve his feigned diarrhoea.

'Would you mind holding up my coat?' he pleaded in a distressed voice and as the gunmen's attention was distracted by holding the coat he plunged away from them, sprang towards the river bank, and dived into the ice-cold Liffey. Shots were fired at him as he swam to freedom.

His escape and dripping arrival at the police station were celebrated in a popular ballad of the day ending as follows:

Cried Oliver St. John Gogarty, 'A Senator am I!
The rebels I've tricked, the river I've swum, and sorra the word's a lie.'
As they clad and fed the hero bold, said the sergeant with a wink:
'Faith, then, Oliver St. John Gogarty, ye've too much bounce to sink.'[19]

Not being of a 'turn the other cheek' mentality the hero of this adventure extracted grim satisfaction some days later when he heard that the leader of the would-be murder gang, O'Leary a tram-conductor on the Clonskeagh line, had been apprehended by a party of Free State soldiers and died 'shrieking inappropriately under the wall of the Tranquilla Convent in Upper Rathmines.'[20] Those who live by the sword shall perish by the sword.

A newspaper had said the gunmen might as well have tried to hold an electric eel as to hold Gogarty, but the men of violence were to have their cowardly revenge. Arson carried less risk of reprisal than assassination and many newly-created senators were victimized. Palmerston, County Kildare, the Earl of Mayo's beautiful mansion perished on 29 January 1923; Kilteragh, Sir Horace Plunkett's luxurious home in Foxrock, was destroyed by explosives on the same day — Sir Horace's comment was, 'It is not so sad as if it had been a poor man's one-roomed home.' A restaurant owned by Senator Mrs. Wyse-Power was damaged by fire in February and Dr. O'Sullivan's vacation home in Glenbeigh, County Kerry, was looted and burnt to the ground.

When the venerable Dr. Sigerson was told that his house in Clare Street containing the accumulated art treasures of a lifetime would be sacrificed he responded, as a wit put it, 'like a stoic, with resignation'. But as his resignation was sent to the President rather than to the Chairman of the Senate it was ineffective and he was prevailed upon to withdraw it.

On 23 February Gogarty's political enemies in the West, who had harassed Talbot Clifton until he left Kylemore House, and destroyed historic Moore Hall, the ancestral home of Senator Colonel Maurice Moore, from where John Moore had marched to meet General Humbert in 1798, burnt Renvyle House to ashes, destroying with it many of Gogarty's precious possessions including valuable first editions, paintings by Augustus John and Sir William Orpen and a self-portrait of Oliver's mother as an auburn-haired girl of sixteen. Nothing but ruin remained of a gracious setting where generations of Blakes had lived and the Gogartys dispensed the 'fáilte Ó Ceallaigh', creating a gathering-place where talented people discussed art and ideas, and gossiped, and raised ghosts — for Renvyle House was haunted by the ghost of Athelstone Blake — against a unique background of rocks and heather, of white-tipped ocean and white-flecked sky. 'Nothing left but a charred oak beam quenched in the well beneath the house. And ten tall square towers, chimneys, stand bare on Europe's extreme verge.'[21]

11

An Offering of Swans

Reluctantly Gogarty carried his colt again and was accompanied by an armed guard. But patients also had to be searched which disrupted the sacrosanct doctor-patient relationship. He took a holiday in Scotland where John Talbot Clifton on his immense deer forest, introduced Gogarty to stalking. He proved a reluctant pupil. His sympathy as a child at Farrell O'Reilly's shoots at Kilbeg, as we have seen, had been with the ducks; he was known to fish with an unbaited hook, and when he shot a stag he experienced remorse, 'What had I destroyed? Grace and speed and an untameable heart!'[1]

In *The Heart Grown Brutal*, a study of the Irish revolution in literature, Peter Costello refers to Gogarty's choice of quotation to round off his account of the death of Griffith: *I perish by the people that I made*, Tennyson's words on King Arthur's parting for the Isle of Avalon. 'Nothing sums up the Free State more aptly than that an Irish poet should quote an English one on a British hero in memoriam of a Dubliner of planter stock whom he sees as creating the Irish people.' It was something of a paradox, too, that a member of Sinn Féin who had inveighed against England, when threatened by Irish extremists should now seek safety in London.[2] Temporarily Gogarty settled there and opened consulting rooms in Grosvenor Street. When his wife decided that the upset of settling into new quarters would be too much for her, Lady Dunsany's pertinent comment was, 'She has married a charming flibbertigibbet and a sacrifice is required if she is to keep him.'[3]

He learned to admire England's ordered greatness. 'London is a university with ten million undergraduates qualified to live and let live.'[4] He called on old friends, the Earl of Granard who from time to time entertained the King in his Halkin Street home, Lady Leslie, Dermot Freyer, Tancred now confined to a mental home, Compton Mackenzie owner and editor of *The Gramophone,* and Christopher Stone who had purchased Field House, Horsham, Shelley's birthplace which Gogarty visited.

He made many new acquaintances amongst whom 'Sludge', that

figment of his youthful imagination, was a notable absentee. He owed his entry to London society to well-disposed friends such as Lady Leslie, Lady Lavery, and other hostesses with a keen eye for an unusually pleasing guest, Lady Leconfield, Mrs. Benjamin Guinness, and Lady Islington. He was greatly impressed by Austen Chamberlain and thought Lord Birkenhead an example of a rake becoming a success. The elderly Duke of Connaught, hearing that he was a doctor, boasted that he had played eighteen holes of golf that day and spent two hours in the saddle. 'You are threatened with immortality, Sir!' was Gogarty's pleasing comment.

At Petworth House where he was Lord Leconfield's weekend guest he was introduced to a 'blub-faced fellow', Winston Churchill.

'Now that you've got your liberty, Gogarty, what are you going to do with it?' asked Churchill, speaking as if he had a cleft palate.

'Discriminate between our friends, Mr. Churchill,' said Gogarty. Grunting, Churchill rose as if to leave the room.

'Why is your guest so unamiable?' Gogarty asked his host.

'Nobody can trust that fellow,' Lord Leconfield replied in his usual stentorian voice, with Churchill still within earshot. 'He crossed the floor twice.'[5]

Meeting the British parliamentarian on the stairs later Gogarty was cut by him.

He had been introduced to Lady Ottoline Morrell earlier in Dublin by Sarah Purser but Lady Diana Cooper was a new friend. She wrote to him with a request for some poems of Yeats; if the publisher could not send her copies she pleaded with Gogarty to write them out legibly. 'I feel that I have waited long and patiently — but that phase is over — send them with all speed or I'll undermine your health, your practise [sic], your fun —'[6]

Seymour Leslie attributed Gogarty's taking London by storm to mere caprice and to his arriving at a time 'when London had nothing better to do'. Leslie's cynicism amused Gogarty but did him less than justice for what bowled over the Londoners was the same charm that captivated his Dublin friends, the fund of stories, some divertingly dirty, and a mind richly stored with poetry. Padraic Colum remembered Gogarty declaiming English, Latin, Greek and lowlands Scots poetry throughout an afternoon's walk in the Dublin hills and how 'he could take hold of, say a strophe of Pindar's, recite it, bring you the whole performance of what would have been the performance of one of the great odes.'[7]

During this London interlude Gogarty returned to Dublin weekly when the Senate was sitting. It may have been on one of those

journeys that he was greatly impressed by the amenities of the
Royal Mail Steamer *Munster* which he described to Seumas O'Sullivan:
'...There is a more delightful pub than we have reached in life or
vision. It is called, as one should dream — "The Hope and Anchor".
Having realised one's Hope what else but cast Anchor? so that "that
heart may be truly fixed where true Joy is only to be found" '.[8]

He was home for his birthday in August 1923 and wrote to Lady
Leslie: 'I am having a birthday to-day! And about 80 people are coming to tea in a garden of rain! The Governor-General, President and
all the rest of them. The widow who was Lady Waterford and is now
Osborne Beauclerk (I think) Lady Arnott, Lady Fingall and so on. I
do hope it won't rain.'[9] It did for half an hour and then the rain
clouds cleared.

His visits to Dublin also provided an opportunity to arrange for the
publication of *An Offering of Swans* a slim volume which the Cuala
Press had ready by 20 October 1923. 'Here are but a few pages that
a few months have made,' W.B. Yeats wrote in the preface, considerably distorting the facts for many of the twenty-two poems had been
written years before and some were included in the earlier collections.

The new poems included the exquisite 'Golden Stockings', inspired
by the sight of his little daughter running through a field of butter-
cups, which won the favour of anthologists, and a very fine poem 'To
the Lady — ' (She was Lady Ottoline Morrell and the poet W.B.
Yeats):

> *In the most intimate years your gables grew*
> *And stood by Oxford on their watery hill;*
> *When all the days were spacious, they were still*
> *A country home of music undisturbed.*
> *You keep your life aloof from common things,*
> *Lovely and strange in beauty of its own;*
> *Like a tall Saint who clasps upon her breast*
> *A Pindar hidden by a palimpsest,*
> *And both ordain a life austere and curbed;*
> *Fixed in the change, and timeless like a shrine*
> *Upon the border of a Grecian town*
> *Where there is calm beyond the reach of gold.*
> *My mind seeks beauty and it dwells on you*
> *Under the elms — and all the air was spring's,*
> *A leaven of silence in the misty dew*
> *Leavening the light, the shadow leavening,*

Your cloak and that tall feather, white under blue —
Walking beside a poet in the evening.

The volume took its title from a vow made when escaping from his
I.R.A. captors that should he survive he would present two swans
to the Liffey:

Keep you these calm and lovely things,
And float them on your clearest water;
For one would not disgrace a King's
Transformed beloved and buoyant daughter.

And with her goes this sprightly swan,
A bird of more than royal feather
With alban beauty clothed upon:
O keep them fair and well together!

As fair as was that doubled Bird
By love of Leda so besotten,
That she was all with wonder stirred:
And the Twin Sportsmen were begotten!

He sounded out Lady Leslie as to George Moore's and Bernard
Shaw's reaction to Yeats's Nobel Prize and mentioned that Price,
the Harley Street doctor whom she had consulted, was tipped for
a knighthood. 'He is a sad little man and I learn that he has his heart
set on what is a great prize to an English doctor. It should be equally
a prize for an Irish one if Lady Aberdeen and others had not selected
the Sancho Panzas and left the Dons out. Now they say in Dublin,
"Work while you're not a Knight, for the Knighthood cometh when
no man doeth work".'[10]
Eventually the novelty of London palled. 'The town where somebody knew me was drawing me from the town where I only knew
those who were somebody.' He resumed practice in Dublin in 1924
and served on the General Council for the revival of the Tailteann
Games to be held between August 2nd and 18th.[11] He was also
chairman of the Archery Committee and vice-chairman of the
Distinguished Visitors Committee. He was commissioned to write
a Tailteann Ode which was printed in the official programme.[12]

The guests he invited personally included his cousins Margaret
and Katherine Burke, from Santa Barbara, California, whom he
urged to come to Ireland for the great occasion.

My wife desires me to write to you at once and invite you
to stay with us here for the Festival. Very likely we shall
have Mann the German novelist and H.G. Wells the English
novelist staying with us at the time: but there is plenty of
room. If you come you will be Guests of the Nation as well.[13]

To his delight they accepted his warm invitation and he arranged
to have a two-seater car available for them as a runabout.

A small but distinguished party comprised of the President of the
Irish Free State, Mr. W.T. Cosgrave, Senator W.B. Yeats, Mrs. Gogarty
with Noll, Dermot, and Brenda assembled at Trinity boathouse on
26 April to see Senator Gogarty fulfil his vow to liberate a pair of
swans on the Liffey, a ceremony duly photographed by Mr. Cashman.
The event attracted press coverage, and casual comment; a wit said
that a swan was a good symbol for Gogarty, 'cold feet and plenty of
neck', another suggested that the Liffey should henceforth be called
the Swanee River.[14]

The return of political stability permitted a resumption of the
Gogarty's Friday evenings with W.B. Yeats, AE, George Redding
and James Stephens in weekly attendance. Others who came less
regularly included James Montgomery, Lennox Robinson, F.R.
Higgins and politicians such as Desmond Fitzgerald and Eamon
Duggan. The company was predominantly male but visiting celebrities such as Lady Leslie, Anna Mae Wong the film star, and tennis
champion Helen Wills were invited if known to be in the city.

On a typical evening [Noll, the elder son, recalled] AE would
arrive just a little bit before nine o'clock. He was usually the
first to come. My mother sat to the right of the fireplace in a
position in which she could later dispense tea from a silver pot
with water boiled in a spirit kettle on a silver tray. Often there
was a guest who was more a listener than a talker who came
along to hear the great. Such a one or my mother or father,
who was inclined to be in and out before the gathering was
complete, might make a remark to get AE going. This was not
difficult to do because he was a master talker; nowadays some
glib writer might suggest that he was a compulsive talker. Anyhow, once started, he would talk on and on. One had the feeling
that he was trying to say as much as he could before W.B.
arrived. No one must think that AE was not a charming talker.
He spoke probably more rapidly than W.B., but like the modest
man he was, he deferred on certain subjects to the arch-poet

and gave him, so to speak, the right of way. There were, however, certain subjects on which AE was the expert. He was big, brown bearded and baggy. He wore small gold-rimmed spectacles and used to peer over these and under his brows when speaking to you. He gently stroked his broad brown beard and could recite, at will, verses by any author whose name was likely to be mentioned. He had an impeccable memory for verse. When I became aware of W.B.'s appearance more accurately, I recalled that he usually wore a sand or cement coloured suit with a blue shirt and blue socks and a broad, loosely tied black tie. My sister tells me that she remembers that he had small feet and small shapely hands. He carried pince-nez on a ribbon, but I recall him with these off rather than on. On one hand he wore the large Dulac ring of blue-green enamel. He made a studied entrance and seated himself not in any special place as AE did, but generally in front of the fire or in mid-circle. He would slightly raise his right hand to catch the speaker's (AE's) eye and join the conversation.[15]

Naturally the discussions touched on a host of subjects, but there were favourite topics and Noll Gogarty who was present on many of these evenings recalls the Plotinus-Porphyry period derived from Stephen McKenna's translation of Plotinus, a Yoga and Yogiman period, a Berkeley period, an Upanishads and Bhavagad Gita period. These were the high-lights; there was also less philosophical chat about recent books, and presumably at least a smattering of gossip. Sometimes those who had been on lecture tours in America made fun of their patrons and on one occasion gibes of this type annoyed John McCormack and caused an angry outburst. Gogarty broke the ensuing silence by recalling an old lady he knew who used to end such embarrassing moments by putting the question whether it would be preferable to be eaten by a crocodile or an alligator.[16]

Despite his gifts as a raconteur Gogarty was not a conversational monopolist; he never ignored a shy person but would draw him out, praising whatever he said and making much of it. His basic good nature and kind heart were obvious to his guests and the style of the Friday evenings in which his wife played an important part can be gauged from Lady Leslie's gracious tribute.

Glaslough, Co. Monaghan. Dec. 8th.

My dear Mrs. Gogarty,

I must send you one line to tell you how very much I enjoyed
Friday evening at your house — you are a perfect hostess, and
I look on yours, as one of the few remaining 'Salons' in the old
meaning of the word. When I came to look for you at the gallery,
you had left — so I had no chance of telling you all this!

Yours affectionately,

Leonie Leslie.[17]

Archery was a sport in which Gogarty and his family were skilled
and which they cultivated assiduously.[18] 'The bow that will be employed at the targets at Ballsbridge in the Aonach Tailteann Archery
Competitions on August 16,' he wrote, 'will weigh about five pounds.
Nevertheless these are quite sufficient to kill a man at eighty or a
hundred yards with a sharp arrow. Tipped as they are, they will
penetrate a sheet of canvas, and three inches of straw matting for
about a foot at one hundred yards.'

The distinguished visitors invited to assist in judging the literary
competitions included G.K. Chesterton, Compton Mackenzie, Sir
Edwin Lutyens, Sir Henry Hadow and Augustus John. Gogarty met
some of them at the North Wall. Compton Mackenzie and G.K.C.
were to stay with Tim Healy, the Governor-General, in the former
Vice-Regal Lodge now known as 'Uncle Tim's cabin'.

Billetted on Lord Dunsany, Augustus John was victim of Gogarty's
mischief for he warned him that Dunsany was a fanatical teetotaller
and above all things he must not offend him by taking a drink in
his house. Dunsany in turn was informed that John held strong
views about alcohol and should not be given it. After a few nights
of unwonted asceticism John fled the Castle and walked to Dublin
arriving as Gogarty was shaving. But he was not altogether at ease
in 15 Ely Place and wrote '...Mrs Gogarty has developed into a
sort of Duchess. I must get out of this.'[19] Talbot Clifton, also an
official guest, in extenuation of John's behaviour, said that he was
a man with all the faults of all the gods.

The revival of the ancient Aonach Tailteann, the great fair or festival formerly held at Tailte near where the Blackwater joins the
Boyne, was planned on a grand scale to include events as diverse as
athletics and chess, hurling and handball, billiards, literary and musi-

cal competitions. The Saturday afternoon opening ceremony at
Croke Park, attended by the distinguished guests, was appropriately
elaborate. High above the Park four planes dived and wheeled in an
aerial display culminating in a salute of guns supported by the sirens
of ships and factories. Then at 3 p.m. a fanfare of trumpets announced the arrival of the procession of competitors, led by some of
Ireland's most famous retired athletes. It filed past the saluting base
to be received by Mr. J.J. Walsh, the Minister for Posts and Tele-
:raphs, who stood between Sir Henry MacLaughlin and Senator
W.B. Yeats.

Among the foreign and Irish notabilities gracing the great ban-
quet at the Metropole none was more impressive than the turbaned,
blue-robed 'Ranji' the famous Indian cricketer who had purchased
Ballynahinch Castle in Connemara, once the home of 'Humanity'
Martin.

John McCormack the celebrated tenor was the chief attraction
of the following evening's concert at the Theatre Royal. Having given
renderings of songs by Handel, Bach, Donardi, César Franck and
others he sang lighter favourites such as 'The Bard of Armagh' and
'The Short Cut to the Rosses'. His singing of 'Kathleen Mavourneen',
a tour de force, was rapturously acclaimed by audience and critics
alike. 'It rang true and poignant with all the greatness and nobility
of Brahms' "Sappische Ode".'

The Gogartys revived the custom of having guests to breakfast and
also gave a garden party.[20] Oliver's personal triumph was to be
awarded the poetry prize for *An Offering of Swans*.[21]

The archery competitions held in the Iveagh Gardens were attended
by the Governor-General who with his party was received by Mrs.
Gogarty. The large attendance included the Earl of Fingall, The Earl
of Granard, James Stephens, Susan Mitchell and Mr. and Mrs. Padraic
Colum.

The most distinguished archer at the games was Mr. W. Andrew,
the English champion, who after his demonstration was presented
with a silver arrow with gold leaves. Mr. H.A. Cox of Terenure
(335 points) and the Hon. Cecil Barry (239) of Lambay won
the gold and silver medals respectively. Oliver Gogarty (121 points)
was placed third. His sons Noll (99 points) and Dermot (54 points)
also competed. Brenda Gogarty (55 points) came third in the ladies'
event. Afterwards the competitors were entertained to tea by Lord
Iveagh and met the Governor-General. (Incidentally, from time to
time it was rumoured that Gogarty was to be Tim Healy's successor.)

When the games were over Gogarty set out with some misgivings for Talbot Clifton's stronghold on the Isle of Islay. His host, a man of action, was almost too much for him and he once said, 'A thought has the effect on Clifton that a swallowed eel has on a horse'. He sent Lady Leslie a gossipy letter from Kildalton Castle with particular reference to the anniversary of the death of Michael Collins. 'We had an amusing time in Dublin. I rejoice to say that the Nation's Widow contented herself with laying a wreath *privately* on the Grave of Love — only one equerry and the press photographer witnessed the grief for that loss of love on the wire. Lady Fingall found that misconduct was confined to the telephone. Mr. Guthrie rudely shattered romance by asking: "How many times?" People are so practical nowadays!'[22]

Early in 1924 Thomas Seltzer, a New York publisher had expressed interest in bringing out an American edition of *An Offering of Swans* but Gogarty's enquiry from Ernest Boyd concerning the would-be publisher's credentials elicited an off-putting reply. Seltzer was the nearest thing to George Roberts that America had produced; he had little capital and good authors avoided him, his only asset was D.H. Lawrence.[23] Boyd offered to find Gogarty a publisher and meanwhile he should not choke off Seltzer completely. 'I assume that half a Seltzer is better than no bread.' He added his thanks for the doctor's professional skill. 'I have been so well for the past nine months that I realise I was never really well before. This winter is passing and I have not had a cold.'[24]

In January 1925 Boyd reported lack of success; he had failed to find a publisher either in New York or Chicago for it was felt that the really interested American readers would already have acquired the Cuala Press edition. He mentioned, too, that following her visit to the Tailteann Games Molly Colum had said that there were no longer any writers of the slightest interest in Dublin and had gone out of her way to belittle Gogarty. 'I could see that you had — very naturally — failed to take this typical product of an Eccles Street convent as seriously as a few of her friends do here.' One of Mrs. Colum's allegations was that as every Irish writer was under a professional obligation to Gogarty none of them dared speak impartially of his work.

Meanwhile, writing to Seymour Leslie in March 1924, Gogarty mentioned Eyre and Spottiswoode's projected publication of *An Offering of Swans and Other Poems:*

Spottiswoode is about to publish a book of verse of mine with

30 additional pieces. They have up to this published only bibles. I am such a suitable successor to that rather inconsequent volume that I look naturally forward to all the parsons and village libraries stocking me. If you wrote to them from your bookshop to enquire when you may expect it and order a dozen, you will help. They say they are taking a risk in publishing 1000. But 3000 sold out in a month here.[25]

After London Gogarty found Dublin a comfortable city. 'The size of Edinburgh and Athens and we are all somebodies here or dream it.' Foreign travel has its own delights, however, which he enjoyed, his journeys varied and purposeful. He had gone to Sicily in June 1921 to see a performance of a play by Aeschylus in the Greek theatre. 'I met Scipio Borghese in Rome and lunched with him and his Oxfordised daughter.' He visited the Holy City on a later occasion in the company of President Cosgrave and Dr. Fogarty, Bishop of Killaloe, who had been a strong supporter of Arthur Griffith. His card home read: 'Yesterday His Holiness the Pope received the Most Reverend Dr. Fogarty and the most irreverent Dr. Gogarty.'

He visited Germany, Greece and Spain. January 1925 found the Gogartys in St. Moritz where Noll came second in a race on the Cresta run. Oliver *père* was not permitted to remain a spectator. 'Even I had to partake owing to a remark of my wife's about preferring a corpse to a coward in the family.' Existence at 6,000 feet did not agree with Mrs. Gogarty who after some days opted to continue her holiday in Paris leaving her husband in charge of the young people. 'I like the altitude of the place,' he informed Lady Leslie. 'The de colleté dresses compensated for the great height, and the bob-sleighs and other things provided the only thrill a middle-aged man can indulge in that does not lead to the divorce courts.'[26]

Referring to the Tailteann garden party, Ernest Boyd remarked, 'The Irish illustrated papers showed you looking very happy on your lawn, and Mrs. Gogarty was the one really chic representative of her sex in sight.' She ran 15 Ely Place on lavish lines, welcoming a stream of callers from the diverse areas of her husband's interests, writers, politicians and aviators, local notabilities and distinguished visitors from abroad. 'Who is one Bracken who suggested that he is Winston's Secretary?' Oliver asked Lady Leslie. 'Yeats brought him here. Red-haired, bone-spectacled, energetic, argumentative, names people freely and owns an hotel in Cromer partnered by Oliver Locker Lampson; Generous type.'

For a time the Gogartys employed a butler, Rider, a paragon

who impressed George Moore, but the cook, Mrs. Keely, who stayed with the family for years ruled longest in the servants' quarters. A capable woman, skilled in culinary arts, her general dependability more than compensated for occasional irregularities. But now and then Mrs. Gogarty lost patience.

'The master wouldn't have spoken to me like that,' the cook protested.

'Very well, Mrs. Keely, just go to the master and tell him what you've been up to.'

Equipped with the armour of a clean apron and cap, Mrs. Keely bustled into Gogarty's study to explain her fall from grace. She blamed a colleague from a neighbouring kitchen overcome by a fainting fit that had taken a dozen of stout to combat.

Generally known as Neenie, and to her husband as Nin, Mrs. Gogarty had a will of her own and did not warm to all his friends. She disliked Dr. Joe Boyd Barrett for pronouncing his name Alliver and a number of his cronies also earned her disfavour. On the other hand James Valentine Nolan Whelan, S.C. often took her to the races and she had a very soft spot for Lord Fingall a no-nonsense type who confided to her, 'My poor bwain can't cope with Daisy's clever fwends.'

An Oxford soccer blue, Nolan-Whelan ran through two fortunes retaining only delusions of grandeur. 'If you don't mind, old chap,' he said to his host one evening in 15 Ely Place after dinner, waving away the box of cigars, 'I'll call a taxi and send to my club for one of the Nolan-Whelan specials.'

Neenie Gogarty was impressed by the telepathic powers of W.B. Yeats. One afternoon as she sat alone by the fire thinking of the west of Ireland and of a favourite pastor, Canon Canning of Ballyhaunis, County Mayo, the parlour-maid showed the poet into the drawingroom.

'I must not interrupt you,' Yeats intoned, turning to leave. 'There is a man of the cloth, a clergyman of your own church about...'

Dublin's social whirl included Lady Ardee's Ball at Woodbrook for the Dudley Nurses and the Ward Hunt Ball which he described for Lady Leslie. 'I danced with the Dowager Lady Conyngham only to find that she had another partner dancing away vigorously. She is not as there as she was! Was that monogamy or polyandry?'

When Oliver's projected holiday in Paris in May 1925 fell through because of surgical commitments he insisted that Neenie and Noll should go there as planned. He sent Mrs. Gogarty's address to his cousins, the Burkes, who were again in Europe: 'I do hope you will meet. She would be fearfully disappointed if you didn't. She was putting a meeting with you forward as the greatest incentive to my accompanying her, but business interrupted. It always does!'[27]

He referred to a senate debate when writing to Glaslough in June. 'Yeats's speech about Divorce caused a mild flutter. He has taken on himself to defend the "stock" which he imagines the Kildare Street Club thinks itself to be.'[28] Finding in the following year that castles in County Galway were cheaper than Corporation cottages Gogarty purchased Dungory Castle, Kinvara, which was in a state of disrepair.

Early in 1926 Miss Nannie O'Rourke, a life-long friend of Neenie Gogarty, died at four o'clock in the morning, and as a result of rushing round to her home in freezing cold Oliver developed an attack of bronchitis. To favour his recovery the Gogartys stayed at the seaside in Greystones, County Wicklow, but his convalescence was disturbed by the delivery at three-thirty a.m. of a cablegram bearing the sad news of Harry Gogarty's death in San Francisco.

He had known for some time that his bachelor brother's health had broken down and had told his sister, Mayflo, with whom he corresponded regularly, that Harry was dying. Nevertheless, the unwelcome cablegram came as a shock. He wrote to a cousin, Joe Oliver, Harry's executor, asking him to distribute his personal effects among his staunch and considerate friends.

A law officer to the Southern Pacific Railway Company, Harry Gogarty had recently been put on the promotion list for an unusual piece of work expertly done in Oregon. He was not, however, a man of property and Oliver sent the executor a disclaimer on whatever funds, some few hundred dollars at most, might remain in the bank.

His postcard from Las Palmas in April 1928 to his elder son alludes to another death, that of his friend John Talbot Clifton:

To-day I got some Spanish shawls for Mummy and Brenda. There is one to be sent direct so as to save the English tax on silk. Mrs. Clifton sailed from this with the body of J.T.C. She came here for a Union Jack to wrap round the coffin and sailed on a Norwegian ship.[29]

Increasingly interested in aviation and not content to remain a passenger he joined the Irish Aero Club and became Ireland's first medically-qualified pilot. When a lady member, discussing planes, said 'You should get a Moth,' he smiled and replied, 'Oh no, I'm afraid you wouldn't hold a candle to it.'

At a time when the average traveller was unlikely to look for better than ship and rail, Gogarty whenever possible opted for the quicker way. 'I may fly over to Hendon with my wife,' he informed Shane Leslie in 1928, 'if I can hire an Army plane at single fare rate i.e. £15.'[30] To attend a motor rally in Heilbronn in August he caught the 7 a.m. plane from Croydon to Stuttgart.

A collection of twenty-seven of Gogarty's poems entitled *Wild Apples* was published by the Cuala Press in a privately-commissioned edition (fifty copies) in 1928.[31] Some of the poems had appeared in the *Irish Statesman,* others were new; almost half of them were to be included in the *Collected Poems.*

The book took its title from its first poem 'The Crab Tree' — *Here are wild apples/Here's a tart crop* — but the tartness was not a dominating feature, the poet's lines still largely inspired by the Muse he had addressed in *Hyperthuleana:*

> *Flushed is your bonnie face,*
> *Cambered your belly*
> *Muse, like the straying Grace*
> *In Botticelli.*
> *Wild with the fruit and blooms'*
> *Mystical birth*
> *Which the dark wood illumes,*
> *Drunken with mirth.*

Wild Apples contains some of Gogarty's most notable poems including 'Aphorism' (renamed 'Ringsend' in *Collected Poems*) with its haunting ending —

> *And up the back-garden*
> *The sound comes to me*
> *Of the lapsing, unsoilable,*
> *Whispering sea.*

The judges of the Tailteann Games poetry competition, equally impressed, according to F.R. Higgins, with *Wild Apples* and Monk Gibbon's *The Branch of Hawthorn Tree,* referred the final decision to Yeats. Understandably the younger poet hoped he might be lucky, for Gogarty had been given the prize in 1924, but to his disappointment he received the silver medal, the gold going again to Gogarty who seemed to Gibbon to be rubbing it in when at the prize-giving ceremony in the Iveagh Gardens, splendidly arrayed in formal morning dress, he shook his hand and said, 'Ah, yes, you got some-thing in the Dramatic Section, didn't you?'[32]

On 2 December 1928 Higgins wrote from Knockmore, Ballina, to thank Gogarty for praising recent work in the *Irish Statesman* and to compliment the surgeon-poet on his own work. 'I can only pray for countless copulations in a mind that's a marriage bed for Beauty!'[33] Higgins enclosed 'Grace before Beer — for Sportsmen, Poachers and other mute Poets', an inscription for one of the snugs in Renvyle House Hotel.

For what this house affords us
Come, praise the brewer most,
Who caught into a bottle
The barley's gentle ghost;
And may our praise be sweeter,
When we're beneath our stools
With drowning tongues and reasons
Serene as rock-lit pools.[34]

Having been compensated for the destruction of his Connemara property Gogarty was re-building Renvyle House which he planned to open to guests on a commercial basis thus adding the role of hotelier to his other commitments. But before we see him as mine host it is convenient to devote a chapter to his years in the Senate.

12

The Upper House

On Monday 11 December 1922 soon after midday Eamon Duggan (Minister without Portfolio) entered the Chamber to administer the Oath prescribed by Article 17 of the Constitution of the Irish Free State to the forty-five members appointed to Seanad Éireann. In this ceremony Gogarty was preceded by his older colleague Dr. George Sigerson and his friend W.B. Yeats and was followed by Mrs. Alice Stopford Green. Then Sir Thomas Esmonde moved that pending the election of a permanent chairman the oldest member, Dr. Sigerson, should be appointed chairman 'for this day only', a resolution seconded by Mrs. Stopford Green who said that 'it would be to us an honour if so learned and faithful an historian of Ireland would take the chair for this day.' The next business was the appointment of a Committee on Standing Orders.

It was, as Donal O'Sullivan has pointed out, a historic occasion: 'For the first time representative Irishmen irrespective of racial origin or religious belief, were assembled together in a Second Chamber to enact laws for their common country.'[1]

On the following day Lord Glenavy and Mr. James Douglas were elected Chairman and Vice-Chairman of the Senate respectively for a twelve-month period. Oliver Gogarty contributed to the brief discussion preceding the uncontested elections. He insisted that elections need not be unanimous. 'I should be very worried to see anything unanimous even in the Seanad, because I have been on many Boards and a unanimous verdict upon any candidate almost always means that there is a compromise.'[2] He balanced a compliment to Arthur Griffith — 'who lived a life of obscurity with a clear vision of realising what a Nation is with the result that we owe to his work the fact that we are meeting here to-day in the Seanad' — with a condemnation of 'that sink of acidity' Lord Carson who 'used the enemies of Ireland as a springboard, and is now safely deposited on the English Woolsack... Lord Carson's spiritual life has been exaggerated by a chronic attack of gall-stones.' Such considerations, however, must not now influence them; the Senate, Gogarty insisted, should be 'an entity without any antecedent'.

Moving a vote of congratulations to W.B. Yeats in November 1923 Gogarty said, 'To my mind, since the Treaty the award of the Nobel Prize to Senator Yeats is the most significant thing that has befallen this country...' But his enthusiasm rather carried him away and the Chairman asked him not to forget the text of his motion. It is interesting that in alluding to famous men of other nations he included among the great modern Italians 'men like Marconi and Mussolini', the latter being then a generally-admired figure.

During its early years the Free State legislature necessarily devoted much time to the regulation of its institutions which were additionally complicated by the state's bi-lingual aspirations. W.B. Yeats[3] discussing an amendment proposing to add the term 'Civic Guard' to Garda Síochána said, 'the question troubles me very much. If I am attacked by a foot-pad and wish for protection how can I call for that protection by using words I cannot pronounce?' This comedy turn was an exception to Yeats's policy of confining his comments to subjects on which he could speak with authority: 'I do not like to speak in the House unless on things I have studied — letters and art.'

Perhaps unwisely Senator Gogarty set himself no such limitations; he attended regularly, spoke frequently and reference to his contributions occupy almost seven columns in the General Index to the *Reports of the Senate Debates 1922 — 1936*. Inevitably his assertive nature led him to occasional pronouncements very wide of the mark. His contributions to a debate on the Customs Duties (Provisional Imposition) Bill caused Senator Michael Comyn to say sarcastically: 'It is very refreshing to hear a very able and skilful Senator discussing a subject on which I can say and without offence, he has a perfectly virgin mind. The observations he has made show me at least that he does not understand the constitutional position of this Bill, the economic position, or the financial position.'

More often than not, however, Gogarty spoke constructively and was far-sighted concerning transport and industrial potential. Despite the Minister for Finance's argument that an Irish pavilion at the British Empire Exhibition in 1924 would be too costly Gogarty supported Sir Thomas Edmonde's proposal for Free State representation. Absence would be construed as sulking in our tent, 'and sulking in our tent in the presence of the greatest collection of visitors that is likely to occur anywhere in our time.' It would be an immense advertisement at little cost and would draw attention to products perhaps not recognised as ours. 'Not so many years ago I heard a soldier in a Crewe restaurant ask for a bottle of "Guinness's Twenty". I said, "Guinness's Twenty? We call that Guinness's double X in Dublin." "Just like you Irish", he said.'

However hard the times, however compelling the need for economies, the government's Old Age Pensions Bill, 1924, seen in retrospect was a mean expedient and it is disappointing to find Oliver Gogarty giving full voice in its support.

He referred to the introduction of old-age pensions by 'that extraordinarily generous democrat, Mr. Lloyd George' and said 'That was one of the most unwelcome heritages we had to accept when the Free State was being formed.' Party loyalty and the belief that what he described as 'the vote-catching device of an English politician' was being abused and paid to middle-aged persons hardly excuse his attitude which merited Senator Foran's rebuke: 'I would like to say something on the point raised by Senator Gogarty, who describes the old age pension as an alien imposition. I would like to say that if the aliens had imposed more legislation of this kind on the country I would regret their leaving it, and how any Senator can get up in this assembly and actually disagree with the pensioning of the aged poor in this or any other country I cannot understand.'

Dr. Gogarty deserved to hang his head in shame but instead with twenty-six others, including W.B. Yeats and wealthy men such as the Earl of Wicklow, the Marquis of Headfort, and the Right Honourable Andrew Jameson, he voted to reduce the old age pension by a shilling.

Gogarty was among those who enthusiastically supported the new government's ambitious hydro-electric project, the so-called 'Shannon Scheme' which, surprisingly, encountered considerable opposition. As he saw it the question was not so much 'can we afford the scheme?' as 'can we afford to delay it?' To those who were insistent that the scheme must pay for itself in a few years his argument was to draw attention to the enormous benefit that would ensue from a general rise in living standards. 'I think that if the Government made a gift of five and a half million pounds to the people of Ireland to raise their standard of living they would be doing a thing that nobody could criticise.... This Shannon Scheme would be of benefit to the country, even if it never paid a penny.' Another reason for supporting the Shannon Electricity Bill was that it would improve education. 'It is said that wherever there is a bulb there is a book.'

He dismissed the suggestion that a river other than the Shannon could be adequately harnessed: '...the Liffey is to the Shannon as a halfpenny dip is to an arc lamp.' He strongly opposed Sir John Griffith's amendment, seconded by Sir John Keane, referring the project to a special commission composed of various bodies including the Irish Farmers' Union and the Institute of Civil Engineers.

Gogarty maintained that it was a matter in which the government must be trusted, and destructive and self-interested critics ignored. The farmers had nothing to contribute. 'The Farmers' Union is a body whose alacrity is more or less confined to opposing tariffs, the Summer Time Bill, the Land Bond Bill, and I believe they were not very much in favour of the Railways Bill, while they were altogether against the Enforcement of Law Bill....I do not think the Farmers' Union is a body to which this matter be referred. If it is to be referred to the Farmers' Union why not the Abbey Theatre, or the Sick and Indigent Roomkeepers' Society who are also interested in electric lighting?' The engineers, on the other hand, and through no fault of their own, had no experience of such massive projects. 'They never had much encouragement in the direction of developing the resources of Ireland... if some years ago a proposition were put forward to send current over copper cables, and if that proposition was brought to "Buckshot" Forster, or if a water-power scheme was brought to "Bloody" Balfour, or even to our friend the lumbering Greenwood, it never would have been met in an encouraging spirit.'

There is considerable individual friendship between members of the medical and legal professions but the degree of pomp with which lawyers surround themselves is irksome to doctors and Gogarty did not spare them in the Senate. When it was moved during a discussion of the Courts of Justice Bill, 1923, that the retirement age of judges should be seventy-five rather than seventy he said, '... it is not to be suggested that all the senility of the country is to be monopolised by the Bar. It is almost antiscriptural to carry on after seventy years of age. I heard of an excellent Judge in India who frequently condemned the advocate to death, and sometimes addressed the criminal in equal terms.' Subsequently he mentioned that the Chairman having described himself as 'the father' of the Bill 'then more or less put himself in the position of the father of Oedipus who proceeded to expose his own child, and is now like a cat left biting its own tail, instead of being sent on its business of rat-catching.'

Along with others Gogarty thought that an opportunity should be taken 'to allow the law to appear in Irish garb made of Irish materials' rather than continue to dress our judges in the English fashion of which W.B. Yeats had said: 'When you think over the present costume, that great gray wig and that gown, if you try to see it without historical associations, is it not something incredibly fantastic?' Gogarty maintained that, 'the important things in the country are often the little things, like the flag, for instance, which are of the utmost importance — more important than words can express, because they are the spiritual symbolic things. The costume of our lawgivers is one of those little important, significant things.... We want to see a change of heart accompanied by a change of costume. Who can tell the thousands of our fellow-countrymen who faced the wig and gown before being condemned to death, transportation or penal servitude, for political offences in the old evil days?... The ingratiating barrister, the transporting judge — all were clothed in this ridiculous remnant of the eighteenth century.'

He opposed General Sir Bryan Mahon's motion censuring District Justice Goff for remarking in Castleblayney courthouse that soldiers in the Great War had to take rum to brutalize them before being sent into action. He did not think the Senate 'should be turned into an instrument to teach manners to badly-mannered justices' and was realistic in deploring an attitude of mind that would have us believe that soldiers should go into action on buttermilk. 'If I were required to go over the top, I would require more than a tot of rum, and I would be inclined to linger until it was brought up to the front line.'

He voted against Senator Douglas's amendment to the Intoxicating Liquor Bill, 1924, proposing the closure of public-houses on St. Patrick's Day and expressed the fear that we would find ourselves, like America, 'in the hands of a rigidly righteous, puritanical set of cranks....' He thought publicans should be given the freedom of choice:

Hitherto I felt a little bit of a hypocrite when I had to vote for the curtailing of the hours for the sale of drink, but when the Minister pointed out that it was really an increase of half an hour I felt I could support the Government. I visited many taverns in the city in my youth, and I did not see any extraordinary occurrences such as would warrant their being closed. But to be perfectly fair, I try to put myself in the place of St. Patrick. What would he say to it? He visited Ireland at a time when there was no word in the Irish language to explain the condition of sobriety. I believe this is a fact. I do not know that there is any Irish word for 'sober'. Although he could not have been extraordinarily shocked at the hilarious reception and subsequent entertainment he must have received in the houses of the chieftains I am not perfectly certain that he would agree for a moment to close these houses compulsorily.

Nevertheless it was generally agreed that the custom of 'drowning the shamrock' had been carried too far and that the unfortunate plant should be given a chance of survival. Senator Douglas's amendment was carried by 18 votes to 9 and the feast day was turned into a fast day, remaining so until comparatively recently.

Gogarty also advocated the abolition of super-tax as an inducement to attract wealthy residents from abroad; proposed that a motor-way to be supported by tolls be established between Dublin and Cork and as early as 1925 forecast that 'soon the roads will replace the railways.'

He asked an interesting question anent the railways: 'Is there a solitary instance where a decrease of traffic has led to the dismissal of a director?' (On another occasion he said he was inclined to think that the directors' minds were running on a single track.) He stressed that despite the supreme advantage which Ireland possesses in the Atlantic 'we are no better than a mud bank in the Mersey' unless our western harbours, potentially the greatest in Europe, are developed.

During the discussion on the Gaeltacht Commission Report Gogarty crystallized problems which remained neglected until very recently, and are still largely unsolved:

The Congested District Board built harbours that are sometimes reached by a strong-winged sea-gull, and it endowed the congests with fishing-boats, but the Board forgot the fact that the congests are not fishermen. If there is a storm they work on the farms, and if fine they go out to sea, and they only pay a couple of months' instalments on the fishing boats. I have seen French poachers come in fishing in Irish waters in weather that was considered impossible by the native fishermen. These fishermen have no ice or proper means of sending their fish to the market. Just as the cattle markets are in England, the fishing markets are in Billingsgate and Grimsby, and the irony of it is that we have to send over to England for fish that should be caught on the west coast of Ireland.

He underlined the importance of creating indigenous industries by a reference to Mr. Henry Ford that would have surprized the motor magnate. 'Ford, excellent though he may be as a wage payer, is, after all, a magnificent but itinerant tinker. He is not a native product of Ireland and Cork could quite possibly be left in the position Belfast was left in, if Ford took his folding factory and went away, because I believe it is in sections and could go away at any moment.'

Many other commonsense pronouncements could be quoted if space permitted. 'One director of the Bank of England could conquer this country by a stroke of the pen, because politics are now changing into economics....' We must supply the best meat to the English market until we have secured an incontrovertible name for supplying the best meat in the world. 'At present some of the credit due to Irish meat goes to Scotland for the finished article, for Irish cattle are finished there in six weeks.'

He approved of maintaining the Imperial connection and suggested that at a forthcoming Imperial conference Ireland's connection with the Empire should be frankly acknowledged and played for what it was worth. 'You cannot sell a man a bullock and give him a black eye at the same time. Though some of our extremists who have furthest removed themselves from reality have told the farmers of Ireland many things, many fairy tales, there is one thing that no political party dare tell the farmer, and that is to forbid him to sell his product to the British Empire.'

When the Censorship of Publications Bill, 1928, came before the Senate on 11 April 1928 the Minister for Justice, Mr. J. Fitzgerald-Kenney, opened the discussion. The Bill, he reminded the House, prohibited the circulation of indecent and obscene books and those advocating the unnatural prevention of conception or the procurement of abortion and applied also to journals and newspapers. It had received the unanimous support of the Dáil and while amended in some respects (the 'recognised associations' which, it had been hoped, might report books to the Censorship Board were not approved and the number of Censors was not to be increased from five to nine) but remained unaltered in principle.

Sir John Keane's was the major voice of opposition. After a long and reasoned speech he asked the Dáil and Senate 'to think twice before they impose upon even an unwilling few, to say nothing of the passive and unheeding mass, the fetters of a mediaeval code.' Senator John Bagwell declared it to be 'an interfering and inquisitorial type of legislation' but others supported it. Colonel Maurice Moore, a brother of the author of *Hail and Farewell*, admitted that having read over many years what came to his hand, proper or improper, he had difficulty, initially, in understanding why he should prevent others from doing likewise. But when he read the Bill it did not seem harmful. 'We all know that if indecent books and papers are published they will have a great effect on the youth of the country.'

It is surprizing to find that Dr. Oliver St. John Gogarty, too, had mixed feelings. Since the death of George Sigerson and the resignation of W.B. Yeats he was the Senate's principal literary figure. His chief objection to censorship was that he 'did not like any men to exploit a kind of lay vocation at the expense of their neighbours'. He said that the Bill was 'attributed to two barristers who, with half an eye on God and two on better business, concerned themselves about the moral welfare of the nation'. Despite these misgivings he approved of the prohibition of contraceptive literature and referred to England as 'the land in which heroes were contra-conceived'. Further evidence of his Catholic orthodoxy was the suggestion that the banned books should include those on the *Index Librorum Prohibitorum* of Rome.

At the end of Gogarty's speech Senator Thomas Johnson said he wondered whether the Minister for Justice 'was better pleased with the support the Bill got from Senator Gogarty or the attack on it by Senator John Keane'. Gogarty's approval was, indeed, qualified by neutralizing clauses. He approved of the control of contraceptive literature — 'No one who has any care for a nation's welfare can for one moment countenance contraceptive practices which are a contradiction of a nation's life' — but said that this should have been met by a Bill of its own. He condemned the pettiness of the customs officers who examined schoolboys' books even before the Bill was made law. This would make us as ridiculous as the customs officers in Italy where Plato's *Republic* was confiscated because the word 'republic' was on the cover. He insisted that the Bill must not be retro-active; it should not seek to include the classic masterpieces of the world. Sir John Keane, incidentally, with perceptive anticipation of what was to happen, singled out *The Midnight Court* as an example of what was likely to earn the Censors' displeasure.

Digressing, Gogarty referred to the freedom of the press. 'What this country needs is freedom from the Press...' and not only from the English newspapers. The Irish daily papers had done more harm than good. 'One paper, the one with the compulsory Latin, had a formula of "all good Irishmen" and tells us what all good Irishmen should do, while at the same time it tries to belittle the authority that upholds the citizenship of Ireland.' Editorials were unduly influential and might need to be checked, especially if the newspaper was irresponsible. Hysterical headlines could be harmful. 'Probably it would be enough to direct the Bill against pamphlets, advertisements, and newspapers, and leave books out.' In order that the Censorship Bill would be 'practicable and less unpleasant' he intended, he said, to introduce amendments to strengthen it during the committee stage.

In the event, however, Gogarty proposed no amendments. When the Committee stage was reached in the Senate on 25 April 1929 he enquired, with the theatre in mind, if typewritten books of words could be excluded. The Chairman decided that his question was irrelevant to the amendment under discussion.

Senator J.C. Dowdall's amendment proposed that the Board of Censors should be comprised of five rather than nine persons; Gogarty said that in his opinion 'the ideal would be zero'. He opposed an amendment favouring the reintroduction of 'recognised associations': 'The proposal is that we should make use of our recently-won liberty to fill every village and hamlet with little literary pimps who will be "recognised". We all know the people who lay themselves out to be self-appointed moralists, greasy-eyed little fellows with a sensitive conscience and a strong stomach for drink.'

He seconded Sir John Keane's amendment (subsequently with-drawn) to restrict censorship to material published after 31 December 1927 but opposed Keane's amendment to remove sensational matter relating to crime from the concern of the Censors. The excitement and thrills provided by the press were harmful. 'It presents the world each day to the public in a manner which produces a panicky and injurious effect on the readers. It displays the tragic and appalling in leaded type, and it makes these happenings to appear as more or less ordinary daily occurrences.' He asked if measures could be taken against 'deleterious advertisements'.

Because it would help to break the secrecy of the Board he favour-ed an unsuccessful amendment giving the author the right to appear before the Board in person and later deplored that 'the author is not entitled to an appeal in what is tantamount to a confiscation of his private property'. He expressed a fear that Dublin's printing trade, which did a good deal of over-flow printing work for English publishers, might find their overseas work affected.

Discussing another of Sir John Keane's amendments Gogarty ex-pressed apprehension regarding a Bill which 'even in its present state, is rather sinister'. He though that there really should not be a Bill of this kind at all. 'It is simply super-imposing a worthy attempt

11 'The Happy Hour: Sinclair, Orpen & Two Babies'. A cartoon by Sir William
Orpen. Courtesy of Oliver D. Gogarty.

12   Oliver St John Gogarty from an etching by Gerald L. Brockhurst, R.A., *c.*
1941. Courtesy of the artist.

13 Neenie Gogarty, 1945.

14 Oliver Gogarty with his grandson Guy Williams.

15   Memorial to James Joyce, Flüntern Cemetery, Zürich.

16   Martello Tower, Sandycove.

17   5 Rutland Square, birthplace.

18   Fairfield, Glasnevin.

19   15 Ely Place, Dublin, from a water colour by Flora N. Mitchell. Courtesy of Oliver D. Gogarty.

20   Renvyle House, Connemara.

21 East 61st Street, New York.

to get rid of certain practices that are coming in here from England. We have had all this hullabaloo about sex. I think it is high time that the people of this country found some other way of loving God than by hating women.'

He stressed the importance of the preservation of ancient monuments but believing that the enthusiasts for the revival of the Irish language were wrong-headed he said so repeatedly. 'Take the fallacies which underlie all this irrational enthusiasm about Gaelic. One fallacy is that the Gaelic-speaking parts of the country are the centre of civilization. Nothing of the kind. These parts are the centre of the most amazing decadence.' He opposed the idea 'that there is no possibility of being an Irishman except you are in the middle of the Gaeltacht' and pointed out that in the towns the inherited languages included Danish, Norman-French and English. 'I am not inspired by vindictiveness against Gaelic, but I say that the enemy of the native language is the march of progress.' Very sensibly he protested against teaching other subjects through the medium of Irish: '... it seems to me a very difficult and unwise thing to filter through the veil a language which is in the condition of being created, and make that the only avenue to the knowledge of the outer world for the children.'

He voted with those who successfully opposed an amendment to the University College, Galway, Bill, 1929, limiting tenure of office to five years in the case of persons not competent to teach through Irish. 'Nobody who is worth his salt as a university professor is going to take the position if the appointment is to be limited to five years.' The logic of the amendment demanded the provision of Irish texts on all branches of art and science; this might cost two million pounds if confined to one dialect or three times that amount if the three dialects current in the country were to be represented. 'If I had six million pounds to distribute in Galway I would spend it in Galway, for Europe begins at Galway; but this sort of thing will make Europe and culture end in Galway. It is pathetic to think that people's patriotism is supposed to have this climax in a dialect or three dialects.'

A throwaway comment about the third estate raised a laugh at the expense of George Bernard Shaw. 'A good many people take up journalism for the purpose of being able to enter certain places and sometimes to evade certain responsibilities. The story is told that on one occasion Bernard Shaw attended a religious function and when the collection box went round he simply said: "Press".'

The Wild Birds Protection Bill presented Gogarty with another opportunity for humorous indulgence. 'There is one bird omitted from the Bill, and its omission is extraordinary for it is the only bird of which I know to which there is a statue. In the eighteenth century in the Phoenix Park they erected a beautiful statue to the phoenix. I think something ought to done to prevent people from shooting it. It is a bird that only appears at rare periods when there is something in the air.'

When Senator Comyn proposed an amendment to insert at the appropriate place the word 'Kingfisher', Gogarty said 'I do not often find myself in agreement with Senator Comyn but his action in moving this amendment shows apparently a change of heart when he wants to put the word "King" anywhere. According to his mentality, one would think that it is the word "President fisher" that he would desire to insert at the appropriate place.'

On another occasion, referring to a speech in which Gogarty had spoken of many things, including the habits of fish, Comyn said he hoped codfish were included. This pair gave each other little quarter but Senator Gogarty was the major aggressor:

> In the heyday of Greek drama it was usual to mollify the drama by a satire or kind of harlequinade, and when Senator Comyn whom I am glad to see present, because I should hate to talk behind his back, finds that the government has not got a leg to stand on, he is employed as a kind of genial reverend Punchinello. It would not be a very great want of chivalry to fail to talk before Senator Comyn because there was a time when if you were behind his back you were in danger of being run through by his Court sword on the way to Dublin Castle, so I think though it be courteous not to talk behind his back it would require more courage to talk behind it.

Discussing the Local Government Bill, 1924, he insisted that 'there are certain cases and certain things that should not be subject to the public franchise and public vote. The people's health should not be put to the vote of the people.' The authoritarian voice of paternalism perhaps, but Gogarty had strong views on the virtues of preventive medicine.

> The state of public health in this city is a scandal.... Certainly, high rates affect the poor to a greater extent than many people imagine. The higher the rates are the worse becomes the state of child mortality. The mortality rate amongst children in Dublin is a thing one should be even ashamed to ventilate. In the

month of August there were 250 deaths out of every thousand; that means that one out of every four died.

On the other hand he voted against an amendment proposing the formation of a public health council, believing that 'very little is to be gained by invoking or inviting from a district the chief medical man, or the most prominent agitator to sit in conclave with a midwife'. He believed that consultation does not always make for efficiency. 'We are told by the papers — for that reason I take it with a grain of salt — that in Russia lately they got all the master artists, put them in a room, and told them to produce a masterpiece. You lose a good deal of initiative if you have to democratise every single human activity....'

He reiterated his belief that the prevention of disease must begin in the schools. He voted against the motion because he thought it would increase administrative difficulties. 'Public health is hard to deal with, no matter what plenary powers the Minister may possess, and a Minister in no circumstances can be considered a tyrant in public health matters, except, perhaps, in the sense of Lord Iveagh, who evicted people from Bull Alley and put them into the Iveagh Buildings.'

He advocated that medical officers of health should hold fulltime appointments which would make them independent. He advised that the county medical officer of health should not be excluded from the urban district; it should be a dual appointment. Concerning the qualifications needed by a sanitary inspector he suggested that an extremely technical or involved diploma was unnecessary to estimate the sanitary condition of a house. 'One's nose is nearly qualified to do that.'

When the Medical Bill was discussed in 1925 he stressed the urgency of defining and legalizing the position of the medical profession. 'Behind the whole matter lies the fact that the question may arise as to whether or not the medical profession in Ireland, and those entering medical qualifying bodies are to have the power to practise freely in the British Empire.' To wish to do so was not to pocket one's pride but, when Ireland's contribution to the Empire was considered, to claim one's rights. Otherwise 'it would mean the debasing of the degrees of famous medical institutions in Ireland and the closing of them possibly. For the wear and tear, so to speak, of the Irish medical profession, only twenty men would be necessary annually in Ireland. That is to say, Trinity College, the National University and the Royal College of Surgeons would be given less than seven men each to qualify.'

In the debate on the School Attendance Bill he maintained that Dublin lacked the accommodation for more than a quarter of the children who should be at school. 'I visited many schools in 1912 to examine children for another purpose. In one school in High Street the playground was the crypt of St. Audoen's Church. There are bye-laws existing defining the cubic space to be provided for each child but they have not been enforced. To compel children to attend these concentration houses — I know conditions are modified by the Bill — would be an inhuman thing to countenance.' He said that the schools should be in the most beautiful parts of our towns and cities instead of in the slums. 'Except the schools run by the religious bodies, I do not suppose there are in the city schools fit to send children to.' On another occasion he said, 'I am more interested in the school building than in the curriculum.'

He lost no opportunity to stress the importance of healthy housing. 'A war memorial is a comfortless thing. I do not know of any greater monstrosity than the Wellington Monument. There is not shelter on it for a sparrow. If the money subscribed for the war memorial is to be turned into stone, the best thing would be to provide houses for the ex-Servicemen.'

Speaking of housing conditions in the Gaeltacht he said, 'It is sad to think that there are houses unfit for human habitation but the medical officer cannot condemn them because it would mean putting the people out on the roadside, though they would be far healthier on the roadside than in those cesspools and tuberculosis-breeding homes.'

We who have grown up with the Irish Hospitals' Sweepstakes are surprized to learn that its introduction met with stormy opposition. Senator Comyn said that we were called the Cinderella of the nations, a name we did not resent but if this Bill were passed we would be called the beggar of the nations. Others disapproved of it as a form of gambling.

'Behind the objection to this Bill,' Gogarty said, 'there seems to be a mentality that I thought long ago sailed out with the Mayflower.... The idea that betting is immoral is a mediaeval or puritanical outlook.' He supported the Bill which was neccessary because the hospitals lacked funds and the state had not come to their assistance. He went on to point out that the position could have been ameliorated by commonsense mergers. 'At present we have eleven hospitals, all overlapping one another in the city. The Rockefeller Grant some years ago made us an offer of two million pounds if we could come to agreement in that regard. Of course, we could not come to an agreement, because some of the hospitals are endowed on a definite basis, religious or otherwise, and they could not be merged. If they were merged there would be no necessity for this system of raising money.'

He returned to this theme: 'It is monstrous to have this city splattered all over with lazar houses. It must be a strange thing to come to a city where you see nothing but saints and doctors and cinemas.' Vienna a city with two million people had only one hospital which was so successful that it attracted people from the ends of the earth. But we had this multiplicity of hospitals, laundries, x-ray rooms, staffs. 'One big central hospital should be built near the mountains, up at Kilbride, say. That is only a matter of eight or ten minutes in a modern bus. Of course that will never be done. They will prefer to go on enlarging the hospitals.'

Departmental procrastination has delayed even a part of the amalgamation he recommended, but not even the FitzGerald Report dared to advise the drastic pruning of provincial facilities that Gogarty had in mind when he said that if services were to be efficient they should be centralized in Dublin which could be reached from any-where in the country within five hours. 'I am strongly of the opinion that the revival of certain country hospitals should not take place.'

His amendment during the second stage of the Public Hospitals' Bill, proposing the establishment of a lending library supplying books for the use of patients, was accepted. In due course he was to suggest that, 'It should be at the option of the Minister to employ part of the fund in doing preventive work....It is pathetic the way hospitals have been thrust upon people while so little is being done to prevent disease. It is homes the poor want: houses, not primarily hospitals.' He deplored the possibility that politicians might find their constituents bringing pressure on them relating to the disposal of funds and suggested, tongue-in-cheek, that the existence of government could depend on the Manchester November Handicap.

His insistence on the importance of preventive methods and ade-quate housing may have become something of a hobbyhorse; if so it was a steed worth riding, hardly meriting Senator Comyn's rebuke, 'Dread the man with one idea, above all the specialist,' a rebuke which Gogarty ignored.

The slums are really out-patients' departments of the nineteen Dublin hospitals. The slums are that and disease factories. I do not often take credit to myself for saving life but I do give credit to myself for saving a child's life this year by insisting on the mother leaving the child in hospital, by preventing the child being taken home. The child is alive today, but in my opinion it had not a week to live if it had to get near its home, which was portion of some ancient Georgian mansion. Everybody knows the horror of the human shelter in Dublin. I need not urge it further. Occasionally we all work ourselves into a condition of indignation in connection with horrible conditions in which many of our citizens are condemned to live. The figure still is, I believe, 52,000 people in single-room tenements. Unchanged for thirty years! Let our indignation become effective now.

When the Illegitimate Children (Affiliation Orders) Bill designed to impose maintenance orders on the fathers came before the Senate in 1929 Gogarty was among those who favoured the hearing of such cases in camera because of the girls' natural reluctance to appear in public court. He saw the measure as one which would reduce infanticide. 'There is an appalling condition of affairs in this country, and that is infanticide. Anything that will give the mother a chance and will encourage her to preserve the life of the child and not strangle it deserves our consideration. It is as important for us to keep these innocent children alive as to prevent contraceptive practices.'

When six years later he congratulated Senator Mrs. Clarke who, in the debate on the Criminal Law Amendment Bill, had declared her opposition to the prohibition of contraception (though personally supporting the Church's attitude), his antagonism towards contraceptive methods seemed to have lessened. Mrs. Clarke believed that control should be achieved by an appeal to the higher, nobler and more spiritual side of the human mind. Gogarty, while not positively supporting contraceptive measures, appeared to stress their prophylactic value. 'There's a worse thing than racial suicide,' he said, 'and that is racial syphilis. That is the one thing that undermines and saps away the vigour of the race, not in the third or fourth, but even in the twentieth generation.' He thought it absolutely impossible to stop the use of contraceptives and it would be difficult to differentiate nicely between the medical and the religious aspect if their purchase were to be permitted under medical orders. 'It is an impossible thing,' he said, 'to hold back the little scientific knowledge that goes to the use of these things.'

He reminded the Senate that after the introduction of anaesthetics there were those who declared it an outrage to use anaesthesia in childbirth. Who could say how attitudes might not have changed in regard to 'these so-called contraceptives' in ten or twenty years time? Then cynicism intruded and he referred to more homely and primitive methods of birth-control: '...it is a very easy thing to destroy the male element; any vinegar will do it; you cannot take all the cruet-stands out of the country.'

Other public-health matters on which he spoke were the use of artificial preservatives in milk and the scandalous condition of some of the abattoirs.

He supported the merger of the College of Science with the National University of Ireland. 'The College of Science has been a bone of contention for many years with the other universities. Trinity College, by the way, has not as broad a curriculum as the National University of Ireland, however deep, intense and excellent it may be. There are certain faculties in the National which are not in Trinity. For instance there is architecture. When the College of Science becomes merged in the National University it will therefore broaden its curriculum.'

Fianna Fáil's accession to power in 1932 and the Economic War which followed Ireland's refusal to pay the Land Annuities provided the opposition Senators with abundant reasons for complaint as tarriffs were imposed and the cattle trade was imperilled. 'We should not have carried the war into the treasure house of the Irish people,' Gogarty insisted and in the debate on government policy towards England he moved 'that this Seanad is of opinion that it is time for the Government to return to a policy of love for Ireland instead of hatred for England'. In the course of his speech, referring to President de Valera's absence on League of Nations' business, Gogarty said, 'our Celtic Calvin, pre-destined failure, has gone to Geneva. We must wait until the people find out that Meath is nearer than Manchuria.'

Gogarty argued that it is bad to hate anybody, but worse to hate England, not for fear of reprisal 'for how can she possibly imagine we have any hate left over when we have done so strangely by ourselves?' But England had become identified with all that comes to us from Europe and civilization, and humanitarianism and all those things which are indispensable for human life are pilloried in the general hate. 'Everything becomes anathema save ruin and vulgarity. We are to be fed on the negations of a progressive people — pauperism and plainness. Is there no other way of not being English? Is there no other way of being Irish?' Looking at the situation in which the nation found itself Gogarty asked: 'What death-watch beetle has crept into the timbers of our. roof-tree? What channering worm is underground?'

As the recession became more acute he pointed out 'instead of being a land flowing with milk and honey, as we are promised ours should be, it is flowing with mulct and humbug.' 'Already they say in Clare blacksmiths are shoeing the cattle so that they may gallop round the fairs on the look-out for a purchaser.' He declared, too, that the Irish equivalent of Nelson's famous message 'England expects every man to do his duty' was 'de Valera expects every man to pay his duty'.

Speaking in the presence of Senator Connolly, the Minister for Lands, he said: ' "Skin-the-Goat" was a patriot but "Skin-the-Calf" is the greatest enemy this country ever had and he's not very far away from us.' Connolly dismissed his critic as 'a dilettante in politics who blows in here occasionally.' He protested that he refused to take him seriously which, if he meant it, was probably just as well for Gogarty accused him of having at Edenderry 'added barrenness to the Bog of Allen' and remarked that to Senator Connolly prosperity 'is like a red rag to a bankrupt'.

He stigmatized de Valera's speech on the Emergency Imposition of Duties Bill, 1932, as 'the voice of a mathematical madhouse, from some algebraical world of minus values where everything is upside-down and all the quantities are negative. It would be tolerable if it remained in its dimension, but it is terrible when such dreams overflow into life. He solemnly suggested that this country with all its poverty, would be better if it were poorer still....' Elaborating his theme he likened the President, who had failed to seize the opportunity of Plenty, to a fanatical edition of St. Francis who is to wed his Lady Poverty 'by proxy, of course; we who are hard set enough to live are to tighten our belts'. Then casting any pretence at humour aside he delivered himself of a blistering peroration:

> Therefore I tell you to have a care, President de Valera, lest your silhouette may come to be regarded as the most sinister which ever darkened the light in genial Ireland and that it may not be without significance that, during the election, your name was written on the dead walls of the roofless ruins of this our country.

On another occasion he said, 'the popular President has the strongest bodyguard that any man in this country had, except Lynchehaun,[4] and I mention Lynchehaun because he turned on the hand that fed him and put his benefactor on a hot seat.' Naturally this comparison with a notorious escapee infuriated the Fianna Fáil senators.

'It is odious, hideous,' Senator Foran said, 'it is outrageous for a man to get up in an assembly like this and draw such a comparison.'

'I have the greatest pleasure,' Gogarty replied, 'in withdrawing any comparison between the criminal Lynchehaun and President de Valera. I was only comparing the strength of their bodyguards, but I will alter it and say that the President is the greatest national fiasco since Jem Roche.'

He was quite unrepentant; it was merely a matter of time until his next outburst. 'Since the betrayal of Kinsale by Don Juan del Aquila there has never been a calamity comparable to the calamity that our Spaniard has brought on the country this month.' He made no concessions: 'The President ran the Irish treasureship on the rocks in spite of many warnings from the Seanad and he wants it to be applauded because he gets away in the lifeboat with a quarter of beef and a lump of coal.' Gogarty would neither forget, nor forgive: 'He cost Ireland the blood of Collins, he broke the heart of Arthur Griffith, and he has now broken the heart of Ireland itself.'

Senator Comyn said that Gogarty's utterances reminded him of a little boy who goes to a dirt heap, makes little pellets of mud, and flings them at decent people as they pass. Sometimes he had been witty and for the sake of his former sallies he was more or less tolerated. But the day comes when wit ceases and only buffoonery remains. 'I think he has passed his little hour upon the stage. He is no longer amusing. He is getting old and dull.'⁵

They were, all of them, getting older and for them all the opportunities for strutting and fretting were ending. President de Valera had seen to that with his Bill to abolish the Senate which in itself was reason for further contention. Those who approve of de Valera's policies in the 1920s and 1930s will see Gogarty as a deplorably vituperative figure in the Upper House but it can be reasonably argued that his consistent attacks were logical and courageous.

It was Eamonn de Valera's good fortune to live to a great age, an elder statesman, a venerated figure who won even the grudging admiration of his political opponents. He became a subject for hagiography in which the controversial figure from the past loses its angularity. Gogarty was not alone in his animosity. Frank O'Connor has described AE in an outburst of emotion, arms raised above his head, beside himself with anger as he called down maledictions. 'I curse that man as generations of Irishmen to come will curse him —

the man who destroyed our country.'[6]

A substantial body of de Valera's contemporaries, intelligent, disinterested men, saw in him a monument to casuistry and blamed him above all others (for he alone might have prevented it) for the civil war. Such men would have thought that Gogarty gave de Valera no more than he deserved and applauded his determined courage. But sooner or later the shrill voice of opposition grows tedious and finally, on the subject of de Valera, Gogarty was a bore. Fortunately there were limits to his animosity; hearing that one of the President's sons had been killed by a fall from a horse he said, 'I'm a father myself. I can feel sorry for Dev.'

13

Hey, Ho Me Randy O!

Is there a professional climacteric? Does a time come when problems which used to fascinate seem irksome, and the demands of life-and-death interventions are unbearably wearing? Is there a moment of realization that life viewed by the sick-bed and in the clinic is but a fraction of the whole?[1] If so this could explain why in the early 1930s Gogarty began to reduce his practice, having, as he said, looked down throats and up noses long enough. He played host at Renvyle House Hotel, began to make some money with his pen, writing topical articles and reviews for the *Daily Express,* the *Evening Standard,* the *Observer* and other English newspapers, and tried himself on the American lecture tour circuit.

He was in his fifties now, but in his prime, for according to a friend he was 'twenty-five years younger than anyone should be at his age at any particular time — in outlook, in physique, in everything about him.'[2] The Minister of Defence, Mr Frank Aiken, referred to him as 'a lazy body' and was challenged to a duel to take the form of an athletic contest in the air, on the earth and in the water, a challenge which the Minister did not accept, although he was by far the younger man.

Pilgrimage in the West by the Italian philosopher, Mario Rossi, gives a vivid description of Renvyle House: '...the most westerly hotel in Europe, beaten by all the Atlantic winds, crowded with guests, a peculiar combination of the great Alpine hotel and the hospitable home. It is not easy to say who is there as Gogarty's guest and who is there as the guest of the hotel. You fail to understand how so many people have arrived there across eighteen miles of an impossible road; nevertheless you find there a sort of mundane tone which couples insensibly with the wildest nature.'

The day-to-day running of Renvyle House was in the hands of Mrs. Gogarty and a manager. The original guest register is a relic of spacious days with the usual columns for name and address and other spaces for 'registered number and make of car' (left empty in the main except for owners of Rolls Royces and Packards) and 'number of servants in party'.

The first names entered on 26 April 1930 are those of Mr. and Mrs. F. Heyn of Craigavard, County Down, and as the months pass notabilities appear: E. O'Mahony ('the Pope'); Liam T. McCosgair; Count and Countess McCormack; Augustus John; Lord and Lady Longford; W.B. Yeats; S.V. Furlong; Vyvyan John; Dr. and Mrs. Tweedy; Willard Connely of New College, Oxford; W. Lambton, KCB, Turf Club, London; Miss Frances Hays, New York; Mr. and Mrs. Churchill, London; Lady Gibson and so on....The guests at Christmas included Dudley Walsh to whose registration a wag added in the respective columns for motor car and servants, 'Tricycle' and '10'.

Early in the New Year Dr. George Maguire of Claremorris arrived with a party. Later Lord Hemphill came over from Ardrahan and as the hotel's second year progressed distinguished names were added to the register: Denis Johnston, the author of *The Old Lady Said 'No'!*, and his first wife, the actress and producer Shelah Richards; the Countess of Fingall; Lady Glanusk of Glanusk Park, South Wales, and Lady Caroline Agar; Stephen Gwynn whose *A Holiday in Connemara* was published years earlier; Colm O'Loughlin, the founder of The Three Candles Press; Frank and Elizabeth Pakenham; Meriel Moore, a leading actress with the Dublin Gate Theatre Company.

On 30 December in good time to see the Old Year out, Surgeon and Mrs. H.L. Barniville arrived. The following year added more illustrious names: Mr. and Mrs. Bronson Albery; the O'Conor Don; Francis Hackett; Dr. Henry Moore, University College, Dublin's diminutive professor of medicine; 'Beckett, Foxrock', with indecipherable initials (on 11 August 1932); Mr. and Mrs. More O'Ferrall with their son Roderic; a distinguished San Francisco radiologist and his wife, Dr. and Mrs. H. Garland; Ireland's finest medical editor, Surgeon William Doolin and Mrs. Doolin; Lord and Lady Glenavy and the Hon. Michael Campbell; Adrian Stokes, the London critic; Professor J. Bronte Gatenby, Trinity College's professor of zoology; Sir William Wilde's future biographer, T.G. Wilson and Mrs. Wilson.

As one skims the register a pageant of the 1930s unfolds: Richard Best; Countess Metexa of Oughterard; Elizabeth C. Yeats, the driving force behind the Cuala Press; Professor and Mrs. Savory; Lord Oranmore and Browne of Castlemacgarret, Claremorris; Gogarty's close friend Dr. Joseph Boyd Barrett; the architect Michael Scott; Margaret Burke Sheridan, the famous soprano; Bip Pares, who illustrated *I Follow Saint Patrick*.

To publicize the hotel Oliver thought up a plan which was as

unlikely as it was unrealizable. Having learned that Edgar Wallace was
arranging to holiday at Rosapenna in County Donegal, Gogarty planned that someone should 'get in touch with that facile fellow Edgar
and to send him to our more beautiful hotel at Renvyle. Once there,
I shall invite him to stay in my cottage 1½ miles away from Renvyle
House and on an island in a lake — meanwhile informing the Civic
Guard that he is missing, Kidnapped! It would suit both parties for
their "Press" — hotel and horror-mongers.'³

His expenses were high, his family was educated expensively —
Noll had been to Downside and Christ Church, Oxford, before reading
law, Dermot rowed for Pembroke College, Cambridge, and studied
architecture under Sir Edwin Lutyens in London — and travel, entertaining and incidentals such as re-roofing Dungory Castle made
inroads on his income which from time to time he supplemented by
the sale of a rare book or valuable painting. When planning to sell
a perfect copy of *Leaves of Grass* to Rosenbach or send it to Sothebys,
he had an offer of four thousand dollars from Amherst. More disappointing, as he explained to Shane Leslie was the outcome of other
negotiations: 'I had the portrait of Yeats by Augustus John sold to
the Gibson Bequest in Cork last week for £1,000 but the Technical
Committee refused to ratify *because Yeats insulted Daniel O'Connell!*
The poem about the 3 statues in O'Connell Street, O'Connell, Nelson,
Parnell....'⁴

His ideas about developing Ireland's amenities expounded in the
Senate were discussed at greater length in the Beaverbrook Press:

The cost of constructing a terminal port at Galway would be
about a third of the cost of the Shannon Scheme. To my mind
it is three times more important because it would let us out on
the Atlantic Ocean, or rather let the highways of the Atlantic
converge on our shores. At present we are marooned in the
midst of the busiest and richest stream of shipping in the world.
We watch the world's ships with our relatives and friends borne
past our shores, and we will not spend less than the price of one
of those ships to open our country to the Atlantic. The principal
stream of shipping goes up channel to Liverpool, Southampton
and Hamburg.

What cannot really be called a second edition of *Wild Apples*
(only eleven of its thirty-three poems are included in the 1928
edition), and should have been retitled, was published by the Cuala
Press in 1930. The selection was chosen by W.B. Yeats who contri-

buted a preface in which, having admonished Gogarty for carelessness, he asks, 'Why am I content to search through so many careless
verses for what is excellent, I think I am not so disinterested; but
because he gives me something that I need and at this moment of
time.' He recommended 'Aphorism' (later renamed 'Ringsend')
to Irish anthologists; for 'being clear and inexplicable' it would
be the most misjudged. Elsewhere he declared it to be about the best
thing Gogarty had written and like everybody who has read it he
could not forget it.

One of the new poems, the sonnet 'To Moorhead, Blind', requires a note of explanation: Dr. Thomas Gillman Moorhead, Trinity's
Regius Professor of Physic and a leading Dublin consultant crossed
to England in July 1926 to attend a meeting of the British Medical
Association; stepping down from the train at Euston he slipped and
fell. Helped to his feet he was conscious but blind. A bilateral retinal
detachment had occurred when his head struck the platform.

The permanent loss of sight which would have terminated the
careers of most men was a prelude to Moorhead's greatness. Clinical
work being necessarily curtailed (though, with the assistance of a
colleague to elicit certain clinical signs, he still undertook some
consultations), he gave more time to teaching and was in demand as
chairman of a number of committees. He remained gregarious. He
played bridge with Braille cards and was a regular theatre-goer.
Gogarty's admiration was well merited:

> *It takes us all our time with all our eyes*
> *To learn, to know, since knowledge comes from sight;*
> *And long before we give light back for light,*
> *The hour of sunset strikes and daylight flies:*
> *But you had swifter thought, your faculties*
> *Gathered more quickly, so the mind is bright*
> *That met, before the dial struck, the night;*
> *And that black darkness bids me moralize.*
>
> *When we old friends, old pupils have been sent*
> *Out of the brittle brightness of the air,*
> *If succour follow in such banishment,*
> *Gleams of your fortitude shall find us there*
> *Amidst the sudden vague beleaguerment*
> *Of that great darkness where you, living, are.*

With characteristic kindness, Gogarty organized a 'panel' of
friends who took it in turn to walk in the country with 'T.G.' on

Saturday afternoons. One of these, William Doolin (the editor of the *Irish Journal of Medical Science* for which Moorhead dictated an already commissioned paper on medical education immediately after his accident, in a nursing-home with his head fixed between sandbags), recalled how he came to know his former teacher during these walks and to realize the man's courage and determination to use his mind as if nothing had happened.

Doolin also remembered Moorhead's weekly dinner parties at the Royal Irish Yacht Club. 'One such *nox ambrosiana* in particular comes to my mind, when Robin Flower had been his invited guest; Dr. Alton, William Fearon, "Kirk" and Oliver Gogarty came to join them, and "T.G." kept the ball rolling between all. Gogarty at one stage had told one of his more scabrous efforts, to which Flower, seated between "T.G." and Alton, reminded the company present that there are still extant in the folklore of European literature the seven original "naughty stories" of which all present day versions were derivatives; turning to the Provost, he appealed to him as a classical scholar for the original of Oliver's particular version!'[5]

Meanwhile Gogarty had not forgotten AE's demand for a larger collection of his verse, a project towards which Yeats gave his encouragement and advice:

> Via Americhe 12—8
> Rapallo,
> Italy.
> Feb. 20.

My dear Gogarty,

An attack of rheumatism confined me to my bed for some days but I am now up again and at my desk where your poems are.

I suggest that you allow me to select from the collection, and from the privately published Cuala book and from that part of Spottiswoode's book, verse which my sister's edition of 'Swans' did not contain. This would make a fine book for Cuala and one helpful to your own reputation. If you like I will take responsibility for the selection and declare that all your erotic verse is dramatic as Swinburne said of his own, or that it contains a cryptogram declaring the hiding place of the crown jewels or anything you like. The present little batch — some 14 of the 20 poems would not overflow the page — is too small, and only two or three times do they come off. I have gone through it all and made suggestions of all kinds on the margin. Of course you could publish it privately with my sister — giving only your best. Lennox Robinson tells me you are getting a great reputation in America especially among people who collect things hard to get at. Another little Cuala book — 300 copies — would be just the thing to keep this interest — Let me select you. I want to praise you —

Yrs.
W.B. Yeats.[6]

During 1932 W.B. Yeats's project of establishing an Irish Academy of Letters caused much discussion and speculation in Irish literary circles[7] and many of those who were left out were intensely disappointed. Monk Gibbon (who was not a founder member), describing a visit to Yeats in *The Masterpiece and the Man,* implies that Oliver Gogarty used guile to ensure his inclusion. 'Gogarty arrived and amused me. He had no sooner sat down than he remarked to Yeats that he would sooner be left out of it all, he did not want to be a member, he was a Catholic and for a Catholic there might be complications. "Leave me out Yeats. Leave me out". This was the right approach to W.B. Yeats. There was never anyone with whom Brer Rabbit's technique of "Don't throw me into the briar patch Brer Fox" was more effective.' The evidence is slender and redolent of sour grapes. Did Gibbon still resent the imagined snub at the Tailteann prize-giving ceremony? Be that as it may, Gogarty agreed to join and served on the Council of the Irish Academy of Letters, the formation of which was publicly announced on 18 September 1932.

In November he acknowledged a gift from John Drinkwater: 'Dear Drinkwater: Your poems arrived and I am reading them now and then, when the chance comes aloud. I think that is the only way poetry should be treated: otherwise it is scriptive and unworthy of the sweet air. I admire your perfect artistry.'[8]

He sailed for America in the S.S. *Lancastria* at the end of the year and was the guest of Judge Richard Cambell in New York City. The details of his first American lecture tour were arranged by the Pond Bureau which issued an appreciation of Gogarty by A.E. He spoke first in Princeton, was guest speaker at the Poetry Society's dinner on 26 January, and had numerous other engagements before his tour ended in March.[9]

Gogarty told his audiences that 'the meanest nursery rhyme

outlasts other poetry; "Sing a song of Sixpence" is indestructible.' The comment recalls G.K. Chesterton's selection of 'Over the hills and far away' as an example of great poetry. Gogarty maintained that the human brain contains rhythm-hungry cells. 'Originally all poetry was a chant or charm to alter destiny, and destiny seems to be as amenable to the rhythm of nonsense verse as to the moralities in the rhymes, say, of Wordsworth, which shows that though destiny may be a fool it exercises a certain amount of taste.' Nonsense rhyme may have existed in Eden before the interference of 'the tree of weary knowledge'; to Gogarty who adopted the rhythms of nursery rhymes for some of his best verses — Goosey Goosey Gander lent its rhythm to 'Leda and the Swan' — it was 'just as incumbent to us to be as little children to climb Parnassus as to enter the Kingdom of Heaven.'

Lecture tours are wearisome even for fluent speakers. Irritation at finding a disproportionately large share of their monetary rewards going to agents is a common reaction which Gogarty did not escape. Irked by the percentage deducted he sent the following on a postcard to his own agent, Mr. Clarke Getts, from the Middle West —

> *They named Clarke Getts, my agent, well.*
> *For all for which his client sweats*
> *On lecture tours with long travail*
> *Clarke Gets.*[10]

— and understandably received no reply.

Many years before, in a letter to his American cousins, Margaret and Katherine Burke, he wrote, 'The Gods may in time bring me to California. I feel that if I got there I would never return and I have not yet reached the time for going West! But I hope some day to see Santa Barbara.' His itinerary permitted him to do so during the lecture tour. He spent three days on an ice-slowed train between Minneapolis and Tucson, Arizona where his sister-in-law lived. He then proceeded to Los Angeles and visited the Burkes in Santa Barbara and his sister, Mayflo, in San Francisco. On the eastbound train he recognized an acquaintance of his hosts in Santa Barbara travelling with a case of hysteria. To his consternation, Gogarty found the hysterical lady committed to his care at Chicago to escort to Pittsburgh.

By now his movements were news but when, on board the *Lafayette* bound for Europe, he saw a report of his attendance at a dinner of the Society of the Friendly Sons of Saint Patrick, he was surprized to find himself designated a firm Protestant and nationalist. Immediately, he cabled a correction: 'I am a Catholic Irishman not given to change.'

His doings which were observed more critically at home were uncharitably reported by Father P.E. Magennis in *The Catholic Bulletin*:

Dr. Gogarty, Senator under the Cosgrave regime, has arrived, and the Yankee interviewer has been at work. We are told that 'AE' is a brilliant talker, but only a patch on Dr. Gogarty, whom he has dubbed 'the master of magnificent conversation' — The Yankee loves such phrases. Lest the American people might doubt the excellence of 'AE', he came himself and did the rounds a la mode. Mabel Greene — one of the authorities on Irish affairs forsooth — tells us that Dr. Gogarty's ability may be judged from his friends, whom she names. — James Joyce, who in return for a life-long friendship, made him (Oliver St. John Gogarty) Buck Mulligan of Ulysses fame. Then come men like Walter Starkie and Synge and Moore, whose Confessions of a Young Man are so idyllic. Mabel Greene knows what will go down with her American readers, so she adds: 'Dr. Gogarty was educated at Oxford and received his medical degree at Trinity.' Should we remark that either of those homes of learning gives him every right to be called a great Irishman? Mabel Greene, for we are sure it was never the Doctor himself who did it, has given to the readers of this same journal the deathless lines aptly named 'The Swan Song'. With this latter testimonial to superior literature and modern ethics, who can doubt about the Doctor being a true representative of the new spirit in Irish literature!

One of the best pieces of advertising on the part of Oliver St. John Gogarty was being featured in a New York daily with John MacCormack and Yeats and Joseph Campbell. It is quite possible that Campbell may not know of what discerning Irishmen think of Yeats, Gogarty and Co., but John MacCormack's recent sojourn in Ireland gives him no excuse. All that was wanted to complete the scene was John giving a vocal expression to the 'Swan Song', and during that performance wearing, of course, the *signa* of all conferred honours.[11]

During the American visit he arranged with George P. Brett of the Macmillan Company of New York for the publication of a substantial

book, *Selected Poems,* and with the publisher's consent asked Bip
Pares (who later prepared the striking dust jacket for *I Follow Saint
Patrick*) to design a wrapper.

Commenting on a poem to James Stephens which concludes with
a question: 'What can have happened James?' Brett wrote, 'How you
have hit the nail on the head with that poem to our friend James
Stephens. It isn't only Ireland that misses him; his public misses
him. If he could only be persuaded to give his anxious and waiting
public something real again!'[12]

His fear that parts of 'The Old Woman of Beare' might give offence

> *Now each bargain driving clown*
> *Wants two ups for one go down;*
> *God, if I reciprocated*
> *They would think themselves castrated!*

— was eased by Horace Reynolds: 'Incidentally I don't think you
have to worry about that poem's reverberations in Amherst: Amherst
is a pretty liberal place, and people, even College presidents' wives,
are getting more and more accustomed to seeing written what they
daily — nay, nightly — think.'[13]

On 12 May 1933 Brett expressed bright hopes: 'I think this collection is going to make a very fine book. I hope we shall be able to do
well with it. Things seem to be changing over here somewhat. Book-
stores are more optimistic and it is my fond hope that by the time
your book is ready for publication we shall be able to get a sale for it
which will be commensurate with its merits.'[14]

(The good fairies who presided over Gogarty's birth cannot have
been far away on 25 July 1933 when the plane he was flying crashed
when landing at Baldonnel. The plane nose-dived, ran into a sheep
and turned upside down. Gogarty was thrown clear and escaped with
a few bruises.)

In those days, untroubled by computers, events in publishing
moved more quickly than at present and by December *Selected
Poems* was out. Gogarty expressed his satisfaction to Brett: 'The
form of the volume has been much admired by those who are competent to judge such matters and the contents by those who are not.
So I am not only satisfied but personally indebted and very grateful
to you and your firm....'[15] He wrote again on 31 January 1934
to draw attention to an error in 'Leda and the Swan' where *hardness*
should read *harness* and arranged for a presentation copy to Augustus
John to be inscribed 'The only copy sent to Europe'.[16]

Brett sent good news in February: 'The sales of your *Selected Poems* go on. Neither of us is going to wax rich from the publication but it is an awfully nice addition to our list. We are proud to have it.'[17] Horace Reynolds wrote to say, 'Your Selected Poems had nothing but praise. It has made its way surely to a deserved place near Yeats's recent volumes.'[18]

In 1934 he contributed an epilogue to a projected book of poems by Scharmel Iris (for which W.B. Yeats wrote a preface) but the manuscript was mislaid and not until 1953 was Iris's *Bread Out of Stone* published. 'Why have I not heard of Scharmel Iris before this?' Gogarty asked. 'Because of the critics who are like eunuchs posing as authorities on procreation. They don't know a thing about it. It takes a poet to appreciate poetry. They alone have the receiving sets that are attuned to brave translunary things.'

Sean MacEntee, Minister for Industry and Commerce in the Fianna Fáil government, said that Senator Gogarty reminded him of a surgeon operating with a pickaxe. His outspokenness made him an unlikely choice for office in the Upper House despite which he had ambitions to become Vice-Chairman and had wished to put his name forward as a candidate for the position in 1932 when Senator Michael F. O'Hanlon was elected. At a party meeting in December 1934 to select a candidate for the forthcoming election of Vice-Chairman, the Chairman, Dr. W. O'Sullivan, suggested that it should be 'the old horse for the same post' meaning O'Hanlon, but Gogarty stood up, wishing to nominate Senator Duggan as an alternative.

'Sit down Gogarty or clear out', the chairman said peremptorily. Gogarty left the room. Some days later he sent an indignant letter to President Cosgrave complaining that free discussion of a choice of candidate had not been permitted and that rather than obey the party whip and vote for O'Hanlon he wished to resign.[19] In his reply Cosgrave pointed out that it was not his business to accept the resignation of a senator. He ended his letter on a note of moderation: 'I want you to support O'Hanlon — if you have definitely made up your mind that you won't please let me know early to-morrow and whether you do or not stop that nonsense about retiring.'[20] The senator did as he was asked and supported O'Hanlon but on 19 December 1934 Michael Comyn secured one vote more than O'Hanlon (26 to 25) and displaced him as Vice-Chairman.

The aspirants to literary fame who had been unsettled by the foundation of the Irish Academy of Letters were again disturbed, but now on a much wider scale, by the news in May 1935 that W.B. Yeats had been appointed editor of the *Oxford Book of Modern Verse.*[21] The recognition of inclusion would be a much-prized consummation, whereas to be passed over was a possibility, to think of which, cast the established poets into the depths of despair. 'Exclusion from the Academy was a disappointment...' Monk Gibbon admitted. 'But exclusion from the anthology was a definite blow.'[22] Gogarty was to have a prominent place among the elect.

Dear Gogarty: The Oxford University Press has asked me to prepare a collection of modern verse, from Gerard Hopkins to the present day. I should be glad if you would kindly give me permission to include in it the poems on the attached sheet. Full acknowledgements would of course be made in the book. Your permission will, no doubt, cover America. Yours faithfully, W.B. Yeats.

Yeats added a handwritten postscript: 'This letter is the work of the Press sent for my signature. I think you are perhaps the greatest master of the pure lyric now writing in English. I am asking for a lot, but don't charge me too much. I can get you a thousand readers for every ten your publisher can get you.'[23]

On 24 October 1935 Yeats wrote to thank Gogarty for his permission 'and for your nobility in omitting the "jingle of the guinea". You need not be afraid of being put too near Hopkins; I do not even mention him in my introduction and I do mention you with much praise.'[24]

When Shane Leslie sought Gogarty's help in preparing an anthology of verse he agreed to co-operate but insisted that the terms of reference must not be drawn up to exclude Yeats 'who brought the Pre-Raphaelite movement to the Celtic twilight and no one has diagnosed it but I. If you read his wholly inordinate and undeserved "featuring" of my poor verses in The Oxford Book of English Verse due to day, you will see how ungrateful I would become (not that I cared a damn if he had left me out with Dunsany and the rest) were I to exclude him from an anthology with which I was associated.'

Considering the delays inseparable from publishing it seemed unlikely that their book would appear in Yeats's lifetime. Nevertheless, Gogarty was determined to keep the faith he had:

in the greatest lyrist and Kalliurge, the most procreant creator

of Beauty within an Irish landscape that Dublin or for that
matter, Ireland produced. So long as 'The Host is riding from
Knocknarea' I must keep bit by bit. Even to look at him in
his old-age is to see the King of the fairies, to see Angus of the
Birds.[25]

The *Oxford Book of Modern Verse* was published on 19 November 1936. Its most furious detractor was Lord Alfred Douglas who
sent a telegram to Yeats:

> Your omission of my work from the absurdly-named Oxford
> Book of Modern Verse is exactly typical of the attitude of the
> minor to the major poet. For example Thomas Moore, the Yeats
> of the 19th century, would undoubtedly have excluded Keats
> and Shelley from any anthology he had compiled. And why
> drag in Oxford? Would not shoneen Irish be a more correct
> description?

So many critics expressed surprize at the omission of the war poet
Wilfred Owen that Yeats explained to Dorothy Wellesley that he had
not realized that he was excluding a 'revered sandwich-board man of
the revolution' but he was unrepentant. 'He is all blood, dirt and
sucked sugar stick.... There is every excuse for him, but none for
those who like him.'[26] Notable Irish omissions were Austin Clarke
and Seumas O'Sullivan. Six of F.R. Higgins's poems were included
and seventeen of Gogarty's, a number which caused raised eyebrows
some of which remain lifted to this day when by a curious reversal
of any ordinary standard of awards the apparent disproportion is
usually held to Gogarty's discredit.

James Stephens who had none of the spite of 'the blind and ignorant
town' in his make-up was a welcome exception. He sent Gogarty
a congratulatory note ('I think that after Yeats himself you are the
best poet of our land') to which he added these few lines:

> *This is all rather out of the blue:*
> *Take it as meant, as friendly, as true,*
> *Good poet! tis good to do homage to you.*[27]

which supports the earlier judgement of AE whose reference to
Ireland's 'best singers' goes some way to explaining Gogarty's de-
valuation in our own day. The lucidity of his 'lighter lyric line',
the melody of rhyme and rhythm which he so prized have less appeal

in an age when a strident cacophony prevails. It is interesting that Ernest Dowson, another poet to whom Yeats may have been over-generous in space, is equally *démodé*.

While it is generally accepted that no anthology can please every-body it seems that Yeats's *Oxford Book* pleased nobody. Even Gogarty knew that he had been disproportionately favoured and mentioned it to Horace Reynolds: 'Yeats's *Oxford Book of English Verse* which he is editing is said to be very odd: only titled ladies and a few friends admitted. This however does not include Dunsany! I am in 14 times,'[28] but he could not, however, have foreseen how this would continue to rankle. More than forty years later when his name is mentioned this old story of Yeats's resented generosity is brought up immediately. As if it mattered a fig! What matters is that in Yeats's judgement (surely not lightly to be set aside?) Gogarty was a superb lyric poet.

Besides, in retrospect is not the furore over this book nonsensical? Could poetry be weighed in grammes, or measured in millimetres, to balance eminence and achievement, all would be well, but its appreciation depends on the varying scale of human affect; the line or stanza delighting one reader is banal, sentimental or flat to another. An anthology is an extended expression of personal choice and Yeats's choice deserves to be defended. He himself defended it when writing to Dorothy Wellesley:

Recent attacks have concentrated on my putting in you & Gogarty — the last because he sings a brave song & so makes a whinging propaganda look ridiculous. You because you are a woman of rank (their hatred is, to use a phrase of Balfour's intemperate youth, 'a fermentation of their desire to lick your boots') & because I have left out Wilfred Owen who seems to me a bad poet though a good letter writer. One American fury mentions neither you nor Owen but denounces Gogarty & Wilfred Blunt (Wilfred Blunt did seversl anti-pacifist things including Bull-fighting).[29]

The verses of Pound, Eliot, Auden and poets whose work had the substance of philosophy did not really appeal to him. 'These new men are goldsmiths working with a glass screwed into one eye, whereas we walk ahead of the crowd, its swordsmen, its jugglers, looking to right and left.' Ahead of the crowd with 'swift indiffe-rent men' like Oliver Gogarty, the swashbuckling surgeon-poet, and Ernest Dowson the dissolute Bohemian of the Rhymers' Club. It was a valid expression of preference.

By this time Gogarty's first major prose work should have been published but some days before the *Oxford Book* came out he explained the delay to Shane Leslie: 'By the way, Rich and Cowan have broken their agreement to publish within 9 months of Jan. 13th last. One of their agents showed uncorrected, unrevised and unexpurgated galleys round the Law Library and United Arts Club roughly bound!'[30]

The original intention was to call the book *The Flashing Phoenix* but he eventually took the title from an old Dublin ballad which, he informed Horace Reynolds, 'Joyce found and rescued from oblivion and obloquy'[31] in Faithful Place —

> *As I was going down Sackville Street*
> *Hey, Ho me Randy O!*
> *Three bloody fine whores did I chance to meet*
> *With me gallopin', rearin' Randy O!*

Unfortunately, instead of becoming the best-seller he hoped for, it earned him notoriety.

As I Was Going Down Sackville Street was published in London and New York in 1937. The illustrated American version was the more handsome book with an introduction by Francis Hackett[32] who adopted something of Gogarty's own trenchancy, declaring him to be 'at once sensitive and savage, poet and ghoul, hero and knave'. There are, too, some textual differences, perhaps editorially determined with the object of avoiding ennui (certain characters would have had little relevancy for American readers) and placating enemies. Even so, both contained passages which, as Hackett said, 'in olden days would very likely have provoked a duel' but unfortunately the London lawyers were less alert to libel.

Sackville Street is an astonishingly outspoken book which even today causes the reader to wince; a record of political disillusion, which at the time of publication may have seemed redolent of vindictive disappointment, it gains credibility from the changed mood of modern Ireland. Not until the 1970s has anyone dared to echo Gogarty's valid defiance of the cult of political martyrology: 'Damn the vampire dead who have left us nothing but a heritage of hatred'.

It is a topsy-turvy book of mixed mood and reversed narrative adopting a pattern set by Endymion, Dublin's wisest fool, who wore cuffs on his ankles to indicate that he did not walk like other men with his feet on the ground. Its happy ending is set in the high hills in the author's early manhood; it commences in a city street some twenty years later. The hills provide an important vantage point from which to view the city, the hero of a book abounding in anti-heroes:

> We were on a high and pleasant shelf. To see the valley it would be necessary to walk a hundred yards to the road; whence to the south-east stood the peaks of the Golden Spears, the Head of Bray, and beyond, a floor of shining sea. Some miles behind, a point might be reached from which Dublin could be seen smoke-veiled in its plain: St. Patrick's Cathedral seemingly still its highest and greyest mass beneath a pall of smoke though Christ Church is higher. The dear and fog-crowned Athens of my youth![33]

From the Golden Age of unrealized ambitions that we return to in the last chapter, Gogarty has travelled far and met a multitude; he retraces his steps with characteristic and unwise exuberance, equally lavish with praise and blame, but never failing to place Dublin in a frame of loveliness:

> Step by step along the deep brown granite footpath we walked, aware of the rose-red city in the evening glow....
> West against the sunset the roofs of Mercer's shone: Union Street, Aberdeen is its counterpart. Again on our left the glory of Spring as the men of Dublin of old knew it; purple with the lilac and gold with laburnum; and the hawthorn about to whiten. Old enough now to be acceptable as natural and not artificial, these old squares must have represented the height of landscape gardening in the days when they were laid out. Powder and peruke and sedan chairs: as gracious as Versailles. The facade of the College of Surgeons gleamed like a Greek temple beyond the lake and waterfall of Stephen's Green. What a magnifying lens was that country that made Parthenons for those who had eyes to see in every city? The pillars on the Acropolis are honey-coloured in the bright air, but these are white and grey, through moving veils of green.[34]

On the first page Endymion, a creature of dreams, sets off to their disadvantage specimens of a new order ('two tall T.D.'s, heavily moustached and carelessly tailored and coiffeured, were bidding goodbye to each other, hiding in the fervour of their handshake all the contempt they mutually reserved',) and on the last we take leave of Professor Yelverton Tyrrell and 'The Master of Those Who

Know', elderly dons of Trinity College, an erudite and incomparable pair who doze in the sun while their irrepressible disciple projects his imagination over the roofs of a Sackville Street that will be renamed, pondering with uncommon honesty what we have gained and lost. The intervening chapters epitomize an epoch which saw the demise of an elite and the birth of the Irish Free State: Gogarty was well placed to witness both the decline and the accouchement with its bitter after-pains, and this gives *Sackville Street* a unique value.

In a laudatory review Austin Clarke[35] pointed to George Moore who made characters of his friends and fellow-authors in *Hail and Farewell* as the originator of a genre: 'Certainly the disconsolate fairies of the Celtic Twilight vanished and the playboys took their place. Even James Joyce, who might have been an Irish Huysmans, was swept into the irresistible comedy of Dublin and gave us the immense Bloom...' Another critic ('M.N.C.') took Gogarty to task in *Ireland To-day* for evading the trouble of supplying a beginning, a middle and an end, but by an odd coincidence James Stephens happened to point out in his notice that 'Dublin has neither beginning, nor end, nor middle'. Stephens's own complaint was a valid one:

> The villain of this book is our own war and wars, and here Gogarty has capitulated. He writes of this in bad temper. A writer must be able to write of bad temper, but not in bad temper, and parts of this fine book are irked by inability to get into this matter by removing himself from it.

Such admirable detachment was alien to Gogarty and besides he wished to present Dublin with all its fantasy, its bitterness and ruth — 'let it portray itself as it is every day'; furthermore, his peevishness is more acceptable in the light of a historian's description of the years in which it was written as 'the most sombre period in recent Irish history.'[36] Donal O'Sullivan, who made that judgment, could not have known that a darker period would follow, or that the generation cradled in the early years of the state would in maturity look askance at the maladroit handling of their inheritance. How interesting to find so many of our present discontents recorded in *Sackville Street*! The changing face of republicanism, the repression of sex and compulsory Irish are topics which columnists and television commentators treat as newly-discovered ills, but these and others — the muzzling of the press, our chauvinism and lack of enterprise, and neglect of art, the plight of Dublin hospitals — are topics which Gogarty discusses without restraint.

The least controversial topic and one where matters have improved is the shameful neglect of writers and authors. Always prepared to couple his complaints, Gogarty bewails money wasted on compulsory Irish:

I thought of the £4,000,000 spent on Gaelic culture which consisted in bemusing children with Esperantisised Irish and making them fall more readily victims to the Communist and Demagogue. And I thought of the fate of Harry Clarke, that supreme colourist in glass, who lived in Frederick Street, to see the window he did for the Irish Hall at Geneva (of course it had to be Geneva, for the eyes of a fool of a Nation are on the ends of the earth) turned down by the Government who commissioned it because a figure of two celebrating Irish exiled authors were in the nude. The money spent is attempting to turn this nation into a race of bilingualists ignorant and gullible in two languages, would have given Dublin spacious streets and boulevards and restored it to the place it held as the Seventh City of Christendom before Napoleonic Paris was Built.[37]

But civic pride remains where it was when Yeats spoke of Paudeen's pence and Biddy's halfpennies. The neglect of our waterways, however, is greater now than when Gogarty pointed out that 'no city neglects its river as Dublin does. There is not a pleasure boat on the Liffey from Butt Bridge to Lucan. If the river and town were in England there would be water-gardens and boat-houses and people delighting themselves in the lovely amenities of the water.'

Within the present decade the news media have been quick to protect their traditional freedoms. Their plight may be more fortunate (or their zeal greater) than their predecessors of the 1930s when, according to *Sackville Street,* it was necessary to read the English papers for unbiased and unsuppressed news — the Irish government has 'freedom from the Press' and owned a Press 'which has no freedom from the Government'.

Passing to a rather abstract discussion which shows how little times have changed, there was a recent storm in *The Irish Times* correspondence columns concerning the relationship between celibacy and holiness, a subject on which Gogarty had spoken, though not on the side of the angels: 'Subjugating their sex becomes an object in itself, as if gelding were godliness.'

More controversial is Gogarty's attitude towards the politics of his times — indeed one would avoid raking embers of the past were it not that their dull glow lights torches to fire other holocausts — but if the growing generation judges that the indictments of *Sackville Street* are admissible then it has lessons to teach them.

Though John Kells Ingram repudiated the sentiments expressed in his 'Memory of the Dead', and Mahaffy — 'Mahaffy is better known in Oxford than in College Green' — and the dons who amused Gogarty were political reactionaries of the most die-hard type, Dublin University has an adequate revolutionary tradition. Whether or not Gogarty's political interests were kindled there, he was, as we have seen involved in Sinn Féin from its foundation.

In espousing the cause of Sinn Féin Gogarty thought he was 'going towards Freedom and breaking down a Bastille', but like earlier revolutionaries he had not reckoned with an aftermath in which erstwhile visionaries appeared in the guise of 'rogues and ruffians calling robbery Republicanism'. The doleful hindsight of more recent years now invests his comments with an element of prophecy:

> Once Republicans get into office, it becomes the turn of the disgruntled to delve deeper for the pay-dirt of the 'Republic' through adits so narrow that they can be counted on to defy anyone drawing a salary as a Minister. They become truer Republicans... So inaccessibly true that the only way one can co-operate with them is by giving them a vote towards office and a thousand pounds a year less Income Tax and free motoring. Then they hand on the baton, or rather, the baton is taken up by a still lower stratum, who in turn become inaccessible or rather, in what is to be next turn, unapproachable...[38]

The buffeting of the war of ideas and ideologies stings less acutely than the hurt pride and injured self-esteem resulting from more personally-directed invective. The following passage (the adjectives used in the American edition are still more offensive) is an example of Gogarty's vituperation and must have incensed his political opponents:

> I could never countenance this euphemism 'Irregulars',[39] They are mostly town riff-raff, misled, or country dupes and discontents whom de Valera aroused when he found that his methods had landed him in a minority.[40]

While the appropriateness of Gogarty's rebukes can be convincingly argued it has to be conceded that their repetition was inartistic.

The ranting and rodomontade of *Sackville Street* have in the end served him ill, drawing attention away from finer qualities of a mind particularly sensitive to the beauty of nature:

> I am aware of the many shades of green which make up to me in exquisite delight for the neglect and want of development of music within me. Is it not a sign of some sort of depravity to be moved overmuch by the shades of green? Maybe, but the harmonies of the tones by which Spring astonishes my eyes are more to me, though transient, than all the vocable glories of everlasting noise.

Nevertheless, this was the effect he was striving for in a Dantesque tour leading from the political Inferno of the 1930s to the far-off Paradise of his youth.[41]

14

Trial by Jury

'Have you read Gogarty's book?' Yeats asked an English friend. 'Here everybody is reading it. A publican down on the quays told a customer: "You can open it anywhere, like the *Imitation of Christ.*" It is not all wit, one can say of it, as somebody said I think of Raleigh, it is "high, insolent and passionate".'[1] The insolence in his own case included the comment that he had at last found the Land of Heart's Desire in the Kildare Street Club but Yeats forgave Gogarty because he showed no hint of self-complacency.

Reminded, like Austin Clarke, of *Hail and Farewell,* Terence de Vere White has said it was Moore again, with less malice and less art.[2] But there was sufficient malice to pepper the pages. Some of his victims were dead and beyond caring, such as Tim Healy, the Governor-General, whom he diminished with the taunt: 'he took the shilling of the Sassenach, without spending in the city the foreigner's pound'; others like W.T. Cosgrave ('whose piety greatly embarrassed His Holiness, the Pope') may have allowed him the licence of an unreliable jester, but one of the Sinclair twins, a Jewish antiques dealer, took him to court.

William A. Sinclair and his brother Harry had a business in Nassau Street. The former, known to his friends as 'the Boss' or 'the Beard' or 'Sink' was the more dynamic of the pair. Beatrice Elvery (later Lady Glenavy), finding him difficult to describe, fell back on the phrase 'a colourful personality.'[3] His temperament was artistic rather than commercial and he disliked his day-to-day work intensely. 'He hated things so much that he hated people buying them', Sir William Orpen recalled, 'and he loved thing so much that he hated to let them go — so as a dealer he was a failure. But as a friend he was a glorious success.'

Gogarty spent a good deal of time in his company during the years of amity with Orpen and addressed friendly lines to him that are a contrast to those written later —

> *Often times of you I think*
> *Sink!*

*And your vision has appeared,
Beard!*

Boss Sinclair's proposal of marriage to Cissie Beckett earned the dis-
approval of the Becketts, and the acceptance of the young woman
herself. She had already shown a streak of independence from bour-
geois values by studying art in Paris with the Elvery sisters and
Estella Solomons. The Sinclairs settled in a tiny cottage on the Hill
of Howth moving later to a larger one to accommodate their five
children. According to Beatrice Glenavy, Cissie and the Boss

> ... kept open house for all the poets, writers and painters
> of Dublin; indeed, for all the freaks and oddities as well. A
> sort of permanent party seemed to be going on there with
> endless talk and drink and intermittent music and dancing.
> It was lively, warm and human, with children tumbling all
> over the place.

Cissie was plain and good-natured; her husband had charm but 'tried
to invest himself with an outsize Walt Whitman-like quality' which
made him seem comic rather than impressive and may explain why
he attracted the mockery of Gogarty and others.

The revels on Howth led to falling profits in Nassau Street where
the antiques shop failed to support two families. Soon after the first
World War, W.A. Sinclair's decision to settle with his wife and
children in Kassell, Germany, astonished Sir William Orpen:

> The very idea of Sinclair leaving Ireland seems inconceivable,
> he loved it so much. I have never known a man who loved the
> hills, the gorse, the sea as he did. He gloried in the summer
> heat, he gloried in the winter storms. Even in mid-winter, he
> would ramble over the Hill of Howth at early dawn, and scramble
> down the cliffs to plunge his body into the waters of the bay.[4]

His intention was to occupy himself writing articles on art and to
buy paintings and antiques for shipment to Dublin, an enterprise
that ended in 1933 when, aware of the growing hostility to Jews,
the Sinclairs forfeited their possessions and returned to Ireland.
Meanwhile, their nephew, Samuel Beckett, had been a frequent
visitor and in 1934 the Boss incurred the icy displeasure of Mrs.
Beckett, who disliked him cordially, by arriving at the Beckett
home, Cooldrinagh, Foxrock, in a state of advanced inebriation
after a long session in the Bailey Restaurant.

A victim of fortune, W.A. Sinclair, whose wife was already ailing with rheumatoid arthritis,[5] now fell ill with pulmonary tuberculosis. He was treated unavailingly in Newcastle Sanatorium and died in circumstances approaching destitution, in the County Home, Rathdrum, County Wicklow, on 4 May 1937. A few weeks before his death he read his former friend's unpleasant comments.

It is hardly possible that when he wrote the controversial passages Oliver Gogarty was aware that misfortune had overtaken the Boss but, inevitably, the circumstances of that death appear to add to the affront and only the cynical will reflect that the opportunity for financial gain now presented to the plaintiff was irresistible although, in Samuel Beckett's opinion, the case taken by Henry Morris ('Harry') Sinclair turned out, more than anything else, to be an opportunity to rake over the family manure.[6]

Pending an action for libel which could not be heard until later in the year, Sinclair sought an injunction against further publication of *As I Was Going Down Sackville Street* which in his affidavit he alleged to be 'a reservoir of filth and the grosser forms of vulgarity'. His application which was supported by the affidavit of Mr. Samuel Beckett of Cooldrinagh, Foxrock, was granted by Mr. Justice Hanna on 7 June 1937.[7]

George Redding referred to the impending case in a letter to Gogarty from Park Royal at the end of September. 'When does Harry claim the pound of flesh? The general opinion was when I was in Dublin that he would get some damages, but nothing excessive as there is a good deal of feeling against Jews owing to the recent influx in Dublin.'[8] He expressed no misgivings regarding his own contributions — the questionable verses were actually Redding's — and it seems that he and Gogarty regarded Sinclair-baiting as a legitimate and praiseworthy activity. For years they had amused themselves at the twins' expense; the following lines written by Redding in 1918 prudently remained unpublished:

> When nature brought forth at a birth
> Two Jews instead of one,
> She saw the work was nothing worth
> And wished it all undone;
> She did not bargain for a pair
> Nor favour either twin,
> From Harry's head she drew the hair
> To put on Willie's chin.[9]

Gogarty's contributions to this unkind game[10] include three poems published in *Hyperthuleana*, 'To a Clever Little Lecher', 'To a Bearded Dealer in Old Objects of Art', and 'The Dandelion':

> *I saw a Dandelion gray in Spring,*
> *The blossom of the ash-pit of the town;*
> *Its thatch, like little thoughts, each puff did fling*
> *Until it bent it half baldheaded down.*
> *But deeply-rooted in the acrid earth*
> *Amongst discarded things it safely grew:*
> *To smite it had but multiplied its birth —*
> *Therefore I left it as I now leave you.*

The hearing commenced in the High Court on Monday 22 November before Mr. Justice O'Byrne and a jury. Incidentally, the only woman called for jury service, Miss Dorothy McArdle the author of *The Irish Republic,* was successfully challenged by the plaintiff's solicitors, Messrs Reddin and Reddin. The courtroom was crowded with lawyers, witnesses, journalists and spectators, the friends and supporters of the plaintiff and defendant and whatever uninvolved spectators could get places in what promised to be the most diverting trial of the year.

The judge, the very symbol of impartial justice, dominated the scene but the bewigged barristers attracted greater attention, vociferous purveyors of what each hoped to pass off as truth to the vitally important but very ordinary looking men in the jury box. The plaintiff, Henry Morris Sinclair, antiques dealer and jeweller, was represented by Albert E. Wood, K.C., Joseph A. McCarthy, K.C. and Ernest M. Wood. The defendant's counsel were J.M. Fitzgerald, K.C., Brereton Barry, K.C. and Oliver D. Gogarty.

The statement of claim quoted two passages alleged to contain an indecent and foul libel, the first:

'And one thing more — where can we buy antiques?'
'Nassau Street, Sackville Street, Liffey Street, where Naylor's is and all along the quays. Have you not heard?'

> *"Two Jews grew in Sackville Street*
> *And not in Piccadilly.*
> *One was gaitered on the feet,*
> *The other one was Willie.*
> *And if you took your pick of them,*
> *Whichever one you choose,*

> *You'd like the other more than him,*
> *So wistful were these Jews.*
> *They kept a shop for objects wrought*
> *By masters famed of old,*
> *Where you, no matter what you bought*
> *Were genuinely sold.*
> *But Willie spent the sesterces*
> *And brought on strange disasters*
> *Because he sought new mistresses*
> *More keenly than old masters.*
> *"The other...."*[11]

Only the first two stanzas appeared in the English edition. The second passage:

'Very well,' said I. 'You must know that George is not only the elegantae arbiter of Dublin, but a critic of the grosser forms of licence. Now, there was an old usurer who had eyes like a pair of periwinkles on which somebody had been experimenting with a pin, and a nose like a shrunken tomato, one side of which swung independently of the other. The older he grew the more he pursued the immature, and enticed little girls into his office. That was bad enough; but he had grandsons, and these directed the steps of their youth to follow in grandfather's footsteps, with more zeal than discrimination. I explained the position to George, who, after due fermentation, produced the following pronunciamento:
"It is a thing to wonder at, but hardly to admire,
How they who do desire the most, guard most against desire:
They choose their friend or mistress so that none may yearn to touch her.
Thus did the twin grandchildren of the ancient Chicken Butcher...." '[12]

Gogarty's defence was that if he did write or publish the words complained of (which was denied) the words were purely fictitious and did not refer to individuals living or dead.

Addressing the jury Albert Wood explained that there were two Sinclair twins, Henry the plaintiff and William who was dead; they were the grandsons of Morris Harris 'the old usurer' of the book who was pilloried by Gogarty.[13] 'With no mercy and with no pity he had pursued the memory of the plaintiff's grandfather as a ghoul, and had applied no mercy and no pity to William Sinclair his one time friend, and to the plaintiff, whom he had pursued with a savagery and ghoulishness which could only fit in with the aberrations of an amoral mind in a pot-boiling scurrility run for the private gain of the author.'

Harris's second marriage, in 1891, to a woman much younger than himself was unhappy; when divorce proceedings we.e instituted in 1906 his wife accused him of enticing little girls into his office for immortal purposes. This was a well-known fact, Wood pointed out. How, then, could the jury believe Dr. Oliver St. John Gogarty when he maintained that it was fiction?

'I wonder,' said Mr. Wood, 'will any literary experts come forward to confuse the plain terms in the case? Will they have the audacity to contend that these vile and venomous libels have the ring of folklore, that they have a high technical character, that they are witty, that they have verbal dexterity, or that they have the feeling of Elizabethan speech? They may, but when they have gone you will be left with this grave and serious libel unexplained. These libels, at most, appeal to the abnormal few who live to perpetuate spicy smut. Is there a hope that a Jew will not receive justice from a Dublin jury? Is it the gambler's throw? Throughout all our chequered history one of the great traditions of our city is that it has never persecuted the Jews, and I know, members of the jury that you will preserve that tradition.'

The first witnesses called were some booksellers whose evidence confirmed that *Sackville Street* was widely circulated; Herbert E. Pembury of Greene's bookshop had sold fifty-five copies of the English edition and a dozen American copies; Walter Hanna had sold eight-six; 136 copies were sold by Combridges; Eason's had sold eighty-two.

The plaintiff was then called. He confirmed that Morris Harris was his grandfather and that he and his twin brother had been adopted by Harris and brought up in the Jewish faith. He recalled that in the winter of 1933, while having a drink with Dr. Gogarty in the smokeroom of the Shelbourne Hotel, the latter read verses in which two Jews figured whereupon Sinclair had said that if they were published he would sue him.

Cross-examining, the defendant's leading counsel, Mr. Fitzgerald, sought to discredit Sinclair and impute unworthy motives. He extracted the information that his father was a member of the Church of Ireland, that Sinclair was not a Jewish name but that of a family dedicated to St. Clair of Assisi and suggested that no one would identify him as Jewish.

'You never carried on business in Sackville Street?'

'No.'

'But there are at the present time members of your adopted Church who do carry on business in Sackville Street?'

'Probably there are.'

'I suggest', said Fitzgerald, 'that there is no warrant for your claim that the two Jews who grew in Sackville Street meant you and your brother, who were flourishing in Nassau Street.'

'But it does mean that,' Sinclair rejoined weakly. 'As I was going down Sackville Street means Dublin,' the plaintiff insisted but counsel's words were for the jury and were not forgotten by them.

'Would you recognise your grandfather as an old usurer?'

'There would be a great many people who would immediately recognise him.'

Fitzgerald then attacked the plaintiff's motives.

'I suggest that there is no justification for the bringing of the action by you and that it can only have one object — you want to make money out of it.'

'I have not brought this case for money. I originally wanted to take criminal proceedings.'

'Why didn't you?' Fitzgerald asked quickly.

'My solicitor Mr. Hays advised me to drop that.'

'He said "drop it",' Fitzgerald said, scoring a point, 'and you dropped him.'

Replying to his cross-examination the plaintiff denied that Samuel Beckett, who had made an affidavit, was a relative. Mr. Beckett's aunt had married the plaintiff's brother.

'I think he is a little more kind than kin,' Fitzgerald rapped out. 'This gentleman who calls himself an author, was the only person you could find to make an affidavit to identify yourself and your brother as the persons hit at in the so-called libel?'

'The time was very short and I wanted to stop this book.'

John Murray, an elderly Duke Street optician who remembered Morris Harris, testified that he had read Gogarty's book and had immediately come to the conclusion that the reference was to the Sinclairs. Morris Harris was an antiques dealer but had been associated with money-lending and might fairly be described as 'an old usurer'.

Brindsley Gerty, formerly a Dawson Street antiques dealer, said that when he read the book he immediately identified the 'two Jews' with the Sinclairs of Nassau Street.

'When you read the lines, "One was gaitered on the feet, the other one was Willie," what struck you?' asked Mr. Wood.

'In business,' Gerty replied, 'we often had a difficulty if the names of the Sinclairs turned up as to which one it was, and it would frequently be asked: "Is it the fellow that wears the gaiters or the fellow with the whiskers?" '

The next witness was Samuel Beckett — the success that lay ahead of this obscure young writer was then totally unsuspected, especially by Mr. Fitzgerald who treated him with great disrespect. Beckett said that on reading the book he immediately identified the persons referred to as Mr. Harry and Mr. William Sinclair.

'How did you get the book?' Fitzgerald asked.

'I purchased it.'

'Was it at the suggestion of Mr. Sinclair that you got it?'

'Partially.'

'When did he suggest to you that you should have a look at it?'

'Early in May, I think.'

'I presume he told you he thought there was a grave libel on him?'

'He told me he thought he had been libelled.'

'You have made an affidavit,' counsel said to the witness, but his words were for the jury, 'in which you led the Court to believe that you were an impartial, independent person, but you forgot to tell the court that it was your uncle-in-law who suggested that you buy the book.'

'I said in my affidavit,' replied Beckett, 'that my attention was attracted to this book because of the notoriety of the author and the attention it had received.'

Having established that Beckett had left Foxrock and lived in Paris, Fitzgerald scornfully examined his credentials as a writer.

'You describe yourself as an author. What have you written to justify that?'

'I have written verse, fiction and literary criticism.'

'I think you have started on Marcel *Prowst* — '

Fitzgerald on purpose mispronounced Proust's name knowing that Beckett would correct him, such smartness alienating a Dublin jury.[14] 'Was he a man who indulged in the psychology of sex?'

'I have not been aware of that.'

'But you have written about him. How long did it take before your book was banned by the Censorship Board of Ireland?'

'About six months.'

'I suggest that it was banned because it was a blasphemous and obscene book.'

'I never discovered why it was banned.'

Counsel read a passage from the book describing a conversation between 'the Polar Bear' and a Jesuit priest and suggested that it caricatured the Redeemer.

'Do you call yourself a Christian, Jew or Atheist?' he asked Beckett.

'None of the three.'

Fitzgerald also established and made much of the fact that Beckett was the author of a privately-printed book, *Horoscope,* with the letter *W* prefixed.

Other witnesses for the plaintiff before the court adjourned at the end of the first day included Mr. Hays, his former solicitor, Mr. J. Mitchel Amers, a friend whom Harry Sinclair had met in Jammet's, and Mrs. Vivienne Ganly, formerly Sinclair's private secretary. When the case was called on Tuesday morning Mr. Wood said that the plaintiff's case was closed. Mr. Justice O'Byrne then pointed out that the defendant denied that he wrote or published the words complained of and that he was not aware of any evidence to go to the jury on that point.

'There is in the book a photograph of the author,' Wood said realizing too late that the technicality of filing a copy of the book as evidence had been overlooked. 'He holds himself out as the author.'

'I have intimated to you,' Mr. Justice O'Byrne said, 'that in my opinion there is no evidence to go to the jury that would justify them in finding that the defendant wrote and published these words.'

For a moment it looked as if the case would collapse but Wood extricated himself from a nasty situation by taking the unusual step of calling the defendant as a witness for the plaintiff. In the witness box Gogarty agreed that he had written a fantasy in fact, *As I Was Going Down Sackville Street,* containing the questionable passages.[15]

'Did you know the late Mr. Morris Harris?' Wood asked him.

'No.'

'You knew Mr. William Sinclair?'

'I did.'

'You knew him by the name of "Willie"?'

'I did not. I knew him as "the Boss" as everybody else did.'

'You knew they were grandchildren of Mr. Morris Harris?'

'I did.'

'You knew they were twins?'

'I was not aware of that then. I may have known it, but it was not a thing that was always in my mind.'

Gogarty denied that Morris Harris was to be identified as 'that old usurer'; it was a composite picture. The twins were a Celtic symbol. The passage which must be considered as a whole was intended to throw discredit on usury and money-lending.

'You knew, of course,' Wood said, 'in regard to the line "one of them was gaitered and the other one was Willie" that William was one brother and that Mr. Henry Sinclair wore gaiters.'

'I think every Jew in Sackville Street wears gaiters.'

Gogarty explained that the name 'Willie' was used to rhyme with Piccadilly.

Wood asked him to explain what Sesterces are, obviously attributing to it some sex-laden symbolism.

'They are Roman coins of about the year 269 B.C. and they were each worth about four asses. They were the lowest form of copper coin known to the Romans.'

'You see no reason why any of the daily papers should put a blank instead of that word?'

'No.'

' "Brought on strange disasters". I take it that comment means venereal diseases?'

'No, it means the liquidation of the firm.'

'That is the Sinclairs?' Wood's quickly interposed question was intended to trap an unwary witness.

'Not at all,' Gogarty said. 'The two Jews who lived in Sackville Street were the symbol for dishonest dealing in furniture.'

When Mr. Fitzgerald opened the case for the defence he referred to the interest aroused by the action and the large crowd seeking places in the courtroom whereas in recent weeks there had been tragic cases attracting no crowds. Nevertheless this case was actually an ordinary case and the fashionable crowds might have their hopes frustrated. All he asked from the jury was that they should act reasonably and judge for themselves what Mr. Sinclair was entitled to for what he alleged to be a broken or damaged reputation. But there was no evidence whatsoever that he had suffered the loss of old friends, or even of a single person.

Mr. Wood had compared Dr. Gogarty to one of those men who dive into ashbins for garbage but Fitzgerald said that the remark was a boomerang that struck at the plaintiff. Mr. Henry Morris Sinclair was engaged in the interesting task of searching the dustbin in the form of Dr. Gogarty's book, but he was not searching for garbage but for solid money from Dr. Gogarty.

'In my submission,' declared Fitzgerald, 'he is not entitled to one copper in this case.'

The jury, Fitzgerald insisted, were entitled to the evidence of reasonable men, witnesses other than those who had been induced, persuaded or cajoled to find .in the book support for the plaintiff and once more he attempted to discredit the latter, especially the principal witness, Beckett, 'the bawd and blasphemer from Paris'. Could the jury imagine 'that wretched creature' making representations to the High Court as an ordinary reasonable man?

With the freedom that barristers seem to enjoy to pillory witnesses Mr. Fitzgerald referred to Mr. Murray 'whose spectacles were, perhaps, useful in finding libels', Mr. Gerty who 'for some reason known to himself had ceased to be in business for twenty years', and Mrs. Ganly who had worked for Sinclair.

The 'reasonable men' called as defence witnesses were F.R. Higgins, ex-Senator Fanning, Professor William Fearon, R.M. Smyllie and Edmund Mooney.

Higgins could not identify anyone from the verses which he regarded as Dublin folk songs current in literary circles. He described a party in the Dolphin Hotel in 1936 at which Gogarty had recited the verses now said to be libellous. Mr. Sinclair who was present did not protest and the atmosphere was friendly and genial.

Michael Fanning had read the book without connecting the verses with the plaintiff. Fearon, Trinity College's professor of biochemistry and author of *Parnell of Avondale,* recalled verses beginning 'Two Jews' which were part of the current doggerel when he was a student at Cambridge. He could not identify *Sackville Street* with the Sinclairs and it had not occurred to him that the passages referred to any living person.

Smyllie, the editor of *The Irish Times,* had read the typescript before publication and in his opinion the passages were not defamatory. He did not relate them to any living person.

'There are rather vulgar verses in the book?' the cross-examining counsel said.

'Yes.'

'And anybody who is perpetuated by this smut or vulgar verse — would you agree that a very great wrong would be done to that person?'

'If I suspected for a moment that they did refer to anyone, I would agree with you.'

Edmund Mooney, a solicitor who knew Sinclair, but not Gogarty, was interested in Dublin life and manners. He had read the book with attention within a week of publication, including the particular passages.

'Did they point to Mr. Sinclair?' Fitzgerald asked.

'No.'

Charging the jury to deal with the matter with their minds and not their emotions Mr. Justice O'Byrne said they had to answer three questions: Were the words written and published by Dr. Gogarty? Did they apply to the plaintiff? Did they constitute libel? Of these the second was vital. There could be little doubt that the defendant was the author; if the passage referred to a particular individual it was certainly libellous; the question at issue, then, was whether these words were properly understood as referring to the plaintiff.

'When you come to consider this question,'the judge directed, 'it is not a question as to whether or not Dr. Gogarty, when writing those words, intended that they should apply to the plaintiff. Neither is it a question as to whether an outsider reading those words without any knowledge of the circumstances would understand them as referring to the plaintiff. It is a question of whether a person with a knowledge of the circumstances did accept these words as referring to the plaintiff — reasonably accept them. Now you must ask yourselves what would any reasonable person think of them — a reasonable person who knew all the circumstances.'

Reviewing the evidence the judge pointed out that Mr. Hays, the solicitor, had never read the book until Sinclair took it to his office to institute proceedings and for this reason he thought the jury would attribute less weight to Mr. Hays's evidence than they otherwise would have done. And Mr. Beckett had been cross-examined with reference to his own work: 'You heard the cross-examination,' Mr. Justice O'Byrne said. 'You saw the witness in the witness-box, and I have no doubt but that you will be able to apprise very accurately the amount of weight which you ought to attach to his testimony. He did not strike me as a very satisfactory witness. He did not strike me as a witness on whose word I personally would place a great deal of reliance. But when it comes to a question of weighing up the evidence and dealing with the weight to be attached to the testimony of different individuals, that is a matter entirely for you and not for me.'

On the question of damages, assuming that the words referred to the plaintiff, they must have regard to the identity of the defendant, a man whose identity lent greater import to the words than if written by somebody of lesser significance.

Having retired for an hour and three-quarters the jury's verdict, on their return, favoured Sinclair... They found that the passage containing four verses in the American edition did not refer to the Sinclairs and did not constitute libel but paragraph three of the statement of claim including the passage commencing 'Now, there was an old usurer' was libellous. They awarded the plaintiff £900 damages.

Later it was said that a juryman insisted, 'Whatever about the jewman he must be made to pay for what he said about de Valera.' Be that as it may, one cannot quarrel with the verdict but it was a regrettable episode, harming Gogarty's pocket, hurting his pride and damaging his literary career; and all the more regrettable because it could so easily have been avoided had the publisher's lawyers been more alert or had the author heeded Sinclair's warning that he would sue him.

Another regrettable aspect of the libel case is that it is used by those who accuse Gogarty of anti-semitism, a charge which in the real sense of that term cannot be sustained. He had many Jewish friends. He dedicated *Elbow Room* to Philip Sayers, a Jewish business-man, and Bethel Solomons who had a motor car with a sloping bonnet was amused when Gogarty said, 'What a Jewish-looking car!' In every country (even in every family) certain members, however unfairly, serve as comedy turns or come in for more than their share of mild abuse. This is inherent in the nature of human be-haviour and unrelated to the malignant segregations of the ghettos. It is ill-mannered, but not racist, to call a man a 'Culchie'; Gogarty's brand of 'anti-semitism' is the parallel of today's Kerryman jokes.

Finally, the legal action is to be regretted for highlighting the caus-tic at the expense of his more genial qualities. The late Sir Maurice Bowra pointed out in *The Greek Experience* that 'The Athenians had almost no laws of libel or slander, and their political debates were as candid and vituperative as their private and forensic quarrels. They seemed to have welcomed a remarkable degree of outspokenness, and to have felt it was part of the game to vilify one's opponent.'

Mahaffy, Tyrrell and the Trinity dons had tutored Gogarty in this tradition. What a pity that a pleb had the effrontery to object! A blistering comment gains a winged life of its own while a smile and a bantering joke are ephemeral. Gogarty's vituperative remarks and George Redding's fable 'Two Jews grew in Sackville Street' survive while the former's friendliness is easily forgotten; his penchant for the cutting quip is recalled while his kindly acts are rarely mention-ed. A retired policeman[16] who had guarded Gogarty in 1923 re-marked on his generosity and how he gave money to the poor. 'He spent money like jackstones.'

15

The Friends thou Hast

If AE's dictum that we are 'a microcosm of our friends' is correct
it is evident that Oliver Gogarty's character was enriched by the very
numerous friends whose affections he held so effortlessly, and in
many instances for most of his adult life. In the nature of things
the older friends of his youth and manhood stepped one by one
into the shadows but contemporaries such as Seumas O'Sullivan,
Shane Leslie, T.G. Moorhead and others survived to provide evidence
of Gogarty's capacity for reciprocated and lasting friendly relationships.

Terence de Vere White recalled meeting Gogarty, who knew him
by sight, if not by name — 'Hello, Pearson', he sometimes said when
he saw the younger man in the street — and being taken into the
doctor's study and given a signed copy of a recently-published
book. Despite his position and achievements Senator Gogarty showed
no trace of pomp or conceit.[1]

When someone said to Mrs. Yeats that 'at this minute he's sitting
somewhere saying scandalous things,' she said, 'And don't you know
that a man can do that and still be the most loyal friend you ever
had.' She knew this better than most: Gogarty was instrumental in
arranging an American benefaction which relieved Yeats from
financial worries; his influence placed Yeats in the Senate; years
previously when Dowden died he had failed narrowly in obtaining
for him the chair of English at Dublin University.

In Gogarty's scheme of things life's absurdities were intended
to be proclaimed; derision was perfectly in order if witty. 'Drink
to me with thine only eye,' he said to a friend with a glass eye,
and he explained Yeats's decision to have the so-called Steinach
rejuvenating operation by saying, 'He's come to an age when he
can't take "Yes" for an answer.'

'Ashe is a fine fellow,' he remarked of a colleague, 'but he's
inclined to think he's the whole cigar.' Seeing Lennox Robinson, tall,
wraith-like and dissipated, he said, 'Poached eyes on ghost.'[2]

'He never got under the surface,' he said after Orpen's funeral, 'until he got under the ground.'

This Athenian outspokenness had a native Irish counterpart which caused Cyril Connolly to retreat from the Palace Bar exclaiming, 'An alligator tank!' There were many others whose tongues depending on mood and circumstance could sting or lacerate.

'The coffin was Chippendale,' said George Moore after the funeral of Sir Thornley Stoker, 'but the lid was reproduction'. On another occasion, addressing his host, he said, 'My dear fellow, if you enter tain a friend don't take the good out of it by having a butler with such awful feet.'

Noting Austin Clarke's arrival in the Bodega, Seumas O'Sullivan said, 'A depression is moving in from Templeogue.'

Standing at the front window of his house in Morehampton Road O'Sullivan saw a man passing with a cart of manure.

'I see Paddy Kavanagh's moving,' he said. 'There go his furniture and effects.'[3]

Yeats, echoing Lenin's remark that religion is the opium of the masses, said, 'In England H.G. Wells is the opium of the middle-classes.'

Samuel Beckett referred to a rising Irish representational painter as, 'a Veronicist who would wipe the face of Christ with a sanitary towel'.

Gogarty was an easy companion to whom fellow poets were prepared to pay a tribute of admiration. F.R. Higgins wrote:

> *Against your strut, your headstrong hop,*
> *Gogarty, none of that shadowy troop*
> *Could tumble among the sun-splitting crop*
> *Of verse stalked in your pages,*
> *Where drunk with song, your foot is sure*
> *And, not of bog latin, you give to the poor*
> *The sacred drop, the rare liqueur*
> *Unearthed from the ages.*[4]

Seumas O'Sullivan dedicated *Mud in Purple* to Gogarty:

> *Since you have loved my city well*
> *Accept the book wherein I tell*
> *Of common things that you and I*
> *Held sacred in the days gone by.*[5]

These two had been friends since the beginning of the century. With the exception of a period reflected in *Ulysses* the Martello Tower in Sandycove lacks a chronicler but, long before literary pilgrims visited it to evoke Joycean associations, it was a place of pilgrimage for Arthur Griffith's American admirers. Seumas O'Sullivan has described the morning swim from the Forty-Foot to Bulloch Harbour and how at breakfast, when they were entertaining a Trinity don, Oliver Gogarty mistook an omelette for a pancake. 'He looked on it and sniffed his approval, but (I still believe that he somehow confused in his mind the idea of pancake and omelette) he insisted that it should be thrown into the air and thus "turned". I protested, he insisted, and sent the lump of fragrance towards the roof. He unfortunately failed to field it on its downward journey — and in the end, we breakfasted that morning on bacon — without the eggs.'[6]

The goings-on in the 'Arch', a nearby tavern, remain conjectural but Gogarty has left a portrait of the bronzed Carson, an all-the-year-round swimmer who ritually recorded the temperature before immersing himself.

> *True, his strokes are not divine,*
> *Are not strokes of such true art,*
> *As, say, Starkey, yours or mine*
> *In regattas taking part,*
> *But his skin! and the time in!*
> *The thermometer and twine!*

Writing to explain his inability to visit Galway, Seumas O'Sullivan thanked Gogarty for the loan of the Tower: '... the past week has been a perfect joy, bathing 2 or 3 times a day and lying in the sun, reading the remnants of the Tower Library and "inviting my Soul"... these days have been a sort of resurrection of my first visit to Sandycove when I found you with that Oxonian Invalid trying to put into him some of the over-plus of your own ever-abundant life.'[7]

Gogarty's letters to Seumas O'Sullivan written over some decades are a light-hearted mixture related to their mutual literary concerns.

5 Rutland Square.
12. v. '05.

My dear Starkey: Stimulate your strong mind. I have been considering your idea for a book of original Essays. I'm sure the scheme would work with you — the question is: would I [?] Would I work at all, with myself even? if you could arrange that I bring you an essay every week on one subject you might be able to amass the contents of a book. Of course I'm full of ideas!...

Suppose we devote Sundays and going somewhere with a naggin and a notebook (I supply the notebooks) and trying to get the greater part at least of one completed. Begin next Sunday. Stead [Stad] at XII o.c.

Yrs. O.G.[8]

No more is heard of the essays but in the following year he express-ed displeasure at an editorial blue-pencil. 'I met Griffith imbibing in the Bailey. He told me where you were. I am not yet reconciled to his deletions. A paper to be published shortly in Belfast by the Hobson set — "the Republic" — interests me now. I have taken a 5/- share and will write for it regularly if it is worthy of the name.'

His letters frequently contained verses, early examples of poems that were published later, e.g. 'Medicus Poetae' and others destined to remain unpublished such as 'To the Poets' —

Although you sing of Life and Love
It's strange that where you fail is
In giving us a rendering of
The vita sexualis.[9]

For his friend's amusement he sent some obscene lines on John Eglinton and a poem written on a prescription form entitled 'To Starkey for the second coming' —

When these heavy days are over
Take a ticket for the train.
To where Bank-clerks are in clover
By the soft, seductive Seine.

I can see the footsteps even
See the skirts to ankles cling

> *And above — the heights of Heaven*
> *Fold on fold and string on string.*[10]

O'Sullivan was an enthusiastic upholder of a tradition that links poets and drinking. Thomas Bodkin, in this connection, faulted Gogarty's misplaced generosity — 'I've seen him take Seumas O' Sullivan and fill him with drink at the bar counter in Suffolk Street. Gogarty would perch Seumas on the bar stool, and Seumas in the end had no way of getting off the stool, except by falling so he had to remain there until he'd sobered down a bit!'[11] — but it was a fault that most Dublin tipplers would have welcomed.

A picture postcard of Renvyle House Hotel was despatched on 30 July 1935. 'It is a great thing to have a pub of one's own where never "Time!" blows loudly but it lies. I wished I had seen you on Saturday week last to thank you for the only intimation I had of the serious condition of our friend. Yesterday I dived on to a submerged rock and very nearly joined him.'[12]

Gogarty's letter from Renvyle House Hotel in December 1938 acknowledges the gift of *Poems 1930-38*.

> My dear Stark: That delightful thing that book of yours has just reached me. I am charmed and most grateful. Apart from the praise it is not possible to qualify for De Profundis at Xmas. The lovers — hedge pupils of Love — and the Milkman, it will be hard to equal the Wasp. If it doesn't buzz through the world belted like a troubadour, so much the worse for the World.
>
> I am here 'Beyond the shout' for a few weeks. After the feast obscene I change the scene.
>
> Dear Bard, I hope that your wings, at any rate, will continue to flash the morn no matter what happens to us.
>
> With renewed thanks and with admiration for your sustained song.
>
> Always sincerely yours,
>
> O. St. J. G.[13]

W.R. Rodgers, another poet with a partiality for public houses, thought Gogarty the most generous man he knew and the most gifted raconteur. 'He could put the word on it. He had his poet's ear for words. I first met him in a busy English pub. I was so caught by his fine and scandalous talk that I watched a stranger beside me steal my overcoat, without so much as registering the fact.'

When it was realized that the coat was missing Gogarty wanted to replace it with his own and he pressed a handful of pound notes on the impecunious Rodgers in case his wallet had also been stolen.

'Still, if talk had been cloth,' said Rodgers, recalling the event, 'I'd have had the makings of an overcoat.'[14]

Gogarty's 'most constant and closely united companion' according to Piaras Béaslaí, was Dr. Joe Boyd Barrett. 'During the years when I was a frequent associate of Gogarty's I never met him without Joe being in his company — a gentle, courteous, kindly man who never said a harsh thing about anybody... and one whose knowledge and appreciation of famous paintings amounted to a passion.'[15]

A more tempestuous friend, Francis McNamara, wrote to him in 1917 about a portrait by Gerald L. Brockhurst:

Well in the first place I didn't know that the portrait in question was my property — I know that when Brockhurst asked me to sit he said that the painting should be mine, but as he never referred to it again and I have not seen or heard from him for 15 months, I came to the conclusion that I had misunderstood him — apparently I did not, and the thing is mine to keep or to sell as I like! I haven't the least idea what Brockhurst is getting now for his work, whether it's tens or hundreds or thousands! Ahem, I'll sell you the portrait for a thou — no, I won't sell it to you at all — but I think you ought to have it... for I am a wanderer with no wall to hang it on, while you are a centre of Kultur both in town and country — also shall I not hang beside Yeats, and ultimately hang to the clicking of a turnstile?[16]

Another instance of Gogarty's natural kindliness was his concern for Bryan Cooper who in 1930 lay mortally ill in Khyber Pass, a great mansion perched on a windy eminence overlooking Killiney Bay. With a cynical twist to mitigate the sadness of his tidings, Gogarty reported Cooper's terminal condition to W. B. Yeats on 17 June: 'Yesterday I was allowed to visit poor Bryan Cooper. The only comforting thought (for one detached as an artist and not Human nor All-Too-Human at that!) is that black will be quite becoming to Mrs. Cooper. But I am genuinely sorry for that great lonely gentleman, lonely as some banished Roman in some land where the Eagles were unknown.'[17]

From Paris in the same year, D.B. Wyndham Lewis acknowledged a copy of the *Irish Statesman,* 'That is a woundy slam of yours at the Attributors! I loved it. Why don't you have a smack now at the Art Critics and their jargon? God knows there are not a few ways of fooling all the people all the time, but I have always admired the way the Art Critic gets away with his bluff.'[18]

The company in the pubs and clubs he frequented was exclusively male but the list of Gogarty's friends also included Lady Leslie, Lady Leconfield and Lady Lavery.[19]

He was a frequent visitor at Castle Leslie and corresponded regularly with its chatelaine.[20] His eulogistic 'Churchill's Favourite Aunt' was published in *Vogue* in 1942. She had outstanding charm and wit which like his own could be malicious. 'Dance on your crow's feet,' she said amiably to a valetudinarian who complained that dancing hurt her feet.

Reflecting on charm [Gogarty wrote] I realized that one must have a good heart to possess it. It dwells only with women and men of good-will. If the definition of a gentleman be, 'One who always considers the feelings of others', the equivalent of gentility, is what constitutes Charm in a lady.

And charm engenders gratitude and affection. It has the effect of a blessing and an inspiration for those upon whom it acts. You try to repay it with the best that in you lies. Charm engenders generosity. It is good fellowship at its best.

Lady Leslie wrote from England seeking political news — 'I am told there will be trouble over the Boundary Settlement and I am told the next Gov. Gen. is to be you: Please confirm or deny these statements' — and kept him in touch with goings on in London.

I hear Augustus John had a party last Eve. and at midnight a Policeman came in with a warrant to search everyone for Cocaine!—

Great excitement — Ladies hysterics — men hoping their names would not appear! — but it was an April Fool joke and it seems the Policeman (a real one) is a friend of John's.

I daresay you know him too! But Senators should be careful —

Shane is in Paris. London rather empty but always some friends coming in and cheering me up —

Remember me to Mrs. Gogarty.[21]

Lady Lavery wrote to him from her London home, 5 Cromwell Place, on 18 November 1923:

My dear Dr. Oliver — I had hoped so much to see you and

telephoned on Tuesday only to find you were 'expected on Thursday', that made me hopeful you might stay over for Friday and luncheon at Cromwell place with Mrs. (pro-Irish) William Randolph Hearst, Lord Ridell and Lord Castlerosse and last but not least Lady Diana C. who you may not see again before she leaves for America next week — forgive me for writing an account of my guests like the social column of the Daily Sketch! but it gives me a melancholy, vengeful pleasure to tell you what you have missed.

But *especially* I wished to see you to thank you for your letter which was a masterpiece of wit and in the best Gogarty manner....[22]

From Petworth House the following note was forwarded early in 1924:

Lady Leconfield and Mr. Seymour Leslie present their compliments to Doctor Gogarty and wish to express the deep sense of neglect under which they are labouring.

Throughout Christmastide they awaited, throughout New Year they hoped, but now on the seventh day of January, when the whirr of the expected swans of the Liffey has still not fallen on their anxious ears, they are preparing to abandon hope, but before doing so, feel it is both wise and just to afford Dr. Gogarty a last opportunity of retrieving his position by the only effective explanation.

They are both surprised and grieved at his neglect in view of the more frequent intercourse of other days.[23]

He stimulated Lady Leconfield's interest in Anglo-Irish literature and she acknowledged his help in building up a collection.

I have now got a fine nucleus of an Irish Library which I shall delight in adding to. The copy of the Playboy and the first edition of Yeats are wonderful to have. Thank you so very much. I have also to thank you for the Yeats Mss. which reached me safely and the little Gregory picture which is most amusing.[24]

AE first encountered Gogarty at George Moore's and noted that when he came into the room 'Moore had the rare experience of being brilliantly out-talked in his own house.' As an editor, AE helped Gogarty, to be rewarded by his hospitality and devoted respect, sharing with Griffith and Tom Kettle an immunity from the doctor's stinging witticisms.[25]

George Moore, on the other hand, was something of a butt. For instance, Gogarty said, 'Moore isn't a man's man; he's happiest in the company of women of his own sort.' When Moore left Ireland Gogarty wrote a 'Lament' later published in *Secret Springs of Dublin Song* —

> *Lonely, O'Moore, your old friends are;*
> *We miss you and forgive the banter,*
> *We miss the generous cigar,*
> *The coy decanter.*
>
> *We miss the nights when you were here —*
> *All Ely Place a catacomb,*
> *Where we sat solemn and severe*
> *Denouncing Rome.*

The novelist was a cantankerous man with something in his nature 'that left even his best friends insecure' yet he could be childishly loveable. Gogarty pictured him as he would see him in his rooms in Ebury Street where he called on him from time to time: 'I will find him in his red plush, high-backed armchair with his back to the broad window, closed by heavy curtains, against which his silver white, flossy hair and porcelain pink face will be silhouetted if he moves. His drooping moustache still contains hints of red at the ends and hides an infirm mouth, only the bright, outturned lower lip of which may be seen.'

Moore's wilfulness and vanity amused Gogarty, but he was amiable and knowledgeable and in matters of art his judgement was impeccable.

When I think of the long, low line of the dim hills on the rim of his ancestral Mayo and of that great house, Moore Hall, in which he first saw the light beside the green crescent of its limpid lake, or of the finely drawn line of my old Dublin hills, I know that I owe the beauty of phrase and whatever little delight my retina brings me from those features of my native land, to long traffic with this master of the English language. Now before death, even the little asperities of his character are smoothed away, polished by that pain as the prose into which no asperities crept was polished by his conscientious and laborious devotion.[26]

Gogarty half-regretted his failure to visit him when passing through London on his way to the United States towards the end of 1932. 'Perhaps it was better not. I could not have helped him. His life was closing, with the long beauty of a Lapland night, crystal and undarkened to the end.' Some months later, on 27 May, a warm cloudless day, he paid his last respects at Lough Carra and rowed out to the island where George Moore's ashes were to rest. A day not to be forgotten:

No! That day on that lake by me will never be forgotten: the oars that dipped in silence and the funerary urn held by Moore's sister in the stern of the heavy boat. We two were alone and we spoke but little, for it was a sad passage with the ashes of a man we loved between us; but as the ripples broke the lake's surface, they laughed, danced, sparkled, and laughed again, they were like millions of invulnerable and immortal merrimen rejoicing that a spirit, as native and impish as their own, the spirit of the last squire of Ireland, and unageing artist had mingled with them after a long sojourn on earth in his unparallelable life.[27]

His tributes to AE included two sonnets, 'To a Friend' and 'To AE going to America.' When on a July day in 1935 the Matron's telegram notified Gogarty that the poet and mystic was near his end, impelled by the mixed instincts of a doctor and a friend, Gogarty hastened to his bedside to succour or say goodbye. Next day he wrote in *The Irish Times:* 'The most magnanimous Irishman of our generation is dead... [he] died with his work finished and the contribution of a great soul complete.'

Those about his bedside broke down, pitying themselves for a love of a kind and noble man who was soon to be lost. His courage in the face of death, the assurance and calmness of a just soul was as moving as is the account of the death of Socrates. His friends were broken-hearted, but he was unmoved. The change in his countenance was remarkable, and the way the mind threw off the veils of death to deepen the great blue light in the eyes as he rejoiced at seeing for a moment a friend's face was something to impress the memory for ever. The hero in the man looked out, and it was his friends who had to brace themselves against life with its loss.[28]

A later and fuller appraisal in which Gogarty described AE's multiple talents was published in *Colby Library Quarterly.*

But it is not as painter, poet, or seer that I would acclaim AE and remember him but as a human being in whom goodness was innate and radiantly active.... That he was grateful for his good fortune appears from his words whispered to me as he lay 'conscious of his own eternity' at the point of death: 'I have realised all my ambitions. I have had an astounding interest in Life. I have great friends. What more can a man want?' There are many still alive who, like myself, consider themselves fortunate to have lived while AE was on earth.

A poet whom AE had helped and publicized was the inimitable James Stephens, another friend praised by Gogarty in verse and prose — 'A mind that lit the Liffey could emblazon all the Thames' — the former, 'To James Stephens', written when Stephens left Dublin for London, the latter in *Colby Library Quarterly*. 'I used to meet him of an evening when his work was over. Then he would recite some of the lyrics "on which I have been sitting all day long in the office, keeping them warm like a hen on a nest of eggs". He could keep three or four lyrics in his head until he got the leisure to complete them.'

He was a gleeman who had joy always at his command. 'Stephens is simpler, wiser, less personal and more lyrical than Yeats. Yeats writes of a "more learned rhythm." There is no room for learning in a lyric; but there is every room for wisdom.' Gogarty's unexpected comparison contains an element of truth but he is comparing a minor voice with a major one.

Accustomed since their earliest acquaintanceship to dissociate between Yeats the man and Yeats the artist the images were bound occasionally to coalesce in Gogarty's mind with the inevitable consequence that his amused awareness of the older poet's foibles and affections surfaced incongruously to be misinterpreted as a reprehensible example of *lèse-majesté* not to be expected from an admiring friend.[29] At an Academy dinner in the Dolphin Hotel attended by members of the Harmsworth family he gestured towards Yeats at the head of the table: 'We have seen Shelley plain!' But the poet's need to retire from time to time caused Gogarty to turn to the ladies: 'Read his latest?' And after reciting appropriate stanzas: 'Pure prostatic verse, my dears!'

There can be no question, however, of the warmth of their friendship and if Gogarty stood to gain most from their long association Yeats also benefited. He encountered in Fairfield the inspiration for *Words Upon a Window Pane* and Gogarty's physical vitality and personality appealed enormously to a man so removed from daily life that he had never visited a public house until F.R. Higgins took him to one.

When he was at Trinity Gogarty undertook a verse translation of *Oedipus Rex* for Yeats to be scolded by the master not for metrical defects but for introducing 'thee' and 'thou'. 'I received a long lecture on modern literary languages', he explained to G.K.A. Bell. 'He forgave William Morris for his archaism for it was both original and scholarly. An archaism was only admissable when one had discovered it for oneself: there was no defence for the continuance of mere metrical conventions: "Hast", "shalt", "thou", "thee", "wert", "art", etc. They were part of a language, highly artificial and conscious, a language that would pass for poetry if one found it at a future date in a single instance where the rest of the literature of the period was lost.'[30] It was a valuable lesson though it was some time before he had the technical competence completely to eschew the time-worn conventions.

He also impressed on Gogarty the importance of 'intensity' of phrase, occasionally altering a word or substituting a line. An example in 'Medicus Poetae' was to amend its last line to read, 'The black bird *leap* from the dark hedge and sing'. And Gogarty recalled that Yeats re-wrote almost an entire stanza of 'Palinode'.

When Yeats tendered similar assistance to Lady Wellesley she frowned on his revisals preferring, she said, a bad poem of her own to a better one written by him under her name, but Yeats maintained that such alterations have always been made in a company of poets and that Lady Gregory had written the end of his 'Deirdre'.

Gogarty invariably accepted Yeats's suggestions gratefully. The revisals are discussed by James F. Carens who points out that despite their close association, verbal echoes of Yeats in Gogarty's poetry are remarkably few.[31] 'Even when, as in the 'thirties, Gogarty increasingly shares Yeats's haughty aristocratic ideals, his rhythms, structures, and images are entirely his own.' Carens then goes on to trace Gogarty's influence on Yeats's poetry adducing reasons for seeing him as a catalyst for the imagery of 'Leda and the Swan', 'Byzantium' and 'The Great Day', and identifying him with Malachi Stilt-Jack in 'High Talk'.

Through his friendship with Yeats he came to know Lady Gregory better, purging himself of the instinctive disrespect of his younger days (Joyce in *Ulysses* refers to 'that old hake Gregory'), glad to help her deal with a domestic problem. 'I called the Medical Supply Co. and asked them to send you a quotation for air and water beds.

Their price to me was the same as Fannins to you: 15/- per month and £5 or £6 to buy out. Of the two kinds the water bed is the better.'[32]

Another letter gave her personal medical advice:

> 15 Ely Place
> Dublin.
> 29. v. 26.

Dear Lady Gregory: If your eyes are not quite well by the time this reaches you it would be wise to have them seen to in Dublin. Dr. Dwyer Joyce (whose father wrote 'Irish Names of Places') is the best oculist.

You probably got some acute attack of conjunctivitis which is another way of saying that the transparent membrane lining the eyelids became inflamed.

On the nature of the infecting organism everything depends. If it is virulent and lasts long ulceration may result. So I advise you having given it now nearly 4 weeks trial to consult someone competent to treat you. Any longer irritation is dangerous to neglect.

I was glad to hear of W.B.'s activity; his horse-power is un-impaired. To-day I went to Lough C with Bremen — archaeo-logically bent.

> Kind regards,
> Yours sincerely
> Oliver St. J. Gogarty.

You did well to treat the eyes with boric acid mild solution. Too strong is an additional irritant.[33]

Towards the end of 1929 W.B. Yeats was ailing and coughed blood. He remained unwell and feverish in Rapallo. His doctors were puzzled until an expert in tropical diseases from Genoa was consulted. He diagnosed Malta fever — an explanation which, with the benefit of hindsight, one may receive sceptically. 'The proper injections were ordered and the danger passed,' Yeats's biographer wrote.[34] How fortunate! Actually no specific treatment was available and the half bottle of champagne which the poet was allowed daily could have been as effective as any other nostrum.

15 Ely Place,
Dublin.
2. 2. 30.

Dear Lady Gregory: Very many thanks for relieving my mind about Yeats. Probably bad drainage or bad water caused the attack.

Yesterday just as your letter came I was re-reading with great admiration your translation from Raftery.

Kindest wishes,

Yours sincerely,

Oliver Gogarty.[35]

It is convenient to attribute ailments suffered abroad to 'bad drainage' but the bloodstained sputum in the early stage of the illness suggests a persisting pneumonia which eventually resolved spontaneously. Ambroise Paré's sixteenth-century remark was applicable in the 1930s and even today: 'I dressed him, God healed him.'

Arriving at Yeats's Rathfarnham home Gogarty found him dieting. 'This blood pressure,' he explained, taking a spoonful of melon.

'One of our medical bugbears', Gogarty said. 'What man is worth his salt whose blood pressure is not high?' Comforting words but hardly justifiable; Yeats had severe hypertension, the systolic blood pressure sometimes registering 260 millimetres of mercury, which taxed his heart and caused acute left ventricular failure in Majorca in January 1936.

Creative work was temporarily forbidden. Only with difficulty was his doctor, a socialist, persuaded to consult with a colleague who was a monarchist. When finally they met they disagreed as to the cause of the illness and both theories had to be allowed for in their instructions.

Yeats's doctor's restricted English led him into certain ambiguities of speech. 'I am a bad doctor,' he said, 'but I have done you more good than the good doctors did', which Yeats conceded to be true. Prohibited foods were declared 'not convenient'; he overused the word 'convenient' and said to a lady: 'It will be convenient for me if you sleep with me for a couple of nights,' when he meant that she was to come into his nursing home.[36]

When Yeats returned to Dublin he gave the Spanish doctor's report to Gogarty who read it silently, 'We have here an antique cardio-sclerotic of advanced years.' To Gogarty's dismay Yeats insisted that he must read it aloud slowly and distinctly. Then, ignoring absolutely its prognostic significance, Yeats said, 'Do you know that I would rather be called "Cardio Sclerotic" than Lord of Lower Egypt.'

Yeats remained in indifferent health. An American millionaire invited him to stay with him in Florida, all expenses paid. 'Clearly, an alarum bell is sounding above my head (Gogarty is probably pulling the string). I have cabled my refusal and my gratitude.' He died in a small hotel on Cap Martin on 28 January 1939 and was buried in the municipal cemetery at Roquebrune.

Gogarty named him, 'the greatest guardian of the English language in our time... the fire-born moods of his mind will live on everlastingly and undiminished past that death which men have invented, and be for us a glory and a joy.'[37] Subsequently a commemorative essay on Yeats was included in *Mourning Became Mrs. Spendlove*; a slightly expanded version, *William Butler Yeats — A Memoir*, was published posthumously by the Dolmen Press.[38] His most fitting tribute, however, was the 'Elegy on the Archpoet William Butler Yeats Lately Dead'.

> *Now that you are a Song*
> *And your life has come to an end*
> *And you wholly belong*
> *To the world of Art, my friend,*
> *Take, for well it is due,*
> *This tribute of my rhymes*
> *With mind unswerved from you*
> *In these enormous times;*
> *Not that I wish to intrude*
> *To mix with mine your leaf,*
> *But that I would entwine*
> *In your magnificent sheaf,*
> *After sad interlude,*
> *A spray cut from that fine*
> *And rare plant, Gratitude.*[39]

Like Yeats, Oliver Gogarty could 'say my glory is I had such friends'; they warmed his days and were repaid by his irrepressible humour. A London newspaper columnist picking companions, a baker's dozen, for a desert island stranding selected Socrates, St. Francis, Leonardo da Vinci, Villon, Rabelais, Shakespeare, Dr. Johnson, Burns, GBS, Ninon de l'Enclos, Florence Nightingale, Mrs. Beeton and Oliver St. John Gogarty.[40]

But if friendships make life worthwhile a broken friendship is a cause for embitterment which Oliver Gogarty did not escape when he and James Joyce fell out.

16

A Roland for your Oliver

By giving his former friend a villain's role in his *Commedia* James
Joyce consigned him to hell with such finality that, with few exceptions, Joycean scholars[1] have hardly bothered to consider critically either Gogarty's 'crime' or his punishment.[2] It is, therefore,
of some importance to examine their relationship impartially, and
possibly to seek a mitigation of sentence, or even a retrospective
pardon. The evidence shows that Gogarty must be credited with
many acts of friendship and that Joyce's general disaffection found
a particular focus in the former's affluence and success, an envy
which Stanislaus Joyce made every effort to magnify, being jealous
of their companionship.

As we have seen they met for the first time in 1901, probably
in the National Library, and soon found that they had much in
common besides a mutual interest in poetry and a facility for versifi-
cation. They were, in a word, Bohemians. More than that they were
rebellious; they had the same endless capacity for ribald laughter,
the same sardonic humour, and an identical talent for blasphemy;
they both leaned towards low company and had a partiality for
taverns. These bonds initially proved stronger than the sundering
differences which eventually led to their estrangement.

Gogarty was more adaptable, more open-minded, less introspective,
less pricked by pride. His comfortable position and background made
him sure of his identity and he had attained a considerable measure
of personal success when Joyce was still a nobody. The latter was
single-minded, sure of his destiny, unable to compromise. Gogarty
grew to be a big fish in a little pond; Joyce's international acclaim
disturbed rather than restored his equanimity. Gogarty expanded as
an establishment figure; Joyce shrank within the chaos he had
caused. Against such a background of psychological and circum-
stantial differences it is not to be expected that mutual toleration
could be sustained, and having forked tongues they used them.
'James Joyce was not a gentleman', Gogarty told an English critic.
'God help anyone who gets into the hands of that fellow', said

211

Joyce, when an Irish visitor mentioned Gogarty's success as a surgeon.

Under the summer skies of youth, friendship seems bound to be eternal, and Gogarty and Joyce responded to whatever each admired in the other's character and style. In another sense, acting like flint and tinder, each sparked off the other's extravagances. Gogarty's easy elegance contrasted with Joyce's seedy hauteur, his inconsequent chatter was balanced by the other's enigmatic utterances, and his sociability differed from Joyce's alienation which evoked a playful Limerick:

> *There is a weird spectre called Joyce*
> *Re-arisen from Monasterboice*
> *His whole occupation*
> *A walking negation*
> *Of all his acquaintance's choice.*[3]

Through *Ulysses* their names are inseparably associated with the Martello Tower, Sandycove, but the earlier background to their friendship was the Library in Kildare Street, the literary assembly rooms, the streets and suburbs of the North Side, Fairfield and the Bull Wall, a favourite swimming-place where over a short distance Joyce was faster than his more robust friend.

That Joyce was indebted to Gogarty, as to many others, for small sums of money is evident in their surviving letters, in one of which Gogarty wrote:

> Be not distressed at my sudden disappearance subsequent to my presenting you with that cheque. It is on *my* head. You would be foolish not to cash it as I know I have yet 20£ or 15£ in the Bank.'[4] [Again in January 1903:] I sent the money Thursday 22 by wire to you c/o W.B. Yeats, 18 Woburn Buildings, Euston Rd., London. With the wire was an order for you on the nearest Post Office....Perhaps your note which I am answering by this was written during the period of despair which you must have suffered on Wednesday at not receiving my promised letter. Only yesterday did the College pay their penurious poet.[5]

They corresponded regularly during Joyce's absence in Paris where he had hoped to study medicine in the winter of 1902–3, and when Gogarty was in Oxford in 1904. Gogarty's epistles vary in length from the briefest card — 'O preposterous Poet! write to thine impossible friend' — to affectionately bantering letters of several pages of fine script with afterthoughts, postscripts, and phallic symbols decorating the margins.

On his return from Paris Joyce affected a broad-rimmed Latin Quarter hat and favoured a popular French song, 'Cadet Rousselle', inspiring Gogarty to a new nickname. His friendship with J.F. Byrne (the 'Cranly' of *A Portrait of the Artist as a Young Man)* cooled and he spent much time in Gogarty's company.

The victims of their secret mockery included the celibate Assistant Librarian to the National Library, W.K. Magee, the refined author John Eglinton, who when a question of sexual indulgence was under discussion said primly, 'I never did it', which became a catchphrase for the students. One afternoon, finding a bag of samples left by George Toberts (then a commercial traveller in ladies' underwear) in the rooms of the Hermetic Society, they played a practical joke in very bad taste. Tying a pair of open drawers to a chair, with the legs apart, they fixed the handle of a broom in the opening and hung a placard beside it with the legend, 'I never did it: signed John Eglinton.'6

Following the death of his mother Joyce began to drink heavily, egged on, according to Stanislaus Joyce, by Gogarty who had told John Elwood he wished 'to break his spirit.'7 Before accepting this accusation at face value as so many Joycean scholars have done it is important to know that Stanislaus Joyce hated Gogarty as he hated J.F. Byrne, whom he called 'Thomas Square-toes' and endowed with 'an impenetrable mask like a Cistercian bishop's face', because they came between him and the brother he worshipped. Their father said unkindly that Stannie was his brother's jackal and his awareness of James's superior mind gave him an inferiority complex. Even the brother whom he so admired rubbed it in by saying that Stannie reminded him of Gogarty's description of Magee, 'that he had to fart every time before he could think'.

Stanislaus Joyce was something of a prig and six years younger than Gogarty who did not conceal the fact that he found him boring —

> *Poet Kinch has a brother called Thug*
> *His imitator, and jackal, and mug.*
> *His stride like a lord's is*
> *His pretension absurd is*
> *In fact he's an* awful *thick-lug.*8

Stannie, in turn, called the Trinity student 'Last-lap Gogarty' and secretly eased his anger by depicting him in his *Diary* as 'shallow' and 'a dangerous ... a most demoralizing person'. Gogarty called him 'Jim's Flemish brother' and Stannie had his revenge by turning him into an unlikely grotesque. 'Gogarty's hooked nose and pointed chin and round form remind me of Punch.'

The relatives of alcoholics are quick to find a scapegoat; it is understandable that Stanislaus should wish to project his brother's lapses on to Gogarty's shoulders but when one looks at the Joyces' mean house in Cabra where on any evening of the week John S. Joyce and Charles Joyce, father and brother, were likely to be as drooling drunk as James, it is hardly necessary to blame an outsider.

Gogarty influenced Joyce in superficial ways: by drawing his attention to a portrait of a clean-shaven Dante he persuaded him to shave off his straggling beard; his habit of making a fair copy of his poems in the centre of a folio sheet of paper was adopted by Joyce. He gave him articles of wearing apparel, lent him a dress suit, and allowed him to borrow his rifle which Joyce promptly pawned. He praised 'Kinch' to all and sundry — even to Fresh Nelly a whore who said he had 'the fuckin'est best voice' she'd ever heard and she'd be glad to help him only 'he's too fuckin proud' — and built him up as a character.[9] The egregious Stannie in more candid moments was prepared to admit that 'Gogarty has friendship for Jim' and to concede that 'in the drab streets of Dublin, the stolid masks of secret and disappointed lives, he and Gogarty make a vital pair'.

The warmth of Gogarty's friendship is apparent in the letters he sent to Joyce from Oxford some of which have been quoted in an earlier chapter. His great desire was that Joyce should visit Oxford.

> Worcester College,
> Oxford.

Be Jaysus Joyce! You must come over here for a day or two next fortnight. I want your advice and criticism on something literary. The fare single to Oxford from Dublin is 27/-. Boat leaves N. Wall at 11 a.m. 1st class. 3rd cl train gets here 11.30 pm and I shall send you your travelling expenses. (I couldn't trust you with more.) I ought to send you the ticket perhaps. Let me know if you will come Thurs. I want to get Drunk! Dhrunk![10]

Unable to raise the wherewithal Joyce remained in Dublin where he fell victim to the perils of Nighttown; when he appealed to Gogarty the latter directed him to a local colleague.

Worcester College
Friday 10 III

My dear Mick,

A friend of mine has been seeking employment as a water-clock and as he has not met with much success would be glad if he could re-convert his urethra to periodic and voluntary functions. I take the liberty of asking you to advise him from this note as I cannot introduce him myself; being busy teaching the language to the natives here. Mr. Joyce is the name of the tissues surrounding the infected part if you will cure him you will delight me. He may have waited too long and got gleet.
   'Rusticus expectat'

With every pleasant thought

of you I remain

Archaeologically yours

Oliver Gogarty[11]

His letter to Joyce was more lighthearted than suited an occasion which must have been worrying and dispiriting to Joyce but ended on a warning note.

My dear Joyce,

I am indeed sorry to have forsaken you in whom I am well pleased. Congratulations that our holy mother has judged you worthy of the stigmata. Pray fervently O my brother that you may gain increase of grace to remain worthy of them and bear the favour with becoming humility. As it would be absurd and pernicious for me to prescribe for a penis in a poke so to speak I enclose a letter for you to hand to my old friend Dr. Walsh one of the best. He will see you all right for me and if you can be repaired repair you. How is the novel progressing. I have written a poem and am on a play.
   If I would venture an opinion — you have got a slight gleet from a recurrence of original sin. But you'll be all right. When next writing be careful not to wish eternal blasting as the pro-

cess is intermittent. Won't you write and tell me all the news.
I have planted a whore and a lamp-post in the back garden here
and things are now quite homely. Don't let any laziness prevent
you from presenting the letter as it may become incurable if
neglected or if you drink.

Write 'de moechis'

I am writing against the Gnostics.

Adieu!

Staboo!

Yrs.

O.G.[12]

The outcome of 'original sin' is not mentioned again and presumably responded to Dr. Walsh's treatment but it may be relevant
to Joyce's later health problems; the subsequent illness in Trieste
characterized by iritis and arthritis would today invite a diagnosis
of Reiter's syndrome.[13]

When Gogarty returned to Dublin he had no idea that the palmy
days of his friendship with Joyce had ended. He was ready to re-
assume his protective role and by providing a regular lodging for
Joyce in the Tower enable him to finish *Stephen Hero*. They met
from time to time; outwardly Joyce was unchanged, raising funds
a major preoccupation. 'I never borrow anything but *guineas* now,'
he told Gogarty.[14]

Actually, for the first time Joyce's mind was in the turmoil of
requited love for a maid-servant in Finn's Hotel. His courtship
of Nora Barnacle, his future wife, had begun on June 16; it was
a relationship which provided a sense of security (though its con-
sequences were to lead to years of insecurity) which allowed Joyce
to give vent to his strongly entrenched persecutory complex towards almost all his former friends, particularly Byrne, Cosgrave
and Gogarty. 'He himself', as Ellman puts it 'was a blend of celebrated victims (Christ and Parnell), light-bringing malefactors
(Lucifer and Giordano Bruno), and exiles (Dante and Daedalus),
while they were Intensities and Bullockships.'

His love for Nora Barnacle made other ties of the affections unnecessary and as he had cast off Byrne for Gogarty he now cast off
Gogarty.

Because your voice was at my side
I gave him pain.
Because within my hand I held
Your hand again.

There is no word or any sign
Can make amend —
He is a stranger to me now
Who was my friend.

The lines from *Chamber Music* are regretful, almost apologetic, but Stanislaus has said that Joyce could shock Gogarty and in 1904 the twenty-two year old's 'Holy Office' was understandably shocking and his pillory of the established writers who had tried to help him intolerable —

But all these men of whom I speak
Make me the sewer of their clique.
That they may dream their dreamy dreams
I carry off their filthy streams
For I can do these things for them
Through which I lost my diadem,
Those things for which Grandmother Church
Left me severely in the lurch.
Thus I relieve their timid arses,
Perform my office of Katharsis.
My scarlet leaves them white as wool:
Through me they purge a bellyful.

Towards the end of August Gogarty told G.K.A. Bell 'I have broken with Joyce'; he complained of his want of generosity and resented his lampooning of AE, Yeats and others.[15] Nevertheless a semblance of amity was restored when Joyce took up residence in the Tower in September.

'This is the man,' Gogarty said, introducing him to Trench, 'who intends to write a novel in fifteen years.'

They drank in their local, the Arch, and in the city pubs. Encountering John Butler Yeats in the street Joyce urged Gogarty to touch him.

'Good morning, Mr. Yeats,' said Gogarty, 'could you lend us two shillings?'

'I have no money', the old man said, 'but had I money I should not give it to you and your friend to spend on drink.'

'We cannot speak of that which is not,' said Joyce preparing to philosophize but the indignant artist was hurrying away from the upstarts, as he would have classed them.

Occupied by thoughts of his 'particularly pouting Nora' Joyce can have had no intention of staying for long in the Tower; silently he was preparing for his so-called exile — the true Irish exiles are those of Lady Dufferin's 'The Irish Emigrant' or the nationless wanderers of the Hon. Emily Lawless's 'Clare Coast' — and with innate cunning contrived that it should appear that he was victimized by Gogarty. The 'black panther' episode was heaven-sent and by fleeing into the night Joyce dramatically removed his physical presence almost finally from Gogarty's life. They were to meet again once or twice but like the Montagues and Capulets they huffed and blew for a lifetime.

Gogarty's offhand comment was that had Joyce used the rifle instead of pawning it, he would have been less gun-shy and when he bolted to the Continent in October 1904 the medical student failed to see this as other than one more of Joyce's predictable and temporary aberrations. 'The Bard Joyce', he informed Dermot Freyer, 'has fled to Pola on the Adriatic. A slavey shared his flight. Considering the Poet's teaching and propensity the town he has chosen for his future living is not inappropriately named.'[16]

The birth of Joyce's son in Trieste on 27 July 1905 fully restored Gogarty's affection for his wayward friend — 'Gogarty, I believe even waxes sentimental over you,' Stanislaus told his brother — and he talked about a reconciliation, unable to believe that Joyce could still harbour a grudge.[17] He had no conception of Joyce's capacity for vindictiveness and self-delusion; the latter's latest fantasy, as described by Stannie in September 1905, evoked by Lermontoff's *Hero of Our Days,* was to identify with the author's hero and imagine himself killing Gogarty in a duel. Fortunately his vengeful thoughts had no power to hurt, and serene in his basic good-humour and ability to see life as a series of jokes, Gogarty, as Vincent Cosgrave noted, took 'a great deal of credit to himself about the success of the ménage à Trieste the town of the Man of Sorrows.'

Some measure of communication was re-established and in June 1906 Gogarty wrote to him from the Waldorf-Astoria, New York, an address which must have set the impecunious Joyce's teeth on edge.

Dear Joyce: I hope to be able to accept your kind invitation which you gave me as an alternative; I am making a tour of the world and I hope to be on the continent of Europe in the Autumn sometime.

I would much like to see Tokio — Yokoyo, Yokoyo, Yokoyo — but it is 17 days from San Francisco and the accommodation is not luxurious in that town just now. If I fail to afford to go far West to East you may see me in August, as I will be journeying to Italy then. I suppose I will be gladder to see you than you to see me but I miss the touch of a vanished hand and the sound of a voice that is still. When I mention voice, I may say that a journey to New York on your part would not be a risk, that is: you would not fail to make money rapidly: there is much money here.[18]

As we have seen, Gogarty's honeymoon plans were vague; the projected visit to Italy did not come off and Joyce scanned the Italian papers in vain for notice of his arrival.

'Guess the latest, guess who's married!' Nora held out an Irish newspaper in August to Joyce who first thought it might be his brother Charlie and then decided it must be another of Gogarty's practical jokes for he had not mentioned the impending nuptials in his letter. The formality of a legal and religious ceremony would have struck Joyce, who remained unwed, as further treachery. He pondered Stannie's suggestion that Gogarty would not have married had he, Joyce, remained in Dublin, wondered how he looked in a tall silk hat, and grudgingly wished 'Mr. & Mrs. Ignatius Gallagher health and a long life.'[19]

The Irish newspapers kept him in touch with Dublin happenings and to his chagrin he became aware that many of his fellow-students, men like Kettle, John Marcus O'Sullivan and 'even Dr. O.S. Jesus Gogarty' were by now public figures. Their lives, he maintained, nauseated him to the point of vomiting. He was sufficiently intrigued, nevertheless, to purchase *The Lake* and read about Father Oliver but when he heard from the honeymooner his cold comment to Stannie was, 'Of Gogarty's card I can make nothing. I don't understand why he desires that we should exchange short notes at long distances and at different angles to the equator.'

When, surprisingly, Stannie suggested he should reply to Gogarty's card he said he would do so only in the event of *Dubliners* being accepted for publication when it would be useful to recruit his services. He did, eventually, send Gogarty his best wishes but added no personal news and made matters worse rather than better by saying that he saw little profit in their 'exchanging any more curt notes'. His intention was to close the correspondence. Gogarty had asked that he should forget the past: 'a feat beyond my power. I forgive readily enough.'

It was not very easy for him, however, to exclude Gogarty from his mind and for some time his letters to Stannie were peppered with derogatory comments. He classified him with Yeats and Colum as 'the blacklegs of literature', a judgement which gives us a measure of the degree of his general disaffection; he dismissed the articles in *Sinn Féin* as 'stupid drivel', not allowing for the fact that little more could be expected from the purely polemical.

Prepared to make infinite allowance for Joyce's temperament Gogarty remained full of good-will and their correspondence was briefly resumed in 1907. Gogarty's letters from Vienna express the wish to help him by arranging pupils among the English-speaking post-graduate students, the hope that they can meet somewhere, and serious concern for his health.

Dear Joyce, I am very sorry to hear you had such a little time in bed to fight rheumatic fever. At least 6 months are necessary to ensure safety of the cardiac valves. If you could come to this place they would give you the best medical advice. London has done most in the attempt to cure the disease and there Paignton [F.J. Poynton] isolated the bacillus: but Vienna is first rate.... Avoid strains and physical work as much as may be, in order that your heart may 'compensate' for the longest possible period.[20]

When Joyce's reply assured him of satisfactory progress Gogarty began to plan a meeting in Venice or Athens.

> IX Spitalgasse, 1,
> Vienna.
> 2 XII '07.

Dear Joyce: Thanks very much for your quick response to my letter. At present my plans are open to change: but I am thinking of going to see Athens and Venice before I finally leave for home. Could you come with me on a trip to Athens returning to Trieste or Vienna within a week or 10 days? Would you care to do it? Your health would not suffer by the rest and change and (if I go) I would put up all expenses....

I wonder would the end of February or beginning of March be too cold. It's so cursedly *cold* now that if this weather continues into March I could go nowhere. Look out for some 1st class passenger vessel or some boat in which we would be the only passengers — there are some plying for wine and currants into the gulf of Corinth — and get an inclusive estimate for the trip as I would like to know how much to keep over after all the hellish expenses of this place....[21]

This plan did not materialize but two years later when Joyce returned to Ireland on 29 July the first person he saw was Gogarty (his uncomplimentary description in a postcard to Stannie was 'Gogarty's fat back') who happened to be on Kingstown pier. He avoided a confrontation but two days later received an invitation to lunch at the Dolphin Hotel —

31-VII-'09   15 Ely Place
                                                      Dublin.

Dear Joyce: Curiosis Cosgrave tells me you are in Dublin. Before trying to get you to come to lunch at Dolphin on Monday next at 1 o'c I would like to have a word with you. My man will drive you across (if you are in). I leave town at 5 each evening: but there can be changes if you turn up.
He will call about 3.20. Do come if you can or will. I am looking forward to seeing you with pleasure. There are many things I would like to discuss and a plan or two to divert you. You have not yet plumbed all the depths of poetry; there is Broderick the Bard! of whom more anon.

                                                      Yours,
                                                      O.G.[22]

— an invitation which was cancelled because of a professional engagement.
When they finally met by chance in Merrion Square Gogarty was shocked by Joyce's appearance and blurted out, 'Jaysus, man, you're in phthisis.' Joyce walked on and tried to cut him but Gogarty followed, took his arm, and persuaded him to call to Ely Place. In the event he proved a stiff guest refusing all forms of hospitality.[23]
'You have your life', he said. 'Leave me to mine.' Finally Gogarty ran out of patience:

'Well, do you really want me to go to hell and be damned?'

'I bear you no ill-will', Joyce said. 'I believe you have some points of good nature. You and I of six years ago are both dead. But I must write as I have felt.'

'I don't care a damn what you say of me so long as it is literature.'

'Do you mean that?'

'I do, Honest to Jaysus! Now will you shake hands with me at least?'

'I will on that understanding.'

Actually their reluctant handshake was a farewell gesture rather than a reconciliation. Remaining intractable, Joyce refused to join the Gogartys for lunch in Enniskerry and left the house. His animosity was increased by F.J. Byrne's innuendo that Gogarty was partly responsible for Vincent Cosgrave's boast that Nora Barnacle had responded to Cosgrave's amorous advances, a false claim designed to break up the Joyces' marriage. The suggestion was even more groundless than Stannie's charge that he was responsible for his brother's drinking but Joyce was by now prepared to believe anything nasty about Gogarty.[24]

They never met again but continued to display a baleful interest in each other's doings, Joyce losing no opportunity to scoff. He referred to *An Offering of Swans* as 'a quartet for sea brass' and when 'The Mill at Naul' was published in *The Irish Times* he dismissed Gogarty as a 'baker's roundsman'. And yet after Joyce's death one of the two books that were found on his desk was Gogarty's *I Follow Saint Patrick*.

Constantine Curran, a friend of both, has said that Gogarty's hostility did not exist until he was pilloried in *Ulysses*,[25] whereas Joyce's envy is recorded in an 'epiphany' written in 1903 or 1904. If one is to apportion blame, Joyce's notorious capacity for turning on well-wishers must be remembered, while credit goes to Gogarty for many kindnesses. The truth of the matter, however, may be that they had out-grown one another, the ribaldry that united them worn thin, the obscenities becoming tedious. Neither man had succeeded in revealing himself to the other, the true personae hidden by their regularly assumed masks of mockery. Gogarty expressed himself more fully and more naturally in his letters to G.K.A. Bell which reflect deeper thought and, surprisingly, an element of melancholy, aspects of character not apparent in the Buck Mulligan of *Ulysses* which is a brilliant and malicious caricature.

Gogarty was also the model for Doherty in *Stephen Hero* and Robert Hand in *Exiles*. He lent something, too, to the creation of a number of characters in *Dubliners,* the self-satisfied Ignatius Gallagher, the ne'er-do-well Jimmy Doyle in 'After the Race' and Lenehan in 'Two Gallants'. Joyce etched his friends and acquaintances pitilessly and it is interesting to compare his version of John Elwood ('Temple' in *A Portrait*) with Gogarty's description of the student from County Roscommon. Joyce describes him as 'a lean student with olive skin and lank black hair', a provincial with 'an indistinct bleating voice' and uses Cranly to damn him further: 'Sure, you might as well be talking, do you know, to a flaming chamber pot as talking to Temple. Go home, Temple, for God's sake go home.'[26] Gogarty regards him more affectionately and speaks of his dancing eyes and beautiful mouth, and of 'his exaltations and exclamations at the wonder of the world and his adventures in it.'[27] He succeeds in adding stature to a friend who was something of an oddity, rather than diminishing him, as Joyce did, to expand and justify his egotism.

George Moore's reply to Mrs. Gogarty when she objected to his misappropriation of her son's name in *The Lake* was, 'Madam, find me a name composed of two joyous dactyls and I will substitute it for Oliver Gogarty.' The inspired Joyce found just such a name — Malachai Mulligan — crowned it with the eighteenth-century epithet 'Buck' and created a character which a few further touches of humanity might have made acceptable.

Understandably, Gogarty, who by now was a public figure, was more angry with Joyce than his mother ever was with Moore. He said, 'that bloody Joyce whom I kept in my youth has written a book you can read on all the lavatory walls of Dublin' and he may have counted it a blessing that *Ulysses,* though never formally banned in Ireland, was not available in the book shops. He said no more than Bernard Shaw and Shane Leslie and the majority of his generation had said already and when an exceptional note of appreciation by A.J. Leventhal was accepted for publication by the *Dublin Magazine,* the printers refused to handle it.[28] The book was a scandal and Gogarty was incensed that he should appear in it as a major character.[29] The passage of time which rehabilitated *Ulysses* lent no ease to his case: his fictional role as Malachai St. Roland Mulligan threatened his separate identity as Oliver St. John Gogarty. His further strictures were, from his viewpoint, entirely justifiable.

17

Elbow Room

Reacting to a dismal occasion Oliver Gogarty said, 'As for weeping
— I feel more inclined to turn upon the toe.' He would have been
at home in the company of Villon or Ben Johnson and upheld the
tradition of the literary pubs that it is better to lose a friend (or a
libel action) than a jest such as the following unkind comment:
'I think "Wild Earth" interred Colum, or was it tame flesh in his
convent-cooled wife.' Worse still (but how accurate!) that remark,
worthy of a maliciously-inspired cartoonist, that de Valera looked
like a cross between a corpse and a cormorant.

Reading in the evening paper that a solicitor he disliked had been
involved in a traffic accident, knocked down by a Rolls Royce, he
said, 'At last, struck off the Rolls!' When a young man named Story
was introduced to him he shook his hand and said, 'Welcome to our
rough island, Story!' Having said that a critic had read the wrong
edition he was asked what edition he should have read: 'the Braille
edition!' Condoms, he said, might be called Roger Casements.

He said of a colleague that, 'His lips were juicy with self-appre-
ciation' and he referred mockingly to Synge whose style he disliked. 'A fellow who could write "Flames, he's winning" without
a smile. The humour of the phraseology was lost in the utility he
saw in it. All he needed to make him look the Puritan was a steeple
hat.' He spoke of Molly Colum as 'one of the rancid women who
shake one's belief in the juniper berry'.

He refused a subscription to the Maynooth Mission to China,
saying he'd prefer to contribute to the Chinese Missions to Maynooth.
Echoing the catechism definition of Purgatory he described Ireland
as 'a place or state of punishment where some souls suffer until
the time comes when they can go abroad.'

The sale of 15 Ely Place to the Royal Hibernian Academy confirmed that his surgical career in Dublin was ending. 'The Senate
cost me my practice,' he told Shane Leslie[1] but the loosening professional ties gave him his freedom to spend more time in Connemara where on an April morning in 1938 a dripping ship's boy

who had swum ashore from the *Daisy Star* in the early hours brought the news to Renvyle House Hotel that the Westport trawler had gone aground on a submerged reef.

Gogarty and his son dressed and rowed out to the ship where they helped the crew to throw ballast overboard and staunch the leak in the bows. When a reporter spoke to him he said, 'it was an ideal morning for a shipwreck. Dawn was breaking. Incidentally, so was the ship.'[2]

Dawn in Renvyle reveals a matchless seascape framed to the northwest by the grey-blue smudge of Achill and in the middle distance by the vast mass of Muilrea. On a clear morning the pitted cone of Croagh Patrick catches the light, mysterious and remote 'like a mountain in Elysium'. Closer to the Connemara coast, in the centre of the bay, Clare Island holds the eye and beside it tiny Caher Island seems insignificant, a desolate whale-shaped slab of barren rock, the most westerly point of Saint Patrick's journey.

Gogarty toiled to the summit of Croagh Patrick and sailed to Caher Island while writing *I Follow Saint Patrick* which was published in 1938 after a lengthy gestation. He had mentioned it in 1930 to Lady Leslie[3] — 'Ulster calls me because I have to do "In the Steps of" series and I am stalking Saint Patrick!' — but he had the project in mind much earlier and discussed the manufacture of swords with Richard Lane-Joynt his colleague at the Meath Hospital who died in 1928.

This book is an exercize in geographical history rather than biography. What he lacked in basic scholarship he no doubt intended to make up by inquiry and an application of commonsense. Relating an expert's reply to a question he observed: 'No, that's the whole thing in a nutshell. But we don't want things in a nutshell, for ancient history is too prone to crystallise itself into nutshells, and so prevent an expansive view.' Well-equipped to take the broadest view, Gogarty recalled Claudian on sea-raiders, consulted a metallurgist on old weapons, and visited Wales and the West Country; the relevant Irish landscapes, already familiar to him, were revisited. Placing reliance on tradition, he selected his premises:

I put forward the suggestion that it was a fleet of Nial of the nine Hostages which captured Patrick in the year of that King's death at sea 405, and presumed it to be possible that the raid took place on the return journey of the fleet rather than on its outgoing....Many scholars agree in naming Nial as the raider, and many, too, agree with the conjecture that the scene was 'in the region of the lower Severn'. Having tramped these regions with the results set out, I came to rest in the one place in the neighbourhood where there .is not only a living tradition but also witnesses in stone to testify to the Saint's having dwelt in and been venerated in St. David's. And from this he was taken in a raid.[4]

The harsh horror of the raid is brilliantly evoked. 'Shouts in a hoarse language that was heard in the Welsh hills for a thousand years before the first word of English, give orders for the bestowal of the captives.' They wade out to the waiting ships for transport to the slave market at the mouth of the Boyne. But by selecting the twelfth of July ('because I wished to get as near as possible to the mentality of the fifth century') for his visit to Slemish, Gogarty indulges himself, and not only at the expense of the drum-beating Orangemen: 'May they never be merged with the South....Athens might as well attempt to bring in Sparta — leave them alone. We want no drums in Dreamland.'

Gogarty admits using conjecture almost to the point of invention but the immemorial landscapes of his book have changed only superficially since Patrick saw them. It was then 'A land of waving woods, hidden rivers and palisaded mounds', but from the heights it is today unaltered:

When you look south from Slemish you see the Mountains of Mourne like pale amethysts, rising in four increasing summits to be crowned by Slieve Donard beyond the shores of Strangford Lough. It is to the west of these hills that the traveller must keep, for the mountains fall sheer into Dundrum Bay and forbid passage by its shores. Further to the west the hills rise again, so the road must have run, as it runs to-day, through the Gap of the North.[5]

Gogarty proposed to strip back the centuries and disclose those horizons which formed successive back-drops to the dramatic life of Saint Patrick. In no way inferior to the best landscape painters, his eye resolved the vistas before him into their elements, his command of language transmitting impermanent retinal images to a new medium enabling their transfer into the more durable repository of the printed page. Examples to illustrate his conspicuous talent have already been given and space permits no more than one more, a fine depiction of the Hill of Slane at dusk:

From the East, cerulean clouds lay low upon the world. The Hill of Slane was lessened by the rising ground dimly seen beyond, crowned by the wood en brousse on the hill of Cullen and by an intervening hill. Earth loomed bluer than the sky, and so blue was the land that a faint mist caused a lake-like water to spread between the hill and Tara's height, as if the submerged and invisible valley of the Boyne were flooded as in the days when it first overflowed from its uncovered source.[6]

He drew, too, on his historical imagination to present an unforgettable picture of the confrontation between the emissary of the new religion and the pagan High King:

Robed in but one colour, robed in ghostly white, crowned with the golden fillet of his mitre, from which a flat disc like an axe-blade rose over his forehead, the solemn figure, greater than all magicians, appeared. In his chasuble and mitre he looked like a Roman Caesar, crowned, divine, triumphant on the Capitoline Hill; and Tara heard the mystic voice of Eternity, the everlasting words of Rome, Latin, the strongest spell of all:

'Hi in curribus, et hi in equis, nos autem in nomine Domini nostri ambulabimus...

Some in chariots and some on horseback, but we in the name of the Lord!'

Adzehead had come! The Druids were face to face with their destiny.[7]

Unfortunately, the secondary purpose implicit in his title, the description of his own itinerary, introduced a second hero into a book with room for only one, and afforded opportunities for discursiveness which Gogarty could not resist. An anonymous reviewer complained, tongue-in-cheek, that 'occasionally the pious pilgrim slips away to take a little stroll down Sackville Street.'[8] Nor does Gogarty's style, inclined to the informal and conversational, always do justice to the theme.

To venture into the disputed byways of Patrician studies was a risky enterprise from which Gogarty does not emerge unscathed. The reviewer already mentioned took him to task for introducing wrong forms of Irish names and 'equally courageous independence of the rules of orthography and grammar in the German language' but to the general reader less concerned with minutiae, however important, the book should continue to appeal.

I Follow Saint Patrick provides a taper to hold against the not quite impenetrable shadows of the past, reducing them a little, and among other things Gogarty's repudiation of the conventional representation of the Saint 'bedight in modern chasuble, mitred and senile' is refreshing:

> His energy must have been as terrific as his endurance, so *pace* our artists, for all their piety I cannot see the Saint as they see him, frail, elderly and emaciated; but rather do I call him up to the mind's eye as an active man between forty-five and sixty, in the full vigour of his years. And most of all I think of him as a man of commanding presence.[9]

Having followed Saint Patrick the author's enduring impression was of 'a definite living force and spiritual personality unique in the Calendar of Saints'. A cynic might question Gogarty's familiarity with that particular Calendar. Nevertheless, do not the following generalizations, written more than forty years ago, have augmented meaning in our own troubled times? 'His presence is a bond, a common heritage, an obligation of goodwill.... It comes to this, then: that an Ireland without Saint Patrick is unthinkable. Every person in our island shares something of the personality of that steadfast and enduring man who is spoken of more frequently with affection than with awe.' Do they not recall a message neglected by violent men, and by others in the clamour of the hustings?

He was pleased with the reception of *I Follow Saint Patrick* and wrote to Dr. Patrick McCartan from Connemara in August:

> Before coming down here to finish 'Tumbling in the Hay' I sent you two periodicals containing reviews of St. Patrick. All the reviews were astonishingly favourable....It should have good sales in the U.S.A. though I find that I get better returns from Europe as well as better advances of royalties. I wish I knew the addresses of some U.S.A. publishers other than Reynal and Hitchcock to whom I might offer my next book on Oliver Goldsmith which will bring in the Dr. Johnson group, the state of Ireland in 1740-60 and debunk Boswell.[10]

He had another American lecture tour in mind and asked Mc Cartan for the address of Feakin a New York lecture agent, mentioning that he had refused Curtis Brown's offer of £2,000 and £400 travelling expenses for an eight-week tour. He referred, too, to

Yeats's illness. 'From all sides the opinion is that the poor old man will not last long but you and your committee will be forever remembered for having made the burden of his declining years easy to bear. If he can move — and I shall be in Dublin living on the strength of St. Patrick with the Vicar Apostolicus — next week I will bring him down here for a rest by lake and sea.'

Others to Adorn, which was almost identical with *Selected Poems* in format and content, was published by Constable in 1938. A reviewer in the *Dublin Magazine* complained that his technique was sometimes uneven, but 'at his best in such poems as the classical and crystalline "Good Luck" and the drowsily beautiful "Mill at Naul", he can hold his own with any poet writing today. It is a volatile book, varied and in different modes; there are poems to the Irish countryside lit by a bright clarity and youthful freshness of vision; poems to lovers and poems to friends; those to Lorcan Galeran are vivid and robust portraits; there are elegant pastiches of the cavalier poets such as "Begone Sweet Ghost", which would not disgrace a contemporary of Waller or Suckling.'[11]

Nineteen-thirty-nine was to be an eventful year for Gogarty, a fateful year for the nations menaced by Hitler. Wintering on the Riviera, W.B. Yeats died in January closing an epoch and leaving an immortal name. A few weeks later *Tumbling in the Hay* was published. The discursive and anecdotal style which detracted from *I Follow Saint Patrick* suits this book in which autobiography is lightly disguised as an impressionistic novel.

Set at the beginning of the century when Gogarty's hopes were as yet untarnished by disillusion, *Tumbling in the Hay* is free of the combativeness that mars *Sackville Street.* In this joyous book the protective comedy of medical-student life see-saws with the aspirations of the timorous disciples of Aesculapius, and the irreverence of youth cocks a snook at the wiser counsels of their elders. The author presides as 'Gideon Ousley' and despite his statement that 'all the characters are fictitious' many are well-known university dons and undergraduates.

For better or worse, continuous assessment and intransigent attitudes towards academic sluggards have put an end to the 'chronics', formerly the most colourful fauna of the Dublin medical schools, but the schools, too, have changed and in *Tumbling in the Hay* we retrieve a vanished city, the Dublin, incidentally, of Bloomsday, and readers of *Ulysses* will recognize the genesis of the Oxen-of-the-Sun episode in Gogarty's chapter on Holles Street Hospital. The Hay

Hotel has disappeared into legend like its wayward customers:

> *Though it is 'hotel' all right,*
> *No one ever stayed the night*
> *For we always came so late*
> *That the night was out of date,*
> *When the sun indecent lit*
> *Summerhill and Britain Street.*

Gogarty assembles a variegated cast of well-rounded characters including a rascally coroner who regularly breakfasted on 'an aspirin and a naggin of malt', Hosanna the barrister who 'could rant like a street preacher or whisper as insinuatingly as a charwoman ordering a glass of plain', Weary Mac, Silly Barney and other feckless medicals, and there are repeated allusions to an intriguing and insubstantial worthy, Jack Lalor the Barber — 'But he will forever be unmet, fresh brushing through the grass behind his dog before the dew has lifted in the morning air.' The narrative commences with a cab-ride and takes Ousley and his socially-conscious mother away from the Catholic University Medical School in Cecilia Street; it ends six years later with another cab-ride, a journey of carousal which breaks off at the Dolphin Hotel, a further almost forgotten landmark. Meanwhile, much of the action has taken place in Golly's pub with visits to a friendly pawnbroker, to Mrs. Mack's in Nighttown and to the Hay Hotel.

Something of the sentiment which inspired Sir Toby Belch's 'Dost thou think, because thou art virtuous, there shall be no more cakes and ale?' permeates *Tumbling in the Hay*. The abandon and absurdity of that unusual hostelry allowed Ousley to look at life afresh: 'This must be the explanation of my desire for "low company" — one gets away from sophistication, one savours life nearer to the bone. It is only by living above moralising that we can become innocent enough to enjoy life.' Nevertheless, he remains conscious, as a medical student must, of dangers abounding in Nighttown, moralizing a little on that score '... as we walked through the long rancid hell, the frowsy pores of whose awful denizens tainted even its polluted air'.

The Hegelian dialectic which Professor Macran, 'the Master of Those who Know', loved to dwell on may be constituted in the contrast between the ordered erudition of Trinity College and the unlettered patrons of the Hay Hotel but in his novel, Gogarty, whose own life encompassed many opposites, treats us to both. The inhuman examination for Fellowship, as he points out, broke the intellects of some of the Fellows leaving them 'solitaries or eccentrics fit for nothing but to be tutors, palaeographists, mathematicians or musicians, a browbeaten banished race, sending out by night furtive notes from quad-surrounded flutes, all but inaudible but fairy-like music in the silence under the moon when the College was supposed to be asleep'. Not so with his heroes, Mahaffy and Macran, or 'the benign Doctor', Robert Yelverton Tyrrell of whom he wrote:

> He looked out upon the world from a sustained viewpoint of lofty irony and agreeable disdain born of a classical self-sufficiency, a kind of Epicurean stoicism before which the common and undistinguished ways of men appeared as hardly to be borne, and the ways of the pretentious and the self-righteous not to be borne at all, but to be encountered by sarcasm. But even his sarcasm was benign.[12]

Tumbling in the Hay, a comic masterpiece, a wonderfully funny book with its population of oddities and geniuses, each clearly presented and individually endowed with his appropriately intricate dialect or superbly modulated tones, is unique and uncontrived. Gogarty never again came so close to perfection.

An undue sensitivity may have prompted M.J. MacManus's censorious complaint that 'the bad taste of many portions of this book is indisputable' for the *Times Literary Supplement's* reviewer found that the author 'maintains an agreeable discretion long lost by the modern novelist'. Harold Nicolson stressed that far from being merely frolic memoirs it was 'a work of very competent art':

> All creative artists have been driven to despair by the impossibility of conveying in written words either the intensity of their own feelings or the mobility of life.
> Yet to some curiously gifted artists (to Smollett and Fielding, and, in our own days, to Joyce and Virginia Woolf) has been accorded a faculty of reproducing upon the printed page an illusion of life's dynamic fantasy. Dr. Gogarty belongs to this rare and honourable category. His *As I was Going Down Sackville Street* was a feat of exceptional vitality. His new book *Tumbling in the Hay* is even more astonishing.[13]

The distance the reviewer lived from Dublin and the warmth of his notice of Gogarty's books were often directly proportional; the

Dublin Magazine's critic complained of anatomical jokes and detected in the highlighting of youth an assertion of outgrown values. 'Hence his book is a symbol and beneath the verbal juggling is an emotional fantasy. Stephen Daedalus searches morbidly for a father. Here the father becomes his own son and mistakes a ghost for himself.'[14] Sir Hugh Walpole, on the other hand, made a complimentary reference to *Sackville Street* and said that *Tumbling in the Hay* was 'a kind of annexe to that remarkable decorated building'.

It appears that Gogarty harboured ill-will towards Samuel Beckett for supporting Harry Sinclair's libel action and after the publication of *Murphy,* a *roman à clef,* he urged Austin Clarke to institute proceedings against Beckett for featuring him as Austin Ticklepenny. Clarke glanced at the novel but found it such heavy-going that he decided that few in Dublin would read it. Wisely he refused to make a fuss about it.[15]

With Gogarty in this litigious frame of mind an opportunity for taking offence presented when Patrick Kavanagh mentioned him by name in *The Green Fool:* 'I mistook Gogarty's white-robed maid for his wife — or his mistress; I expected every poet to have a spare wife.' The author was, in the legal sense, a man of straw but Gogarty sued the publishers, Michael Joseph, Ltd., and the printers William Brendon & Son Ltd., for defamation of character.

When the action was heard in London in the King's Bench Division before Mr. Justice Macnaghten and a jury on 21 March 1939 he was awarded £100 damages and costs but despite the apparent vindication of the judgement for the plaintiff the episode was unfortunate. Today Patrick Kavanagh's many readers (forgetting his assaults on others in the 'Paddiad') resent what they regard as an established writer's attack on an obscure provincial still struggling to make his name.

The allegedly libellous words seem so innocuous that one wonders if a tender spot had been touched. The lines 'To Catullus' in Gogarty's unpublished papers hint at something of the sort —

> *Until I felt, I never knew*
> *What torture she had put you through*
> *Who held you on Love's rack.*
> *How could I sympathise before*
> *I loved just such a lovely whore*
> *A whore and nymphomaniac?*[16]

— but remain unexplained. No suspicion of romantic irregularity attaches to his name in Dublin where his contemporaries regarded

22   National Maternity Hospital, Holles Street.

23   The Richmond Hospital.

24   Allgemeines Krankenhaus, Vienna.

25   Meath Hospital.

SELECTED POEMS

OLIVER
ST·JOHN GOGARTY

26   Dust jacket of *Selected Poems* by Bip Pares.

AS I WAS
GOING DOWN
SACKVILLE STREET

A
Phantasy in Fact

BY
OLIVER ST. JOHN
GOGARTY

With an Introduction by
FRANCIS HACKETT

AN EXTRAORDINARY BOOK by a
distinguished Irish doctor, senator, wit
and man of letters—an amazing combination
of memoirs, fierce and witty commentary and
sheer mad imagery, portraying Dublin, Irish
and English life as he has known them. "Here
at last is Gogarty", says Mr. Hackett in his
introduction, "and for those who have been
watching the Irish literary scene it is a stroke
of fortune."

27   Dust jacket of *As I was Going Down Sackville Street* (American edition).

TELEGRAPHIC ADDRESS:
"PROXIMITY, LONDON."

TELEPHONE NO.
466, KING'S CROSS.

GOWER HOTEL,
GOWER STREET STATION,
N.W.

9·3·VI·06

Dear Joyce

I shall be in the overwhelmed city tomorrow Wednesday. If I rise in time I shall call up to the fortress of all the Joyces about 7.45. We must solve the importunate particle-reason, together. You will be glad to see me again & I reciprocate your feelings

Yours

Caddie Rouselle.

28   Letter to James Joyce signed 'Caddie Rouselle'. Courtesy of Cornell University.

15, ELY PLACE,
DUBLIN.

To T Gillman Moorhead.

It takes us all our time with all our eyes
To learn to know, since knowledge comes from sight;
And long before we give light back for light
Evening is on us, and the daylight flies:
But you were swifter, and your faculties
Gathered more quickly, so the mind is bright
That, long before the evening, fell on night,
And it shall comfort you to realise
That, when we all are into darkness sent,
The dark of which you had more than your share,
If there be succour in Time's banishment,
Pre-eminent again, you'll help us where
The sudden dark, the vague beleaguerment,
Calls for such fortitude as you can spare

Oliver St J Gogarty
Christmas 1929

29 Holograph of *To T. Gillman Moorhead* by Oliver St John Gogarty. Courtesy of the Royal College of Physicians of Ireland.

To his Friends when His Prostate Shall have become Enlarged.

Bear with me, Friends, when, ill-defined,
The mortal part shall touch my mind,
And men shall think askance at me
And my postcocious potency.

If I, a philosophic freak,
On "Cruelty to Children" speak,
Remember that, in point of fact,
My thoughts may dwell beyond Stead's Act.

When the gland sets my mind on fire,
Urging inordinate Desire,
And, from the Sea 'neath which it lies
A Thousand Venuses arise,

And I am contemplating rape,
And growing careless of escape,
And Lust, not Art entrances me -
For who writes old men's poetry?

And I am guarded down the Street,
Then let your kind Committee meet:
"We loved him, young, for his large heart -
Stand by this hypotrophic part!"
Thus may the Town be set at ease
And learn to pity my disease
Till I, with undishonoured head,
Join the uncopulating Dead.

NATIONAL MATERNITY HOSPITAL,

HOLLES STREET,

DUBLIN,

This is to Certify that
Mr Oliver Fogarty has attended
the practice of The National
Maternity Hospital from 1st July 03
1903 to the 7th January 1904
and has attended 32 Cases
Having had personal Charge of 12

Signed .... A.B. ....
Jany 18th 1907

31   Certificate of attendance at National Maternity Hospital, 1903.

the motivation of the regrettable action as the desire to take a bumptious upstart down a peg. Like the former libel suit it has had a disproportionate effect on Gogarty's reputation and should be seen as something quite out of character, for on many occasions he went out of his way to help fellow-writers.

To celebrate his victory he lunched on 22 March with Sir William Rothenstein who described him to Enid Starkie as 'a joyous, wise libidinous companion, with a Rabelaisian note, which I like.'[17]

In retrospect the most notable literary event of 1939 was the publication on 4 May of James Joyce's *Finnegans Wake* which a few days later was reviewed by Gogarty in the *Observer*. His notice was both perceptive and confused, eulogistic and condemnatory. He called it 'the most colossal leg-pull in literature since McPherson's Ossian' but cited Yeats's opinion 'that this kind of prose made any other colourless'; he dismissed it as 'the language of a man speaking, trying to speak, through an anaesthetic' but, with physiological insight, said, 'It is an attempt to get at words before they clarify in the mind.' Whether it be civilization's panegyric or its funeral celebration it certainly is literary Bolshevism.

Despite Gogarty's equivocations his review pleased Joyce:

When I think of the indomitable spirit that plodded on, writing *Ulysses* in poverty in Trieste, without a hope of ever seeing it published, I am amazed by the magnitude of this work, every word of which in its 628 pages, twisted, and deranged in order to bring up associated ideas in the mind...The immense erudition employed, and the various languages ransacked for pun and word-associations is almost incredible to anyone unaware of the superhuman knowledge the author had when a mere stripling. In some places the reading sounds like the chatter during the lunch interval in a Berlitz school. Every language living and dead in Europe gabbles on and on.

Gogarty's tributes — 'indomitable', 'erudition', and 'magnitude' — delighted Joyce who said to Frank Budgen that Gogarty was an athlete and knew the value of staying-power. One is tempted to believe that in this last brief communion of minds, Gogarty had warm recollections of the knowledgeable 'Kinch' before life changed him, and that Joyce had unrancorous memories of his former drinking-companion.

Towards the end of the year the Cuala Press published *Elbow Room*. The poem which gave the collection its title describes a remote attic 'in the vault of Space', a dark uninviting place, but a place offering relief from the pressing discontents of his present environment:

> *Oh! what a place to speak your mind*
> *Without disquieting mankind!*
> *There's where I would find elbow room*
> *Alone, beyond the crack of doom.*

Provoked originally by local irritants, principally the narrow-minded political regime against which he had waged verbal war, by the time of its publication 'Elbow Room' could also serve as a symbol for the turmoil of European conflict and the war against totalitarianism in which Ireland stood officially neutral but thousands of Irishmen participated.

The defence of democracy cannot, however, have been Gogarty's most pressing concern in the summer of 1939 and despite his decision to volunteer for service as a medical officer in the British forces it would be foolish to explain his subsequent actions on this basis. But would it not be equally incorrect to accept the frequently-made assertion that Sinclair's victory in the libel case was a determining factor in Gogarty's self-imposed exile? Had the costly legal proceedings been financially crippling this reverse of fortune could have been easily mended by re-directing his energies into remunerative surgical practice. Instead his decision led him into a hazardous living by his pen.

His reasons for leaving Ireland are conjectural but as he was physically fit and temperamentally optimistic, a spirit of adventure may have been the strongest motivating force. His disenchantment with his role as a cipher in the political party in opposition is registered in a letter to Shane Leslie and is also relevant:

Saddened by the drabness, misery and meanness of my natal city under the exclusive Commune, I, finding myself the only householder in a cul-de-sac of tenements, sold Ely Place to that treble contradiction in terms the Royal Hibernian Academy. The Institution is to turn my garden into a non-Platonic Academe and build its picture gallery thereon.[18]

There is really no evidence that his initial intention was permanent residence abroad and it is to be presumed that his decisions were moulded by the opportunities that presented. By now his sons were married and self-supporting — Noll was a rising barrister, Dermot an architect with a growing practice — and Brenda was making a name for herself as a sculptress with busts of such notabilities as Jack B. Yeats, Colonel Maurice Moore, Lennox Robinson and Eric Shipton, the explorer and mountaineer, to her credit. Mrs. Gogarty, a stay-at-home with none of her husband's restlessness, was happy supervising the running of Renvyle House Hotel which should have provided an ample income. He was on a free rein and meant to enjoy himself.

PART THREE

18

There is a Happy Land . . .

At sixty-one Oliver St. John Gogarty was too old to enroll in the armed services. When to his disappointment his application to join the Royal Air Force was rejected he went ahead with plans for a lecture tour. His intention was to spend some months in the United States but like John Butler Yeats, another great Irish talker earlier in the century, he found New York City so congenial that he settled there.

His visa was granted on 14 September 1939. Shortly after this, to the envy of his Irish aviator friends, he made the transatlantic crossing by seaplane from Foynes. In many ways it was a liberation, and experiencing a surge of energy he set about recording his impressions and looking up the friends he had made during his earlier visits. Then he commenced an arduous and badly-arranged lecture tour which took him five times to Canada, three times to Chicago, and south to Charleston, Dallas, and steamy New Orleans.

From the Book-Cadillac Hotel, Detroit, he wrote to Miss Marilla Freeman, President of Cleveland's Women's Club:

Dear Miss Freeman,

This is a line very sincerely to thank you for your splendid sponsoring of me last evening and for inviting me to that enjoyable dinner.

Very kindly convey to your friend and colleague how I regret being unable to visit him as arranged.

How I wish that the remainder of this itinerary could be such fun!

> Believe me to be
> Dear Miss Freeman,
> Yours sincerely,
> Oliver St. John Gogarty.[1]

239

Writing to Noll, his barrister son, from Amarillo, Texas, he described how the editor of the local *Daily News* had taken him hunting rabbits with a bow. 'I am getting extra money for articles. One could live here well but I will stay only as long as I can send cash home to relieve the bad times that must come.'[2]

On the completion of the tour, in mid-December, he visited his recently-widowed sister in Hollywood which he found to be a charming city of illusion where he met a number of the anonymous scholars who were masters of the new art of turning prose into pictures. He failed to interest any of the producers in his own work and was led to the conclusion that to be selected a book had to be such a best-seller that the producers are forced to screen it. He did not meet Sam Goldwyn but reported his latest to Shane Leslie: 'I assure you it is the *mucus* of the whole situation. If you don't believe me, include me out.'[3]

The novelty of air travel, difficult for present-day readers to appreciate, is expressed in Gogarty's 'High Above Ohio' which described how, god-like he can behold East and West in a glance and —

> *See alternate valleys gleam*
> *Each one with its little stream,*
> *And the undulant, immense,*
> *Free, American expanse.*[4]

The physical vastness of America appealed to him as did the breadth of outlook of its forward-looking people, a people who had originally been nomadic and whose towns, as a result, are 'tepees enlarged and luxurious'.

The trees, rivers, and mountains of America delight me. All smallness was forever driven out of me. Even though the inhabitants have not as yet dominated the landscape (it is the other way round just now), signs are not wanting that the landscape is entering into American literature. The trees of America are more varied than those of the Old World. Among them is the female yew tree from which bows are made for the best archers in the world.... Of trees in bloom who can speak? Acre after acre of apple orchards in bloom — a sight that can hardly be sustained such is the joy it transmits.[5]

According to Francis Thompson: *Our towns are copied fragments of our breasts/And all man's Babylons strive but to impart/The grandeurs of his Babylonian heart.* New York City, the apotheosis of the urban and the modern Babylon, has its detractors and admirers. Gogarty became a fervent and perceptive admirer.

What if the evolution of the skyscraper was determined by the exigencies of space and the dictates of financiers? The architects and engineers were silent and unrecognized poets. 'From blue drawings they built compliant to commerce, yet not unmindful of Art.' Their masterpieces were the response to an unprecedented challenge, the outcome of daring imaginations assisted by unbounded prosperity. 'Art is the manifestation of the mind of a nation and from it the character of that mind may be judged and the chance of the survival of the nation appraised.'

He thought Manhattan, with the blessing of deep water on both sides, the 'lordliest Venice of the world'.

Venice with its far-famed Giotto's tower,[6] what is it to the towers of New York? It is beaten even for very grace. This tower town is unequalled in the mind of man. And it knows something of the romance of towers. There is the Ritz Tower, Beekman Tower, Waldorf Tower and Tudor and Windsor Towers. Towers and towers and it towers to the lofty sky. That is what I meant when I said that 'skyscraper' was a misnomer in New York, for the sky is so lofty that it stands far above its towers. How well they balance each other, these soaring pavilions of the sky. The loveliest building on earth is the Chrysler building. Who dreamt of that mighty tower lightening off into that tenuous pinnacle as tapered as the snout of a sword-fish? How it conceals the great mass of the mighty pile. And the way its roof is designed: shell upon shell, dark as lead during the day but see it with the sun from the East River upon it and it can hardly be endured that brilliance supernal making invisible the exquisite spire that is lost in light.[7]

He could not tire of watching the Chrysler building; he liked to linger in 43rd Street just off Fifth Avenue feasting his eyes on it; he studied it from Tudor City and looked at it down Lexington Avenue. Unforgettable, bathed in sunlight, unimaginable at nightfall. 'When the lights come out in New York they are like so many fire-flies shining in a honey-comb. Light after light a delight to the beholder. They climb up through the thin air until they constellate the sky. Symbols of the aspirations of the people of this soaring city.'

He admired the young American women, 'tall and slight and *bien soignée,* with large orbits and beautifully formed lips and slender calves and feet.' He liked the chatty informative taxi-drivers and the Irish policemen.

'Have you ever heard of Balla?' an Irish cop asked him, stopping the whole street with a wave of his hand like the London bobby in the Percy French song.

'Balla in Co. Mayo, is it?

'Now you're talking!', the policeman released the pent-up traffic. 'If you ever go to Balla tell them that you met me, and the boys will treat you well.'

One thing was missing, Gogarty reflected, that would have made it perfect. 'If there were only a river flowing down Park Avenue about as wide as one of the islands there, a river with a low wall on which you could lean your belly the way the boys do it in Westport, County Mayo, what a town it would be!'[8]

Expecting to sail for home in April 1940 and puzzled by the authorities' refusal to name the port they were bound for he said, 'Perhaps we will never make haven (only Heaven)!' A well-paid sale to Lippincotts encouraged him to stay for a further six months which he planned to prolong if he could have his visa extended. Meanwhile, as he informed Professor William Lyon Phelps of Yale, he had again volunteered for war service.[9] 'I tried to join up in Canada but they found out my age as if it mattered to me any more than Time touches you.'[10]

For a time he stayed at the Ritz Tower and later at Beekman Tower but eventually, becoming an American citizen, he settled in an apartment at 45 East 61st Street. This. too, though cramped and lacking air-conditioning, was a 'good address', pleasantly situated between Madison and Park Avenues. A short stroll westward provided the trees and greenery of Central Park stretched like a carpet flanked by the palaces he admired; a walk in the other direction took him within moments to Third Avenue where in one or other of the Irish taverns Gogarty was sure to find the transatlantic equivalent of the kind of company that made G.K. Chesterton, in London, exclaim, 'Will someone take me to a pub!'

Asked if he intended to return to Ireland he replied, 'Why should I? In Dublin I'd spend most of my time sitting in pubs talking to people for nothing. Here I make a comfortable living saying the same thing for money.' Now his reminiscences were saleable, a considerable advantage for a man who had turned his back on his profession but inhibitory to true creativity, especially at a time of life when nostalgia rules. An Irish friend who occasionally met him in New York has said, with a candour worthy of Gogarty himself, that he tended to spoil his charm as a companion 'by continually telling stories that he had already published in his books'.

His memory held the material on which he drew for lectures and articles. These were remunerative — the *Atlantic Monthly* paid him $300 for an essay on Lord Dunsany; Messner and Company offered him $250 per month for a twelve-month period while writing a book; *Harper's Bazaar* paid $200 for thirty-two lines of verse; he received $350 for a talk to the Library of Congress and Joseph Grace, a shipping magnate, paid him $1,000 for editing his daughter's poems. It was an improvement on Dublin where remuneration for an article 'would be only a pound or two'.[11]

Going Native, a novel published in 1940, and the least successful of his books, derives from the period during the Irish civil war that he spent in England. A conversation between his surrogate Gideon Ousley and W.B. Yeats in the latter's garden in Rathfarnham — 'Grandeur is gone, Ousley, Grandeur is gone' — is a prelude to Ousley's departure for England to play a part in what aspires to be a comedy of manners that contrasts English and Irish attitudes. 'There is no Kingdom of Heaven over here; the British Empire has replaced it.'

Estella Ruth Taylor[12] has praised the author's portrait of Yeats in *Going Native* — 'I looked closely at the face covered with its unageing ivory-brown skin and at the imperial brow so white and calm. His eyes were hard to catch directly. They were deep and bright, quick glancing as if a glance were all they needed for complete understanding of any mortal on whom they looked.' — and the book contains some fine descriptive passages, for instance his beautiful representation of a stately English home or his rumination on landscape:

If you lie back in a punt under a willow and watch the branches, pollard and all as they are, swaying very gently, almost imperceptibly, in an unfelt breeze, it is quite possible that you will be mesmerised to sleep. I was hard at work getting myself reconciled to the pollarding of the willows, to me another reminder of the orderly hand which is at work over the whole country and has been at work from time immemorial bringing all things, even the landscape, within the law; and thinking how different are the black and sour sally trees which grow in Connemara of the little lakes and flourish solitarily upright and untamed on the central island which nearly every lake possesses. Black, sour, choppy willow trees, good for a heronry or to shelter the red-berried mountain ash, stiff and ungraceful, unaccommodating trees....[13]

It is interesting, too, to have a glimpse of the infant Irish airline which provided a service between Baldonnel and Croydon but the fictional aspects are inferior to the factual. The book contains much that would do credit to an essayist but its fictional characters are unconvincing.

Even Ousley tires of his adventures within a few weeks:

The question is how long can I abide this civilisation, the greatest civilisation on earth? How long can I live with the pirates who have put on dinner jackets? How long can I live with the inventors of From Friday to Tuesday, the inventors of the long week-end?

Can I go native here for long, here where the larks sing beside factory chimneys, where the wild birds and the deer and even the poets are tame? I fear that my soul is sprouting again. I can hear the tinkle of the streamlets in the granite hills of home.[14]

A reviewer ('M.D.') in the *Dublin Magazine* who found in *Going Native* an 'unsatisfactory blend of fiction and biography' scolded the author for purple passages which 'suggest that Dr. Gogarty is parodying the essay of a schoolgirl who has just read the worst passages of Donn Byrne. It is some time before one realises that these pages are not a parody.'[15]

Mad Grandeur, a long historical tale published in 1941, was a logical and ambitious extension of Gogarty's habit of drawing on memory for the stuff of his books, but he presents an eighteenth-century tableau rather than a novel. A well-drawn and variegated tableau, to be sure, highly coloured and densely populated with French emigrés, Irish highwaymen, tapsters, fishermen, coachmen, starveling peasants, a numerous cast of horsemen, gamblers and villainous soldiers, all decked in period costume and moving against a background that includes hovels, country mansions and town houses, a canvas with so many distracting set pieces — the duel, the prize fight, the great race at the Curragh — that Hyacinth Martyn Lynch the young Connaught landlord, who is the author's somewhat priggish hero, fails to command our attention.

The *Dublin Magazine's* reviewer's sugar-coated complaint was that *Mad Grandeur* 'trails its length somewhat in the manner of Pope's famous Alexandrine.'[16] A less kind critic who found it 'false as history and unconvincing as fiction' refers to 'glaring anachronisms' which he does not detail but would include Denis St. George's use of twentieth-century methods of artificial respiration and the diagnosis of his semi-invalid mother's ailment as 'largely of the spirit, since no doctor had been able to find an organic cause for it'.

What strengths and interest the book now has reside in its descriptive passages — the account of the ash wood at Martyn Hall, for instance — and the light its final chapters shed on Gogarty's own character. Though his hero, Martyn Lynch, may refer to eighteenth-century French *sans-culottes,* his own mind is occupied with thoughts of twentieth-century Irish irregulars, and the flames that destroy Martyn Hall and Attymon House are those that brought down the roofs of Moore Hall and Renvyle House.

A civil war generation does not forgive its enemies. Gogarty was no exception and though writing ostensibly of 1798, rankling memories of his own political lifetime guided his pen. 'In the bitter mood that obsessed him he wanted to shut out forever the ominous sight of his slow-moving, lowering countrymen. They always hung about yards and back doors. Never did they come straight forward on any errand.'[17]

Ireland has won her freedom, but at what price? The illusory walk of a Queen reverted to the walk of a slattern. 'A revolution that succeeds is acceptable. What Cornwallis can never clean up is the feeling I have for what are, after all, I suppose, my own people. Why should I be made to entertain so much hate? It divides a man against himself.'[18]

Reading between the lines it is evident that young Martyn Lynch's sentiments are those which Gogarty had experienced; one is surprized (and relieved) to find that the caustic-tongued ex-Senator had such insight into his disaffection. With Griffith, Collins and Kevin O'Higgins dead, men of his own class whom he had admired endlessly, he was drawn increasingly into the company of men whose hour was also ending. Through his remarkably gifted personality he had earned a high place in Irish society at a time when bureaucracy was replacing aristocracy.

Perhaps at the bottom of all his troubles was the fact that he was a remnant and a freak. His ancestors should have left their land in the Flight of the Earls or have spread a wing with the

Wild Geese after Aughrim's fatal field. His friends originated from a different stock: Cromwellians and Williamites, whom the ruinous genius of the Old Lands had caught and infected with its out-of-date and heroic virtues — liberality, prodigality and mad grandeur.[19]

Hyacinth Martyn-Lynch, with his wife Ninon and their friend Denis St. George, engaged to Mabs Lynch (a prototype of Constance Gore-Booth), plan a fresh start in the New World and Toucher Plant, a dubious but resourceful character, helps them to find a ship. 'Anything is possible in America.'

The pace of the modern adventure story would leave *Mad Grandeur* at a standstill but it delighted James Montgomery who in the course of his occupation as film censor had seen more pictures than anyone in Dublin. He despatched a postcard: 'You should send *Mad Grandeur* to John Ford, Hollywood.'[20]

Among the old friends Gogarty met in New York was Frank Mac Dermot who was broadcasting about the necessity of making the Irish ports available to the British navy, propaganda which did not meet with Gogarty's approval. Another was Gerald Brockhurst, the Birmingham artist, who had settled in Manhattan as a leading portrait painter. His etching of Gogarty made an impressive frontispiece for a special collector's edition of *Elbow Room*.

The many new friends included André Michalopolus, professor of classical literature and civilization at Fairleigh Dickinson University and formerly Governor of the Ionian island, Kerkyra; Dr. William Spickers, a leading surgeon with whom he often lunched at Sardi's or the Russian Tea Room at West 57th Street; and Mrs. Mary Owings Miller, editor of *Contemporary Poetry*.

He spent some days in Barnert Memorial Hospital, Paterson, New Jersey in February 1942 and had treatment for rectal polypi which he described to Shane Leslie. 'I had them fulgurated, that is destroyed by tame lightning. "Some shall be saved: yet so as by fire," St. Paul. They were 10 inches from the surface. It would have filled Freud with consternation had he beheld my proctoderm turned into a thurifer to send up incense to Asculapius.'[21]

He also referred to this illness when writing to Mrs. Mary Owings Miller:

Your generosity and that of your husband is outstanding even in this open-hearted and openhanded country. Very many thanks to you both....I am glad to say that the operation, examination, preparation and every other botheration was within my means at the moment. All's well that ends well. But I shall be flippant when it comes to writing epitaphs. What intestinal trouble I had proved to be "benign": "full of benignitie" like the babe in Dunbar's 'Timor Mortis Conturbat me'. I was equally perturbed by the chance of malignitie.[22]

He mentioned to Mrs. Miller that he had seen only two reviews of *Elbow Room* including a rather irrelevant one from Molly Colum who had sent him an apology beforehand with the assurance that she would see that any objections he cared to make were published in the *New York Times* book review. 'It went on to say [Gogarty wrote] that she was in effect saving me from "lambasting" by another writer who did not like my attitude to James Joyce. Her idea of reviewing is odd. It is but a slight book. One does not expect poetry to pay even though they [sic] may expect to be reviewed on merit and not on attitude.'[23]

By now his decision to remain in America was hardening. Indeed, as he explained to Noll, in war time this was to follow the line of least resistance.

If I were to return to London I would find myself without an identification card....And I could earn nothing nor get out. Food will be Ireland's problem for the coming year. I hope that there are potatoes and beef enough on the farm [in Renvyle] to keep Mummy and Bee. You may have to fall back on the land before this war is over. I have finished a book and am starting another. Also giving 'lectures'. There's a livelihood in it and no banks to worry one. I wish I could get Mummy and Bee over here just to see the country through a year. There is every climate....[24]

He was at Trudeau near Saranac Lake in the Adirondacks during the hot summer weather of 1942 where by chance he encountered the grave of Hazel Lavery's first husband 'dead at 30 in 1904'.

News of wartime Dublin reached him through his numerous correspondents. Early in 1941 Dr. T.G. Moorhead who had married Stephen Gwynn's daughter wrote: 'Here in Dublin we carry on quietly, rather depetrolised and daily more or less petrified by censorship and rumour. The latter is the only untaxed and uncensored product of the Gael. We read your last book with much enjoy-

ment, it was lent to us by a lucky owner for 48 hours. It is, of
course, not obtainable in the Irish market.' His wife added a postscript: 'Dublin misses you and Academy dinners are grown very
staid and respectable.'[25] George Redding complained: 'I get no
word of you or your books....Have you deserted all your friends
and really Gone Native?'[26] Later in the year he described an evening
in Fanning's, then under new management, with a number of cronies
including Brinsley McNamara 'who is shockingly puffed up regarding
a reference by Smyllie in the Irish Times who printed the assertion
that he is a great conversationalist....There were also a couple of lads
junior to your generation. Your ghost was stripped of its shroud and
subsequently buried with full honours and many a bon mot.'[27]

Inevitably the news from time to time included unwelcome
tidings of illness and death; the dispersed Bailey coterie was in
the winter of life. 'I am hovering between wife and death,' James
Montgomery quipped. He died in the Mater Nursing Home after a
prostate operation on 14 March 1943. Some days earlier, knowing that
he was dying, he asked his son to write to Oliver Gogarty and George
Redding. 'I hope all goes well with you', wrote Dr. Joe Boyd
Barrett, 'I miss you very much. "Perdere amicum est damnorum
maximum" as the old Romans truly said. The "strong unmerciful
tyrant" has been very busy here in Dublin. Dear Old George Bonass
has left us....'[28] Bonass, in his heyday, had been a cricketer and bon
vivant; warned off alcohol when a patient in the Meath Hospital,
Gogarty came to his rescue and deceived the unsuspecting nurses
by bringing him whiskey in a hot water bottle.

> *Now that the stumps are drawn for you,*
> *Whom shall I tell my secrets to?*
> *You've gone where all good Fellows go,*
> *You've gone to join the bucks and beaux*
> *The florid boys with full-eyed faces*
> *And girls who know not what straight-lace is.*[29]

A desultorily-kept diary[30] for 1943 reveals Gogarty as an inveterate 'diner-out' (a term which includes other gregarious meals):

January 14th:	Lunched at Lyons 50 W with Major and Jim Healy. Had cold bad. Sinal pain and insomnia.
January 15:	Supper with Tischa Ling. Given five pints of Crystal Lake Water. Read the Phaedo until morning.

January 17th: Dined with Dr. John Erskine. Wonderful music
by Mr. Williams organist of St. Bartholo-
mew's — Liszt, Chopin, Beethoven on John's
Steinway grand piano.

January 18th: Went to Sonia Henje's skating company with
S. at Madison Square Gdns. Supper first. Home
11 pm. bus cross town and transfers to Madison. Show amusing. Madison Sq. Gdns. amazing.

January 19th: Dine with Major Montgomery Hyde to meet
the Millers 7.30.

January 24:   Lunch with Editor of Vogue 1 Gracie Sq. 1.30.
Dine with Harry Ericksen. Talked chiefly
about Walter Starkie recalling his eager and
avid ways. 'He smiles as if you and he knew
the whole world were a farce that may be
allowed to go to the devil provided that you
and I have a good time.' Ericksen.

Other gleanings show that a polyp was removed from the right
maxillary antrum towards the end of January and that he saw
Katherine Hepburn — 'tall, gaunt, big eyed and big mouthed' —
in *Without Love* at the St. James's Theatre. His regular friends included Dr. Vincent Hurley, F.R.C.S., Major Kinkead, James A.
Healy, Connie Neenan, Mrs. Ethel Mann, Mrs. Arthur Comstock and
her daughter Mabs, later Countess Moltke.

February 6:   Dined with Dr. Hurley in Chinatown, on, God
or Con-fu-ko knows what.

February 9:   Took out 'First Papers' accompanied, conducted
and greatly helped by James Healy who must be
related to me through great grandmother Healy
whose portrait used to hang in my Da's study in
No. 5 Rutland Square, Dublin. I remember how my
grandmother, Father's mother, had Mrs. Healy's
keys painted out and a bunch of grapes substituted.
It seems the keys suggested housekeeping!

He lectured to Boston's Eire Society on 14 February and spoke
in Binghampton, N.Y., two weeks later. A note of a dinner engagement for 17 March — 'Mrs Grenville Emmet 3 E94 dinner 8 pm black
tie' — is followed by a rueful entry, 'It was tomorrow!'

May 7th: Went to Panther Creek with Dr. James Krouk, Casper — Sheriff, Hill — Magistrate, Cuff and Hurley. I caught the one and only fish, 3 in.!

June 2nd: Went to Zoo.

On 8 July he took a train at Grand Central Station for a six-hour journey to Brattleboro to stay with Robert Flaherty at Black Mountain Farm in the Green Mountains of Vermont.

July 9th: Spend time adjusting myself to wider prospects and mountains.

July 18th: Swam in and sat by the forest pool. Had tea from a thermos.

July 27th: On horseback to West Dummerston. Balestrier's house — Mr. Miller. Horse given to rearing which was corrected by tapping him lightly between the ears.

He wrote to Neenie from Black Mountain Farm hoping that his letter would arrive in time 'to wish you many happy returns of your birthday and my love':

Vermont was settled by Scots and English and it is a farming country with fields and fences that recall Ireland. In Winter the temperature falls to fifty five below zero! The barns for the cattle are therefore close to the homes. It is the only State in which the population is decreasing because the Middle West is more fertile so Bob Flaherty picked up 120 acres of meadow and pine hills for £600 and transformed the barn into a huge studio with immense fireplace and windows that can slide and leave open one wall. The silver grey timbers he turned inside out or rather put the weathered side in, heated and plumbered the place and, with his freezing apparatus can live off his chickens, ducks and garden-produce all the year round. Mrs. F. knows nearly as much about running a place as yourself but with the swift ripening Summers and the assured sun and the methods of preserving and no labourers to deal with, has an easier time.

For forty miles the wooded mountains fold on one another as far as the eye can see. The effect is monotonous, so is the tone of their forests' green. A bare summit would refresh the eye...[31]

Despite the monotony of its scenery, Gogarty was delighted by the Green Mountains. 'The human body', he told a newspaper reporter, 'is at its best in certain parts of America, notably Vermont. In Vermont you could forget you had a body altogether.' He also expressed his enchantment in 'Dawn in Vermont':

> *The sun is rising mistily,*
> *The valley fills with gold*
> *I lie and wonder sleepily*
> *How many suns of old*
> *Arose and filled the valleys*
> *and lit each tree from tree*
> *Along the forest alleys*
> *And not a soul to see!*[32]

George Redding wrote to him in August 1943: 'Many thanks for (1) the "Bill Bavelier" poem — a very pleasant effort (2) your last letter and its break into song (3) the parcel containing ham and tea, which arrived all right and was greatly appreciated especially by my wife who asked me to send you her special thanks. I also received a copy of "Contemporary Poetry" containing your verses on the projected event which we hope will never take place.'[33]

Another poem written in 1943 was addressed to Madame Chiang Kai-shek (then in the United States at the height of her popularity) whom he saw as a modern Helen of Troy:

> *Madame, to-day that lady's place*
> *Is yours, the world's outstanding lady,*
> *With roles reversed: you ask for peace...*
> *To save from grim forbearing lords*
> *The delicate and gracious things:*
> *Wisdom and truth and forms of thought*
> *The immemorial ages wrought,*
> *From Vulpine and foresworn war lords*
> *Who still for all their vaunting brings*
> *Are savages in heart and brain*
> *Who mix with chivalry chicane...*

Like many others he changed his mind about the Kuomintang, coming to admire Mao Tse Tung 'the greatest man since Ghengis Khan' or even greater because he liberated the Chinese peasantry, the most down-trodden folk on earth. 'His actions cannot be included in the word "Communism". He is not Stalin's stooge. Hatred against the exploiters of China is what energises him.'

252 Oliver St. John Gogarty

The diary entries were resumed in the fall with some regularity:

October 10th:	Campbell and I walked under star-skied N.Y.
October 13th:	lunch Carmel Snow [editor of *Harper's Bazaar*] meet Ross of the New Yorker. Chateaubriand 1.15.
October 31st:	Trip no further, pretty sweeting/Girdles end in lovers meeting/ Every old maid's son doth know.
November 4th:	Went to 122 E.36 to meet Dr. Jimmy Yen of China.
November 23rd:	Wrote in a few hours 'Poets and Little Children'.

The article was accepted promptly by *To-Morrow* but to his disappointment he learned that he was to receive $150 instead of the expected $250.

December 7th:	Cold.
December 8th:	Max Ryan washed out sinus.
December 20th:	Met Dr. Murphy cancer expert Rockefeller Institute.
December 25th:	Lunched at 540 [Park Avenue]. Turkey, cranberry sauce, turnips, string beans, sauce, Dined 541 East 72. Dinner ditto.
December 26th:	Slept.

Countess Moltke who had stayed in Ely Place when visiting Dublin in her teens and is featured as a wide-eyed American girl in *Sackville Street* had an apartment in East 61st Street opposite Gogarty's. He used her first name, Mabs, for a character in *Mad Grandeur* a book dedicated to her mother, Mrs. Arthur Comstock, who had placed a house at his disposal in Wycoff, New Jersey looking on to 'the continuous woods of the Ramapo range of mountains, which from afar girdle twice five miles of paradise with a double wall of translucent blue'.[34]

From time to time he availed of a standing invitation to dine with the Comstocks, either in Mabs's small apartment across the street from his own, or in her mother's at nearby 540 Park Avenue but in an unambitious way he was a competent self-caterer. An acquaintance recalled seeing the ex-Senator in Lexington Avenue, a tin of sardines in one hand, a bottle of milk in the other and his hat set squarely on his head.

Gogarty's easy manner, vitality and versatility impressed Countess Moltke; on one level she remembered him swapping examples of onomatopoeic verse with P. D. Ouspensky, a Russian scholar, on another his uncondescending friendships with truck-drivers and other working-class men in the Third Avenue bars. He had a special quality as a counsellor for the young, or for those of any age who were in trouble; with these he was endlessly patient and infinitely painstaking in his efforts to solve their problems. This was only partly related to a medical training for he had an instinctive facility to communicate with the rising generation whom he never patronized but treated as independent-minded adults.

In a public lecture in New York, Ouspensky referred to the St. Matthew parable of the rich man and the eye of a needle; it was not a matter of material wealth, the Russian philosopher explained, but the indulgence of diversions which conflicted with the cultivation of God-given talents. Turning his head a fraction of an inch, Gogarty exchanged a questioning glance with his companion, Mabs Comstock. She felt it was a tacit admission from this man of many talents that by dispersing his energies so widely his poetic talent never reached its full potential.

He spent the spring and early summer of 1944 at the Rocky Ridge, Maryland, where one night he had a vivid dream that someone was writing his life and that he read 'Such was the transcendant success of the amplitude and versatility of his talent that we find him at the age of 65 washing his own pyjamas in Maryland and hanging them on a cherry tree to dry. Here we note a sharp and a characteristic contrast between the subject of this *Life* and George Washington: one utilises the tree, the other fells it and proceeds to make capital out of an unconcealable act. Yet the latter in spite of an avowed and overwhelming handicap became Father of his Country.'[35]

His principal publication in that year was *Perennial,* a collection which included the Yeats Elegy and had as a frontispiece a reproduction of a bronze of Gogarty by Stuart Benson. For New Year's Day 1945, he sent Professor and Mrs. Owings Miller a poem in lieu of a greeting card:

> *Pindarus said, as I surmise*
> *Twenty five hundred years ago,*
> *Happiness is the Chiefest Prize;*
> *And Glory second comes thereto.*
> *For him who has lighted upon both*

> *And taken both to be his own,*
> *Life has no greater need: in truth*
> *He has achieved the Supreme Crown.* [36]

This year saw the publication of another period piece, *Mr. Petunia,* set in Virginia, re-introducing a more self-assured Toucher Plant and featuring as anti-hero, a paranoid clock-maker who gave the novel its title. Incidentally, it earned the displeasure of the dismal Irish censors, Gogarty's only banned book, for despite his reputation for writing bawdy Limericks none of his contemporaries was less salacious.

Early in June he heard a rumour that Lady Leslie, Sir Shane Leslie's wife, was in New York at the Hotel Plaza, but being under twenty-four hours notice of sailing to Europe on his first visit home he could not call. He made the Atlantic crossing in the Queen Mary, then converted to a troop-ship, a miserable voyage which ended with two seemingly unnecessary days at anchor in the Firth of Clyde. He travelled by train to bomb-scarred London, which he found greatly changed, crowded, expensive and dominated by queues. Among the friends he met was Norah Hoult who, remembering his Dublin entourage, George Redding, George Bonass, and Dr. Boyd-Barrett, asked him did he have a similar entourage in New York. He replied, 'Yes, Lord Astor's butler'.

Difficulty in getting a 'sailing-ticket' delayed his arrival in Dublin until 22 June and he missed his daughter's wedding. [37] He also missed what he irreverently called 'the greatest farce since the High Pontifical Crowning of Lambert Simnel in Dublin in 1487', the ceremonial of Sean T. O'Kelly as President of Ireland: 'semi-divine now but later to be deified like Tiberius etc.'

When he woke in the Shelbourne Hotel on the morning after a late arrival he experienced a feeling of rare anticipation and excitement — 'Back to my unfriendly, friendly, bitter Ithaca after six years!' His bedroom window overlooked Kildare Street but by looking sharply to the left he could see the lake in St. Stephen's Green and beyond the park and the houses the faint curves of the Dublin Mountains which, according to James Stephens, were conceived by God and sculptured by Praxiteles.

The first caller, the 'Pope' Flanagan (a brother of the 'Bird' Flanagan, a notable practical joker), arrived when he was still in the bath. He brought news of Dermot Freyer who had opened a hotel on Achill Island and, seeking a paragon, had placed an advertisement in a Dublin paper: 'Young (18–30) lady companion-housekeeper, some knowledge and taste for cooking, preferably capable drive car, fond of country life, wanted; comfortable, modern, country house hotel, remote West Eire; work not hard; must have pleasant looks, lively, cheerful personality; willingness to try hand at anything; interest, pictures, music, Irish national culture — dancing, language; also bathing, games, etc. an advantage; preferably no nail pigment, lipstick, ultra-modern, stupid fashion audacities; personality, character. Good looks more important than certificates, diplomas. — B.C. 1009, Box 60.'

After breakfast Gogarty walked along Merrion Row. He turned into Merrion Street, and into a past century.

The air was crystal clear, even the thin blue plumes of turf smoke could not stain the sky as the soft coal had done before the town had won back to its own. I could see the wide greens of Leinster Lawn and Merrion Square. In front of me was Number One where the forceful and brisk father of Oscar Wilde practiced and won an international reputation as an oculist and aurist. Here his wife, Speranza, held her exotic salons.[38]

His way took him past a lawyer's office where James Stephens had earned a pittance as a scrivener, and past a house formerly owned by his late colleague, Sir Lambert Ormsby, who used to say as he grew older, 'All I want is a little respect'. In Lincoln Place he noticed a building which had been Finn's Hotel from which forty years previously Nora Barnacle had eloped with James Joyce.

Memories crowded more thickly as he entered Trinity College through the back gate and walked by the School of Chemistry where he had been instructed by Professor Emerson Reynolds. Ghostly cyclists circled on the level greensward of College Park, cheered by laughing youths and long-skirted ladies with gaily-coloured parasols. Savouring his wine in a grey, stone Queen Anne house Henry Stuart Macran whiled away the morning, and most welcome of all that host of shades who greeted Gogarty as he walked over the cobbled square was Robert Yelverton Tyrrell 'the sweetest cynic of all time'. Passing between the statues of Edmund Burke and Oliver Goldsmith he regained the modern city.

Meeting Tom Casement, the original of 'George' in Denis Johnston's *The Moon in the Yellow River,* in the Palace Bar he reminisced and they deplored the passing years.

'Well, then, Oliver', Casement said, 'you and I are old men. God help us both, the best is behind us.'

'Too true, Tom,' admitted Gogarty, 'too true' —

> *Gone are those days I well remember*
> *Gone are those days so full of fun*
> *Now all my limbs are growing stiffer,*
> *Did I say all? Well... all but one.*[39]

Other friends he looked up included Stephen Gwynn, Dr. T.G. Moorhead and E.H. Alton, the Provost of Trinity. He told a newspaper reporter, tongue in cheek, that he was thinking of calling on the two Japanese representatives in Dublin to condole with them on the oncoming death of Hirohito but he realized it might embarrass Mr. de Valera. The Irish premier, it will be recalled, had called on the German Minister to express his condolence on the death of Adolf Hitler.

After a few days in Dublin, and having visited the Exhibition of Living Art in which many of the exhibits seemed to him like 'illustrations for the dermatology of a leper colony',[41] he joined his wife in Renvyle where he spent the remainder of the summer in the neighbourhood of Hy Brasil.

What territory could be more worthy of lordly vision than this land beyond the Shannon and the slowly winding Suck? Far away rise the tumbling mountains diamonded by a flash of sunlight or merging into majesty in purple and gold. Beyond them, the illimitable Atlantic with its spectral islands seen once in seven years. There floated the Isle of Inis Bofin, the Island of the White Cow, until it was accidentally disenchanted by some fishermen who touched it with fire. It could no longer float about, hidden in mist from mortal eyes, for fire with its power to disenchant fixed it forever on its base.[41]
base.[41]

He spent a night at Brenda's new home, a few miles outside Tullamore, and in October the newly-weds visited the Gogartys in Renvyle. Oliver found his son-in-law well-read and efficient.

To his irritation he was held up in Limerick waiting for a plane to make the nine hours flight to Goose Bay, Labrador. Back in New York he wrote 'Dublin Revisited' for *To-morrow Magazine* (republishing it in *Mourning Became Mrs. Spendlove,* 1948, his first collection of essays) and resumed his occupation of itinerant lecturer, his repertoire including 'Poets I have met', 'Dublin and the Irish Renaissance', 'The Romance of Medicine', 'The Rarer Ballads', 'What is Poetry?', 'William Butler Yeats', 'James Joyce', 'Mad Grandeur — Ireland in the Eighteenth Century'.

He wrote to Noll from Lincoln, Nebraska, on 26 November: 'This is the heart of the Middle West one of the growing agricultural and cattle states. The men of the soil speak a weird dialect. They are mostly descended from Swedes a nation capable of bearing the infinite boredom of the endless flat fenceless fields.'[42] But the prospect of yet another long train journey to Chicago was equally unattractive.

He continued to help Irish writers at home in every way he could and among others spoke of Brinsley MacNamara and Maura Laverty to publishers looking for short stories.

E.H. Alton wrote to him in May 1946 from the Provost's House from where he could see the rain streaming down on College Park which made him envy Gogarty in a warmer and sunnier climate. 'I cannot find words to thank you for what you are doing for the Library. I think that Trinity is a big thing in Ireland and I think the Library is one of the biggest things in Trinity, and any attention paid to it touches my heart of hearts.'[43]

When he visited Dublin again in 1947 the blossoms were profuse, the sun was shining and the people smiling. The promise of warmth had brought out a profusion of light summer frocks. 'You would think to see so many pretty cyclists steering for the seashore that an orchard was moving in a breezy morning of May.'

Meeting Richard Best, the librarian, in the street he arranged to spend an evening with him at his home, 57 Upper Leeson Street. The house was set back from the roadway and a folding door between the main reception rooms was drawn back to form one long chamber; the front windows looked on to lilac and laburnum while at the rear the fruit trees were in flower. A Renaissance copy of a fourth-century B.C. statuette of the Listening Dionysius, which had once been in Sir Thornley Stoker's collection, graced a black marble mantlepiece. It was an elegant setting, and silent as became a scholar's dwelling.

When old friends meet the talk is of the past. They spoke of George Moore and of his pagan funeral, and of the coldness between Yeats and Seumas O'Sullivan. Yeats had said, 'Where is the wild dog which ever praised his fleas?' but O'Sullivan's reply was less well

known. 'Where is the wild dog which ever knew his father?' They
discussed James Joyce's 'Holy Office', so offensive to many who
had befriended him. Gogarty's copy had perished when Renvyle
House was burned. 'I tore it up', said Best.[44]

Later they looked at Best's collection of paintings which included
works by Nathaniel Hone, Jack B. Yeats, Abigail Mosser and others.
It was eleven o'clock when they parted but it was still twilight.
Going back to his hotel Gogarty turned down by the canal where at
the lock gates a white cascade of water was rushing.

On another evening he dined at the Dolphin Hotel especially
favoured by the racing fraternity who on a memorable occasion
held a wake there for a greyhound. Its owner, Jack Nugent, knew
anyone who was worth knowing and had more than his share of
self-assurance.

'There's no soap in your toilet, Nugent', a drunken guest complained.

'Get out of here! How dare you come into any man's house with
dirty hands? Go home and wash yourself!'

As usual he called on the Provost of Trinity and accompanied E.H.
Alton to dine at the American Embassy. The Grays and their guests
were greatly taken by him and impressed by his knowledge of American literature and persons.

He made his way by train and bus to Galway and Connemara.
'Were it not for the clouds off the Atlantic that bring in rain, I would
never leave Renvyle with its glimmering islands and its assured faith
in wonders of the deep.'

Economic necessity had also to be considered and he wrote to
his wife on 25 September from the *Queen Elizabeth:*

My dear Nin: We are locked up in the ship until she sails in
the morning, but letters will be taken ashore... I hope that
you met Bee [Brenda] and that you had good weather for
your trip...

Constable is placing another £110 to my account before
Xmas. The ship is crowded so there is little room for my type-
writer.

I am sorry to have been so self-absorbed while I was with
you. It seems worse now in view of my enforced freedom.

Mrs. Phillimore gave me tea at the Ritz. I saw the Americans
only for ten minutes. Dulanty on whom I called appeared (as
usual) optimistic.

> Love to you & Bee
>
> Oliver.[45]

His concern for Mrs. Gogarty's well-being is evident in his letters to Noll. 'A hundred pounds of white flour is on its way to you. Kindly give some to the Cosgraves, Dr. Lane, Bee and anyone you like. See that Mummy gets first cut.'[46] And five days later on 15 October: 'Let me know how Mummy is. Dr. Cyril Murphy is an alarmist. In my case anyway. I hope that he proves to be as wrong about Mummy's heart.'[47]

When the novelty of travel had worn thin it might have become arduous for a man of his years but he seems to have undertaken his journeys light-heartedly even when, as in January 1948, a flight from New York City to Norfolk, Virginia, encountered tempests and icy blasts and took two days to accomplish.

The winds may have reminded him of the inclemency of Renvyle in winter, and the depredations of its weather, for in his letter to his barrister son he reminded him that the roof needed slates here and there and some of the windows were in bad condition and lacked paint.

In writing to Mummy I asked her to tell Dermot that the fire extinguishers in Renvyle are probably useless by this time. They get corroded and the valve sticks when they are most wanted.... I learned the danger of effete extinguishers from an apartment curator here.[48].

A course of lectures at New York University kept him occupied until May. Meanwhile, with a projected collection of biographical essays in mind, he had written to Noll on 20 March: 'If you see Miss Kettle at the Four Courts' Library ask her to let me have a specimen of her father's handwriting for inclusion in my Nine Worthies.... Last night I went to a preview of Bob Flaherty's new picture, Louisiana Story, and there I met Lady Leslie, Shane's wife. She and Anita are over in this country.'[49]

In order to 'point a bone at the censors' he decided that in future the English editions of his books should be marked 'not for sale in the Irish Free State'.

He sold a story to the *Atlantic Monthly* and an article to *Town and Country* in April but was increasingly aware of a diminishing market. Despite financial strictures he remained a model of generosity to his wife and the flow of gifts to others in Ireland included shooting boots, fishing reels, nylon lines, shoe-trees, a U.S. navy life-saving kit, books and magazines. Irish Sweepstakes tickets were given to local friends and when an editor admired Gogarty's light yellow hand-made shoes he ordered a pair for him in Dublin.

A presentation copy of Lynn Doyle's *Green Oranges* reached him later that year. The author enclosed a note hoping he would find 'a little glimpse of reality here and there among the old farce. Farce does not thump so easily with his bladder-at-the-end-of-a-string as the years go on.... We miss you. The gaiety of the nation is eclipsed by your penchant for the Yanks.'[50]

He looked up this old friend when he was in Dublin in 1949 and subsequently Lynn Doyle expressed his admiration for Gogarty's poem 'Between Brielle and Manasquin' wishing it had been 'Between Skerries and Malahide'. 'How charmingly and how easily it reads. Add envy to my acknowledgement of deadly sins!'[51]

As usual on his return trips he spent most of the summer in Renvyle and on 16 September he and Mrs. Gogarty drove to Rockfleet, County Mayo, a distance of fifty miles, to visit Sir Owen O'Malley and his wife Anne Bridge, a distinguished novelist.

During the holiday, for one reason or other, he was 'dry' as he explained to Denis Johnston. 'I did not care to go to the Pearl [Bar] for when one is on the wagon one feels like a pariah. I shall change all that in a few weeks.'[52] He flew to New York on 29 September.

Hoping, perhaps, to escape from New York during the worst of the winter cold he enquired from Padraic Colum early in January 1950 about opportunities for lecturing in Florida, only to be informed 'It is very pleasant on the beaches, and you would probably enjoy that side, but you must remember that that part of Florida is frontier and there is hardly anyone you could have a conversation with.'[53] He was not put off and in due course in Key West he saw the most southerly house in the United States, the most southerly beauty parlour, the most southerly poulterer and the most southerly bar where he had 'a couple of slow ones'.

The bookstore was owned by a Commander Breden, ex-British navy. Gogarty told him his books sold well in England. 'It rains in England', said Breden.

He was taken for a flight by Colonel Pen Edgar proprietor of a yellow-winged sea plane with dark blue floats and 'got the overall view of the area that a pelican might get if not intent on food'. He felt relieved not to be a painter for he would have suffered frustration 'endlessly trying to get the electric aquamarine or the dissolved faint emerald into which the water turns when the sun is low setting, in tremulous light'.

A letter to Mrs. Comstock expressed discontent with Florida:

You can have too much sun. That is being borne in on me; but when I come to examine the cause, I find that it is the neighbours of the burnished sun that are the problem. There is not an abstract thought in Key West. This means that happiness depends on neighbours as it to a large extent does. So I won't grouse at the cold and slush of New York when I get back in a few weeks' time. I can't go sooner because of the tenant who kindly took over from me. ... The air line costs only $35 which with tax comes to $40.25. And there is no charge for food in the air. Theoretically it takes 5½ hours but in reality it is about 8 and then there is the delay at the air port getting luggage and the hour's trip in the limousine to New York. But still a day does it.[54]

Business reasons brought him back to Ireland in 1950 and writing from Renvyle he congratulated Denis Johnston on his election to the Irish Academy of Letters. To his pleasure Enid Starkie, the other candidate he had supported, was also elected.

He sent Johnston a verse, 'On the Sale of St. Nicholas's Church, Fifth Avenue' —

> *To set mankind a clean example*
> *Christ scourged the cashiers from the fane*
> *But their revenge was sly and simple:*
> *The money-changers bought the Temple*
> *The hard bright eyes are back again*[55]

— coupling with that almost simoniacal transaction the threatened sale of Renvyle House Hotel, forced on the owners by unaccommodating bankers.

His visits to Ireland in 1945 and 1947 had provided material for *Rolling Down the Lea*. When it was published in 1950 he thumbed his nose at the Censorship Board by requesting that it should not be distributed in Ireland.

E.H. Alton thanked him for 'your very amusing book'.

Those who have read it think it is a fine contribution to Dublin's social history .... My son has asked why you have put me in a chapter that is lewd as well as learned. He thinks it is a reflection on my moral character. I explained that you were using it in the ancient sense in which the laity were contrasted with the really respectable level of society, the Church. Or perhaps you were thinking of poor Ovid, whom we could hardly recognise as being a man of very high character though he was undoubtedly a man of learning, and wasn't he a splendid poet?[56]

The lewdness really was negligible and if *Rolling Down the Lea* can be placed in any genre it is a travel book which celebrates Dublin and Connemara. *Intimations,* also published in 1950, was another collection of light readable essays. No claim of lasting literary importance can be made for either; the only significant publication of Gogarty's third phase is *The Collected Poems* published in London in 1951 and in New York three years later.

19

The Day of the Lyric

The publication of his *Collected Poems* is a vital event for any poet and should provide the body of work he wishes to leave to posterity; henceforth only the curious will turn to the earlier 'slim volumes' and he is fortunate if time permits the hoped for *Last Poems*. In Gogarty's case the latter did not materialize and *Unselected Poems* (1954) was an unrepresentative collection.

The English edition of *The Collected Poems of Oliver St. John Gogarty*, containing 143 poems, was limited to 500 copies; the larger American edition was identical in format and content. The press notices, on the whole, were favourable. Ian Hamilton paid a warm tribute in the *Manchester Guardian:* 'At his best, usually his briefest, Dr. Gogarty comes close to justifying Yeats's description of him as "one of the great lyric poets of our age".'[1] Austin Clarke's praise was more qualified but the rule that the nearer home the harder to satisfy was better exemplified in the *Dublin Magazine* by 'W.P.M.' who concluded a cynical review by observing of some quoted lines, 'Not much of "the fascination of what's difficult" was felt in their making.'[2]

The taunt cannot be wholly repudiated. The poet's social and professional interests were time-consuming; writing verse was an intermittent and casual occupation — among his papers one encounters lines scribbled on a sheet of Dáil notepaper, on a prescription pad, on a library slip. Yeats complained that he was a careless writer 'often writing first drafts of poems rather than poems.'[3] Had he applied himself more rigorously he could have eliminated faulty lines and emended facile rhymes. Had he chosen more critically he would have excluded what 'M.N.P.' not unfairly called 'the lamentable *Ode* for the Tailteann Games' and some other inferior poems. Even so the *Collected Poems* musters far more than the 'score of lyrics' which AE asked for, promising that they would place him in the first rank of Irish poets. But twenty years or so later when the *Faber Book of Irish Verse* was published it was left to an English poet to remark on the niggardly way he had been treated, asking 'can he be sensibly cut down, however delicious it is, to no more than "The Hay Hotel"?'[4]

In the Preface to his own *Collected Poems* (1926) James Stephens wrote, 'It is said that this is the day of the lyric, and the fact that it has been said indicates some displeasure on the part of those who make the discovery.' Actually, the day of the lyric as Stephens and others like him understood the term was already over, a fact which helps to explain Gogarty's present neglect.

Two Irishmen, James Stephens and Francis Ledwidge, were represented in Mr. (later Sir) Edward Marsh's popular Georgian anthologies, so called because they contained verses written in the early years of the reign of King George V. Gogarty had much in common with the group of writers for whom Marsh was editor and if a label helps evaluation he could be placed with the Georgian poets using the term in the sense that Marsh and Harold Monro intended it to be used, as a hallmark to excellence. By the time that his *Collected Poems* appeared, towards the end of a long life, younger poets writing in the modern idiom would have seen him as a super-annuated Georgian, employing the word in an altered and derogatory sense.

The metamorphosis of a word conveying the expectation of 'a new strength and beauty' which in due time could rank with gone-by major poetic ages (an expectation, moreover, which attracted immense popular support as judged by the sale of the various editions of *Georgian Poetry*) into a term of obloquy and reproach occurred within a dozen years and after a major war; it entailed the elevation of obscurity and varied shades of meaning to a virtue, abolished rhyming other than the most muted. and introduced altered forms attractive to an elite rather than a popular readership. The modern mode encountered disbelief, disdain, even a sense of outrage (G.K. Chesterton said that free verse had as little to do with poetry as sleeping in a ditch had to do with architecture) and its protagonists employed their own condemnatory propaganda. In the struggle for attention many practitioners of poetry are no less frenetic than their contemporaries in the battles of the '-isms', or, (dare one say it?) in the strenuous partisanships of the soccer terraces.

The virtues of the Georgians — vitality, a sense of buoyancy and optimism — were at variance with a mood of cynicism and disillusion prevailing in the aftermath of the first World War. Increasingly, they were decried as 'week-end poets' indulging in pseudo-pastoral-ism. The good were lumped with the bad, some of whom, according to Middleton Murry, had merely 'a desire to write poetry rather than the urgent need to express a perception'.[5]

The revolution proved to be an organic movement and prevailed over the earlier one which, too, had served a purpose. Robert H. Ross in *The Georgian Revolt 1910-1922* concludes: 'But by 1925 time had inexorably decreed, and Edward Marsh had wisely bowed to the inevitable. Georgian poetry was allowed to cross its Acheron. There were few to remark — and fewer to lament — its passing in the new world of Sweeney and Mrs. Porter.'

The destruction of the Georgian occurred rapidly in England but the moderns made headway more slowly in Ireland where, apart from W.B. Yeats, the established poets favoured the forms they had learned to handle in their youth. Thomas MacGreevy, Ireland's first modern poet,[6] did not publish *Poems* until 1934.

The divisions between schools of poetry should not constrain the uncommitted general reader for whom an eclectic attitude brings greater gain. Besides, fashions change and just as hem-lengths go down and up, moods of aesthetic appreciation alter. There are indications that before long the Georgians may be restored to favour for, as James Reeves points out, they 'can offer virtues which seem to have deserted modern poetry and which might be re-gained if we want to see poetry once more in its wholeness.'[7] The virtues he refers to include emotional warmth and natural simpli-city, to which may be added Gogarty's particular strong points: euphony, clarity, and an elegant concinnity —

> *What should we know,*
> *For better or worse,*
> *Of the Long Ago,*
> *Were it not for Verse:*
> *What ships went down;*
> *What walls were razed;*
> *Who won the crown;*
> *What lads were praised?*
> *A fallen stone,*
> *Or a waste of sands;*
> *And all is known*
> *Of Art-less lands.*
> *But you need not delve*
> *By the sea-side hills*
> *Where the Muse herself*
> *All Time fulfils,*
> *Who cuts with his scythe*
> *All things but hers;*

> *All but the blithe*
> *Hexameters.*

His definition, *Poetry's a rhyming spell/ Telling more than words can tell,* incorporates his invariable use of rhyme, a partiality which is usually delightfully effective (except for those inalienably opposed to it), but occasionally betraying him into banality.

He was not an experimentalist. He had a vast acquaintance with verse, particularly the ancient classics, Elizabethan and seventeenth-century verse and was strongly influenced in his youth, as we have seen, by Swinburne. He admired the work of A.E. Housman, whom he called 'that master of terseness', John Masefield and Vachel Lindsay. Characteristically, his strong dislikes and prejudices were voiced unhesitatingly; they included Browning[8] ('Browning is only suited for reading in banks'), and Gerard Manley Hopkins ('who introduced the hiccough into English prosody') whose name was so close alphabetically to his own that Yeats had to promise him they would not be neighbours in the anthology. Predictably, like many in his age group, he disliked Eliot and his followers, saying, 'Poetry is courage and theirs is the opposite.'

For the most part Gogarty's poetry deals with facts rather than fancy, with occasional exceptions:

> *If sight were sound,*
> *O the blazon of the gorse bush*
> *Calling from the granite where the heavy air is scented,*
> *Challenging the Summer with its golden clarion;*
> *And how can Summer answer, the Summer silken tented,*
> *Drowsed by Paynim perfumes in its blue pavilion?*

Like the Elizabethans his inspiration was 'in the lust of the eyes and the pride of life' and the sustained note of his verses proclaims —

> *... the knowledge that embraces*
> *Beauty yet to come, Beauty gone before;*
> *The uninterruptible implacable procession*
> *Of Beauty moving onwards from the Fountain to the*
> *Bourne.*

That knowledge is best expressed in his verses on ladies and landscapes. He had made Dermot Freyer a Christmas gift of *Sixteen Poems* by William Allingham in 1905 and remarked in an enclosed letter: 'They are perhaps the first to give the "sentiment" of Irish scenery in English verse. It deals with your ancestral West.'⁹ His own pastoral verses, likewise, were mostly reflections of Connemara in the West of Ireland or Wicklow where he was delighted by Kiltymon, 'The Waveless Bay':

> *I close my eyes to hold a better sight,*
> *And all my mind is opened on a scene*
> *Of oaks with leaves of amber in the green,*
> *A mist of blue beneath them: to the right*
> *A long cape fades beyond the azurite*
> *Of one calm bay to which the pastures lean.*
> *The rounded fields are warm, and in between*
> *The yellow gorse is glaring stiff and bright.*
> *It matters little what distraction drives*
> *Clouds through my mind and breaks the outer day.*
> *For all I know that distant water strives*
> *Against the land. I have it all my way:*
> *Through budding oaks a steadfast sun survives:*
> *Peace on the fading cape, the waveless bay.*

Feminine enchantment and allure are vividly depicted, and at all ages; his daughter in 'Golden Stockings', a neighbour's child —

> *Now in your apple-tree*
> *In your sun bonnet*
> *(Ribbands upon it),*
> *Dimples that laugh at me!*
> *Thus you came into view*
> *Over our hedge,*
> *Blithe as the light on you*
> *At the lips' edge!*

— the nubile wenches of his youth, and older more self-assured women.

'Tis love that counteracts decay/And lights and makes all Beauty last may be special to pleading with a lady inclined *To starve the light-heart man of rhyme,* a lady very different from the raucous but often good-hearted and uncalculating damsels of Nighttown. These feckless girls are modern versions of the old woman of Beare *(This to-day had fresh Nellie,/ For she had as wild a belly;/ Or a kind of Mrs. Mack/ For she had a bonnie back)* whom we encounter dwelling on her past —

> *Of the men for whom I stript*
> *None was weaker when we clipt,*
> *But the fury of my flame*
> *Magnified the man in him.*

Like most medical poets Gogarty's verses contain few professional tokens. An x-ray and a 'flickering skiagram' are used as similes. 'High Tide at Malahide' is mirrored intra-cerebrally: *And every axon in my brain/ And neuron takes the tide again,* while 'Suburban Spring' '(It's dust or sinus) sneezes' can be a time of nasal irritation. 'All the Pictures' is an exception:

> *I told him he would soon be dead,*
> *'I have seen all the pictures', said*
> *My patient 'And I do not care'.*
> *What could a doctor do but stare*
> *In admiration half amused*
> *Because the fearless fellow used*
> *'The Pictures' as a metaphor,*
> *And was the first to use it for*
> *Life which he could no longer feel*
> *But only see it as a reel?*[10]

A social sense only rarely obtrudes:

> *Build not in lanes*
> *Where the thought of an angel*
> *Is one with a tombstone;*
> *But out where Raheny*
> *Gives on the Howth Head*
> *And the winds from Portmarnock;*
> *Or build where Dundrum,*
> *With its foot set in granite,*
> *Begins the long climb*
> *To the hill which O'Donnell*
> *Crossed ages ago*
> *In his flight from the city.*

Just as mountain peaks are buttressed by declivities the summits of achievement of even the greatest poets give way to slopes of indifferent quality. Gogarty was no exception but the unevenness of the *Collected Poems* could have been avoided. It contains the best

of his lyrics, the great Yeats elegy and the fine four-stanza elegy
for Robert Yelverton Tyrrell:

> *Old friend, long dead, who yet can thrive*
> *More in my heart than men alive*
> *Because in you the flame lived more*
> *Than ever since the days of yore*
> *When, everywhere that Rome was known,*
> *The post-triumphal silence shone,*
> *And in the vespertinal hush*
> *The trumpet yielded to the thrush;*
> *Because those days you could restore;*
> *Aeternae lucis Redditor.*

There are sufficient examples in it of the mock-heroic and satiric
but a more selective approach to the compilation of the collection
would have eliminated a number of faulty poems. The gaps could
have easily been filled with better verses. As it is one asks why was
'Medicus Poetae' not included? And his gift for light humorous verse
is at its best in 'A Line from Rabelais' and 'To his Friend the Apothecary Poet'.

The gallery of girls may be full but a poem from *The Venture*
(1905) merited inclusion, if only for the vowel-music of the black
'a's —

> *My love is dark, but she is fair*
> *And dark as damask roses are,*
> *As dark as woodland lake-water,*
> *Which mirrors every star.*

His experience of the laws of libel taught him something and he
did not use unpublished lines evoked by a Dublin lawyer's novel
which referred to 'Griffith and his fleas.' According to popular
report the lawyer and his doctor brother stayed at home on Easter
Monday 1916, their rifles locked under the stairs by their mother.

> *You talk of Griffith and his fleas*
> *Remember for you ought*
> *That you were also with the 'flees'*
> *When Ireland rose and fought.*
> *When Dublin's streets ran red with blood*

> *With your embattled brother*
> *You were with the also rans*
> *Assisted by your mother.*

Gogarty's notebooks and papers contain some interesting poems and fragments —

> *Tell each pleasant little harlot*
> *Tho' her sins be black as scarlet,*
> *Noted by an infant scrivner*
> *All her sins shall be forgiven her!*[11]

On 1 August 1936 he wrote to W.B. Yeats: 'I found myself pitying myself this morning so to cure the mood I wrote the following bawdy poems.' Allegedly by Simon Swishback and Piano Mary, and with possible relevance to Yeats's Crazy Jane period, one or other would find a place in a present-day edition of *Collected Poems*: Piano Mary's equivalent of Dowson's 'faithful to you in my fashion' is the better of the two.

> *He lay upon me head to tail*
> *And wriggled in his joy*
> *But it was all to no avail —*
> *I'm true to Billy Boy!*
>
> *He put me standing on my head*
> *More muscle to supply*
> *But little cared I what he did*
> *I'm true to Billy Boy!*[12]

A revised *Collected Poems* would also repair a notable exclusion, the omission of 'On First Looking into Kraft-Ebbing', Gogarty's send-up of Keats which has been said to be the most brilliant parody in the English language.

'The One Before Breakfast', an amusing unpretentious *jeux d'esprit*, was an extemporization in the Shelbourne Hotel bar in the presence of a few friends one of whom took down the words as recited and arranged for the hotel typist to make copies which Gogarty signed.

> *The one before breakfast*
> *Alone in the Bar,*
> *Will slide down your neck fast*
> *And ease the catarrh:*
> *Your glass with its end up*
> *Will scarce leave your jaws,*
> *When your body will send up*
> *A round of applause.*
>
> *If Dawn is distressful,*
> *The morning's far worse*
> *When they who were less full*
> *Call drinking a curse;*
> *And ask you to chuck it.*
> *You certainly shall*
> *When you kick the bucket*
> *'A large Catch-me-Pal'!*

Finally, *'Wie geht es Gagenhofer?'*, Gogarty's only war poem merits quotation in full, the version given being that written by Gogarty on the blank leaves of a copy of Seumas O'Sullivan's *Requiem* (1917) now in the British Library.

> *King of the Iron men*
> *In shining armour dight*
> *Where did your heart look when*
> *Whelmed in the roaring night,*
> *The travail of things transferred*
> *Storms of the splendidest springs?*
> *Whom did you seek full armed*
> *Whom but the men who could sing?*
> *Child of the land of laws*
> *Son of the lyric land —*
> *In the mid battle a pause*
> *A grasp of the straining hand;*
> *What have the fates to offer*
> *How goes it Gagenhofer?*
>
> *The bard is of the heights*
> *He sees when all is blind*
> *The heart of passion lights*
> *The prophesying mind.*
> *The sea heaves up, the land*

With ruinous guns is rocked,
What in the dark is scanned,
What in the future locked?
What have the fates to offer
How goes it Gagenhofer?

To banded nations rage
In Earth and land and sky
Death is the equipage
Lovers of women die.
A blood-red bird careens
Through chaos unperturbed
Suns in his plumes he screens
When shall his flight be curbed?
What have the fates to offer
How goes it Gagenhofer?

To wonderful goals impelled
The legions bleeding strain
Is Energy dispelled
Can Life flow forth in vain?
What have the fates to offer
How goes it Gagenhofer?

Of old the legend ran
The soldier far renowned
That Macedonian man
When for the battle bound
Brought with him for the song who sang
Of Thetis' child the wrath
And how the archer rang
And none withheld his path;
Who shall against you bring
A word time disabuses?
An Appollonian King
Who counsels with the muses
What have the fates to offer
How goes it Gagenhofer?

By rhythm the gods are bound
The fates in the skein are noosed
The soul is kin to sound
And first by sound was loosed.
Four million march in time

To the sound of the guardian song
Who breaks or binds the Rhyme
A Nation's soul keeps strong
What have the fates to offer
How goes it Gagenhofer?

May no Tiresian word
Plower who plows for Peace
Whose Ploughshare is the sword
Whose terrible gifts are these:
Courage the first of things
Logic the word of god
Law like a song that sings
Equal and just, unaw'd, —
With doubt your hope forbode
Doom with ambiguous breath
The breakers of the road
That leads to life past death —
What have the fates to offer
How goes it Gagenhofer?

Remote in the west we dream
Aloof from springs newborn
What in your East shall gleam?
What stars rise with your morn?
What has your warsong roused?
Send of your heart housed speech
A word we may keep heart housed
Here till the end's in reach.
Poet our land is fair;
Rich fields with beauty mated
The fairest fields that e'er
Injustice devastated.
What have the fates to offer
How goes it Gagenhofer?[13]

Obviously a first draft, this poem contains inversions and archaisms needing removal. It is an interesting statement on the morale-boosting contribution a poem can make and Gogarty's attitude is very different from the mood expressed by W.B. Yeats in 'On being asked for a war poem'.

There need be no doubt that he could have polished and perfected 'Wie geht es Gagenhofer?' Gogarty had considerable craftsmanship.

There are revisals confirming this in the notebooks in Bertrand Library, Bucknell University, and it is enlightening to follow the evolution of 'To the Moon' from the first version —

> *O born before our birth began*
> *Throughout thy clear and frozen vales*
> *Beyond the listening ear of Men*
> *Aloft may sing — what nightingales*

— through six re-writings to the perfected version —

> *O Born before our birth began!*
> *Through all your blanched and listening vales*
> *Far from the echoing shores of man*
> *Aloof, may sing — what nightingales!*

Because the early editions of his poetry were limited Gogarty was first read locally and his critics, official and unofficial, were friends in Dublin's literary coterie. AE called him 'our Irish Herrick.'[14] F.R. Higgins, in a letter, wrote: 'Poetry has many tablelands; yours are peaks scarred with gold — rhythm's mountain ranges illuminated by fastidious craft.'[15]

Reviewing *An Offering of Swans* in *The Dial* James Stephens observed: 'His poetry is not breathed in the Irish manner. It is more carved than flowing.'[16] Stephens thought that Gogarty's vast memory for Scotch ballads, English lyrics and Latin verse sometimes influenced his creativeness adversely, as did his antic temperament. 'Wit becomes a scholar, but it is a mark of ill-breeding in a poet....' Nevertheless, he selected 'Golden Stockings' as a poem to be included in all forthcoming anthologies, and one suspects that Gogarty may eventually have become as tired of that exquisite lyric as Yeats did of 'The Lake Isle of Innisfree'.

The Yeats anthology gave him a wider readership. The notice of *Others to Adorn* in the *New Statesman* by G.W. Stonier said, 'One of the merits of Mr. Yeats's "Oxford Book of Verse" — it had a few — was that it introduced us to Dr. Oliver St. John Gogarty'.

Austin Clarke,[17] reviewing the *Collected Poems,* praised the lyrics ('A poem such as "Begone Sweet Ghost" must be regarded as perfect of its kind') but rebuked him for 'taking every care to avoid the difficult, scarcely-known ways of Irish tradition.' One is left with the feeling that he is finding fault with Gogarty because his Muse does not link arms with his own. And finding Gogarty's poetic face-tiae 'guarded and frequently learned in their references', he blames this on 'the sombre moral tradition of the medical profession', apparently forgetting the levity of *Tumbling in the Hay*.

But what Clarke sees as weakness is viewed as a positive advantage by a British critic relieved by the absence of 'the note of complaint', and 'the thin screech of self-pity, self-absorption, self-disgust and self-bamboozlement'. Ian Hamilton wrote: 'The Celtic twilight cast little of its purple glow over Gogarty: he loved the blinding sun too much...'

Gogarty is a classical poet, not merely in the lesser sense that he moves with sufficient ease between Praxiteles and Petronius Arbiter, but that he has the unmistakable air of one bringing a vastness of passion under control, subjecting it to strict proportion, working down as it were, from the surface on the rough matrix towards the potential perfection at the core.[18]

Terence de Vere White[19] cited 'Dervorgilla' as evidence that Gogarty 'seemed to despise his own people' but scorn can be a poet's legitimate purpose, scorn for a people who adopted the vices but never the virtues of their conquerors, Swift's Yahoos, Joyce's rabblement, the slayers of Kevin O'Higgins and, in our own day, the despoilers of our architectural and archaeological heritage, the sectarian assassins, the petrol-bombers and knee-cappers.

In addition to the many relatively brief notices of Gogarty's poetry in newspapers and little magazines there are a few more extended studies. Cornelius Weygant gave high praise to 'Golden Stockings' — 'This is as winning a poem about a child as we have in all English literature' — finding it as fresh and fetching as a Mozart air. 'It contents us as do all discoveries of beauty.'[20] He thought 'Good Luck', of which the first stanza is perfect and the best of the three —

> *Apples of gold the Hero dropt*
> *As he was in the race outstript*
> *And Atalanta, running, stopt,*
> *And all her lovely body dipt*
> *A moment; but she lost her stride —*
> *And had to go to bed a bride.*

— 'in the very vein of the Cavalier lyrists' though remaining a thoroughly original creation with Gogarty's clarity and fall of words.

Like others he observes that a fragment can possess a greater measure of delight than the entire poem. 'It is a bit here and a bit there that you enjoy on turning his pages. You savour the lines that catch and imprison beauty. "There's hope in the masts at the end of the street" haunts you, and every time you look at poplars after you have read "Sandymount" you recall his "votive poplar trees".'

Weygant responded to Gogarty's images with such excitement that he feared it had unsettled his critical faculty.

> When it so happens that a poet cares greatly for many of the things for which you, reading, care greatly, you are perhaps prone to set his value higher than less prejudiced sympathy would. Gogarty cares greatly for a damson plum in blossom:
> > Out of the dark of sleep I come
> > To find the clay break into bloom,
> > The black boughs all in white!
>
> His care is my care. His experience is my experience. Every time I pick him up I find some image that has always been a delight to me.

Vivian Mercier begins a critical essay by pointing to some of his faults — 'Gogarty was prone to write a poetry of statement rather than suggestion, of rhetoric rather than sensibility leaning too heavily on ready-made symbols and facile literary or mythological allusions.'[21] These he attributes to an education in ancient classics but to have read Horace, Catullus, Propertius and other Latin poets with insight was to have models for wit, precision, and cadence, virtues which Gogarty possessed. Wit is easier to talk of than to create, Mercier finds Eliot's

> *When lovely woman stoops to folly and*
> *Paces about her room again, alone,*
> *She smoothes her hair with automatic hand,*
> *And puts a record on the gramophone*

mere facetiousness compared to the true wit of Gogarty's

> *Begone, sweet Ghost, O get you gone!*
> *Or haunt me with your body on...*

He refers to Gogarty's affinity for Horace, a man whose temperament and divided mind were not unlike his own.

Such a talent may well be at its best in mock-heroic writing. Pope's masterpiece is *The Rape of the Lock,* and Gogarty's may yet prove to be *Leda and the Swan.* A masterpiece of sustained tone it certainly is, running a razor's edge between irony and farce:

> *Of the tales that daughters*
> *Tell their poor old mothers,*
> *Which by all accounts are*
> *Often very odd;*
> *Leda's was a story*
> *Stranger than all others.*
> *What was there to say but:*
> *Glory be to God?*
>
> *And she half-believed her,*
> *For she knew her daughter;*
> *And she saw the swan-down*
> *Tangled in her hair.*
> *Though she knew how deeply*
> *Runs the stillest water,*
> *How could she protect her*
> *From the winged air?*

Why do the critics who like to talk about wit, irony, and ambiguity never take up this poem, though they love to study Yeats's companion piece? If you think Gogarty's poem was easier to write than the Yeats sonnet, just try to produce a similar tour de force. A man who can write like that need not be considered too boastful when he claims to have learned something of the art of poetry from Yeats.

A. Norman Jeffares took the 'ear, nose and throat specialist with an ear for melody, a nose for the ridiculous, and a throat unashamed of emotional speech and song' as the subject of his Chatterton Lecture to the British Academy in 1960.[22] 'The Ship' reminded him of Flecker and he placed Eliot's 'newspapers from vacant lots' in amusing juxtaposition with the Irishman's more optimistic *By an old lot a cherry tree/ An, old wild cherry blooming brightly/ A sight of joy in the unsightly;* he found the clarity and excitement of Marvell's 'green Thought in a green Shade' in Gogarty's 'Fresh Fields'. It would not, however, have gratified the poet to know that Jeffares detected echoes of Browning in his verses.

One presumes that Gogarty was not being quite truthful when he told Horace Reynolds in 1930: 'I would give all my lyrics for your seat on a horse!' It was an example of an inability similar to Goldsmith's to take himself seriously, unlike Yeats who invariably projected himself as a poet. Jeffares has suggested that because of their medical education the two Olivers 'did not share Yeats's need to strike throughout his life self-encouraging gestures in the face of death. Both lived perhaps more in the present than Yeats...' This attitude towards his own work may have influenced its reception.

Gogarty has probably eluded serious critical attention because of this habit of being gay about matters in which he feels deeply. He was not solemn: he hated to run the risk of boring by portentousness. The solution lay for him in a quicksilver mind, in a cavalier attitude: it naturally demanded that he write with ease:

> *No wonder Pegasus cast a shoe*
> *When I succumbed to the English curse*
> *Of mixing philosophy up with verse.*
> *I can imagine a poet teaching;*
> *But who can imagine a poet preaching?*

Jeffares drew a parallel between 'Thinking Long' and Yeats's 'When You are Old and Grey' but there is a closer parallel between the latter and 'When it is too late' *(Wild Apples)*. Both, incidentally, are echoes of Ronsard's 'Quand vous serez bien vieille, au soir, à la chandelle' and knowing that to recall it increases the poignancy of lost beauty, Gogarty ends his poem harshly:

> *When your looking-glass no longer*
> *Throws enchantment back again,*
> *That enchantment which was stronger*
> *Than you guessed, on lives of men,*
> *Take my book to find reflected,*
> *Safe from ravage of the years,*
> *All the pride by time rejected:*
> *Only then, break into tears.*

Addressing the Yeats Summer School, Sligo, in 1970 James F. Carens who had access to unpublished material discussed the influence on Gogarty of Yeats (and the reverse) reaching conclusions some of which have been mentioned in Chapter Fifteen. 'His influence on Gogarty confirmed the latter's disposition to express himself in traditional forms — and to succeed. Like his friend, the painter, Augustus John, Gogarty has paid a penalty for finding his freedom within a set of conventions: his genuine accomplishment has been largely ignored by literary critics.' Ambiguity, levels of meaning, tension, the much-prized qualities of the 1930s and later are not found in pages which for Carens reflect 'simplicity, tenderness, delight'.

> The intense ironies that we regard as expressions of our cultural *angst* are nowhere found in his work, but there is the most refreshing and joyous humor... Setting himself against the complexity and obliquity that was characteristic of modernist verse in his time, Gogarty sought to sing with the greatest simplicity and directness possible.[23]

Only obliquely relevant to the theme of Gogarty's poetry is James Joyce's appropriation of three stanzas from the 'Ballad of Joking Jesus' for use in *Ulysses* but Carens has pointed out that by taking an excerpt and altering it Joyce conceals the serious theme underlying the comic blasphemy, a satire on commercial Christianity.

Looking at a number of Gogarty's poems David R. Clark [24] distributes both praise and blame. Quoting 'Ringsend' he declares it 'a very beautiful poem indeed and, for once, worthy of "one of the great lyric poets of our age".'

He devotes most of his article to an analysis of 'The Crab Tree'. The following is the first of its five stanzas:

> Here is the crab tree,
> Firm and erect,
> In spite of the thin soil,
> In spite of neglect.
> The twisted root grapples
> For sap with the rock,
> And draws the hard juice
> To the succulent top:
> Here are wild apples,
> Here's a tart crop!

The verse form is very appropriate to the content of most of the stanzas; the idea of lean strength is conveyed by the short lines with two stresses, the irregular meter, iambic, trochaic and anapestic by turns, the ten-line stanza, and an intricate rhyme scheme which nevertheless contains a number of non-rhymes and off rhymes. Look for a moment at the rhyme scheme. In stanza one 'erect' rhymes with 'neglect', 'rock' (believe it or not) rhymes with 'top' and 'up' (as one can tell from the other stanzas — 'grown', 'alone' and 'gone', for instance, in stanza two), and 'grapples', line five, rhymes with 'apples', line nine. This odd pattern is maintained throughout. I think it is meant to express, in its odd combination of irregularity and uniformity, the ideas of *Chaos contracted/To intricate form* of stanza four. I think it is a clever and successful technical device. The play of feminine versus masculine endings in the poem is also worth looking at.

Clark finds a point of disagreement with Mercier and Jeffares. Like doctors, critics differ, and poets like patients wilt and die, wishing no doubt that instead the condign fate of Goldsmith's dog would occasionally silence their supercilious dissectors.

Poets do not write primarily to satisfy critics; should they desire to satisfy anybody, apart from themselves, it it the general reader. André Michalopolus (if one can place him in this less sophisticated category) paid Gogarty a worthy compliment: 'I love your poetry. You can wrap the simple things of life in a veil of words that have the quality of the morning air on the slopes of Hymettus.'[25]

An admirer from Scotland who had never before written to an author — 'I have never wanted to' — sent an unsolicited letter of appreciation.

It is a good many years since I first came across a selection of your poems in the *Oxford Book of Modern Verse* and finding you in the dry and thirsty Wasteland of most of the moderns was like coming upon a well of water. It was with greatest eagerness that I ordered a copy of your *Collected Poems* as soon as I saw them advertised and it is with the utmost pride that I now possess one. They seem to me to have wit, gaiety, wisdom and courage as well as formal beauty and clarity of language — and heart. I have found enormous comfort as well as pleasure in them; and not a few of them (as for example, Per Iter Tenebricosum) are of that perfection which sends a shiver down the spine, like great music, and seem to me as fine as anything I have come across in English literature. I lent my copy to a friend and the verdict came back, 'These are lovely, lovely poems.'

A soldier's wife wrote to say that she was taking his *Collected Poems* to Malaya: 'I do not know whether you will find the necessity of taking it to a wooden house in a jungle clearing in Pahang a tribute to the poems or an insult to the binding but I promise that it will be valued very much. They are poems to read and re-read until they are kept in the heart, not locked in a dust-proof bookshelf as a collector's edition.'[26]

However tempting to leave the last word with a sincere but untutored critic, she lacks authority, and besides the louder echo of Yeats's praise should not be shut out. Now that the dust has settled on the silly business of the *Oxford Book of Modern Verse*, its crazy apportionments, the indulgence of personal choice must no longer be used inversely as a prejudicial scale of measurement. What matters is the affirmation and the man who made it. 'One of the great lyric poets of his age....'[27]

20

One of the Most Charming Funerals

Insensibly, with their understated mysteries, regenerative and de-
generative, the years moved on leaving Oliver St. John Gogarty older
and obliged grudgingly to admit it.

> *If Ousley were alive to-day*
> *He'd sing of days when we were young;*
> *How Elwood tumbled in the Hay*
> *And how Fresh Nelly champed her tongue:*
> *His fiddle string is long unstrung*
> *And I am in a parlous way*
> *But here's 'The Days when we were young!'*
> *And here's that hostel called the Hay.*

His hair was white but his blue eyes were bright, reflecting alert-
ness and interest, his carriage agile, his appearance dapper. The
younger Irish writers who knew him in New York do not seem to
recall him as an old man, though they invariably refer to him as a
lonely man.[1] Seán Ó Faoláin met him three or four times and thought
him a pathetically lonely figure. 'His tragedy was that he outlived
Dublin's best age and like Tithonus had no option but to die as our
green grasshopper.'[2] Mary Manning came to know him in the last
years of his life when he was lonely, hard-up, and at a loose end in
Manhattan. 'Someone from Dublin would enter the room, and sadness would vanish and the face light up and out would come a
stream of beautiful talk. I thought then, as I still do now, that of
all the Irish Renaissance group he was the most human and the
most endearing.'[3]

Advancing years did not bring the forgiving geniality or resigned
acceptance that might have reduced his antipathy towards modern
art and such popular heroes as Freud and James Joyce. Denis Johnston has described how Gogarty came into a New York tavern,
slapped a literary quarterly down on the counter, pointed at it
indignantly and exploded wrathfully.

'That's what we've come to!' he exclaimed. 'The fellow once spent an evening with me in Holles Street Hospital and now some character in Canada is probably getting a Ph.D. for analysing his profound knowledge of midwifery.'[4]

The offending article, A.M. Klein's 'The Oxen of the Sun' in *Here and Now* (1949), was typical of the scholarly exegesis which *Ulysses* had attracted in which enthusiasm and assertion were sometimes more conspicuous than a sense of proportion. It rankled in Gogarty's mind and led to his ill-advised 'They Think They Know Joyce' in the *Saturday Review of Literature*. In this savage essay he designated Joyce, not without an element of truth, as 'the most predamned soul I have ever encountered', and called *Ulysses* 'one of the most enormous leg-pulls in history'. Carrying the attack to Joyce's readers he declared that America had taken up Joyce because it is 'the country par excellence of the detective story, the crossword puzzle, the smoke signal', all of which are supplied by *Ulysses*. As for those who claimed that *Finnegans Wake* supplied a new speech dimension — 'It is infantile Mairsy Doats!'

The effect, as Denis Johnston has pointed out, was catastrophic. 'It was as if Gogarty had deliberately belched at Mass!' Being grossly overstated it convinced nobody, but by a boomerang effect has done Gogarty lasting harm. More harm, indeed, than his characterization as Buck Mulligan, for the discerning would have realized that this was, as someone has said, 'a portrait of the doctor as a young man' whereas the *Saturday Review* article reflected an unexpected lack of sagacity excusable only in a man in his dotage. It was a repetition, in another context and medium, of his indisciplined utterances in the Irish Senate. Had Gogarty ever learned that words, like arrows, cannot be recalled once they are released, his career would have ended differently and his reputation would have been higher.

His son forwarded a letter from a Dun Laoghaire solicitor in January 1951 — 'Mr. Patrick J. Moran of Dun Laoghaire who was a retired official of the Valuation Office died some time ago and before he died he told me that there was a balance of a fee of £3.3.0d. due to you for an operation on Mr. Moran's nose in the year 1912; and he requested that I would pay this amount to you' — which evoked Oliver's comment that Pat Moran's extreme honesty was the outcome of his work in the Valuation Office: 'He did not wish to meet the Recording Angel with a little omission in the books.'[5]

Neenie's health remained a source of worry to which he referred when writing to Noll in April: 'She complained of the cold. I wish that she had not such an aversion to America and to central heating.

Her head hurts in a hot room. The heart weakness was not a thrombosis....'[6]

By 1952 it was clear that Renvyle House Hotel could not be retained which distressed him enormously.

> I had not the slightest idea that an hotel we got on a large
> compensation grant would not pay. The war, the dishonesty
> of managers and incompetence, coupled with the fact that I
> had to look after my profession in Dublin and not business
> in Connemara; and, above all, the four years of the war put
> everything in this predicament. I do hope that the octopus, the
> bank, will not strangle the place in our (Mummy's and mine)
> life time. It cannot be very long.[7]

He paid another visit to Ireland in 1953 by which time other
dear friends had fallen from the ranks of the living. He contributed
articles on James Stephens ('a gleeman, the most lyrical spirit of
his time') and Stephen Gwynn to the *Dictionary of National Biography*. He described Gwynn as a man whose patriotism 'took a form
almost unique in Ireland; it had little in common with ephemeral
politics; rather was it concerned with the natural beauty and traditions of the land, particularly those of the eighteenth century'.

In the same year when he was awarded the Poetry Society of
America's Annual Gold Medal for services to poetry he received
a congratulatory note from Padraic Colum: 'A line to tell you that
I am happy in your award. At the time you were being presented
with it I was reading the Crab Tree and Leda to the class in Mrs.
Crane's. They felt as I did that it was an occasion. More and more
good wishes.'[8]

In 1954 he was elected Fellow of the Academy of American
Poets and the autobiographical *It Isn't This Time of Year At All*
was published. William Fearon, a literary-minded biochemist, thanked
him for the gift of 'yr. latest bk.' but expressed the opinion 'that your
finest critical work to date is *Intimations*, that paragraph in which
you summarize Joyce is the best key I know to his cuckoo clock, and
I should like the book put on our English course.'[9]

Augustus John wrote from Freyern Court, Fordingbridge, Hants.,
to register his appreciation of the autobiography which he had
read and re-read from beginning to end with delight. '*Your* Dublin
is an inexhaustible well of fish and other forms of life which you
land in your magic net still kicking. You have saved them from
oblivion, honourable or otherwise. I have no taste for Paradise,

but give me Tir na nOg! Let us make a date there where no dates
are! In any case I could never remember them.'

A Connecticut hostess with whom he stayed thought him a
'blazing amazing' man. She found him 'intrepid, scornful, excoriating,
witty', and yet he was as obliging and angelically helpful 'as the nicest
boy of ten who ever lived', grateful for every kindness shown to him
and going out of his way to avoid being a trouble.

In the summer of that year Horace Reynolds temporarily over-
came his misgivings and obtained permission to edit a collection of
his bawdy verses. Understandably, Gogarty waxed warm and cold in
turn but enthusiastically Reynolds hoped that *The Merry Muses of
Hibernia* (Gogarty preferred the title *Levia Carmina*) would make
his friend as famous as Burns.

Having assembled an extensive collection of limericks and verses
of a varying degree of indelicacy it was decided, detecting an in-
compatibility between blasphemy and bawdry, not to include the
'Ballad of Joking Jesus'. Reynolds then imposed further censorship.
'I'm inclined to cut the contents down to "The Hay Hotel", "On
First Looking Into Krafft-Ebing", "The Old Pianist", "The Getting
of Gargantua", "Sackville Street" — No Limericks. I find the more
scatalogical the more tiresome.' If the selection were thus restricted
he thought that Gogarty could publish it under his own name. 'Otherwise I shall have to invent a father for the poems and that won't be
half the fun. Maybe I'll pretend there was a real Malachi Mulligan,
a guy in London, perhaps a barrister....'[10] Later he suggested that the
book should have a foreword from the author Farrell O'Reilly. 'Will
you endite one, saying how it feels to see in type these memoirs of
your dead life....'[11] Finally caution triumphed over value and the
typescript remains unpublished in a Harvard library.

It comes as a surprize, however, to find Gogarty in his correspondence with Horace Reynolds disowning the much-quoted limerick
'There was a young man from St. John's'. 'I wish I had the genius',
he wrote regretfully.[12] He also disowned authorship of a poem in
Irish Society welcoming the return of the troops from South Africa
in 1901 and concealing in the first letters of each line (when read
downwards) the prophetic message 'THE WHORES WILL BE BUSY':
'... which was not written by me but by someone whose name I
cannot recall at the moment — Jack Lester.'[13]

He had known Horace Reynolds now for almost thirty years and
they corresponded regularly. 'So you're off for Europe next month',
Reynolds wrote on 26 March 1955. 'Will Dev let you in? I hope so,
and I hope you have a good time. Go it while you are young, as my

Uncle Sandy used to say.'[14]

During what proved to be his second last visit to Dublin he had the pleasure of hearing his 'Elegy on the Archpoet W.B. Yeats' broadcast by Radio Éireann in Austin Clarke's poetry programme on 16 May. Invited himself to broadcast and given explicit instructions that the talks should each last fifteen minutes and contain approximately 2,000 words he agreed to do so but eventually sent 4,600 words on Arthur Griffith and 3,300 words on Tom Kettle. Nevertheless Radio Éireann agreed to broadcast the extended talks provided that certain specific cuts were permitted. 'I am told to say', Mervyn Wall wrote from the General Features Department, 'that even if de Valera were not alive, we would still prefer not to broadcast these references.'[15] To his surprize and amusement Gogarty found himself presented with a paper to receipt *before* he received payment, but he signed the document as required and posted it to the General Post Office.

A friend who happened to meet him in Anne Street that summer thought he looked thinner and a trifle bent, his manner more serious than in the halcyon days.[16]

Start from Somehwere Else (1955) contains a familiar mixture: reminiscences of Irish and British worthies, most of whom we have met more than once, enlivened by his own wit and the wit of others including Winston Churchill's comment on Sir Stafford Cripps — 'There but for the grace of God goes God'. The chapter on argot is particularly good, reporting a dialogue between two Dublin 'auld wans' that would have done credit to a persisting playwright.

Since the end of the war his visits to Ireland, leisurely holidays in Dublin and the west, were biennial or triennial events but a special occasion, Oliver and Neenie's golden wedding anniversary. beckoned him home in August 1956 when he paid a short visit to Dublin to join his family in celebration. The festive luncheon was held in the Shelbourne Hotel but Mrs. Gogarty's failing health now clouded her mind, preventing her from entering into the spirit of the day. What could have been a triumphant and grateful acknowledgement of survival may have had moments that grieved him. If so he concealed them and with his old gallantry and charm presented a ring to his less resilient life-partner.

If the dulling embers of memory rekindled for him, at that celebratory luncheon, something of the warmth and beauty of the girl he had married half a century ago in the wonderful summer of 1906, or the grace of the more mature chatelaine of Renvyle House —

Tall, on a bare landscape,
Where earth the stone upthrusts —
Holding your exquisite frock
Against the morning gusts
And light is on half the rock[17]

— it can only have underlined their present plight, involuntary victims of life's involutionary phase. There was nothing of the slippered pantaloon, however, about Oliver; Neenie had fared worse although she actually survived him. But their days of glory and wealth, when distinguished visitors (and affluent patients) made their way to nearby Ely Place, were over. With Renvyle House in other hands and Oliver's creativity exhausted, as he himself frankly admitted, the sands were running out.

The rumour that he was thinking of retiring reached ex-President W.T. Cosgrave who wrote on 5 November 1956 to give him the benefit of his own experience: 'With your permission I should like to make a comment on your declared intention of retiring. Don't! Everyone who does steps over a canyon making it impossible to retrace, then they find it lonesome and are prone to lose interest in men and things.'[18]

He was not fated to retire and it was alien to his nature to brood on an inevitability that could not be far away, beyond occasionally remarking with Epicurean detachment: 'While I am, death is not. When death is, I am not.' Man and death never meet, a comforting philosophy.

Towards the end of November Horace Reynolds acknowledged a 'bright and chirpy' letter —

It is plain that you are not like King Solomon and King David. Do you know the rhyme?

King David and King Solomon
Led merry, merry lives
With many, many lady friends
And many, many wives.
But when old age crept onward
With all its heavy qualms
King Solomon wrote the Proverbs
And King David wrote the Psalms.[19]

Cardiac symptoms necessitated a short stay in a New York hospital in April 1957 and he complained to Reynolds, 'It cost me 22 dollars a day and *extras*. Until I recover I will have to defer the pleasure of seeing you and yours.'[20] His friend had issued a warm invitation — 'Better come up and have a ride in the new Plymouth. I'll take you to the sea' — adding a pleasant postscript: 'One of the Harvard librarians tells me he is starting to collect your books. He has just discovered you!'[21]

He appeared to recover from his indisposition and wrote to Denis Johnston on 8 June to arrange a meeting: 'Let it be on whatever day your lecture is over. Say we meet at Donaghue's, 64th and Lexington at a time to suit you.' He poked fun at the James Joyce Society and literary societies in general ending his letter with a swipe at Joyce. 'There is an amount of squalor inseparable from his work which the impertinence of a loose association with Homer will not hide.'[22]

He mentioned his desire to buy a house with three acres near Ticknock, County Dublin, in a letter to Noll on 3 August: 'In this city the noise is so bad day and night that I become distracted. It is the noisiest city in the world because, though others may be as noisy, here they have mechanical gadgets that make noise and noise only. Next year, if I am alive, I intend to go to Ireland for good....'[23]

From the oppressive heat of a New York summer he wrote to Horace Reynolds on 14 August:

I woke up this morning with the following ringing in my head. I must be getting in my second childhood. It is from the Rime of Sinbad the Syphilitic Sailor.

O what a wondrous paradox:
A sailor, who escaped the rocks,
Was wrecked by going down the docks
When safe ashore;
And brought to light a hidden pox
And Hunter's sore.[24]

More fortunately situated, Reynolds replied from Maine describing the view and other vacation delights. 'I bought a bottle of Jameson and had drinks every night before dinner. I also read William Carlos Williams' letters. He's a poet and a doctor, like you. Did you ever meet him?'[25]

His letters home remained cheerfully optimistic. On 15 September he thanked Noll for a gift: 'The pipe arrived on Friday last. It is splendid! I broke it in immediately. Friday is apparently my "lucky" day. Thank you, thank you. How is Mummy? And why has she to go into a nursing home?'[26] Next day he was buoyant and talkative when he lunched with a writer friend, Ben Lucien Burman. They arranged to meet for dinner three nights later in a downtown Chinese restaurant favoured by Gogarty but he failed to turn up. Burman learned later that on his way to keep the appointment Gogarty had collapsed. A policeman called an ambulance and he was taken to the nearby Beth Israel Hospital.

This massive building rising between First and Second Avenues at Nathan D. Perlman Place, a neighbourhood lacking affluence, provides a service for the unpretentious habitants of the East Village and the teeming Lower East Side. Though on a larger scale, it is not unlike Dublin's Meath Hospital on the fringe of the Liberties from where harassed mothers in Kevin Street and the Coombe had taken their snotty-nosed urchins for Gogarty's good-humoured advice in his heyday.

When the shock of arrival was over, the pain relieved by an injection, he felt at ease with his companions in distress, many of them immigrants like himself. When Burman[27] came next day he found him joking with his Puerto Rican neighbours, making them laugh. 'In the few hours since his arrival Oliver had already stamped the bleak ward with his personality. It was like one of his favourite little bars. Oliver had taken over.' Alarmed by the intravenous drip and the oxygen cylinder, Burman concealed his concern but made arrangements for Gogarty's transfer to a private hospital and persuaded the wife of the affable man in the next bed to move their large and noisy television set into the day room.

On the following day it was decided that Gogarty was not well enough to be moved. Outwardly he seemed his cheerful and irrepressible self but the high-spirited mood of *Hyperthuleana* was long since heavily overdrawn. His medical mind must have apprised him of the fact that the prognosis was grave. Born with a caul he had had more than his share of luck, yet there is an end to everything: he was set now for Ultima Thule. He was talking to Burman when suddenly he went pale.

'I think my trouble is coming on me,' he said.

Burman dashed for the intern. Emergency treatment was given and Gogarty rallied but visitors were forbidden to talk to him. When Gustav Davidson, the secretary of the Poetry Society, arrived with

Mrs. Davidson they were allowed to stand in the doorway with Ben Lucien Burman and wave. They could see Oliver Gogarty smiling to them from behind the oxygen mask. The smile concealed the knowledge that 'He had seen all the pictures....' He died next morning, 22 September 1957.

Some days later the bereaved relatives waited at Shannon airport for the plane bearing the remains.[28] Then the hearse and funeral cars drove northwards to Galway and on through Oughterard to Connemara where the coffin was placed overnight in Letterfrack Church. Solemn requiem mass was sung next morning, for in the West of Ireland a burial is a ceremonial occasion, but not necessarily a sad one, except for those most intimately concerned.

The narrow road to Cleggan runs by lakes and meadows and is bordered by golden furze-bushes and scarlet fuschia. The conceit that the dead welcome peace is a happy one and there is no more peaceful place in Connaught than Ballinakill cemetery where Gogarty is buried mid-way between Letterfrack and Cleggan. Set on a green hillside this burial ground slopes steeply towards the reeds and choppy waters of a slate-coloured lough; eastwards, blue and cloud-capped the Twelve Bens dominate the horizon. It is a landscape that would have delighted the deceased, and the knowledge that this was so comforted the mourners, both the close relatives and the friends. The latter included Monsignor Pádraig de Brún; ex-President W.T. Cosgrave and his son Liam, a future Taoiseach; Lennox Robinson bearing a laurel wreath from the Irish Academy of Letters and Dudley Walsh with bay leaves; Sean MacBride, Michael Scott, Professor Liam O'Briain, and Ulick O'Connor a young barrister and poet who was then writing Gogarty's biography.

Liam O'Briain said later: 'This was one of the most charming funerals I was ever at. Everything went exactly as Oliver would have liked it.'[29] The country choir that sang 'Dies Irae', the lake with a swan swimming out of the reeds like an auspicious symbol, the willow tree over the grave... these were details he would have relished, but best of all the Holy Water the parish priest sprinkled from a whiskey bottle.

By then the obituarists had recorded their praise, among them Myles na gCopaleen who in his column in *The Irish Times* — which he termed 'a corner often used for derision' — expressed in measured words his admiration for 'this great man'. His tribute, emphasizing Gogarty's courage, is worth all the rest, for Myles na gCopaleen's customary astringency was such that fulsomeness was beyond him; it merits fuller quotation.

Courage is never enough. One trouble about it is that its possessor is hardly ever out of trouble and requires other skills for self-extrication. The last word is not to be confused with self-exculpation, but if a man wishes to be elsewhere (possibly on a professional medical appointment) and is talking to a friend (the late Alf Bergan, for instance), he does not make a crude or objectionable exit.

Two minutes of that tongue and very subtle mind at the back of it would have convinced anybody of his day that Gogarty's departure involved for the party of the other part something of the nature of a bereavement. To a stranger it may seem that he was glib. Less glib or more honest man I personally never met. Wit, adjustment to an existing situation, improvisation, all those qualities he had, he had in a profusion unexampled. Now and again a remark seemed cruel. Occasionally a handy quotation betrayed him into saying something that seemed unkind. Against whom can this charge not be laid? Even his majesty the sun has spots.[30]

By the time that his widow was laid in the grave by his side in 1958 Oliver St. John Gogarty's reputation as a poet and author was already at a discount in that literary purgatory into which, in the natural sequence of events, so many dead authors are thrust incontinently by living critics. Other factors contributed to a conspiracy of silence which threatened his name with extinction: men of a different ilk from Myles na gCopaleen did not hesitate to denigrate him; political opponents liked to forget him; partisans of Joyce did not forgive largely-imagined wrongs; absorbed in their introspection the younger poets were deaf to his gladder measures.

The publication of Ulick O'Connor's biography of Gogarty in 1964 enabled reviewers to register a diversity of views. Among those who had known him personally, Piaras Béaslaí called him 'one of the outstanding figures of the Ireland of his time — astounding in his versatility'.[31] Sir Shane Leslie, another friendly witness, wrote, 'Thanks to the friends and enemies he made, Oliver Gogarty is the only Dubliner who merits to share the irrepressible, lacerated, challenging epitaph of Swift in St. Patrick's Cathedral. He was as satiric a poet as the Dean and no less fierce as a wielder of the word political.'[32] A younger poet, Padraic Fallon, denied that Gogarty was even a remarkably good 'light' poet. 'The poems have a jejune air. One can see the piece of paper produced during a lecture on anatomy and passed around, or see George Redding, the mild-and-bitter man of the Bodega, scanning it in a corner and mooning over a piece to mate it.'[33]

From a later generation Eavan Boland[34] viewed him as a 'paragon *manqué*'; Brendan Kennelly[35] granted that he had played a part in the making of modern Ireland ('His later disillusion with Ireland does not lessen the dedication he showed to it as a young man. One thing is certain: if Gogarty left Ireland, Ireland never left Gogarty'); in a sympathetic and enquiring critique Augustine Martin concluded that Gogarty's life 'was essentially tragic... he was undone by the very gifts which made him famous — wit, sociability, personal magnetism and the vanity which, inevitably, they brought with them.'[36]

If Groucho Marx is to be believed, 'Time wounds all heels'; the day of the begrudgers is ending and a tentative and sober appraisal can now be made. Oliver St. John Gogarty was a poet in the true sense of that word, and one of the wits of his age; a versatile personality whose mind was too agile for the comfort of many of his more mediocre contemporaries though his warm friendliness delighted others. A surgeon of above average ability, he was acutely conscious of the importance of preventive measures in medicine; a stringent political critic, but too outspoken to be taken seriously, he was insufficiently adaptable to exert a major influence in politics, although constructive and broad-minded. A prose writer of unfulfilled potential, coming too late to an art form in which the unforgivable sin is repetition,[37] his principal claim on posterity[38] is through his verses but the full measure of this claim cannot be gauged until an edition is provided containing his best lyrics and a selection of his Rabelaisian fantasies. AE predicted: 'It is only those of the next generation who will have in the same book the contraries which gained intensity from each other, the laughter of Silenus with the divine grace of the nymph he pursues.'[39] That generation and a later one are still waiting.

Addendum

A Check-list of Oliver St. J. Gogarty's Publications

VERSE

PROSE

SECONDARY WORKS

Even the most meticulous bibliographer expects his work to be augmented by others in due course. Completeness can rarely be claimed and certainly not in the present instance; no attempt has been made to search newspapers exhaustively for Gogarty's articles and omissions are probable in the contributions to literary periodicals. A complete list of his books is presented.

Two books which never materialised, *Ditties of no tone* and *Sinbad the Sailor* are referred to in earlier chapters. *Limestone & water,* a projected verse collection, emerged as *Selected Poems;* a book on Goldsmith remained unwritten, and likewise *Nine worthies.* His expected contribution for *Scattering Branches,* a tribute to W.B. Yeats, failed to turn up.

Nevertheless, Gogarty's publications are far more extensive than generally realized. The early books of verse published in small editions are now rarities; the later prose works published in America may not have reached booksellers in Europe in any quantity so it is to be hoped that a check list, however imperfect, shall have some utility for collectors, research students and that most admirable person the general reader.

Iseult Gonne may have translated some of Gogarty's verses into French; Monsignor Pádraig de Brún translated 'The Ship' into Irish and, as it appeared in *Fion na Fileachta* under the Monsignor's name, he is sometimes given credit for the original.

In view of Gogarty's flair for parody it is a matter of justice that he has been parodied. 'Liffey Bridge by Mrs. J.P. Jameson' and 'The Ship' by 'Gulliver St. John Fogarty' (*The Irish Times,* 11 February 1956):

> *A chap from Valparaiso came —*
> *They kicked him out of Buenos Aires —*
> *He brought a Bentley and a dame,*
> *And lots of Paraguayan shares.*
> *Oh, you must buy my shares if you*
> *Would sail away from gloom and wet*
> *And live just like the film stars do —*
> *Champagne for tea with Crepes Suzette.*
> *Well, Well, I was young and had some dough,*
> *And I believed when I was young*
> *That somehow it should grow and grow —*
> *And so, of course, was badly stung.*
> *Across some golden fools like me,*
> *Impressed by his suave Latin charm,*
> *He slipped a fast one, courteously,*
> *Till he was traced by the gendarmes.*
> *But he will come to me once more,*
> *On his release, to pay his debt.*
> *He's really honest at the core —*
> *My God! I half believe it yet!*

Writing to Shane Leslie on 23 November 1918 Gogarty referred to a play which cannot now be identified:

> Yeats has another stage dialogue of mine. . . as no one may call on him without an appointment in writing I cannot learn if he wants it for the Abbey or not. In Ireland the Abbey is used to bury poets alive. However, I got such a quantity of dramatic advice that I now know I shall never be able to write a satisfactory play. An Abbey for a tomb therefore is no small thing.

One of the recipients of *Hyperthuleana* was Herbert Henry Asquith, Prime Minister of England 1908-1911, who on 12 March 1923 sent Gogarty a postcard signed H.H. Asquith — 'Dear Dr. Gogarty, my best thanks for Hyperthuleana. . .' The number of printed copies of this work has been variously stated but a note on the copy in the National Library of Ireland '25 copies printed. This is no. 2' which is followed by the poet's signature seems authoritative. It is regrettable that this work was never re-issued despite the encouragement of Horace Reynolds who referred to it in a letter to Gogarty in 1930:

> I still cherish the hope of seeing some day a beautiful privately-printed edition of *Hyperthuliana* with additions. You may remember that I asked you to allow me to arrange this, but you refused. Should you change your mind, please let me know. It would give me great joy to see these fine things of yours in fine format.

In the last month of his life Gogarty was preparing a new collection, *Penultimate Poems,* another unfulfilled project.

32   From bronze medallion by Spicer Simpson. Courtesy of National
Gallery of Ireland.

33   Detail from cartoon by Gordon Brewster, 1935. Courtesy
Medical Board, Meath Hospital.

34   86 St. Stephen's Green, Dublin — formerly University College.

35   The Campanile, Trinity College, Dublin.

Royal Humane Society.

INSTITUTED 1774.

Supported by Voluntary Contributions.

PATRON,

His Majesty the King

VICE PATRON,

H.R.H. the Duke of Cambridge, K.G., G.C.M.G.

PRESIDENT,

H.R.H. the Duke of Cornwall & York, K.G. &c.

At a Meeting of the Committee of the Royal Humane Society held at their OFFICE, 4, TRAFALGAR SQUARE, on the 15th day of July 1901 Present Admiral George Digby Morant *in the Chair*

It was Resolved Unanimously

That Oliver St John Gogarty is justly entitled to the Honorary Testimonial of this Society inscribed on Vellum, which is hereby awarded him, for having on the 22nd June 1901 gone to the rescue of Max Harris who was in imminent danger of drowning in the Liffey at Dublin and whose life he gallantly assisted in saving

George

President.

F. A. C. Claughton
Secretary.

W. Digby Morant
Chairman.

36   Testimonial of Royal Humane Society.

37   Left to right: Sir Hamilton Harty, Oliver St John Gogarty, W.B. Yeats and
Count John MacCormack in New York, 1932.

38   Beth Israel Hospital, New York.

39　Ballinakill Lake, Connemara.

40　Connemara — "The lanes that end on hill or strand . . ."

41 Gogarty's tombstone, Ballinakill Cemetery, Connemara.

SENATOR

OLIVER ST. JOHN GOGARTY

⟨1878 – 1957⟩

SURGEON, POET, STATESMAN,

WAS BORN

IN THIS HOUSE.

42   Plaque on 5 Parnell (Rutland) Square.

(A) COLLECTIONS

Hyperthuleana, pp8+58. 8vo. Dublin, 1916. Privately published edition of 25 copies printed by The Gaelic Press, 30 Upper Liffey Street.
The Ship and Other Poems. illustr. 16mo. Dublin, Talbot Press, 1918.
   Review: AE *The Irish Homestead*, 24 August 1918, 561.
An Offering of Swans. pp8+28 8vo. (preface by W.B. Yeats), Dublin, Cuala Press, 1923. 300 copies printed. Facsimile edition Irish University Press, 1971.
   A letter from Gogarty is attached to a copy of *An Offering of Swans* owned by Miss E.C. Yeats, now in the Library of Trinity College, Dublin.

15, Ely Place,
Dublin
18. V. 1928.

Dear Miss Yeats,
   The plays are 'Blight'

'A Serious Thing'
'The Enchanted Trousers'

all produced at the Abbey: all out of print.

   The poems are:
   1 Hyperthuleana
   2 An Offering of Swans
   3 Wild Apples
   4 The Ship and other Poems

1 and 3 are out of print. 4 was burned in the Renvyle Fire. 1 copy exists.
Yours sincerely
Oliver St. J. Gogarty.

All except 2 were very limited editions. I find that the less copies the more readers. My next edition shall be 25.

An Offering of Swans and Other Poems. London, Eyre and Spottiswoode, 1924. Portrait of Gogarty by Augustus John. Through an error 3,000 copies were printed of which 2,500 were sold by February 1929.
   Reviews: A.E., *Irish Statesman*, 1, 4, 36-38, 15 December 1923; Stephen Gwynn, *Observer*, 13 January 1924; James Stephens, *The Dial*, June 1924; S.O'R, *Dublin Magazine*, 2, 281, 1924; *New York Times Book Review*, July 1925.

Wild Apples. pp33, 8vo. Dublin, Cuala Press, 1928. 50 copies printed.
   Review: A.E., *Irish Statesman*, 13, 299-300, 14 December 1929. New York edition 1929. Jonathan Cape & Harrison Smith; differs in format and content.

Wild Apples. pp8+30. 8vo. (Preface by W.B. Yeats). Dublin, Cuala Press, 1930. 250 copies printed. Despite the identical title this is not a second edition with poems added. Both republished by Irish University Press in facsimile editions 1971.

Selected Poems. New York, The Macmillan Company, 1933; reissued 1943. Wrapper drawing by Bip Pares.
   Reviews: Time, 27 November 1933; *The Irish Times,* 23 February 1934.

Others to Adorn. ppxxxviii+184. 8vo. Preface by W.B. Yeats. Foreword by A.E. & Horace Reynolds, London, Rich and Cowan, 1938. This is almost identical with *Selected Poems.* Galley proof in British Library.
   Reviews: Times Literary Supplement, 4 June 1938; G.D. Stonier, *New Statesman and Nation,* 11 June 1938; M.G., *Dublin Magazine,* 81-83, 1938.

Elbow Room. pp32. Dublin, Cuala Press, 1939. 450 copies. Contains 12 poems. Facsimile reprint, Shannon, Irish University Press, 1971.

Elbow Room and Other Poems — with an etching (dry point) of the author by Gerald Brockhurst, R.A. Edition limited to 75 copies. 1941. N.Y. Duell, Sloan and Pearce. Printed 60. *Elbow Room.* New York, Duell, Sloan and Pearce, 1942. 21 poems.

Perennial. pp 48. 8vo. portrait, Baltimore, Contemporary Poetry, 1944 — 14 poems; reissue 1949.

The Collected Poems. ppxxvii+212. 8vo. portrait. London, Constable & Co., 1951 (500 copies); New York, Devin-Adair, 1954.
   Reviews: Austin Clarke, *The Irish Times,* 23 February 1952; Ian Hamilton, *Manchester Guardian,* 21 March 1952; W.P.M., *Dublin Magazine,* 27, 52-54, 1952; A.K. Feiling, *The Spectator,* 5 December 1952.

Unselected Poems. Contemporary Poetry. pp. 8vo. Baltimore, Maryland, 1954.

(B) INDIVIDUAL POEMS
* Indicates unsigned

1902   In Memoriam Robert Louis Stevenson; Vice-Chancellor's Prize Poem. Printed by The Official Guides Ltd., Printers & Publishers, 28 Bachelor's Walk, Dublin. (The copy in the National Library, Dublin, is a presentation copy to the Librarian, T.W. Lyster.) Gogarty was awarded the Vice Chancellor's Prize for English Verse in 1903 for a poem 'The Death of Shelley' which does not seem to have survived.
1903   The Death of Diogenes the Doctor's Dog.* *T.C.D., A College Miscellany,* 14 February.
   Virgil.* *Ibid,* 21 November.

1904 Foreword* *Ireland*, 2 April.
To Stella. *Dana*, 4 August, 144.
The Horse Show.* *Ireland*, September, 280.
Ireland's Welcome to the Fleet.* *Ibid*, September, 283.
Song. *Ibid*, September, 303.
On the death of a favourite race-horse.* *Ibid*, September, 311.
Winifred. *Dana*, 7 November, 208-9.
O'Connell Bridge. *Ibid*, November.
1905 Cervantes: Tercentenary of Don Quixote; Vice-Chancellor's Prize Poem. Privately printed.
Molly, *Dana*, February, 308.
Two Songs (My Love is Dark and Gaze on Me). *The Venture*, ed. John Baillie.
Ringsend: A sonnet. Privately printed.
1906 In Haven. *Oxford Magazine*, 7 March.
1909 The Isles of Greece. *The Gambolier*, 1, 14, 18 February, 170-171.
1911 [Oscar Grunwald] A line from Rabelais. *The Irish Review*, Vol. 1, May, 128-129.
1912 Ode on the Bicentenary of the Medical School, T.C.D. *Souvenir Programme, Dublin University Dramatic Society*. It was also included in a memorial volume, edited by T.P.C. Kirkpatrick, presented to those few who delivered orations.
[Selwyn Merle] To his friend the apothecary poet. *The Irish Review*, Vol. 1, 5 February, 79-80.
1917 The Rebels.* Included in a collection of anonymous verse, *Aftermath of Easter Week* with Foreword by Piaras Béaslaí, Dublin, Irish National Aid and Volunteers' Dependents Fund.
1920 To Seumas.* *T.C.D., A College Miscellany*, 3 June.
Spirat adhuc. *The Athenaeum*, 27 August, 265.
1922 Galway. *An Saorstat — the Free State*, Vol. 1, 4, 18 March 1922.
Arthur Griffith. *Free State*, 19 August, Vol. 1, 27, 1.
Micheál Ó Coileain. *Free State*, 1, 28, 30 August, p.1.
Earth and Sea. *Ibid.*, 4 November, p.3.
1923 Ode for the Tailteann Games. *The Irish Statesman*, 1, 171-2.
Sunt apud inferos tot milia formosarum. *Ibid*, 1, 331.
To W.B. Yeats, to build a fountain to commemorate his victory. *Ibid.*, 1, 427.
1924 Ode. *Aonach Tailteann Souvenir Program*, 183-91.
Aonach Tailteann Prize Ode. Music by Louis O'Brien.
The Casting. *Irish Statesman*, 1, 585.
Centaurs. *Ibid*, 1, 809.
In the Garden. *Ibid.*, 2, 233.
To Some Spiteful Person. *Ibid.*, 3, 267.
1925 The Weathercock. *Ibid.*, 3, 718.
T.W. Wilson on homophony. *Ibid.*, 3, 814.
Portrait. *London Mercury*, June.

1926   Mettus Curtius. *Irish Statesman*, 6, 292.
1927   To George Redding. *Ibid.*, 8, 398.
       To James Stephens. *Ibid.,* 9, 201.
       To a Friend. *Ibid.*, 9, 247.
       Wild Apples. *Ibid.*, 9, 320.
       Galway.*Tuam Herald*, 2 June.
1928   To A.E. Going to America. *Irish Statesman*, 9, 457.
       Fresh Fields. *Irish Statesman*, 10, 386.
       To the Fixed Stars. *Ibid.*, 10, 87.
1929   Verse. *Ibid.*, 11, 342.
       The Plum Tree by the House. *Ibid.*, 12, 188.
       The Phoenix. *Ibid.*, 12, 370.
       Clouds. *Ibid.*, 12, 469.
       To Helen Beauclerk. *Ibid.*, 13, 10.
       What should we know. *Irish Statesman*, 3 March.
       To Emily Miner. *Irish Statesman*, 13, 51.
1930   Goodbye. *Irish Statesman*, 14, 47.
1932   Hey Nonny. *Dublin Magazine*, 7, 2, July-September.
       Leda and the swan. *Atlantic Monthly*, 149, March, 325-6.
1933   Connemara. *Dublin Magazine*, July-Sept. VIII, 2-3.
       (An off-print of this poem was issued by Alex Thom & Co., Dublin).
       If Helen burnt the topless tower. *American Spectator.*
       Thrush in Ash. (To E.H.). *Atlantic Monthly*, 152, August, 195-6.
1934   In Memoriam of my friend Arthur Russell, Soldier and Airman. *The Irish Times*, 4 October.
       Fog Horns. *Dublin Magazine*, IX, 3-6.
       The Mill at Naul. *Atlantic Monthly*, 153, 579-80.
       The Irish Times, 21 July.
1935   Glenasmole. *Dublin Magazine*, 10, 3-4, July-September.
1937   The Forge. *Dublin Magazine*, XII, 1-3.
       [Amicus] To the memory of R.Y. Tyrrell. *The Irish Times*, 20 March.
1940   Spring in the desert. *New York Times*, 19 April.
1941   Elegy to W.B. Yeats. *The Irish Times*, 13 October.
       Tailteann Ode. *Poetry*, August.
1942   High above Ohio. *Contemporary Poetry*, 1, 4, 3-5.
       Panegyric. *Ibid.*, 2, 1, 6.
       Fellow victims. *Ibid.*, 2, 2, 12.
       Perennial. *Ibid.*, 2, 3, 6.
1943   Suburban Spring. *The New Yorker*, 8 May 1943.
       To an old tenor. *Poetry*, October.
       Farrell O'Reilly. *The Bell*, 11, 658-60.
       To Madame Chiang Kai-Shek. *The Montreal Gazette.*
       To a critic. *Contemporary Poetry*, 11, 4, 8.
       To his friends when his prostate shall have become enlarged (dedicated to Dr. Young of Johns Hopkins Hospital). *Ibid.*, 111, 1, 10.
       Song made by Sir Dinaden. *Ibid.*, 111, 2, 8.

Visitation. *Ibid.,* 111, 3, 12.

1944 News. *Saturday Evening Post,* 41, 26 February 1944.

Hesperus, Thou bringer of good things. *Contemporary Poetry.* 111, 4, 10.

If sight were sound. *Ibid.,* IV, 1, 8.

High-tide at Malahide. *Poetry,* May.

1945 The Stream. *Contemporary Poetry,* V, 3, 10-11.

1946 Farrell O'Reilly. *Poetry.*

Glenasmole. *Contemporary Poetry,* V, 4, 10-11.

Psychoanalysis. *To-morrow,* 26 December.

1947 The Dublin-Galway train. *The Bell,* XIV, 4-8; *Contemporary Poetry,* VII, 6-10.

Psychoanalysis. *Irish Writing,* 51.

1948 Report on the sexless behaviours of microscopic immortals. *Atlantic Monthly,* 182, September, 44.

1949 I have seen all the pictures. *The Bell,* xvi, 2.

1950 Noah's Ark. *Atlantic Monthly,* 185, April, 58-9.

Jonah and the Whale. *Ibid.,* 185, April, 59.

Tardy Spring. *Ibid.,* 185, June, 92.

The dispute in the poet's head and heart. *Saturday Review of Literature,* 2 December.

1951. The Ho Ho Bird. *Good Housekeeping,* November.

The Changeling. *To-morrow,* January, 40-41.

Sounds. *Ibid.,* July, 49.

1953 Adam and Eve. *Irish Writing,* 43-46.

Verse. Reproduction of holograph. *Bulletin of the poetry society of America,* 11 January.

1954 The Changeling. *Ladies Home Journal,* April.

The Singing Well. *Good Housekeeping.* November.

1955 The Ship. *Argosy,* 4 June.

1958 The Phoenix and the Unicorn. *New York Herald Tribune,* 29 June.

1960 To T. Gilman Moorhead. *Journal of the Irish Medical Association,* 47, 138, December.

1966 The song of the cheerful (but slightly sarcastic) Jaysus. *Letters of James Joyce* Vol. II ed. R. Ellmann, London, Faber & Faber, 1966. A copy of this poem, written by Gogarty in 1905, was sent to Joyce by Vincent Cosgrave. The *Letters* also contains two fragments of Gogarty's 'Sinbad the Sailor'.

1972 Song. (*The first was Medical Dick/The second was Medical Davy. . .*). This bawdy ditty which Gogarty sent to Joyce in the early 1900s and which echoes in *Ulysses* remained unpublished until less censorious times permitted its inclusion in James F. Carens's essay 'Joyce and Gogarty' *New Light on Joyce from the Dublin Symposium,* ed. F. Senn. Bloomington, Indiana University Press, 1972.

The delightful item of Gogarty's bawdy quoted on page 270 came to light in 'Gogarty and Yeats', Carens's contribution to the Festschrift for William York Tindall, *Modern Irish Literature* ed. R.J. Porter and J.D. Brophy, New York, Iona College Press, 1972.

(C) ANTHOLOGIES

1. *Secret springs of Dublin song.* Preface by Susan L. Mitchell. Dublin, Talbot Press; London, T. Fisher Unwin, 1918. 500 numbered copies. Contains unsigned poems by Gogarty (fifteen or possibly sixteen), Seumas O'Sullivan, Lord Dunsany and others. (Jack B. Yeats was asked to do a wrapper for *Secret Songs* but declined, offering instead a frontispiece for £5, the drawing to be returned.)

2. *A golden treasury of Irish verse,* ed. Lennox Robinson. London, Macmillan 1925. (Golden Stockings; Perfection, Non Dolet).

3. *The Oxford book of English verse,* ed. Sir Arthur Quiller-Couch. Oxford, Clarendon Press, 1925. (The Plum Tree by the House; The Image-Maker).

4. *The Oxford book of modern verse,* ed. W.B. Yeats. Oxford, Clarendon Press, 1936. (Portrait with Background; Ringsend; Marcus Curtius; The Conquest; Per Iter Tenebricosum; Verse; After Galen, With a Coin from Syracuse; Non Dolet; O Boys! O Boys!; To Petronius Arbiter; The Image-Maker; Palinode; To Death; To a Boon Companion; Dedications; Colophon.)

5. *Rose Window,* a tribute offered to St. Bartholomew's Hospital by twenty-five authors. London, Heinemann, 1939. (The Blackbird in the Town.)

6. *A new anthology of modern verse 1920-1940.* Chosen and with an introduction by C. Day Lewis and L.A.G. Strong. London: Methuen and Co., 1941. (On Troy; Time, Gentlemen, Time!)

7. *Other men's flowers,* selected by A.P. Wavell. London, Jonathan Cape, 1944. (The Boon Companion; To Death.)

8. *Poet physicians.* Compiled by Mary Lou McDonough. Charles C. Thomas, Springfield, Illinois, 1945. (The Blackbird in the Town; I Tremble to Think; Palinode.)

9. *T.C.D.: an anthology,* ed. D.A. Webb. Kerryman Ltd., Tralee, 1945. (On the Death of Diogenes the Doctor's Dog; To Seumas.)

10. *Poems of our time: 1900-1942,* ed. Richard Church and M.M. Bozman. London, Dent, Everyman Library, 1945.

11. *1000 years of Irish poetry,* ed. Kathleen Hoagland. New York: The Devin-Adair Company, 1950.

12 *An anthology of Irish literature,* ed. David H. Greene. New York: Random House, 1954. (The Crab Tree; Ringsend; Exorcism; To the Liffey with the Swans; Per Iter Tenebricosum; Verse; To W.B. Yeats who says that his Castle of Ballylee is his Monument.)

13. *Anthology of 20th century narrative poems,* ed. Maurice Wollman. London, Harrap, c. 1954. (Croker of Ballinagarde.)

14. *Reading poetry aloud,* ed. Edward Hodnett. New York: W.W. Norton and Co., 1957. (The Image-Maker; The Plum Tree; After Galen; Death May be Very Gentle.)

15. *The Oxford book of Irish verse,* ed. Donagh MacDonagh and Lennox Robinson. London: Oxford University Press, 1958. (Non Dolet; Golden Stockings; Per Iter Tenebricosum; The Crab Tree; To the Liffey with the Swans.)

16. *A book of Ireland,* ed. Frank O'Connor. London, Collins, 1958 and Fontana Books, 1971. (Non Dolet.)

17. *The Mentor book of Irish poetry,* ed. Devin A. Garrity. New York: New American Library, 1965. (Non Dolet,; Leda and the Swan; O Boys! O Boys!; The Three; The Casting; Kingdoms.)

18. *Familiar medical quotations,* ed. Maurice B. Strauss. Boston: Little, Brown and Co., 1968. (To Death; Non Dolet.)

19. *The Penguin book of Irish verse,* ed. Brendan Kennelly. Harmondsworth, Penguin Books, 1970. (Ringsend.)

20. *The New York Times book of verse.* New York: The Macmillan Company, 1970. (A Prayer for His Lady.)

21. *Poems from Ireland.* Selected by William Cole. New York: Thomas Y. Crowell Company, 1972. (O Boys! O Boys!; Back from the Country.)

22. *The Oxford book of 20th century English verse,* ed. Philip Larkin. Oxford, Clarendon Press, 1973. (Ringsend; Farrell O'Reilly.)

23. *The Faber book of Irish verse,* ed. John Montague. London: Faber & Faber, 1974. (The Hay Hotel.)

24. *The Wolfhound book of Irish poems for young people.* Selected by Bridie Quinn and Seamus Cashman. Dublin: Wolfhound Press, 1975. (The Crabtree; Golden Stockings; Galway).

25. *My favourite short stories of Ireland,* ed. Bríd Mahon. London: Lutterworth Press, 1977. (Golden Stockings).

(D) BOOKS

As I was Going Down Sackville Street. pp329. 8vo. London, Rich & Cowan, 1937. Reprinted April 1937. Portrait of author by Augustus John; index. New York, Reynal & Hitchcock, 1937. Introduction by Francis Hackett. Illustrated; lacks index. (Galley proof, Harvard).

Paper-back editions: London, Penguin Books, 1954; Sphere Books, 1968. Do not contain the libellous passage. New York, 1967.

Reviews: Horace Reynolds, *New York Times Book Review,* 4 April 1937; Lewis Gannett, *New York Herald Tribune* 5 April 1937; *Time,* 5 April 1937; Derek Verschoyle, *Spectator,* 9 April 1937; William Soskins, *New York Herald Tribune Book Review,* 18 April 1937; James Stephens, *Sunday Times,* 18 April 1937; Flaccus Kimball, *New York Sun,* 1937; M.N.C., *Ireland To-day,* 2, 80-81, 1937; A.I., *National Review,* 799-802, June 1937.

I Follow Saint Patrick pp336. 8vo. Wrapper drawing and illustrations by Bip Pares. London, Rich & Cowan, 1938; 2nd edition, pp335. 8vo. Constable & Co., 1950. New York, Reynal & Hitchcock, 1938. pp12-321. 8vo.

Reviews: Arthur Kells, *Dublin Magazine,* 13, 72-75, 1938; C.D., *Irish Book Lover,* 26, 48, 1938-9; F.S., *Studies,* 27, 675, 1939.

Tumbling in the Hay. ppxi+324. London, Constable &Co., 1939. Re-printed, February 1939.

Tumbling in the Hay. A Novel. ppx+330. 8vo. New York, Reynal & Hitchcock, 1939, pp296. 8vo.

  Reviews: Harold Nicolson, *Daily Telegraph & Morning Post,* 24 February 1939; Sir Hugh Walpole, *Daily Sketch,* 18 March 1939; Horace Reynolds, *New York Times Book Review,* 18 June 1939; Walter Sidney, *Brooklyn Eagle,* 22 July 1939; A.C., *Dublin Magazine* 14, 85-86, 1939; P.C.T., *Irish Book Lover* 26, 116-117, 1939.

Going Native. pp294. 8vo. New York, Duell, Sloan & Pearce, 1940. London, pp9+294. 19 cm. Constable & Co., 1941.

Typescript of *Going Native* is in New York Public Library. 'Presented to Mary Walsh from her devoted friend Oliver St. John Gogarty, New York, Feb. 22, 1940.'

  Reviews: Iris Barry, *New York Herald Tribune Book Review,* 25 February 1940; R. Ellis Roberts, *The Saturday Review,* 2 March 1940.

Mad Grandeur. pp438. 8vo. New York and Philadelphia, J.B. Lippincott Co., 1941. London, Constable & Co., 1943.

  Reviews: M.D., *Dublin Magazine,* 19, 67-68, 1944; Horace Reynolds, *New York Times Book Review; Irish Press,* 29 February 1944.

Mr. Petunia. pp302. 21 cm. New York, Creative Age Press, 1945. London, Constable & Co., 1946. pp231 19 cm.

  Review: M.D., *Dublin Magazine,* 22, 58-59, 1947.

Mourning Became Mrs. Spendlove. pp6+250. 8vo. New York, Creative Age Press, 1948.

  Reviews: Milton Crane, *Chicago Tribune,* 28 March 1948; W.H. Hull, Mankato, Minn., *Free Press,* 23 April 1948; *Fort Worth Star & Telegram,* 16 May 1948; Pierce Atwater, El Paso, *Texas Herald Post,* 29 May 1948; C.B. Abernethy, *Birmingham News,* 29 May 1948; J.R.M., *Pasadena Star-News,* 20 June 1948; Sibyl C. Hayes, *San Jose Mercury-News,* 25 July 1948.

Rolling Down the Lea. pp8+278. 8vo. London, Constable & Co., 1950. With errata slip and note 'By request of the author, this book is not for sale in the Republic of Ireland.'

James Augustine Joyce. pp6. 8vo. Dallas, *Times Herald,* 1949.

Intimations. pp6+268. 8vo. N.Y. Abelard Press, 1950.

  Review: Richard Harrity, *New York Herald Tribune Book Review,* 31 December 1950.

It Isn't that Time of the Year at All. pp224. 8vo. Author's portrait by Augustus John on dust-jacket. London, Macgibbon & Kee, 1954; New York, Doubleday & Co., 1954. pp256. Reprinted by Greenwood Press, Westport Connecticut, 1970.

Reviews: Orville Prescott, *The New York Times,* 5 February 1954; William Y. Tindall, *New York Herald Tribune Book Review,* 7 February 1954; Margaret Parton, *New York Herald Tribune,* 9 February 1954; Horace Reynolds, *Christian Science Monitor,* 11 February 1954; Vivian Mercier, *The Commonweal,* 12 February 1954; Harrison Smith, *Saturday Review of Literature,* 13 April 1954.

Start From Somewhere Else. pp 189. 8vo. New York, Doubleday & Co., 1955.

Review: H.A.W., *Trenton Sunday Times — Advertiser,* 25 September 1955.

A Weekend in the Middle of the Week. pp285. 8vo. Introductory essay by Ben Lucien Burman. Photograph of Gogarty on dust-jacket. New York, Doubleday & Co., 1958.

Reviews: Horace Reynolds, *New York Times,* 2 March 1958; Leslie Hanscon, *New York World-Telegram & Sun,* 6 March 1958; Horace Reynolds, *Christian Science Monitor,* 3 July 1958; Frank Swinnerton, *Bookman,* 1958.

W.B. Yeats: A Memoir. Preface by Myles Dillon. pp27. 8vo. Dublin, Dolmen Press, 1963.

Reviews: Stephen Fanning, *Kilkenny Magazine,* 127-131 Autumn/Winter 1963; Rivers Carew, *The Dubliner,* 3, 82-83, 1964.

(E) SOME ARTICLES AND REVIEWS

1903 A word on criticism and 'Broken Soil'. *The United Irishman,* 19 December, 6.
1904 Review of *New Songs,* 3rd edition, ed. AE. *Dana,* 1, 32.
1905 [Omega] Talk for Talk's Sake — 1. How I dined with the Duchess. *The United Irishman,* 14 January, 3.
The Irish Literary Revival. *Evening Mail* (Dublin), 1 March.
1906 [Oliver Gay] Richard Talbot. *The Shanachie,* 2, 127-29.
[Oliver Gay] The Gardeners. *Sinn Féin,* 26 May, 3.
[Oliver Gogarty] Ugly England. *Sinn Féin,* 15 September, 3; 24 November, 3; 1 December, 3-41.
[Mettus Curtius] 'On keeping shop'. *Sinn Féin,* 10 November, 3.
'Parliamentarianism & Power'. *Sinn Féin,* 17 November, 3-4.
1907 [Oliver Gay] An Interpretation. *The Shanachie,* 4, 96-99.
1910 Empyema of the ethmoid cells with symptoms of trigeminal-neuralgia. *Dublin Journal of Medical Science,* CXXIX, 224-5.
A case of thrombosis of the lateral sinus with resection of the jugular vein. *Dublin Journal of Medical Science,* CXXX, 212-14.
1911 The need of medical inspection of school-children in Ireland. *Dublin Journal of Medical Science,* December, CXXXII, 409-20.

1912   The need of medical inspection of school-children in Ireland. Illustrated. *Irish Review*, 2 March, 12-19.

1914   Latent empyemeta of the nasal accessory sinuses. *British Medical Journal*, 2, 1020.

1921   *A suggested operation for turbinal catarrh.* Dublin: Printed for the author, 1921.

1922   The Nation's Loss. *An Saorstat*, 19 August, 1, 27, 1.

1923   Literature and Civilization. *Irish Statesman*, 1, 11, November, 23.

1924   Review of R.H. Towner's The Philosophy of civilization, *Irish Statesman*, 1, 758-760.

Style. *Ibid.*, 814-815.

Review of H.D.'s *Heliodora & other poems. Irish Statesman*, 3, 50-52.

Review of H.W. Wells's *Poetic imagery. Ibid.*, 3, 504.

1926   Review of *Facsimile reprints. Irish Statesman*, 6, 18.

Review of R.B. Ince's *At the sign of Sagittarius. Ibid.*, 7, 284.

Review of *Songs from British drama. Irish Statesman*, 6, 190.

Review of W.H.R. River's *Psychology & ethnology, Ibid.*, 7, 260.

Review of *Twilight in Italy* by D.H. Lawrence. *Ibid.*, 7, 260.

1927   Review of H.W. Household's *Hellas. Ibid.*, 8, 192.

Review of D. Langley's *Anacreon. Irish Statesman*, 8, 43.

Review of Sir A. Cobham's *Australia & back. Ibid.*, 7, 435-6.

Review of Goethe's *Faust. Ibid.*, 7, 556.

Review of *Pomona. Irish Statesman*, 8, 46.

Review of *Robin Hood* by E.C. Vivian. *Irish Statesman*, 9, 356-357.

Mid air. *Ibid.*, 9, 151-153.

Review of Ormond poems. *Irish Statesman*, 9, 212.

Review of E.M. East's Heredity & human affairs. *Ibid.*, 9, 357-358.

Review of *Pilot & plane* by C.A. Lindbergh. *Ibid.*, 9, 541.

1928   Review of T.W. White's *Guests of the unspeakable. Irish Statesman*, 11, 257.

Review of W.P. Ker's Form & style in poetry. *Ibid.*, 11, 173-174.

Review of *The Vicar's daughter* by E.H. Young. *Ibid*, 11, 342.

1929   Review of *A glossary of French. Irish Statesman*, 13, 219.

The Charioteer. *Irish Statesman*, 12, 406-408.

Review of T. Benson's *Glasshouses. Ibid.*, 13, 283.

Masks. *Irish Statesman*, 12, 327-328.

Lest we forget. *Ibid.* 13, 91-93.

Stumpfoonery. *Ibid.*, 13, 29-30.

Wisdom singing. *Ibid.*, 13, 316-319.

1930   Galway as the Gateway of Europe. *Daily Express*, 25 July. 15.

The Attributors. *Irish Statesman*, 14, 36-37.

Enjoying Dublin. *Daily Express*, 3 September.

1933   George Moore — A Conversation in Ebury Street. *Saturday Review of Literature*, 28 January.

Tribute to George Moore. *Daily Express*, 22 May.

Moore's funeral. *Ibid.*, 29 May, 2.

1935   AE — An Appreciation. *The Irish Times*, 18 July.
Mr. de Valera's Ireland. *Evening Standard*, 28 October.

1936   Memories of George Moore. *The Observer*, 4 October.
(Review of Joseph Hone's *Life of George Moore*.)
Next Door to George Moore. *Saturday Review of Literature* XIV. 3-4.

1937   De Valera and the Kitchen Table. *Evening Standard*. 24 June.
Dublin, Seventh City of Christendom. *The Listener*, 6 January, 10-12.
Review of L.A. G. Strong's *The Minstrel Boy*. *The Observer*, 15 August.

1938   In Memoriam — Sir Robert Woods. *Irish Journal of Medical Science*, 633.

1939   An Impression of W.B. Yeats. *The Arrow*, Summer, 19-20. Yeats by Gogarty. *Evening Standard*, 30 January, 3. A condensed version in *Irish Digest*, 111, 2 April 1939, 15-16.
Review of Sean O'Casey's *I Knock at the Door*. *The Observer* 12 March.
Review of James Joyce's *Finnegans Wake*. *Ibid.*, 7 May.

1940   How is poor old Ireland and where does she stand? *Town and Country*, 20 July, 62-3.
How the poets praised women. *Vogue*, July, 58 & 78.

1942   Churchill's favourite aunt. *Vogue*, May, 106-7.
You might call it charm. *Ibid.*, July, 28.

1943   Ireland's greatest poet (review of Hone's biography of W.B. Yeats). *Montreal Gazette*, 24 April.
A new Scots poem. *Contemporary Poetry*, 3, 3, 16.
Culture and continuance. *Vogue*, 15 January.
Sir John Pentland Mahaffy of Dublin. *Ibid.*, March, 104-5.
I like to Remember. *Ibid.*, 15 June, 41, 65-6.
The hero in the man. *To-morrow*, November 459.
Liquid Assets. *To-Morrow*, 12 December.

1944   What's your hurry, anyhow? *Vogue*, 15 January, 57.
Can you shoot in a bow? *Vogue*, 15 September, 215-17.
Poets and little children. *To-Morrow*, March, 12-15.
The wonder of words. *To-Morrow*, September, 45-49.
Mourning became Mrs. Spendlove. (Short Story.) *Ibid.*, May, 21-27.
The empty seat at the table. *Ibid.*, December, 17-24.

1945   Dublin. *Town and Country*, November, 128, 193, 196-8.
Mr. Pirrie, pyrophile. *To-Morrow*, September, 38-41.
There's some that don't believe it. (Short Story.) *Ibid.*, October, 54-56.
Exhibition of Living Art. *The Bell*, —11, 616-618, October.

1946   Now let us praise famous men. *Vogue*, November.
Ireland re-visited. *To-Morrow*, April, May.
My favourite forgotten book. *Ibid.*, May, 78.

1947   James Joyce: a portrait of the artist. *To-Morrow*, January, 20-7.
My friend Flaherty. *To-Morrow*, March, 42-3.

Reminiscences of Yeats. *To-Morrow*, May, 16-20.
Intimations. *Vogue*, September.
The life of Reilly. *To-Morrow*, October, 44-46.
The merriman. *Ibid.*, December, 37-39.

1948   The pull of Ireland. *Vogue*, August 93-99. Illustrated by Felix Topolski.
Hometown re-visited — Dublin. *To-Morrow*, February, 46-50.
Once Only. (Short Story.) *Atlantic Monthly*, October.

1949   Speranza: that remarkable woman — Oscar Wilde's mother. *Vogue*,
April.
American patrons and Irish letters *To-Morrow*, July, 41-45.
James Joyce as a friend of music. *Ibid.*, December, 42-45.
James Augustine Joyce. *Dallas Times Herald*, 3 April.

1950   Lord Dunsany. *Atlantic Monthly*, March, 67-72.
They think they know Joyce. *Saturday Review of Literature.* 18
March, 89. Condensed in *Irish Digest*, August, 19-23.
Dean Swift as a human being. *Atlantic Monthly*, 186, October, 54-56.
Dictionary of National Biography 1941-1950. Biographical articles on
Stephen Gwynn (1864-1950) and James Stephens (1880-1950).

1951   My friends Stephens and Dunsany. *To-morrow*, March, 22-28.
Key West. *Vogue*, 15 May, 64 and 111.
The contribution of Mr. Theocritus. (Short Story.) *To-morrow*, August,
37-39.

1952   Buck Budgett and the 18th century. *Atlantic Monthly*, March 66-71.
I regard America. *Vogue*, April, 168-70.
I love you pink. *Ibid.*, September.

1954   The downfall of de Valera. *Spadea Syndicate* Inc., New York, 2 June
1954.

1955   An angelic anarchist [A.E.] *Colby Library Quarterly*, 24-28. (Written
for *Nine Worthies).*

1956   Politics in Ireland. *Buffalo Courier Express*.
Ireland re-visited — the country. *To-morrow*, May, 13-17; the town,
Ibid., April, 15-19.

1957   He never hunted geese again. *Vogue*, September.

1961   James Stephens: *Colby Library Quarterly*, Series V: 9, 205-15. (Written for *Nine Worthies).*

1962   The most magnificent snob I ever knew. *The Irish Times*, 10 and 11
July. Gogarty's recollections of J.P. Mahaffy.

(F) PLAYS

Blight: a tragedy of Dublin — an exposition in 3 acts. By Alpha and Omega.
Dublin: Talbot Press, 1917. There is an incomplete manuscript and typescript
of *Blight* with autograph corrections in the Library of Trinity College, Dublin.

A serious thing — a play in one act by Gideon Ousley. pp18. 20 cm. n.p., n.d.
[Dublin, 1919.]

The enchanted trousers — a play in one act by Gideon Ousley. pp30. 20 cm. n.p., n.d. [Dublin, 1919.] (The British Library's copy, the author's presentation copy to Seymour Leslie, has a typewritten letter from Gogarty to Leslie inserted.)

The plays of Oliver St. John Gogarty. Edited by James F. Carens. Newark: Proscenium Press, [1971.] Five hundred copies printed. (A proof copy in Morris Library, University of Delaware.)

(G) PREFACES, INTRODUCTIONS, ETC.

Preface to D. Houston's *The Milk Supply of Dublin.* Dublin, 1918.

Foreword to Harvey Graham's *Surgeons All.* London, Rich & Cowan, 1939.

Foreword to *Poetry of Nora Grace.* Dublin, Cahill. n.d. [c.1946].

Foreword to Daniel Defoe's *The Fortunes and Misfortunes of the Famous Moll Flanders.* London, C. & J. Temple, 1948.

Introduction to Arnold Ussher's *The Face and Mind of Ireland.* New York, Devin Adair Company, 1950.

Epilogue to Scharmel Iris's *Bread out of Stone.* Chicago, Henry Regnery, 1953. (Written in 1934.)

Foreword to Gustav Davidson's poems, *Ambushed by Angels.* London, Outposts publications, 1965.

(H) LETTERS

(a) O.G. to editor *Irish Statesman* 11, 94, 1928. Motor racing and the Phoenix Park.

O.G. to editor *The Irish Times* 31 August 1933, issuing a challenge to Minister for Defence. (See also *The Irish Times* 29 August and 2 September 1933.)

Many Lines to Thee: Letters of Oliver St. John Gogarty to G.K.A. Bell... *1904-7.* Edited by James F. Carens, Dublin, Dolmen Press, 1971.

Letters of James Joyce, Vol. 11. Edited Richard Ellman. London, Faber and Faber, 1966. Contains letter from O.G. to J.J., 14 June 1906.

Letters to W.B. Yeats, ed. Richard J. Finneran, George Mills Harper and William M. Murphy. Vol. 2. London: Macmillan, 1977. Contains three letters from Gogarty, 13 November 1929, 9 April 1930, 17 June 1930.

Literary correspondence of a surgeon-poet ed. J.B. Lyons. *Irish Medical Times* 19 May 1978. Oliver St. John Gogarty- some correspondence ed. J.B. Lyons, *Structure* 3, 15-20, 1978. (O.G. to Lady Gregory, George P. Brett, and Denis Johnston).

(b) The following collections of letters contain letters to Gogarty:

Letters from A.E. Ed. Alan Denson. London, Abelard Schuman, 1961. A.E. to O.G., early 1933.

Letters of James Joyce. Vol. 1. Ed. Stuart Gilbert, Faber & Faber, 1957: J.J. to O.G., 3 June 1904; Vol. 11 ed. Richard Ellmann 1966: J.J. to O.G. March or April 1904.

'Four Letters: Sean O'Casey to Oliver St. John Gogarty'. ed. James F. Carens. *James Joyce Quarterly,* 8, 1, 111-118. All addressed from London dated 30 May 1928, 5 February, 1929; 16 February 1929; 14 April 1930.

Letters of James Stephens. ed. Richard J. Finneran, London, Macmillan, 1974. J.S. to O.G. Dublin 7 July 1917; Dublin May 1922; London 29 June 1933; Eversleigh 26 December, 1936.

The Letters of W.B. Yeats. Ed. Allen Wade. London, Rupert Hart-Davis, 1954. W.B.Y. to O.G. p. 891.

'Letters from Lady Gregory and James Stephens.' Ed. James F. Carens. *Bibliotheca Bucnellensis,* VIII, 1-9, 1970.

(I) ANTHOLOGIES

1000 years of Irish prose. Eds., Mercier, Vivian and Greene, David H. New York: Grosset & Dunlop, 1961. (Tall hats and churns.)

Familiar medical quotations. Ed., Strauss, Maurice B. Boston: Little, Brown & Co., 1968. (Brief extracts from *As I was going down Sackville Street; I follow Saint Patrick* and *Tumbling in the Hay.*)

The Oxford book of literary anecdotes. Ed. Sutherland, James. Oxford, Clarendon Press, 1975. (Extracts from *It isn't this time of the year at all* and *Irish literary portraits,* ed. Rodgers, W.R.)

Dictionary of biographical quotation. Eds., Wintle, Justin and Kenin, Michael. London: Routledge & Kegan Paul, 1978. (Robert Browning, Lady Gregory, George Moore, Jonathan Swift, *As I was going down Sackville Street;* Augustus John, Ode to Augustus John.)

(J) RECORDINGS

Two records of Gogarty's poems were made by Harvard University.

(K) BIOGRAPHICAL AND CRITICAL

Burke's Irish family records. London: Burke's Peerage Ltd., 1976.
Carens, James F. 'Joyce and Gogarty.' *New Light on Joyce from the Dublin Symposium,* ed. Fritz Senn. Bloomington: Indiana University Press, 1972.
Carens, James F. 'Gogarty and Yeats.' *Modern Irish Literature,* ed. R.J. Porter and J.D. Brophy. New York: Iona College Press, 1972.

Carens, James F. *Surpassing Wit*. Dublin: Gill and Macmillan, 1979.

Clark, David R. *Lyric resonance — glosses on some poems of Yeats ... and others*. Amherst: University of Massachusetts Press, 1972.

Colum, Padraic. 'Oliver Gogarty on James Joyce.' *Saturday review of literature*, 22 February 1941.

Eglington, John. *Irish literary portraits*. London: Macmillan, 1935.

Griffin, Gerald. *The Wild Geese*. London: Jarrolds, n.d.

Gwynn, Stephen. *Irish literature and drama*. London: Nelson, 1936.

Huxley, D.J., 'Yeats and Dr. Gogarty.' *Ariel*, 1972.

Jeffares, A. Norman. 'Oliver St. John Gogarty': Chatterton Lecture. *Proceedings of the British Academy*, 46: 73-98. Reprinted in *The Circus animals*. London: Macmillan, 1970.

Joyce, Stanislaus. *An open letter to Dr Oliver Gogarty*. Paris: Editions Finisterre, 1953.

Kain, Richard. *Dublin in the age of William Butler Yeats and James Joyce*. Newton Abbot: David & Charles, 1972.

Lyons, J.B. *James Joyce and medicine*. Dublin: Dolmen Press; 1973.

Lyons, J.B. *Oliver St. John Gogarty*, Lewisburg: Bucknell University Press, 1976.

Lyons, J.B., 'Oliver St. John Gogarty — the early phase.' *Journal Irish colleges of physicians and surgeons*, 5, 62- 1975.

Lyons, J.B. 'Oliver St. John Gogarty — the productive years.' *Studies*, 145-163, Autumn/Winter 1977.

Mercier, Vivian. *The Irish comic tradition*. Oxford, 1962.

Mercier, Vivian. *Poetry*, 93, 35-40, 1958.

O'Connor, Ulick. *The times I've seen — Oliver St. John Gogarty: a poet and his times*, illustr. [13] pp385. 8vo. New York: Obolensky, 1963; London: Jonathan Cape, 1964; reprinted New English Library, 1967.

Reviews: Sir Charles Petrie, *Illustrated London News*, 4 July 1964; Sir Shane Leslie, *Sunday Independent*, 21 June 1964; Piaras Béaslaí, *Irish Independent* 17 February 1965; John Barkham, *New York World-Telegram and Sun*, 16 March 1964; J.P. O'Reilly, *Irish Independent*, 6 July 1964; Eavan Boland, *The Dubliner*, 3, 69-70, 1964; Padraic Fallon, *The Irish Times*, 1964; Brendan Kennelly, *Hermathena* 99, 97-98, 1964; Augustine Martin, *Studies*, 53, 326-329, 1964.

Rodgers, W.R., ed. *Irish Literary Portraits*. London: British Broadcasting Company, 1972.

Smith, Grover. 'Yeats, Gogarty and the Leap Castle ghost.' *Modern Irish Literature*, ed. R.J. Porter and J.D. Brophy. New York: Iona College Press, 1972.

Taylor, Estella Ruth. *The modern Irish writers*. Lawrence: University of Kansas Press, 1954.

Weygandt, Cornelius. *The time of Yeats*. New York: Appleton — Century Co., 1937; Russell & Russell, 1969.

White, Terence de Vere. *The Anglo-Irish*. London: Gollancz, 1972. Subsequent correspondence *The Irish Times* 2 January 1973, Shaemus

O'Haurdeen; 8 January 1973 Vivien Igoe.

White, Terence de Vere. *A fretful midge.* London: Routledge & Kegan Paul, 1957.

White, Terence de Vere. *Dictionary of national biography.* London: Oxford University Press, 1971.

Wilson, T.G. 'Oliver St. John Gogarty, M.D., F.R.C.S.I.' *Archives of otolaryngology,* 235-243, August, 1969.

(L) MISCELLANEOUS

A.E. (George Russell). 'Oliver St. John Gogarty: an appreciation by A.E.' Brochure issued by the Pond Bureau, New York, 1933.

Amory, M. *Lord Dunsany: a biography.* London: Collins, 1973.

'Appreciation' by J.H. *The Irish Times,* 28 September 1957.

Bardwell, Leland. 'Irish literary doctors, 4 — Gogarty.' *Irish Pulse,* 15, 7 November 1970.

Béaslaí, Piaras. *Irish Independent,* 17 February 1965.

Beckett, Samuel. See Belis, Andrew.

Belis, Andrew [S. Beckett]. 'Recent Irish Poetry'. *Bookman,* 77, 241-242, August 1934. Reprinted in *Lace Curtain,* Summer 1971, 58-64.

Blair, Deirdre. *Samuel Beckett.* London: Cape, 1978.

Boyle, Patrick. *Hibernia,* 5 November 1971. (Uncomplimentary reference in a review of *The Green Fool.*)

Breit, Harvey. 'In and out of books.' *New York Times Book Review,* 1954.

Burman, Ben Lucien. 'Leprechaun in a top hat.' *Readers' Digest,* 126-132, 1952.

Cardozo, Nancy. *Maud Gonne.* London: Gollancz, 1979.

Cixous, Hélène. *The exile of James Joyce.* Translated by Sally A.J. Purcell. New York: David Lewis, 1972.

Clarke, Austin. 'The last gleeman' (James Stephens). *The Irish Times,* 15 July 1961. Subsequent correspondence, Oliver D. Gogarty, Robert O'Doherty, and Donal O'Sullivan, 17 July 1971.

Clery, A.B. 'The big three, Myles, Dwyer and O'Carroll.' *The Richmond, Whitworth & Hardwicke Hospitals, St. Lawrence's Dublin. 1772-1972.* Ed. J.D.H. Widdess. Dublin, 1972.

Colum, Mary & Padraic. *Our friend James Joyce.* London: Gollancz, 1959.

Costello, Peter. *The heart grown brutal.* Dublin: Gill & Macmillan, 1977.

Crone, John S. Editorial. *Irish booklover,* 7, 33, 1920.

Curran, Constantine. *Under the receding wave.* Dublin: Gill & Macmillan, 1970.

Curran, Constantine. *James Joyce remembered.* London and New York: Oxford University Press, 1968.

Doolin, William. 'In memoriam: T.G. Moorhead.' *Irish Journal of Medical Science*, 348-350, 1960. (Refers to Gogarty's kindness to Moorhead).

Editorial. *The Catholic bulletin*, 5-7, 1924.

Edwards, Owen Dudley. 'Gogarty: the man behind the folklore figure.' *The Irish Times*, 20 May 1978. Subsequent correspondence: F.X. Burke, 23 May; Brendan O'Brien, 24 May; Mervyn Wall, 24 May; J.B. Lyons, 27 May; Robert O'Doherty, 27 May.

Ellmann, Richard. *James Joyce*. London: Oxford University Press, 1959.

Fallis, Richard. *The Irish Renaissance*. Dublin: Gill and Macmillan, 1978.

Fanning, Stephen. *The Kilkenny magazine*, 10, Autumn/Winter, 1963.

Fitzwilliam, Michael (pseudonym of J.B. Lyons). 'Gogarty, doctor and writer.' *Medical News* (London) 21 June 1963.

Fleming, Lionel. 'Head or harp — 5' *The Irish Times*, 26 November 1965.

Flood, J.M. 'Oliver St. John Gogarty: a memoir.' *The Irish Times*, 1961.

Freeman's Journal, 28 April 1924 illustrations of the swans on the Liffey.

Glenavy, Beatrice. 'Joyce and Gogarty. *The Irish Times* (Letter) 10 July 1962.

Glenavy, Beatrice. *Today we will only gossip*. London: Constable, 1964.

Gibbon, Monk. *The masterpiece and the man*. London: Hart-Davis 1959.

Gwynn, Stephen. *Irish booklover*, 14, 32, 1924.

Gogarty, Oliver D. 'My brother Willie was your father's friend.' *Bibliotheca Bucnellensis*, 7, 1-13, 1969.

Headlam, Maurice. *Irish reminiscences*. London: Robert Hale, 1947.

Hewson, Michael. 'Gogarty's authorship of *Blight*.' *The Irish Book*, ed. Alf MacLoughlainn. Dublin, 1959.

Higgins, F.R. *The gap of brightness*. London: Macmillan, 1940.

Hogan, Robert and O'Neill, Michael J. *Joseph Holloway's Abbey Theatre*. Carbondale: Southern Illinois Press, 1967.

Hogan, Robert and O'Neill, Michael J. *Joseph Holloway's Irish theatre*, Vols I-III. Dixon, California: Proscenium Press, 1968-1970.

Holroyd, Michael. *Augustus John*, Vol. II London: Heinemann, 1975.

John, Augustus *Chiaroscuro*. London: Cape, 1952.

Johnston, Denis. 'A short view of the progress of Joyceanity.' *Envoy*, 5, 17, 13-18. Reprinted in *A bash in the tunnel* ed. John Ryan. Brighton: Clifton Books, 1970.

Joyce, James. *Ulysses*. Harmondsworth: Penguin Books, 1969.

Joyce, Stanislaus. *My brother's keeper*. London: Faber, 1958.

Joyce, Stanislaus. *The complete Dublin diary of Stanislaus Joyce*. Ed. George Healey. Ithaca: Cornell University Press, 1971.

Leslie, Seymour. *The Jerome connexion*. London: John Murray, 1964.

Leslie, Sir Shane. *Sunday Independent*, 21 June 1964.

Lumley, W. 'Gogarty: a memorial.' *The Irish Times* (letter) 3 November 1961.

Lyons, J.B. 'Irish doctors and literature.' *Dublin magazine*, 46-61, Autumn/Winter 1973/4.

Lyons, J.B. 'An inn-keeper's guest book.' *Irish medical times*, 17 June 1977

Lyons, J.B. — 'A defence of Oliver Gogarty.' *Ibid.*, 8 July 1977.

Lyons, J.B. — 'Gogarty on censorship.' *The Irish Times*, 9 September 1977.

Lyons, J.B. — 'Oliver St. John Gogarty — a centenary tribute.' *Hibernia*, 17 August 1978. Subsequent correspondence: Gerry Lawless 24 August, 14 September 1978, 4 January, 18 January 1979; J.B. Lyons 31 August, 23 November 1978, 11 January 1979; Dermot McEvoy 23 November 1978, 4 January 1979; John Feeney 11 January 1979; D.R. O'Connor Lysaght 14 February 1979.

Lyons, J.B. — 'Senator Oliver St. John Gogarty, 1922-1936'. *Journal of the Irish Medical Association*, 72, 162-166, 1979.

Lyons, J.B. — 'Oliver St. John Gogarty Exhibition at R.C.S.I.' *Irish medical times*, 19 January 1979.

Lyons, J.B. 'Oliver St. John Gogarty, M.D., F.R.C.S.I.' *Journal of the American Medical Association*, 30 March 1979.

McDiarmid, Hugh. 'To Oliver Gogarty.' *Irish statesman*, 18 May 1929.

McDiarmid, Hugh. *The company I've kept*. London: Hutchinson, 1967.

McEvoy, Dermot. 'Ecce homo'. *Hibernia*, 24 June 1977. (Review of Tom Driberg's *Ruling passion;* contains a single anecdote concerning Gogarty's alleged anti-semitism.)

Mackenzie, Compton. *My life and times, Octave 6:* London: Chatto and Windus, 1967.

Magennis, P.E. 'Ireland in America today.' *The Catholic bulletin*, 23, 327-331, 1933.

Maguire, William J. *Irish literary figures*. Dublin: Metropolitan Publishing Co., 1945.

Malone, Andrew. *The Irish drama*. London: Constable, 1929.

Manning, Mary. 'Gogarty on stage.' (Review of Collected Plays.) *The Irish Times*, 22 April 1972. Subsequent letter Dermot McEvoy 1 May 1972

Melchori, Georgio. *The whole mystery of art: pattern into poetry in the work of W.B. Yeats*. London: Routledge & Kegan Paul, 1950.

Miller, Liam. *Retrospect: the work of Seumas O'Sullivan and Estella Solomons*. Dublin: Dolmen Press, 1973.

M.N.C. 'Arch-mocker.' *Ireland today*, 80-81, May 1937.

Moore, George. *Salve*. London: Heinemann 1912.

Moore, George. *The Lake*. London: Heinemann 1905.

O'Brien, Darcy. *W.R. Rodgers*. Lewisburg: Bucknell University Press, 1970.

O'Brien, Eoin T. 'The wit of Oliver Gogarty.' *British Medical Journal* 1, 828, 1976.

O'Connor, Frank. *My father's son*. London: Macmillan, 1968.

O'Connor, Ulick. 'Dublin: decline and fall.' *The Listener*, 19 April 1956, 445-446.

O'Connor, Ulick. 'James Joyce and Gogarty: a famous friendship.' *The Texas quarterly*, 3, 189-210, 1960.

O'Connor, Ulick. 'Oliver Gogarty.' *The arts in Ireland*, 2, 3, 52-56, 1973.

O'Connor, Ulick. 'Oliver St. John Gogarty, surgeon, poet and wit.' *Irish medical times*, 12 December 1976.

O'Connor, Ulick, 'Cycle champion and surgical wit.' (Review of J.B. Lyons's monograph, 1976). *Sunday Independent,* 2 January 1977.

O'Connor, Ulick. 'Gogarty's house.' *The Irish Times* (letter), 27 August 1971 and subsequent correspondence: Maurice McGonigal, 30 August; Patrick Layde, Brendan O'Brien, William Russell, 1 September.

Ó Faoláin, Sean. *Vive Moi!* London: Hart-Davis, 1964.

O'Meacair, Art. 'Two legislators on Irish.' *Catholic bulletin,* 17, 374-381, 1927 and subsequent comment from Murphy, J.J. "A programme for certain professors." *Ibid.,* 483-491, 1927.

Orpen, Sir William. *Stories of old Ireland & myself.* London: Williams and Norgate, 1924.

O'Shannon, Cathal. 'Gogarty's notes on Joyce.' *Evening Press,* 27 September 1957.

O'Sullivan, Donal. *The Irish Free State and its Senate.* London: Faber, 1940.

O'Sullivan, Donal. Letter to *The Irish Times,* 24 September 1957; Dan Breen's reply 1 October.

O'Sullivan, Seumas. *Mud and Purple.* Dublin: Talbot Press, 1918.

O'Sullivan, Seumas. *Essays and recollections.* Dublin: Talbot Press, 1944.

'Plaque unveiled at Gogarty's birthplace.' (Illustrated.) *The Irish Times,* 26 July 1971.

Plunkett, James. 'Oliver St. John Gogarty, 1878-1957.' *Our Place: Ballinakill Parish Magazine,* 1978.

Quid Nunc (Seumas Kelly). *The Irish Times,* 8 September 1953; 11 February 1956.

Redding, George. *Irish Statesman,* 8, 469, 23 July 1947.

Reid, B.L. *The man from New York: John Quinn.* New York, OUP, 1968.

Reynolds, Horace. 'A gallant Irish poet.' *Christian science monitor* (Boston), 19 January 1937.

Richardson, Joanna. *Enid Starkie.* London: John Murray, 1973.

Rossi, Mario. *Pilgrimage in the west,* trans. T.R. Hone. Dublin: Cuala Press, 1933.

Rothenstein, Sir William. *Since fifty.* London: Faber, 1939.

R.S.W. 'Dr. Gogarty and his Olivers.' *Daily Express,* 31 August 1929.

Russell, Francis. 'Gogarty: last of the wits.' *National review,* 37-39, 11 January 1958.

Saddlemyer, Ann. *Letters to Molly: John Millington Synge to Maire O'Neill, 1906-1909.* Cambridge (Mass). 1971.

Scarlett, M.B. 'The world of Oliver Gogarty'. *Archives of Internal medicine,* 116, 295-300, 1965.

Scholes, Robert and Kain, Richard M. *The workshop of Daedalus.* Evanston, Northwestern University Press, 1965.

Sheridan, Clare. *Nuada veritas.* London: Thornton Butterworth, 1927.

Stanford, W.B. *Ireland and the classical tradition.* Dublin: Figgis, 1976.

Stanford, W.B. and McDowell, R.B. *Mahaffy.* London: Routledge & Kegan Paul, 1971.

Starkie, Enid. *A lady's child.* London: Faber, 1941.

Stephens, James. *The Dial,* June 1924.
'Take me up to Monto.' *Evening Herald,* 27 April 1972. Subsequent correspondence: Mrs. P. Wilde, 23 June; 'The writer of the Monto articles' 12 July; Ulick O'Connor, 13 September 1972.
Tèry, Simone. *En Irlande 1914-1923.* Paris: Flammarion, 1923.
The motor news, 16 July 1927 (Refers to Gogarty's handsome Mercedes car with its yellow body.)
Trench, C.E.F. 'Dermot Chenevix Trench and Haines of *Ulysses'. James Joyce Quarterly,* 13, 39-48, 1975.
de Valois, Ninette. *Come dance with me.* London: Hamish Hamilton, 1957.
Walsh, Caroline. 'Literary landmarks — 15: Oliver St. John Gogarty and Dublin.' *The Irish Times,* 7 June 1977. (Illustrated.) Subsequent correspondence: Veronica Jane O'Mara, 24 June; Elsie M. Hamilton, 2 July; Peter Costello, 1 July; J.B. Lyons, 11 July 1977.
Weaver, J.W. 'Moore's sainted name for Gogarty in *Hail and farewell.' English literature in transition,* 14, 190, 1971.

(M) OBITUARIES

British Medical Journal, ii, 768, 1957.
Doolin, William. *The Lancet,* 5 October 1957.
The Irish Times, Irish Press, New York Herald Tribune, New York Times, The Times, 23 September 1957.
Janeway, Carol. *The Village Voice,* 2 October 1957.
Mellotte, J.H. *British Medical Journal,* ii, 947-8, 1957.
Myles na Gopaleen. *The Irish Times,* 25 September 1957.
O'Connor, Ulick. 'Oliver St. John Gogarty: An Appreciation.' *Manchester Guardian,* 25 September 1957.
O'Hearn, Walter. 'Nobody Quite Like Gogarty.' *The Montreal Star,* 24 September 1957.
Stonyhurst Magazine, 33, 91-92, 1958.
Time, 30 September 1957.

(N) BIBLIOGRAPHIES

Anglo-Irish Literature: A Review of Research, ed. Richard J. Finneran. New York, Modern Language Association, 1976. Section on Gogarty by James F. Carens, 452-58.

A Survey and Index of the Irish Statesman (1923-1930). Smith, Edward Doyle, Ann Arbor, University Microfilms, Inc., 1966.

The Bell — An Index of Contributors. Holzapfel, Rudi. Blackrock, Co. Dublin. Carrig Books, 1970.

An index of contributors to the Dublin Magazine. Holzapfel, Rudi. Dublin. Museum Bookshop, 1966.

Printed Writings by George W. Russell (A.E.). Denson, Alan. Evanston. Northwestern University Press, 1961.

'Seumas O'Sullivan: A check-list.' Denson, Alan. *The Dublin Magazine*, 7, 9-23, 1963.

The Cornell Joyce Collection. Scholes, R.E. Ithaca, Cornell U.P. refs. to Gogarty's MS. letters to James Joyce, 1961.

(O) CALENDAR

Leo Laboratories Ltd., Dublin 12, Ireland issued in 1979 a calendar featuring four medical authors — 'Famous medical names in Irish literature'. (Oliver St. John Gogarty, Oliver Goldsmith, George Sigerson, Sir William Wilde.) Biographical notes by J.B. Lyons.

(P) DISSERTATIONS

Huxley, D.J., 'A study of the works of Oliver St. John Gogarty.' University of Sheffield, 1969.
Regan, Mary J., 'The poetry of Oliver St. John Gogarty: a study of the Irish and classical elements.' New York University, 1974.

(Q) STAGE AND TELEVISION

The last of the Bucks. A one man show by Ulick O'Connor. Directed and designed by Tomás MacAnna.

An offering of swans. A film created by Ulick O'Connor. Transmitted by Telefis Eireann, 13 November 1978, director, James Plunkett.

Notes and References

Abbreviations. (a) Primary printed sources: *As I was going down Sackville Street* — *S. S; I follow Saint Patrick* — *St. P.; Tumbling in the hay* — *Tumbling; It isn't this time of year at all* — *It isn't; Start from somewhere else* — *Start; Going native* — *G. N.; Mad grandeur* — *M.G.; Mourning became Mrs. Spendlove* —*Mourning; Many lines to thee* —*Many lines; Collected Poems* —*C.P.*

(b) Manuscripts: The bulk of Gogarty's correspondence with Lady Leslie and Sir Shane Leslie, letters written to him by many others, and additional unpublished material were consulted in Ellen Clarke Bertrand Library, Bucknell University (Bucknell). Most of the papers related to my subject's friendship with Seumas O'Sullivan are in the National Library of Ireland (N.L.I.) and the manuscript department of Trinity College, Dublin (T.C.D). Gogarty's letters to James Joyce and to Horace Reynolds are owned by Cornell University Library, Ithaca (Cornell) and Houghton Library, Cambridge, Mass. (Harvard), respectively. The late Major Freyer of Achill Island copied letters written to him early in the century, making them available to Mr. Ulick O'Connor when the latter was writing a 'Life' of Gogarty; these letters and other relevant material which I have used were recently deposited in the Ulick O'Connor Archive in Morris Library, University of Delaware (U.O'C.Arch.). The correspondence with George Brett and Dr. Patrick McCartan is in the New York Public Library (N.Y.P.L.); the letters to Lady Gregory are in the same institution's Berg Collection (Berg). Some other letters are in the Beinicke Rare Book & Manuscript Library, New Haven (Yale).

(c) Printed secondary sources included in the check list are indicated in this section by the author's surname and date.

(d) Additional material in the possession of Oliver Duane Gogarty, S.C. (O.D.G.).

Some obvious errors and inconsistencies of spelling have been corrected; punctuation is occasionally supplied. Now and then it has proved impossible to verify the date or location of a printed source.

INTRODUCTION

1   Carens's *Surpassing Wit* (1979) was published since the present work went to press, too late to allow me the full advantage of his critical study. Carens affirms that, 'In the whole body of Gogarty's poetry, published and unpublished, there are perhaps a hundred poems by which he will live. Of these, at the very least, some two dozen shorter lyrics and a dozen longer poems are exceptional enough to hold their own in the diverse body of modern poetry.'

CHAPTER 1

1.   Graves, Robert J. *A system of clinical medicine*, Dublin, 1843.
2   Burke, 1976.
3   *The medical directory*, London, 1890.
4   O.G./Shane Leslie, 15 November 1919, Bucknell. Oliver's letter to Margaret Burke, an American cousin, on 25 May 1924 is also relevant: 'I have copied out a very interesting document which I got from New Orleans. It takes us back five generations to old James Gogarty who died at 95 years of age. This is a good inheritance.' O.D.G.
5   Henry Arthur Hallam Devereux Gogarty was called to the Irish Bar but emigrated to San Francisco where he was counsel to the Southern Pacific Railway. He died in 1926. Mayflo, who married Dr. Roden Ryan, also emigrated to San Francisco moving to Los Angeles where she still lives at an advanced age. Richard Howard Aloysius Gogarty was Dublin agent for the Argyll Motor Company before emigrating to Argentina where he styled himself Senor Ricardo O'Gogarty. 'So Uncle Dick has written. . . . He is the ony brother I have left, the youngest and the only one who was not given a profession or sent to an University. He left Dublin about 40 years ago in a red shirt to seek his fortune in the Argentine. His idea of it then was that of a cowboy. The last I heard of him he was working for Cook's.' O.G./O.D.G. 25 January 1953. O.D.G.
6   O.D.G.
7   *It isn't*, p. 12
8   *It isn't*, pp 16-17
9   *CP*, p. 197
10   O.G./Mrs. Mary Owings Miller. 1954, Bucknell.
11   *Calendar*, Royal University of Ireland.
12   *The Clongownian*, 1897.
13   *It isn't*, p. 29
14   *The Clongownian*, 1897.
15   His marks were undistinguished: Latin 550/1200; French 263/800; English 476/800; mathematics 250/1200; natural philosophy 271/800; overall result: pass.

CHAPTER 2

1   *Tumbling*, p. 2.
2   His marks indicate failure in all subjects: Latin 307/1200; experimental physics 93/900; chemistry 135/900; biology 341/900.
3   Yeats, John B. *Letters to his son W. B. Yeats and others, 1867-1922*, ed. J. Hone. London, 1944.
4   Ms. T.C.D., Mun. V. 23-7.

5   I am grateful to Dr. Seumas Cahalane for this information from the records of the National Maternity Hospital.
6   Harvard.
7   'As for Limericks, my friends attribute them to me, hence my reputation amongst my friends, but I write none, myself. Do not think by this that I would repudiate "unbaptised rhymes" or that I have "grown uncivil, as narrow natures would And call those pleasures evil Happier days thought good" — as Yeats says — but, for all I know, Limericks have never left the Stock Exchange which I believe is their origin and fountain-head. . .' O.G./Horace Reynolds, 8 March 1927, Harvard.
8   Stanford and McDowell, 1971.
9   *Intimations*. 'By the way, the armistice terms make no mention of compensation to Mahaffy for the loss of so many of his crowned friends.' O.G./Lady Leslie. Bucknell. 16 November 1918.
10   *It isn't,* p. 62.
11   *Tumbling,* p. 68.
12   Stanford and McDowell, 1971.
13   *Start,* p. 73.
14   *Secret Springs,* p. 11
15   *Faber Book of Irish Verse.*

CHAPTER 3

1   O'Connor, 1964.
2   O.G./James Joyce n.d. (c. February 1904) Cornell.
3   *It isn't* p. 64.
4   *It isn't* p 66.
5   O.G./James Joyce n.d. Cornell
6   O.G./James Joyce 11 June 1904 Cornell
7   *Many lines.*
8   *Many lines.*

CHAPTER 4

1   *Many lines.*
2   O.D.G.
3   *Many lines.*
4   N.L.I., Ms. 15, 576.
5   *Letters of James Joyce,* ed. Ellmann, R. Vol 2, p53, 1966.
6   *Many lines.*
7   Clery, 1972.
8   *Tumbling,* p. 245.
9   *Tumbling,* p. 231.

10   'It was the way he envisaged Life that made him great and remarkable.
      And that gave him a greatness which far excelled the greatness of the
      most skilful surgeon. As for surgery he was unsurpassable. In grave
      operations such as laryngectomy his assistant got the impression as he
      advanced step by careful step towards the end that he was taking part
      in some great harmony, so dexterous was the work and so masterly the
      mind that guided it. And what a mind it was, apart from his surgery!
      He was, if it has to be stated in one word, pre-eminently a just man. His
      greatness was moral greatness.' — Obituary of Sir Robert Woods by O.
      St. J.G. *Irish journal of medical science,* 1938.
11   Maurice Joy was Horace Plunkett's secretary and editor of *The Irish
      rebellion of 1916 and its martyrs,* New York, 1916.
12   *Many lines.*
13   *Many lines.*
14   *Many lines.*
15   Writing to G. K. A. Bell on 18 November 1905 Gogarty remarked '. . .
      [Moore] owes me gratitude if such a thing were ever his, for forbearing
      to proceed against him for a libel in that book of his. As long as my
      mother does not hear of it I don't care about Moore's audacious act.
      All he wants, I know, is to make me angry and by my kicking up a row
      advertise it. I told him I rejoiced that he had cast the ring for me: one
      can only die once, and, as I am yet alive in spite of the oblivion he has
      provided, my name must do something now — it cannot die again!'
16   *Many lines.*
17   O.G./Dermot Freyer, 5 May 1905 U. O'C. Arch.
18   According to Lumley (1961) 'The anatomy paper not commending
      itself to him, was discarded. He manufactured a fresh one, the questions
      of which he proceeded to answer. The professor — Alexander Fraser —
      is reputed to have said: "He didn't reply to any of my questions, but
      mon, it was grand anatomy."'
19   Gogarty's name appears in the first list of subscribers to Sinn Féin —
      (10/- O.G.).
20   *United Irishman,* December 1905.

CHAPTER 5

1   O.G./Dermot Freyer, 19 September 1907 U.O'C.Arch.
2   *Many lines.*
3   *Many lines.*
4   Bucknell.
5   *Many lines.*
6   N.L.I., Ms. 15, 576.
7   N.L.I., Ms. 15, 576.

8   Ironically, Mrs. Gogarty did not live to see her son's academic fulfil-
ment. 'The news is that O.G.'s mother is "beastly dead" and that O.G.
is very rich.' (Letter from James Joyce to his brother Stanislaus, 10
January 1907). His inheritance made it possible to specialize in ear-
nose-and-throat surgery instead of becoming a general practitioner as
originally intended. 'I hope to be holding a locum or something of the
kind in England next December.' O.G./G.K.A. Bell 2 February 1906,
Many lines.
9   O.G./Seumas O'Sullivan. N.L.I., Ms., 15573. 12 October 1906.
10   *Many lines.*
11   O.G./Dermot Freyer, 19 September 1907 U.O'C.Arch.
12   O.G./Seumas O'Sullivan, 11 April 1907 N.L.I., Ms. 15, 573.
13   O.G./Dermot Freyer, 5 October 1907 U.O'C.Arch.
14   O.G./Dermot Freyer, 14 October 1907 U.O'C. Arch.
15   O.G./James Joyce, 10 December 1907 Cornell.
16   Newcastle sanatorium for tuberculosis.
17   N.L.I., Ms. 15, 573.
18   Hogan and O'Neill, 1967.

CHAPTER 6

1   Breathnach, C.S. 'Sir Robert Woods.' *Journal Irish colleges of physicians and surgeons,* 2, 48-51, 1972.
2   *It isn't* p. 86.
3   Mellotte, 1957.
4   Saddlemyer, 1971.
5   Leslie, 1964.
6   O'Connor, Frank, 1968.
7   A further amusing summary of his opinion of his E.N.T. colleagues was
recalled for me by Ulick O'Connor:
Down we lay him Mr. Graham,
It's always uncertain with Mr. Curtin,
You never know with Mr. Keogh,
It's only Woods who delivers the goods,
If that's not derogatory to Oliver Gogarty.
8   Mr. J. McAuliffe Curtin, an E.N.T. surgeon who had seen many of
Gogarty's former patients, said at a meeting of the Royal Academy of
Medicine in Ireland on 27 November 1972 that Gogarty seems to have
been above average in surgical technique. Mr. T. G. Wilson (1969)
thought he had good judgement and excellent hands.
9   Piaras Béaslaí (1965) has stressed that when Gogarty was established
in practice he 'became a teetotaller, and continued so through his
medical years. . . . He used to stand drinks to others but did not imbibe
himself. I remember him making jocose remarks sometimes on the ad-

vantage he had over us in abstaining from alcohol. It was only when he lost interest in his medical practice and began to write books that he became a drinking man again — but a very moderate one. His usual drink was lager beer. . . .'

10   O.G./Dermot Freyer n.d. [1909] U.O'C. Arch.
11   N.L.I., Ms. 15, 574.

CHAPTER 7

1   *S.S.,* p. 293.
2   Ben Lucien Burman, a writer who knew Gogarty in America, insisted that far from being a snob he was 'the exact opposite of snobbish — a violent rebel against any kind of pretentiousness.' When the caretaker of a block of flats whom he had met in a Third Avenue bar came down with tuberculosis, Gogarty arranged for his admission to hospital and visited him regularly. His friends included waiters and truck-drivers.
3   Robert Y. Tyrrell/O.G. n.d., Bucknell.
4   Robert Y. Tyrrell/O.G.n.d., Bucknell. Sir Charles Bent Ball, Bt., was surgeon to Sir Patrick Dun's Hospital.
5   *S.S.,* p. 316.
6   *Start,* p. 83.
7   Starkie, 1941
8   An exception to a general rule, Fanning's success was said to derive from behaving on the basis that the customer was always wrong.
9   O'Brien, 1976.
10   *C.P.,* p.67.
11   Yet Sir William Orpen (1924) refers to Gogarty as 'that king of wits'. Also suggesting that this quarrel was mended is a letter to his cousin in California referring to a portrait of her sister: 'Had I thought of it I could have got Sir William Orpen to paint her at a greatly reduced fee while she was over here.' O.G./Margaret Burke, 26 January 1924, O.D.G.
12   'To W.A.S.' N.L.I. Ms. 15, 577.
13   *Start,* p.78.
14   Stephen Gwynn/O.G., Bucknell.
15   This generous offer was not availed of; the bust was the work of Albert Power, R.H.A.
16   *It isn't* p. 198. A statement difficult to credit today. Is one to attribute it to the faulty recall of a septuagenarian or has it a praiseworthy purpose of demythologising? Surely he would have heard of the 'man called Pearse' whom Vice-Provost Mahaffy banned from a proposed meeting of the Gaelic Society in Trinity College in November 1914. And one would expect him to have known the poets Thomas MacDonagh and Joseph Mary Plunkett who edited the *Irish Review.* Plunkett, incidentally, was an 'old boy' of Stonyhurst.
17   Bucknell.

CHAPTER 8

1   An alternative spelling, *Hyperthuliana,* is sometimes used.
2   Carens, 1971. *Many lines.*
3   O.G./James Joyce. Letters of James Joyce, ed. Ellmann, Richard, Vol. 2, 141. 1966.
4   Carens, 1972
5   O.G./Dermot Freyer, 23 December 1908 U.O'C.Arch.
6   *Many lines.*
7   O.G./James Joyce, 20 October 1907 Cornell.
8   O.G./Dermot Freyer, 29 July 1909 U.O'C.Arch.
9   O'Shannon, 1957.

CHAPTER 9

1   Henry Blake and others *Letters from the Irish highlands.* London, 1825.
2   Martin, Violet and Somerville, E. OE. *Through Connemara in a governess cart.* London, 1893.
3   O.G./Lady Leslie, 5 March 1919 Bucknell.
4   Davis, Richard. *Arthur Griffith.* Dundalk, 1976.
5   Piaras Béaslaí (1965) doubted that Michael Collins used Gogarty's house 'to any great extent during the Black-and-Tan days. Of course one cannot be positive as to the movements of such a man as Collins, but Gogarty himself never claimed to me to have met him before the truce.'
6   *S.S.,* p. 188.
7   *C.P.,* p. 26.
8   Holroyd, 1975.
9   The Bucknell Gogarty Collection contains a number of letters from John to his Irish friend. On 22 February 1924: 'One of my many missions in life seems to be converting Lesbians to the cult of Phallus. I have great success in this work and it is splendid sport. In 1925: 'Dear Oliver, It's damn good of you to offer to clear out my catarrh for me. . .' John said of *S.S.* that it was 'the next best thing to having you talk and . . . not quite so exhausting.'
10   O.G./Lady Gregory. N.Y.P.L.Berg.
11   Hewson, 1959. O'Connor wrote a series 'Studies in Blue' for an evening paper. .
12   Gogarty explained that he selected the pen-name Gideon Ousley 'because it is O.G. backwards and because a friend of mine, Citizen Elwood, was always talking about one Gideon Ousley. Also for the reason that I did not wish to be accounted in one-track minds with playwriting when I was supposed to be a surgeon.' O.G./Horace Reynolds 9 February 1956 Harvard.

13   *C.P.*, p. 191
14   'Shaw at lunch on Monday was even better than Shaw on Shaw on Sunday at the Abbey.... He told me things of great interest about Shakespeare.' O.G. /Lady Leslie, 23 October 1918 Bucknell.
15   Lady Gregory/O.G., Carens, 1970.
16   It was successfully revived by a Galway group for Gogarty's centenary.
17   Student lore hints at a farce by Gogarty with characters taken from medical nomenclature — the twins Dia and Rhoea; Umbilicus, a naval officer; the Penis, an upstanding young fellow, etc.
18   N.Y.P.L.Berg.
19   One of the recipents of a presentation copy was Lady Leslie whose favourable opinion pleased him. 'Dear Lady Leslie: Thank you for your letter. It exalts me. Yours was the cheerfullest acknowledgement of all. Some people did not reply: Some didn't like the things I thought they would. Lady Leconfield liked the drawings; I am still wondering whether her silence on the verses be just or merciful or both combined.' O.G./Lady Leslie, 18 November 1918 Bucknell.

CHAPTER 10

1   *S.S.*, p. 265.
2   Lord Dunsany/O.G. n.d. Bucknell.
3   Lord Dunsany/O.G. n.d. Bucknell.
4   *S.S.*, p. 277
5   *S.S.*, p. 260.
6   O.G./The Misses Burke, 2 February 1922 Bucknell.
7   A suspicion which seems to have been unfounded.
8   O.G./Clare Sheridan, Bucknell.
9   Sheridan, 1927. O.G. /Lady Leslie, 3 November 1922. 'What a way Clare Sheridan rounded on me in her American paper! Not up till nine o'clock. And she called at 8 for the ancestral bacon and egg!'
10   Sheridan, 1927.
11   O.G./Shane Leslie, 20 October 1921 Bucknell. 'The P.M's remarks on Collins are interesting: but only Griffith counts. The other is considered an arrogant fellow. Griffith is Ireland at present.'
12   *Free State*, 19 August 1922.
13   *Free State*, 19 August 1922.
14   *Free State*, 29 August 1922.
15   O.G./Lady Leslie, 28 August 1922 Bucknell.
16   O.G./Shane Leslie, 28 December 1922 U.O'C. Arch.
17   O.G./Shane Leslie, 1923 Bucknell.
18   O.G./Lady Leslie, 1922 Bucknell.

19   The ballad was composed by William Dawson and sung at an Arts Club dinner.

20   *It isn't*, p. 214.

21   *S.S.*, p. 198.

CHAPTER 11

1   *S.S.*, p. 215.

2   Someone described him as a one-man war between an English Oliver St. John and an Irish Gogarty.

3   Amory, 1973.

4   *S.S.*, p. 253.

5   *It isn't*, p. 224.

6   Lady Diana Cooper/O.G., n.d. Bucknell.

7   Rodgers, 1972

8   T.C.D., Seumas O'Sullivan papers, 3594.

9   O.G./Lady Leslie, 17 August 1923 Bucknell.

10   O.G./Lady Leslie, Bucknell.

11   Mr. de Valera and his supporters withheld their good will. 'The dominant feeling of all true Irishmen at the moment,' de Valera said, 'is one of sorrow at the condition to which our country has been reduced. In this atmosphere the Tailteann Games must be a mockery.' (S.J.L. *Irish Press*, 24 August 1975).

12   O.G./Shane Leslie, 26 October 1923 Bucknell. 'The delay in answering was caused largely by my visit to Germany, largely by the Tailteann committee insisting on an Ode at a moment's notice for a musical competition. I had hardly time to celebrate our epic scandal — Fergus McRoy and Maeve, when the weak Ailinn could only take the sword of the otherwise occupied Hero — symbol of libido as Jung would say.'

13   O.G./The Misses K. and M. Burke, 10 January 1924. O.D.G.

14   In his correspondence Gogarty mentions that he refused swans from the King's Swan Master when told they were not for sale but would be a gift; he was aware, too, of the hazards of anti-royalists. He purchased a pair from Gurney of Norwich for £5.

15   Gogarty, Oliver D., 1969.

16   de Valois, 1957.

17   Lady Leslie/Mrs. Gogarty, Bucknell.

18   Lord Dunsany wrote to him from Lowndes Square, London: 'If you want to exercise your bow and arrows do take them down to Dunsany any time you care to and assail the rabbits.' Lord Dunsany/O.G., 1924 Bucknell.

19   Mackenzie, 1967.

20   As reported by *Irish Life* their guests included the Governor-General and his house party, and President and Mrs Cosgrave, His Highness

Count von Schlitz Goertz, the Earl and Countess Fingall, the Dowager
Marchioness Conyngham, and the Hon. Edward de Moleyns, Lady
Gormanstown, Lord Dunsany, Lady Vere Foster, Mr. and Mrs.
O'Higgins, Lord Louth, Sir Simon and Lady Maddock, Sir Henry and
Miss Grattan Bellew, the Marquess and the Marchioness MacSwiney,
Senator Sir Nugent Everard and Lady Everard, Mr. J.J. and Mrs.
Walsh, Chief Justice Kennedy and Mrs Kennedy, Sir Conway Dwyer,
the Hon. Cecil Baring and Miss Baring, Mr. and Mrs. G.K. Chesterton,
Senator W.B. and Mrs. Yeats, Major Bryan Cooper, Dr. McCartan
and niece, Mr. Justice Johnston and Mrs. Johnston, Mr. Justice Sul-
livan, Senator Sir Thomas and Miss Esmonde, etc..

21   Gogarty was awarded a bronze medal in the art section of the Paris
      Olympiad.
22   O.G./Lady Leslie, 31 August 1924 Bucknell.
23   Writing to a friend in 1925 Lawrence refers to 'the two little Seltzers
      dangling by a single thread, over the verge of bankruptcy, and nobody
      a bit sorry for them.' (Moore, H.T., *The Priest of Love*, 1976.)
24   Ernest Boyd/O.G. 20 January and 8 February 1925 Bucknell.
25   O.G./Seymour Leslie. Ms., B.M.Cup 403 n.34. British Library.
26   O.G./Lady Leslie, 30 January 1925 Bucknell.
27   O.G./The Misses Burke, 11 May, 1925. O.D.G.
28   O.G./Lady Leslie 14 June 1925 Bucknell.
29   Bucknell.
30   O.G./Shane Leslie, Bucknell.
31   Thanking Gogarty for a presentation copy of *Wild Apples*, Sean O'
      Casey wrote: 'not so wild either, for there's a scent of culture in most of
      them.' He liked the poems 'in which you put your arms around a
      woman the best of all.' O'Casey referred to Gogarty as 'a man who is
      greater than he will permit himself to be'. Carens, 1970.
32   Gibbon, 1979.
33   F.R. Higgins/O.G., 2 December 1928 Bucknell.
34   The version in Higgins's *The Gap of Brightness* has a different ending.

CHAPTER 12

1   O'Sullivan, 1940.
2   The quotations from all Senators' speeches in this chapter are taken
     from the official record.
3   W.B. Yeats found difficulty in establishing common ground (although
     they 'seemed men of skill and mother-wit') with the government
     ministers. 'But their minds knew no play that my mind could play at; I
     felt I could never know them. One of the most notable said he had long
     wanted to meet me. We met, but my conversation shocked and embar-
     rassed him. No, neither Gogarty nor I, with our habit of outrageous

conversation, could get near those men.' *On the Boiler,* Dublin: Cuala Press, 1938.

4   Sentenced to life imprisonment for assaulting Lady McDonnell with intent to kill on 6 October 1879, James Lynchehaun of Achill Island, County Mayo escaped from Maryborough Gaol in September 1902. The judge in the subsequent extradition trial in Indianapolis decreed that Lynchehaun's crime was political and instructed that he be discharged.

5   Reviewing Ulick O'Connor's biography (1964), Paul Kee referred to 'a split in Gogarty's mind between perceptive, intuitive understanding and unpleasantly prejudiced humdrum obtuseness'. Be that as it may, observers of present-day Ireland may discern a prophetic quality in his disillusion and in his mistrust of the new Republican cause'. See Chapter 13, note 39.

6   O'Connor, Frank, 1968.

CHAPTER 13

1   An invitation in 1932 to join the Council of a newly-formed section of laryngology and otology in the Royal Academy of Medicine in Ireland was turned down by Gogarty. 'No thank you,' he said, 'I don't want to be standardized.' Wilson, 1969.

2   Rodgers, 1972.

3   O.G./Shane Leslie, Bucknell. He also tried to interest H.V. Morton (author of the *In the steps of . . .* series) in Connemara. Morton wrote from the Daily Express office on 16 April 1928: 'The only piece of bad luck I encountered in Ireland was missing your letter. Nothing would have given me greater pleasure than to see Connemara with you. Unfortunately when you wrote to me I was already motoring round the country and I did not receive your invitation until I returned to London. I thought the road from Galway to Clifden the most interesting in Europe.' H.V. Morton/O.G., O.D.G.

4   O.G./Shane Leslie, Bucknell.

5   Doolin, 1960

6   W.B. Yeats/O.G., 20 February 1932 Bucknell.

7   'Yeats was in here yesterday mainly about his throat and when he was not, by using it vigorously, disproving the seriousness of his complaint, he was too busy talking about the New Academy for Ireland which he is getting the Government to bless and endow.' O.G./Horace Reynolds, 11 April 1931. Harvard.

8   O.G./John Drinkwater, 3 November 1932 Yale.

9   Gogarty wrote to Horace Reynolds (1896-1965), a Boston teacher, critic and man-of-letters with whom he was friendly over a number of years, from the Hotel Statler, Buffalo — 'I am not human at all or a

member of Society, just a mere projectile of the Pond Bureau 25 W. 43rd St. New York.

I can only go "lecturing" where they will have me. Thus I saw Caufield at Amherst; but I had to use the air service to get to Pittsburg afterwards; and now I leave this for Detroit, Minneapolis, Tucson, Los Angeles before returning for a week — before sailing — to New York. I met Yeats who got enough to keep his contra-censor (not -ception, I hope) Academy going.' 1 March 1933 Harvard.

10   Bucknell.

11   Magennis, 1933. Father Magennis also had hard things to say about the Irish Academy of Letters: 'We hear of a certain member of the "brood of Vipers" returning home with money to endow a phantom Academy. It is nothing to us under what pretensions he received those alms, but it was the lethargy of despair into which the whole movement was thrown by the Cosgrave regime at home which made such doles possible. There are, and have ever been, in America a class which corresponds to what was once called "Castle Catholics". Itinerant showmen, coming to the United States and laying claim to worth which they never possessed, can easily, in times such as we have had for the past few years, perpetrate any kind of *pia fraus*.'

12   George P. Brett/O.G. N.Y.P.L.

13   Horace Reynolds/O.G., 1933 Bucknell.

14   George P. Brett/O.G. N.Y.P.L.

15   O.G./George P. Brett N.Y.P.L.

16   O.G./George P. Brett N.Y.P.L.

17   George P. Brett/O.G. N.Y.P.L.

18   Horace Reynolds/O.G. 17 July 1934 Bucknell. Reynolds was one of Gogarty's most fervent admirers. 'I do not know where else in modern poetry you will find just this rare combination of wit and beauty, satire and song, realism and high adventure, overflowing fancy and precision of form.' '. . .spring is his season, sunshine his light, youth his time.'

19   O.G./W.T. Cosgrave, Bucknell.

20   W.T. Cosgrave/O.G., 17 December 1934 Bucknell.

21   In his letters Yeats sometimes refers to 'my Cambridge book.'

22   Gibbon, 1959.

23   W.B. Yeats/O.G., Bucknell.
24   Bucknell.

25   O.G./Shane Leslie, Bucknell.

26   Yeats, 1940.

27   Stephens, 1974.

28   'The English critics, who have never forgiven Yeats for taking the Nobel Prize from their despairing poets or, rather, poets of despair, are hard on his heels over this Anthology. . . God only knows why I am given such undeserved prominence. Possibly because I set my face against the revival of "folk" poetry and Padraic Columism; and insisted that there were better things to hear and still finer things to see in

Ireland than turf smoke and cottage songs. Now like Joyce, Yeats has put me with the Bucks!' O.G./Horace Reynolds, 23 November 1936 Harvard.

29   Yeats, 1940.

30   O.G./Shane Leslie, Bucknell.

31   O.G./Horace Reynolds, Harvard.

32   When invited to write the Preface Francis Hackett replied: 'My dear Gogarty, I'd be delighted to do it — It cannot repay your kindness to Signe, which I'll never forget, but it will be pleasant to link arms with you before you hurl the bomb — I *must* read it first. Then I'll write what I have to say, and then we'll see if it will do. It's a good moment for you to appear in the U.S.A.' Francis Hackett/O.G., Bucknell.

33   *S.S.*, p. 319.

34   *S.S.*, p. 76.

35   Clarke, *The Observer,* 4 April 1937.

36   O'Sullivan, 1940.

37   *S.S.*, p. 37.

38   *S.S.*, p. 21.

39   'The Irregulars' idea of Ireland is a desert with a robbable bank.' O.G./Lady Leslie, 28 August 1922 Bucknell.

40   *S.S.*, p. 186.

41   Frank Swinnerton called *S.S.* 'the writing of an irresistible talker.'

CHAPTER 14

1   Yeats, 1940.

2   de Vere White, 1970.

3   Glenavy, 1964.

4   Orpen, 1924.

5   Eventually Cissie Sinclair was confined to a wheel-chair existence. Beatrice Glenavy (1964) saw her as the model for 'Hamm' in Samuel Beckett's *End Game.* 'She used to make jokes about her tragic condition. She once asked me to "straighten up the statue" — she was leaning sideways in her chair and her arthritis had made her body heavy and hard and stiff like marble. As I did what she asked I saw tears of laughter in her eyes.'

6   Blair, 1978.

7   An apology was extracted from Gogarty by the National City Bank Ltd. for his reference to the National Land Bank. *Irish Press,* 28 May 1937.

8   George Redding/O.G., 28 September 1937 Bucknell.

9   Bucknell.

10   A letter (MS Yale) to Henry Phelan Gibb on 3 November 1913 contains the remark 'Sanct-Clair is enjoying the Jewish New Year whatever it may be'.

11   *S.S.* (N.Y. edition) pp. 6869.

12   *S.S.*, p.71.

13   Quotations from the trial in this chapter are taken from *The Irish Times, Weekly Irish Times* and *Irish Independent.*

14   O.D.G.

15   'Admirers of Senator Oliver St. John Gogarty are disappointed with his turn in the witness-box during the hilarious Sinclair v. Gogarty libel case... He certainly managed to glance briefly at Celtic folklore, and to say he thought his rhyme of "sesterces" with "mistresses" was pretty good (is it?), but what was wanted was one of those Gogarty disquisitions which are like an explosion at Brock's, a stream of fireworks popping off at every angle and in every direction without pause or intermission, Chinese crackers and Roman candles and Very lights and Bengal fires and set-pieces all streaming and mingling and crackling all at once, causing the dull-witted Saxon to retire from Gogarty's presence feeling as if a train had hit him.' D.B. Wyndham Lewis, *The Bystander,* 8 December 1937.

16   The late Sean Loughran, Dalkey, County Dublin.

CHAPTER 15

1   de Vere White, 1972.

2   Gogarty once said to Lennox Robinson, 'James Joyce got the King's bounty from Asquith when he hadn't written a line.' Lennox asked, 'What line hadn't he written?'

3   'Seumas O'Sullivan who doesn't love either Yeats or F.R. Higgins complained that one poet had swollen feet, the other a swelled head.' O.G./Horace Reynolds, April 1936 Harvard.

4   Higgins, 1940.

5   George Redding (23 July 1927, *Irish Statesman*) and Hugh M'Diarmid (18 May 1929, *Irish Statesman*) also addressed poems to Oliver Gogarty and Sir Francis Meynell, who spent 1911 in Dublin, remembered his Irish friends:

      Ireland, take, if your proud heart can,
      The homage of an Englishman.
      And first those friends — the poets who
      As much as songs had men in mind:
      McDonagh and Pearse of the rebel kind;
      Gogarty, Colum, Stephens too,
      Who with loud angers used to meet
      At the mild house in Merrion Street,
      Holding me, stranger, as their own
      Because I was a poet's son...

6   O'Sullivan, 1944.

7   Seumas O'Sullivan/O.G., Bucknell.

8   O.G./Seumas O'Sullivan, N.L.I., Ms. 15, 573.

9   T.C.D., Ms. 4148 a.

10 N.L.I., Ms. 15, 577.

11 Rodgers, 1972.

12 N.L.I., Ms. 15, 575. The friend may have been A.E. who died on 17 July 1935.

13 O.G./Seumas O'Sullivan, N.L.I., Ms. 15, 575.

14 O'Brien, 1970.

15 Béaslaí, 1965.

16 Francis McNamara/O.G., 23 December 1917 Bucknell.

17 *Letters to W.B. Yeats,* 1977 Vol. 2, 512.

18 D.B. Wyndham Lewis/O.G. 19 March 1930. O.D.G.

19 Although he poked fun at Hazel Lavery in his letters to Leonie Leslie he was on friendly terms with the former who described how she had read something of his 'and entranced the entire company at Lady Cunard's. They declared you were the very wittiest creature ever had come out of Ireland and that they intended never to let you leave this dismal London — as you were essential to their light and happiness — however I explained that you were returning to cut a throat or two from time to time.' Lady Lavery/O.G., 22 May 1923 O.D.G.

20 'Dear Lady Leslie: My heart leapt up when I beheld — not that polychrome commonplace which Wordsworth made worse — but your handwriting. "Something bright and novel and saved from the wreck of time" I said as I opened the envelope. And so your letter proved to be. You call it chaotic but "one must have Chaos within them to give birth to a dancing star" as the Poet has it.' O.G./Lady Leslie, 26 November 1918. Bucknell.

21 Lady Leslie/O.G., n.d. O.D.G.

22 Lady Lavery/O.G. O.D.G.

23 O.D.G.

24 Lady Leconfield/O.G. 15 October 1928. O.D.G.

25 George Moore was less respectful. With Gogarty he attended a meeting of the Hermetic Society during which, after certain incantations, AE declared that although his Hebrew was rusty he still knew enough to recognize that he was on the edge of discovering the lost Fifth Gospel. 'I see it coming up plainer now!' he whispered. 'Amen, amen, amen, amen.' Whereupon Moore returned to his companion and cackled: 'Good gracious, this is pure mumbo jumbo. He sees either the end of the Four Gospels or he has got the Fifth one upside down.' The interruption led to the immediate expulsion of Moore and Gogarty.

26 *New York Saturday Review of Literature,* 387 and 401, 28 January 1933.

27 *The Observer,* 4 October 1936.

28 *The Irish Times,* 18 July 1935.

29   It should, of course, be remembered that Yeats, in turn, could behind
      their backs tell uproariously funny stories about George Moore and
      Gogarty.
30   *Many lines.*
31   Carens, 1972.
32   N.Y.P.L., Berg.
33   N.Y.P.L., Berg. It was Gogarty who advised Lady Gregory to consult
      Mr. Slattery who operated on her for a breast cancer.
34   Hone, J.
35   N.Y.P.L., Berg.
36   Yeats, 1940.
37   *Evening Standard*, 30 January 1939.
38   When *Letters on Poetry from W.B. Yeats to Dorothy Wellesly* was
      published he read it with interest and thought it showed 'how dearly
      Yeats could love a lady even if he disliked a lord in the person of Dun-
      sany.'
39   *C.P.*, p. 200.
40   When asked what six persons he would resurrect from the dead,
      Gogarty selected Wolsley, Shakespeare, Pitt, Wellington, Disraeli and
      Sir Austen Chamberlain 'the man without chicane.'

CHAPTER 16

1   The misinformed conclusions of many Joyceans are typified by Hélène
      Cixous (1972). Under Gogarty in the index to her book one finds
      references to 'athleticism', 'denseness', 'faults catalogued' and 'wealth
      of'.
2   Seán Ó Faoláin has written (1964): 'Joyce did him an immense and
      cruel injustice in *Ulysses* by presenting him to posterity as something
      approaching the nature of an insensitive lout whose only function in life
      was to offset and emphasise the exquisite sensitivity and delicacy of
      Stephen Daedalus. Gogarty was a kind and generous man, full of verve
      and zest .... His essential nature which nobody could ever possibly
      gather from *Ulysses,* was his nature as a poet—and he was a fine poet."
3   Curran, 1968.
4   O.G./James Joyce, Cornell.
5   O.G./James Joyce, Cornell.
6   Ellmann, 1959.
7   Joyce, Stanislaus, 1958.
8   Joyce, Stanislaus, 1971.
9   Joyce, Stanislaus, 1971.
10   O.G./James Joyce, Cornell.
11   O.G./Dr. M. Walsh, 10 March 1904 Cornell.

12 O.G./James Joyce, Cornell.
13 A point discussed in greater detail in Lyons, 1973.
14 *Many lines,* 1971.
15 *Many lines,* 1971.
16 O.G./Dermot Freyer, 23 March 1905 U.O'C.Arch.
17 *Letters of James Joyce, Vol. 2.* ed. Ellmann, 1966.
18 O.G./James Joyce, 14 June 1906 Cornell.
19 *Letters of James Joyce,* Vol. 2. ed. Ellmann, 1966.
20 O.G./James Joyce, 10 November 1907 Cornell.
21 O.G./James Joyce, Cornell.
22 O.G./James Joyce, Cornell.
23 Ellmann, 1959.
24 Presumably unaware that Gogarty was out of favour with his brothers, Charlie Joyce sent him a begging letter on 18 February 1918 from 30 Great Georges Street: 'Dear Dr. Gogarty, Can you lend me £1? I feel I am treating you badly but the pressure is very great.' Charles Joyce/O.G., Bucknell.
25 Curran, 1968.
26 James Joyce. *A portrait of the artist as a young man.*
27 *Tumbling,* p. 138.
28 *Retrospect,* ed. Liam Miller, Dublin, 1973.
29 Brinsley Macnamara placed it to Gogarty's credit that he refused an American publisher's attractive invitation to write a book on Joyce. 'The reason he gave me for this showed the difference between the two men better than any other explanation that I know of. "I just couldn't do it", he said. "The man was too sad. Joyce was the very saddest man I ever knew."'

CHAPTER 17

1   O.G./Shane Leslie, Bucknell.
2   *Evening Mail,* 23 April 1938.
3   O.G./Lady Leslie, 12 August 1938. Bucknell.
4   *St. Patrick,* p. 79.
5   *St. Patrick,* p. 115.
6   *St. Patrick,* p. 177.
7   *St. Patrick,* p. 180.
8   *Studies,* 27, 675, (1939).
9   *St. Patrick,* p. 252.
10 O.G./Dr. Patrick McCartan, 14 August 1938 N.Y.P.L.
11 *Dublin Magazine,* 81-83, (1938)
12 *Tumbling,* p. 72.
13 *Daily Telegraph and Morning Post,* 24 February 1939
14 *Dublin Magazine,* 13, 72-75, (1938).

15   Austin Clarke/James Mays, 19 September 1972. I am indebted to Mr.
      Mays for this information.
16   Bucknell.
17   Richardson, 1973.
18   O.G./Shane Leslie. Bucknell.

                            CHAPTER 18

1   O.G./Miss Freeman, N.Y.P.L., Berg.
2   O.G./Oliver Duane Gogarty, 12 December 1939. O.D.G.
3   O.G./Shane Leslie
4   *C.P.*, p. 79.
5   *Vogue*, April 1962.
6   Is Gogarty misplacing a Florentine tower?
7   'Where things are done.' Typescript, Bucknell.
8   In another mood he said that Americans could not cook potatoes —
      'their's tasted like soap' and complained of the tea bags, 'lingerie tea,
      with a muslin bag'.
9   'I've been wondering how you have [been] progressing in your design
      to enter the army.' Horace Reynolds/O.G., 31 December 1941
      Bucknell.
10   O.G./William Lyon Phelps, Yale.
11   O.G./Oliver Duane Gogarty, O.D.G.
12   Taylor, 1954.
13   G.N., p. 60.
14   G.N., p. 290.
15   *Dublin Magazine,* 17,61-2, (1942).
16   *Dublin Magazine,* 67-68, (1944).
17   M.G., p. 424.
18   M.G., p. 426.
19   M.G., p. 436.
20   James Montgomery/O.G., Bucknell.
21   O.G./Shane Leslie, 25 February 1942 Bucknell.
22   O.G./Mrs. Mary Owings Miller, Bucknell.
23   Gogarty avoided public controversy with Mary (Molly) Colum but in
      Perennial he refers to '. . . ladies, who pen-pecking, mollie coddle/The
      Muse with mash from a bemused noddle.' And in a letter to Mrs Mary
      Owings Miller: 'She said. . . that Joyce would turn in his grave if he
      knew I considered him to belong to the "lower middle classes". For she
      has never quite got over the class distinction that obtains in Dublin
      where she would be kept in her place. Little did I realise how much is to
      be said for class distinction until I saw the disproportionate importance
      attached to such persons when they come over to the U.S.A.' Bucknell.
24   O.G./Oliver Duane Gogarty, 5 February 1941 O.D.G.

25 T.G. Moorhead/O.G., 29 June 1942 Bucknell.
26 George Redding/O.G., 8 July 1941 Bucknell.
27 George Redding/O.G., 3 December 1941 Bucknell.
28 Joe Boyd Barrett/O.G., 26 August 1943 Bucknell.
29 Bucknell.
30 O.D.G.
31 O.G./Mrs. Gogarty, July 1943. O.D.G.
32 *C.P.,* p. 79.
33 George Redding/O.G., 1 August 1943 Bucknell.
34 Dedication, *M.G.*
35 Bucknell.
36 Bucknell.
37 She married Desmond Williams a member of the Tullamore distilling family. The wedding took place in the Church of Christ the King, Tullycross, Renvyle. The ceremony was performed by the Rev. F.M. Hanrahan, P.P., Letterfrack. The bride was given away by her brother, Mr. Oliver D. Gogarty. Her bridesmaid was Miss Olivia Robertson. Mr. Daniel Williams was best man, and the groomsmen in the church were Dermot Gogarty and Dermot Williams.
38 *Mourning,* p. 132.
39 Fleming, 1965.
40 *The Bell,* 616, (1945).
41 *Mourning,* p. 149.
42 O.G./Oliver Duane Gogarty. O.D.G.
43 E.H. Alton/O.G., 21 May 1946 Bucknell.
44 Rolling down the lea.
45 O.G./Mrs. Gogarty, Bucknell.
46 O.G./Oliver Duane Gogarty. O.D.G.
47 O.G./Oliver Duane Gogarty. O.D.G.
48 O.G./Oliver Duane Gogarty, 10 February 1948. O.D.G.
49 O.D.G.
50 Lynn Doyle/O.G., 30 August 1948 Bucknell
51 Lynn Doyle/O.G., 25 June 1949 Bucknell.
52 O.G./Denis Johnston, 17 September 1949.
53 Padraic Colum/O.G., Bucknell.
54 O.G./Mrs. Comstock. Countess Moltke.
55 O.G./Denis Johnston.
56 E.H. Alton/O.G., 25 September 1950 Bucknell.

CHAPTER 19

1 Ian Hamilton, 21 March 1952.
2 *Dublin Magazine,* 27, 52, (1952).
3 W.B.Yeats, Preface to *Wild Apples.*
4 Geoffrey Grigson, *The Irish Times,* 9 March 1974.

5   J. Middleton Murry, 'A poet of the moon', *Athenaeum* 169-170, (1920)
6   Anthony Cronin. 'The first of the few.' *The Irish Times,* 2 January 1976.
7   James Reeves. Introduction to *Georgian Poetry.* Harmondsworth 1962.
8   '...of course you know the only rhyme for "Vichy"? Naturally Browning's...Vichy/is she? After which Comrade Browning ought to have taken a course of intestinal massage himself.' D.B. Wyndham Lewis/O.G., n.d. O.D.G.
9   O.G./Dermot Freyer, 1905 U.O'C. Arch.
10   Having seen the patient he wrote this in Philip Sayers' office.
11   Bucknell.
12   O.G./W.B. Yeats. Bucknell.
13   MS British Library.
14   A.E., 1933.
15   MS N.L.I.
16   Stephens, 1924.
17   Austin Clarke, *The Irish Times,* 23 February 1952.
18   Ian Hamilton. *Manchester Guardian,* 21 March 1952.
19   de Vere White, 1972. An erratum slip in *The Anglo-Irish* substitutes *As I was walking*(sic) *down Sackville Street* for *As I was walking down Grafton Street* leaving an error uncorrected. A small point but one which may show that this author lacks the essential sympathy towards his subject necessary to validate his criticism.
20   Weygant, 1937.
21   Mercier, 1958.
22   Jeffares, 1970.
23   Carens, 1972.
24   Clark, 1972
25   André Michalopolus/O.G., 5 February 1953 Bucknell.
26   Joan Weimer/O.G., 17 April 1952 O.D.G.
27   W.B.Yeats. *Introduction to Oxford Book of Modern Verse.*

CHAPTER 20

1   Speaking at the International James Joyce Symposium in Dublin in 1977, Denis Johnston said: 'In his latter days he became — I was going to say a pathetic figure but you couldn't possibly regard Gogarty as pathetic — but he was a figure that was, as it were, losing faith in himself and it's understandable that he began to do that business of repeating himself in one book after another....falling to some extent into a rut in a downtown district of New York where one would sometimes meet him and he would join you in a pub on Third Avenue. This was, I think, the saddest period of his life because he was alone.'

2   Ó Faoláin, 1964.
3   Manning, 1972.
4   Johnston, 1951.
5   O.D.G.
6   O.G./Oliver Duane Gogarty, 1 April 1951. O.D.G.
7   O.G./Oliver Duane Gogarty, 12 January 1952.
8   Padraic Colum/O.G., Bucknell. When he received another award later Lord Dunsany wrote from Dunstall Priory.
       'My dear Gogarty, Hearty congratulations on your award of 5,000 dollars. I am sure it was well deserved. Also it is another blow at the un-metrical nonsense called "modern verse".' Lord Dunsany/O.G., 4 January 1955 Bucknell.
9   W.R. Fearon/O.G., 11 May 1954 Bucknell.
10   Horace Reynolds/O.G., 9 August 1954 Bucknell.
11   Horace Reynolds/O.G., August 1954 Bucknell.
12   O.G./Horace Reynolds, 1952 Harvard.
13   O.G./Horace Reynolds, 27 August 1954.
14   Horace Reynolds/O.G., Bucknell.
15   Mervyn Wall/O.G., 20 August 1955 Bucknell. The *Irish Independent*'s radio critic found that Gogarty's piece on AE (read by Joseph O'Dea) was not a clear picture: '. . .the writer had employed verbal embroidery to such an extent that no definite impression of George Moore was received. Dr. Gogarty is an enchanting writer but this was a piece which did not achieve its aim.'
16   Flood, 1961.
17   *C.P.* p. 163.
18   W.T. Cosgrave/O.G., Bucknell.
19   Horace Reynolds/O.G., 15 November 1956 Bucknell.
20   O.G./Horace Reynolds, 13 May 1957 Harvard.
21   Horace Reynolds/O.G., 10 May 1957.
22   O.G./Denis Johnston, 8 June 1957.
23   O.G./Oliver Duane Gogarty. When the Martello Tower Sandycove came up for auction he had considered bidding for it. 'If the Tower at Sandycove is for sale separately from the cottage and there is not the 20 pounds ground rent on it, offer 300 pounds for me.' O.G./Oliver Duane Gogarty, 7 December, 1954. O.D.G.
24   O.G./Horace Reynolds, Harvard.
25   Horace Reynolds/O.G., 24 August 1957. Bucknell.
26   O.G./Oliver Duane Gogarty. O.D.G.
27   Burman, Introductory essay in *A weekend in the middle of the week*, 1958.
28   Unaccustomed to the art of American morticians the family was startled when the coffin was opened at Shannon. 'That's not father,' the elder son exclaimed, struck by the resemblance to an actor who used cosmetics. 'That's Michael MacLiammoir.'

29   Rodgers, 1972.
30   Myles na gCopaleen, 1957.
31   Béaslaí, 1965
32   Leslie, 1964.
33   Fallon, 1964.
34   Boland, 1964.
35   Kennelly, 1964.
36   Martin, 1964.
37   Horace Reynolds remarked in a review of *A weekend in the middle of the week:* 'Gogarty wrote as a tiger hunts: if he missed his spring he would not try again, and this refusal to recognise the work in writing meant that some of what he wrote was mechanical and disconnected. But there were always days when he did not miss his target.' *New York Times Book Review,* 3 March 1958.
38   Dr. and Mrs. Gogarty's immediate posterity was two sons, a daughter and three grandchildren. The elder son's marriage to Sheila Flynn (d. 1979) was childless. Dermot and Carmel (née Esmonde) Gogarty's marriage was dissolved; their son Michael now lives in Johannesburg and has two daughters. Brenda Williams (her husband, Desmond, died suddenly in Renvyle some years ago) has two children, Guy and Clare. The former has three daughters.

An affectionate parent and grandparent, Oliver wrote to Neenie on 2 December 1948: 'I am longing to see little Clare and Guy. I suppose Der's boy will be over for the Christmas holidays. I wish I were.' O.D.G.
39   A E, 1933.

INDEX

342   *Index*

Campbell, Joseph, 170
Campbell, Michael, 164
Campbell, Judge Richard, 168, 252
Canning, Canon, 140
Carens, Prof. James F. 90, 91, 116, 206
278-279, 319
Carrowbehy, 37
Carson, Alfred E., 197
Carson, Lord, 144
Carter, Capt. Bonham, 27
Casement, Tom, 255-256
Castleblayney, 148
Castlerosse, Lord, 202
Catholic University, 30
Catholic University Medical School, 29,
230
Cavendish Hotel, 46
Cecilia Street, 29-30, 36-37
Censorship Bill, 150-152
Cervantes, 54
Chamberlain, Austen, 131
Charlemont, Earl of, 22
Charleston, 239
Chesterton, G.K., 136, 169, 264
Chiang Kai-Shek, Madame, 251
Chicago, 239
Childers, Erskine, 126
Childers, Mrs, 126
Christian Brothers, 57
Churchill, Lord Randolph, 107
Churchill, Winston, 42, 107, 131, 139
Clark, David, 279-280
Clarke, Austin, 174, 178, 182, 196, 232,
263, 274-275, 285
Clarke, Harry, 179
Clarke, Tom, 88
Clarke, Senator Mrs., 158
Clifton, John Talbot, 110, 114, 129-130,
136, 138, 141
Clifton, Mrs. Talbot, 141
Clongowes Wood College, 26-28
College Park, 30, 36, 40, 50
College of Science, 159
Collins, Michael, 108-109, 125, 138, 138,
161, 325-326
Colum, Mary (Molly), 138, 224, 247, 336
Colum, Padraic, 115, 131, 137, 220, 224,
260, 284
Comstock, Mrs. Arthur, 249, 252, 260
Comstock, Mabs — see Countess Moltke
Comyn, Michael, 145, 154, 156-157, 161,
172
Connaught, Duke of; 131
Connelly, Willard, 164
Connemara, 43, 63, 65, 88, 105, 137, 143
224, 228, 243, 256, 258, 262
Connolly, Cyril, 196
Connolly, James, 88
Connolly, Senator, 160
Conyngham, Lady, 140
Coole Park, 106

Cook, Thomas, 21
Coote, Col., 81
Cooper, Becky, 38
Cooper, Bryan, 200
Cooper, Lady Diana, 131, 202
Cosgrave, Liam, 290
Cosgrave, Vincent, 36, 94, 216, 218, 221-
222
Cosgrave, William T., 109, 125, 134, 139,
164, 172, 182, 287, 290
Costello, Peter, 130
Cox, H.A.,

Dalkey, 47, 80
Dallas, 239
Davidson, Gustav 289
Dawson, William 327
Deane, Sir Thomas, 71
De Brún, Pádraig, 116, 290, 295
Detroit, 239
De Valera, Eamonn, 109, 120, 159-162,
180, 256, 285, 327
Dixon, Andrew, F., 50, 51
Dolan, 30
Dolphin Hotel, 82, 83, 205, 230, 258
Doolin, Mrs., 164
Doolin, William, 164, 167
Douglas, Lord Alfred, 79, 174
Douglas, James, 144
Douglas, Senator, 148
Dowdall, J.C., 152
Dowden, Prof. Edward 83, 195
Dowson, Ernest, 175
Dresden, 68
Drinkwater, John, 168
Drummond, 21, 22
Duane, Martha, 61
Dublin Castle, 29
Dufferin, Lady 218
Duffy, Bernard, 21
Duffy, Maria Theresa, 21
Duggan, Eamon, 134, 144
Dun's Hospital, 72
Dunsany Castle, 85, 86, 118
Dunsany Castle, 85, 86, 118
Dunsany, Lord, 82, 85, 88, 110, 118, 119,
175, 243, 327, 329
Dwane, Roger, 30
Dwyer, Father, 120
Doyle, Lyle, 268

Easter Rising, 118
Economic War, 159
Edgeworth, Maria, 106
Eglington, John, 198, 213
Eliot, T.S., 175, 266, 276, 277
Ellmann, Richard 216
Elpis Private Hospital, 79
Elvery, Beatrice, 86, 182
Elwood, John, 36, 37, 213, 223, 282
Ely Place, 30, 71, 287

Private

10.X.96

My dear Shane

Lady Leslie told me you were thinking of standing for Monaghan. This is to urge you to do so. Canon & Dean Kerr of Carrickmacross would welcome You; and, if it prevented too much study - work, it would compensate by the provision of study "copy."

I was about to drive up today but as my man went out I couldn't get filled up with the right kind of petrol and I go only 10 miles to the gallon!